D1378139

The Psychology of Shame

Second Edition

 **Gershen Kaufman, PhD,** was educated at Columbia University and received his PhD in clinical psychology from the University of Rochester. Currently he is a professor in the Counseling Center at Michigan State University where he is engaged in providing psychotherapeutic services to university students; consulting to university faculty and staff; clinical supervision and training to psychology practicum students and interns; research supervision to graduate students; and teaching courses on Affect and Self-Esteem and the graduate-level clinical Practicum in the Psychology Department, as well as a course on Lesbian, Bisexual, and Gay Studies in Women's Studies. Dr. Kaufman also maintains a private practice as a licensed psychologist where he sees a broad range of clientele in psychotherapy.

A pioneer in the study of shame, Dr. Kaufman is the author of *The Psychology of Shame: Theory and Treatment of Shame-Based Syndromes* (Springer, 1989); *Shame: The Power of Caring* (1992); and *Journey to the Magic Castle* (1993). He is the co-author with Lev Raphael of *Stick Up For Yourself! Every Kid's Guide to Personal Power and Positive Self-Esteem* (1990); *Dynamics of Power: Fighting Shame and Building Self-Esteem* (1991); and *Coming Out of Shame: Transforming Gay and Lesbian Lives* (1996). He is also the co-author with Lev Raphael and Gerri Johnson of *A Teacher's Guide to Stick Up For Yourself* (Free Spirit, 1991).

Dr. Kaufman has been widely in demand as a lecturer over the past decade throughout the United States, Canada, and England. He has lectured as well as conducted seminars and workshops on the role of shame in personality, psychopathology, and psychotherapy; on shame and self-esteem; and on the significance of shame for gender, culture, and society. He has lectured at universities, medical centers, teaching hospitals, meetings of the American Psychiatric Association, state Psychological Association meetings, state Social Workers Association meetings, addiction treatment centers, and numerous conferences. He has also presented an innovative self-esteem curriculum which can be implemented either in clinical or educational settings.

The Psychology of Shame

Second Edition

Theory and Treatment of Shame-Based Syndromes

Gershen Kaufman, PhD

Michigan State University

SPRINGER PUBLISHING COMPANY

First edition published, 1989

Copyright © 1996 by Springer Publishing Company, Inc.

Springer Publishing Company, Inc.
536 Broadway
New York, NY 10012

Cover and interior design by Tomas Yabut
Production Editor: Pamela Ritzer

96 97 98 99 00 / 5 4 3 2 1

Library of Congress Cataloging in Publication Data

Kaufman, Gershen.
    The psychology of shame: theory and treatment of shame-based syndromes /
Gershen Kaufman.—2nd ed.
       p.   cm.
    Includes bibliographical references and index.
    ISBN 0-8261-6671-7
    1. Shame. 2. Self. 3. Affect (Psychology) 4. Affective disorders. I. Title.
RC455.4.S53K38   1996
616.85'2—dc20362.1'0973—dc20   95-52777
                                              CIP

Printed in the United States of America

To

Silvan S. Tomkins

Man is unique not because he does science,
and he is unique not because he does art,
but because science and art equally are
expressions of his marvellous plasticity of mind.

JACOB BRONOWSKI
The Ascent of Man

Contents

Foreword to the First Edition

In 1980, in the introduction to *Shame: The Power of Caring,* I wrote, "The full range of what I have called the primary affects has not yet become common knowledge." Today, that is no longer true. Infant affect is now under intensive scrutiny, most notably in the work of Demos and Kaplan. The narcissistic self is at the center of Kohut's revision of classical psychoanalytic theory. Empathy for the feelings of the borderline self is now represented as crucial for therapy of the heretofore inaccessible, fragile, beleaguered self.

Gershen Kaufman's *Shame: The Power of Caring,* now in its second edition, is no longer a solitary voice. Broucek, Nathanson, and Morrison have deepened our understanding of the dynamics of shame. The concern with shame has moved center stage within the therapeutic community, and Kaufman's work was influential in that transformation. The present work continues and deepens that contribution. We are once again indebted to Gershen Kaufman for his special sensitivity to the role of shame and its contribution to affect theory and to psychotherapy.

We are further indebted to him for relating the dynamics of shame to the full spectrum of the primary affects and for embedding affect theory within the larger matrix of script theory. In script theory the basic unit of analysis is the scene. The scripts are sets of rules for the governance of scenes. Such scripts include the classical family romance, the object relations of Fairbairn, and the narcissistic self of Kohut, but also include affect management and affect control scripts, ideological as well as affluence, limitation, remediation, contamination, and antitoxic scripts. Script theory purports to match the great diversity to types of scenes that human beings magnify by their various affect investments.

SILVAN S. TOMKINS

Preface to the Second Edition

Shame is no longer the neglected emotion it once was. It is no longer being kept in the closet, either of the consulting room or the laboratory. Interest in the study of shame has, in fact, exploded since publication of the first edition of *The Psychology of Shame*. The focus of this new interest extends in multiple directions, from alcoholism, addiction, and dysfunctional families to narcissism and self psychology. Shame has even filtered into new domains of inquiry, from gender studies to history and anthropology. And the discourse taking place about contemporary social problems also reveals an increased awareness of shame, a sensitivity to the role that shame plays in the problems of the homeless and the aged. It is this recognition of shame itself that is so new and that, in turn, makes fresh insights possible.

By examining not only the operation of shame but of affect in general, we are able to arrive at richer understandings of phenomena that were previously perplexing. The first edition of *The Psychology of Shame* presented an interconnected theory of personality, psychopathology, and psychotherapy based on the affect theory and script theory of Silvan S. Tomkins. If, as Tomkins argues, affect is the primary innate biological motivating mechanism, then affect must be our starting point in constructing a theory of personality. Further, affect must frame our understanding of how psychopathology originates as well as how it becomes maintained over time. But the primacy of affect must also translate into application. Theories must have utility as well as explanatory power. Hence, the psychotherapeutic intervention strategies, which are systematically developed in Part II, are a direct outgrowth of shame theory. These new principles of psychotherapy extend shame theory into action; they also permit other researchers and clinicians to further verify the theory presented in Part I.

What still remain unexamined are several important clinical problems and contemporary issues. Given the unique experience of particular minorities living in American society, we need to examine the role of shame in profoundly shaping the evolving identities of racial, ethnic, and religious minorities. Just as shame is a societal dynamic, impacting the lives of various minority groups that inhabit a given society, shame is equally a force in culture generally. Every culture experiences shame, but differently. Cultures utilize shame as a means of furthering social control, as an important socializing tool; cultures also pattern shame quite distinctively.

Not only are identity and culture held captive by shame, so is ideology. Ideology is rooted in affect. Contemporary society bears witness to the magnification of various ideological disputes that threaten social stability, disputes like those now raging over abortion and the right to die. Affect itself first gives rise to ideologies, and affect also becomes polarized during controversy, propelling ideology itself into a governing psychological force. Here we enter the arena of hatred and violence. The interplay among identity, culture, and ideology can be illuminated in previously unrecognized ways by an affect theory perspective.

Likewise, the concept of *governing scenes,* first articulated in the previous edition, has important implications beyond its original scope. How scenes are first constructed and subsequently reactivated has a direct bearing on understanding the nature of trauma as well as the reenactment of traumatic scenes. Instead of continuously replaying in the form of flashbacks, however, those scenes can be banished entirely from awareness, often for years—resulting in such distinctive and disparate syndromes as posttraumatic stress disorder and childhood sexual abuse.

Memories can be both real and false because of the nature of scene magnification during retrieval from memory. Such an analysis has important implications for the current controversy surrounding recovered memory therapy, a topic that has been attracting increasing attention both in the mental health field and in society generally, particularly given its legal ramifications. The practice of psychotherapy can only benefit from an expanded awareness of the interaction of scene magnification and memory.

The examination of scenes at the individual level takes us back to the level of the group. Just as the individual's governing scenes empower personality development, governing group scenes empower culture. Shared group scenes of intense affect, which remain alive in collective memory over decades and even centuries, have enormous power to capture and dominate an entire people. The humiliation that was experienced in the past by nations or particular cultural groups can be as real today as it was then. It lives on in memory. Governing scenes are as pivotal in cultural memory as they are in personal memory.

Science—encompassing theory and practice—is always an expanding enterprise, and the theory first put forth in the earlier edition of *The Psychology of Shame* is equally evolving. Every theory must remain open, alive, and changing. By testing it against new problems, we experiment with what it can do, what it is able to reveal, and we discover new meanings.

GERSHEN KAUFMAN
East Lansing, Michigan

Preface to the First Edition

The mental health field is plagued by a compelling new generation of psychological dysfunction. The neurotic organizations observed in prior years, described by Freud and subsequently elaborated by others, have largely been replaced. We no longer see such precisely organized syndromes, and perhaps we only thought we did. We could not perceive in earlier years what our language disallowed, just as we cannot perceive now what our language continues to mask, obscure, or deny.

The current patterning of psychopathology reveals a disturbing array of disorder and dysfunction. Just as nature has thrown new and perplexing diseases in our path—AIDS is one example—our psyche has created, perhaps invented, new psychological syndromes which continue to baffle us. The recent acceleration of borderline, addictive, abusive, and eating disorders demonstrates the point. Depressive, schizoid, and schizophrenic syndromes can become so entrenched as to resist therapeutic intervention. Disorders of self-esteem, disorders of mood, compulsive and addictive syndromes, disorders of narcissism, borderline conditions, and schizophrenic syndromes comprise rapidly evolving classes of psychopathology. To be effective with these syndromes, psychotherapeutic intervention requires an accurate understanding of how the self develops, actually functions, and changes.

Psychological theories of the psyche began as useful metaphors to describe the inner experience of the self. Each observer, each theorist—from Freud, Jung, Adler, Horney, and Sullivan to Erikson, Fairbairn, Rogers, and Berne—constructed a particular model of the psyche, and fashioned a distinct language of the self. But what began as a metaphor has unfortunately become reified, disconnected from phenomenological experience. Psychology needs a new vision, a coherent image of the self to guide it. A science of the self must begin by making observations within its domain and then translating them into descriptive/relational language. Other observers must then be able to repeat each observation by working backward from the concept (linguistic symbol) to its referent (phenomenological event). Science inevitably advances by such continual conversation between the intellect and the senses, and by discovering a new potential of meaning in an old concept, whether it be gravity or time, affect or imagery.

This book presents a developmental theory of the self that integrates three distinct theoretical perspectives: the object-relations theory of W. R. D. Fairbairn and Harry Guntrip, the interpersonal theory of Harry S. Sullivan and Bill Kell, and the affect theory of Silvan S. Tomkins. This paradigm is applied first to personality development, next to reformulating psychopathology, and finally to psychotherapeutic intervention. Human development is rooted in affect dynamics because affect is the primary innate biological motivating mechanism, according to Silvan Tomkins. We must attend first to affect and it its vicissitudes, and doing so is a very different way of organizing perceived psychological phenomena.

Shame will be examined from the perspective of affect theory. The affect of shame is important because no other affect is more disturbing to the self, none more central for the sense of identity. In the context of normal development, shame is the source of low self-esteem, diminished self-image, poor self-concept and deficient body-image. Shame itself produces self-doubt and disrupts both security and confidence. It can become an impediment to the experience of belonging and to shared intimacy. Shame always alerts us to any affront to human dignity. It is the experiential ground from which conscience and identity inevitably evolve. In the context of pathological development, shame is central to the emergence of alienation, loneliness, inferiority, and perfectionism. It plays a central role in many psychological disorders as well, including depression, paranoia, addiction, and borderline conditions. Sexual disorders and many eating disorders are largely disorders of shame. Both physical abuse and sexual abuse also significantly involve shame.

We will examine the psychodynamics of shame both in interpersonal relations and within the self's inner life, and explore shame's impact on normal as well as pathological development. We will further examine how the self is shaped by three central, interactive processes: affect, imagery, and language. Effective psychotherapies for specifically shame-based syndromes, as well as other affect-based disorders, evolve directly from this expanding knowledge of how the self develops, actually functions, and changes.

GERSHEN KAUFMAN
East Lansing, Michigan

Acknowledgments

To Silvan S. Tomkins, whose theoretical formulations of affect, scene, and script have profoundly shaped my thinking about the psychology of the self and also about psychotherapy. He has served as a beloved, invaluable, and stimulating mentor. I am deeply indebted for his critical reading of this manuscript, his penetrating critique, his illuminating suggestions, and his warm support, encouragement, and generosity over the last decade. Silvan Tomkins died in 1991, and he will be greatly missed. His genius inspired many.

To all the graduate students who have participated in my advanced graduate seminar on Psychology of the Self at Michigan State University. Over the past several years this has been an especially important laboratory for phenomenologically testing these ideas. I would like to acknowledge the following individuals: Dan Allender, Mark Picciotto, Dave Minder, Victor Nahmias, Shereen Arulpragasam, Barbara Palombi, Chip West, Chet Mirman, Wes Novak, Jan Rosenberg, Terry Bradley, Joel Kelley, Shing Shiong Chang, Melanie Neuroth, Lisa Blank, Sandy Tsuneyoshi, David Harris, Diane Trebilcock-Mitchell, Gary Gunther, Alice Riger, Tim Eaton, Jim Thomas, Cindy Morgan, Cathy Miller, Ted Brewer, Martha Berry, Ginny Duerst, Charles Berthold, Lori Brooks, Michelle Meola, Andy Reisner, Mary Fedewa, Shawn Fulton, Susan Schechtman, Bill Abler, and Wing Shing Chan. Their support and penetrating inquiry provided essential stimulation. They have challenged me to think my ideas through, to rethink what I had already concluded, and to extend ideas into new domains. The intellectual excitement generated by the seminar was central to this endeavor.

To my friends and colleagues in Minnesota, where my work initially found a home. It was their interest in my first book, *Shame: The Power of Caring,* that encouraged me to develop my theories further. It was there that I also learned how well lecturing can stimulate writing.

To Don Nathanson, for his enthusiastic response to my work and his encouragement to develop it further. I am particularly indebted to him for his critical reading of this manuscript and his many helpful suggestions. Several sections have been either added or developed further because he encouraged me to do so.

To Lev Raphael, my partner, who always shared the dream and believed, even before I did. Many theoretical concepts were developed and refined through our collaborative writing, teaching, lecturing, and consulting. I am equally indebted for his critical reading of the manuscript, his challenging ideas and numerous helpful suggestions, and for the shared excitement and enjoyment that are the fruits of writing. He gave so generously of his time and skill, laboring long hours over the manuscript with me, both honing the ideas and sharpening their presentation. To him I am deeply grateful for carefully guiding this book to fruition.

To all my clients, who allowed me to share their lives, their struggles, and their growth. Without them this book would not have been possible.

G. K.

Part I

A Developmental Theory of Shame, Identity, and the Self

> Our experiences do not merely link us to the outside world; they are us and they are the world for us; they make us part of the world. . . . Nature is a network of happenings that do not unroll like a red carpet into time, but are intertwined between every part of the world; and we are among those parts. In this nexus, we cannot reach certainty because it is not there to be reached; it goes with the wrong model, and the certain answers ironically are the wrong answers.
>
> JACOB BRONOWSKI
> *The Identity of Man*

One

Phenomenology and Facial Signs of Shame

Yet justice is a universal of all cultures. It is a tightrope that man walks, between his desire to fulfil his wishes, and his acknowledgment of social responsibility. No animal is faced with this dilemma: an animal is either social or solitary. Man alone aspires to be both in one, a social solitary. And to me that is a unique biological feature.

JACOB BRONOWSKI
The Ascent of Man

At the beginning of this inquiry into the psychology of shame, certain fundamental issues and assumptions must be addressed. Why is shame important to examine? Why construct a psychology based on shame? Since the dawn of scientific psychology, shame has remained an obscure phenomenon. It has never been the subject of scientific inquiry in the way that sexuality, anxiety, or even aggression have. Personality theorists have never accorded shame the status of a central construct. Libido, drive, sexuality, aggression, dependency—these have been the organizing constructs of our science. Observers of psychopathology have likewise universally ignored shame in construing the sources of psychological disorder. They refer to drive conflicts, guilty impulses, interpersonal dynamics, cognitive self statements, dysfunctional family systems, but not shame. Why is shame consistently overlooked? Because shame remains under taboo in contemporary society.

3

Shame actually has been neglected for various reasons. Indeed there is a significant degree of shame about shame, causing it to remain hidden. The cultural taboo surrounding human sexuality in an earlier age is thus matched by an equally pronounced taboo surrounding shame today. But another reason for the neglect of shame concerns the lack of an adequate language with which to accurately perceive, describe, and so bring into meaningful relationship this most elusive of human affects. The failure to attend to shame until quite recently is partially the result of the failure of scientific languages that describe inner experience. Without an accurate language of the self, shame slips quickly into the background of awareness. Our competing psychological languages or theories also have oriented us more toward examining guilt. The consequent reification of guilt as a construct has unfortunately obscured the role of shame, hindering accurate perception of its impact and dynamic complexity. Finally, psychological theorists as well as practitioners have found it both easier and safer to explore "guilty" impulses rather than a "shameful" self.

Why is shame surfacing now? The recent acceleration of addictive, abusive, and eating disorders has shifted the focus of attention. These are syndromes in which shame plays a central role, and the new and growing focus on these particular disorders has moved shame into the spotlight. Another reason concerns the failure of accepted theories and traditional methods of treatment; they have largely failed with shame. Furthermore, a radical transformation of our civilization, of both society and the family, has been under way in recent years. Increasingly, the problems in living now encountered are the result of inadequate parenting. A century ago, the extended family provided each developing individual with a vital supporting network of additional parenting figures. Not only has that been lost, but the nuclear family itself has given way to single-parent families, dual-career families, latchkey children, postdivorce families, blended families, stepfamilies, and so on. Culture is in the grips of a profound transition, and the breakdown of traditional forms of family and interpersonal relations has further intensified the experience of shame, bringing it into new and wider focus. Parents feel burdened and taxed by the demands of living in a complex, technological society and feel equally ill-prepared for the demands of parenting in such a society. In response, many parents simply abdicate. And the schools, which might provide a substitute, feel equally burdened, prompting many of our young people to become discouraged in yet another arena. The continuing evolution of our technological society is creating ever-new pressures that individuals are increasingly responding to with shame. The challenge for the next century lies precisely in creating new and viable forms for the family, for work, for interpersonal relations, for schools, for psychotherapy—for all of the central institutions of a culture.

If shame has been neglected until recently, why is shame important? Shame must be examined for various reasons. To begin with, shame plays a vital role in the development of conscience. By alerting us to misconduct or wrongdoing—to transgression in whatever form—shame motivates necessary self-correction. Thus, an understanding of antisocial or psychopathic behavior must begin with an inquiry into shame. The optimal development of conscience depends on adequate and appropriately graded doses of shame. Conscience will misfire because of too little or too much shame.

Shame alerts us not only to transgression but also to any affront to human dignity. By motivating the eventual correction of social indignities, shame plays a vital positive role. In the history of peoples, shame has always been associated with honor and pride. Even risking death may seem preferable to suffering the intolerable indignity of shame.

Conscience and dignity are certainly important reasons to study shame. The development of identity is another. No other affect is more central to identity formation. Our sense of self, both particular and universal, is deeply embedded in our struggles with the alienating affect. Answers to the questions, "Who am I?" and "Where do I belong?" are forged in the crucible of shame.

Shame is also acutely disturbing to the self. In fact, no other affect is more deeply disturbing. Like a wound made from the inside by an unseen hand, shame disrupts the natural functioning of the self.

Because shame is central to conscience, indignity, identity, and disturbances in self-functioning, this affect is the source of low self-esteem, poor self-concept or body image, self-doubt and insecurity, and diminished self-confidence. Shame is the affect that is the source of feelings of inferiority. The inner experience of shame is like a sickness within the self, a sickness of the soul. If we are to understand and eventually heal what ails the self, then we must begin with shame.

Certain mistaken assumptions unfortunately have continued to hinder understanding and knowledge. These assumptions concern the source and the target of shame. The traditionally accepted view is that shame requires the presence of another person. Either one or more people must be present during shaming, or else the communication of shame must come directly from another, as when, for example, a mother disparages her child in front of peers. Shame generally has been viewed, both in our science and in our culture, as visual and public. In contrast, guilt traditionally has been viewed as essentially auditory and private. This assumption, which is fundamental to formulations of personality and culture, is in error because shame can be an entirely internal experience with no one else present. The source of shame can be either in the self or in another, with the result that individuals can experience shame whether or not others are present and watching. Individuals will also feel shame whether or not others are actually doing the shaming. Only the self need watch the self and only the self need shame the self.

Now consider the target of shame. The traditional view has held that the target is the self. When individuals feel shame their entire self is involved. Contrast this with guilt for a moment. If shame is about the self, then guilt is about deeds or acts. The target of guilt is conceived to be the self's behavior whereas the target of shame is presumed to be the whole self. The assumption that we feel guilty about deeds but feel shame about self is equally in error. The target of shame can be either the self or the self's actions, just as one can feel guilty about deeds or else feel essentially guilt-ridden as a person. From the perspective of affect theory, one can feel shameful about deeds as well as guilty about self.

Implicit in traditional assumptions concerning shame is the belief that shame is a more "primitive" state than guilt. Visual shame has been conceived as developmentally eclipsed by auditory guilt, a more advanced affective state requiring or reflecting a higher level of self-development. Again, this is inaccurate. Neither shame nor guilt is more primitive or advanced than the other. The mistaken conception of guilt as a more advanced state is determined wholly by the particular categories imposed upon inner experience, not by inner experience itself. The language with which we partition inner events, and then rearrange them into meaningful relationship, either hones perception or further masks it.

Another mistaken belief is that shame is inherently crippling whereas guilt is "healthier," presumably because guilt is about the self's acts or deeds, not about the self. Shame is not necessarily crippling, though it can become so. But inherently, shame only amplifies our experience. It can have important positive effects as well, depending on its frequency, intensity, duration, consequences, and remedies. Shame is the experiential ground from which conscience and identity spring.

Examining the dynamics of shame has become imperative. Shame is the principal impediment in all relationships, whether parent-child, teacher-student, or therapist-client. It violates both inner security and interpersonal trust. Shame wounds not only the self, but also a family, an ethnic or minority group within a dominant culture, or even an entire nation. Any disenfranchised, discriminated-against, or persecuted minority group will experience the shame of inferiority, the humiliation of being outcast. Racial, ethnic, and religious group tensions are inevitable consequences of that shame. Just as personal identity becomes molded by shame, ethnic-religious identity and national character are similarly shaped. Shame is also an impediment in international relations, where the dynamics of diplomacy invariably are the dynamics of shame and honor. Shame is a universal dynamic in child rearing, education, interpersonal relations, psychotherapy, ethnic group relations, national culture and politics, and international relations.

PSYCHOLOGY OF SHAME: THE HISTORY OF AN IDEA

The psychology of shame is also the history of an idea. Previous conceptions of shame have suffered from the restrictions imposed by language on accurate perception of inner states. In Freud's work shame receives comparatively little attention; guilt holds the spotlight. Freud views the origin of shame in relation to genital visibility:

> . . . man's raising himself from the ground, of his assumption of an upright gait; this made his genitals, which were previously concealed, visible and in need of protection, and so provoked feelings of shame in him. (1930, p. 99)

In a subsequent paper Freud also relates shame's origin to genital deficiency:

> Shame, which is considered to be a feminine characteristic *par excellence* but is far more a matter of convention than might be supposed, has as its purpose, we believe, concealment of genital deficiency. We are not forgetting that at a later time shame takes on other functions. (1933, p. 132)

Freud's concept of libidinal drives hinders the identification of particular affects, shame being one, but also orients him more toward examining the nature of guilt in relation to oedipal strivings. When the human being is conceived as gripped by imperious drives in perpetual conflict with reality and society, shame is of little consequence. Freud's blindness to shame is partially the result of his drive theory, and partially the result of the general failure of language to partition affect. Any psychological theory is limited by the contemporary language of the day, and by the particular conception of the universe existing at the time.

Adler's work on inferiority feelings and the inferiority complex (1933) reflects an increased awareness of the importance of shame-related phenomena. His concept of inferiority represents one of the first attempts to accord shame a central role in the development of personality. Adler, in contrast to Freud, certainly perceives the effects of shame, but lacks an affect theory and an accurate language to partition and rearrange the perceived data.

The concept of inferiority reappears in the work of Franz Alexander (1938) where it is reinterpreted within psychoanalytic theory. For Alexander, inferiority is "a self-accusation based on a comparison, on the simple fact that one feels weaker than another person" (p. 44). Although his purpose is to distinguish between inferiority and guilt, Alexander concludes by suggesting that these feelings represent two different types of shame, each with its own remedy, aggressive/competitive behavior versus atonement.

In the work of Karen Horney (1950), shame is not itself accorded the status of a central construct. However, the effects of shame are described in terms of Horney's concepts of "neurotic pride" and "the pride system." Horney relates shame directly to pride: "The two typical reactions to hurt pride are shame and humiliation. We will feel ashamed if we do, think, or feel something that violates our pride. And we will feel humiliated if others do something that hurts our pride, or fail to do what our pride requires of them" (p. 95). Her concept of pride is not a positive one; pride is the enemy of love, inseparably linked with self-hate and self-contempt:

> The development of pride is the logical outcome, the climax and consolidation of the process initiated with the search for glory. The individual may first have relatively harmless fantasies in which he pictures himself in some glamorous role. He proceeds by creating in his mind an

idealized image of what he "really" is, could be, should be. Then comes the most decisive step: his real self fades out and the energies available for self-realization are shifted to the actualization of the idealized self. The claims are his attempt to assert his place in the world, a place that is adequate to the significance of the idealized self and one that supports it. With his shoulds, he drives himself to actualize the perfection of this self. And, lastly, he must develop a system of private values which, like "the Ministry of Truth" in *Nineteen Eighty-Four* (by George Orwell), determines what to like and accept in himself, what to glorify, what to be proud of. But this system of values must by necessity also determine what to reject, to abhor, to be ashamed of, to despise, to hate. It cannot do the one without the other. Pride and self-hate belong inseparably together; they are two expressions of one process. (1950, p. 109)

Subsequent inquiries into shame largely concentrate on the distinctions between shame and guilt, as though these two particular communicative symbols now have been forever stamped into human experience. Furthermore, shame and guilt continue to be viewed predominantly from a psychoanalytic perspective. Psychoanalytic theory, however, is more accurately understood as a *linguistic system:* it is simply one language among many for describing the domain of inner experience.

In their classic monograph, Piers and Singer (1953) conceptualize shame as arising from tension between ego and ego ideal while guilt stems from tension between ego and superego. Guilt accompanies transgression and the implicit threat is one of punishment, that is, castration. Shame accompanies failure and the implicit threat is abandonment.

In his pioneering study of identity, Erik Erikson (1950) places shame in the second of eight stages or identity crises that span the life cycle. The genesis of shame is related directly to the arena of toilet training and the outcome of that stage is autonomy versus shame and doubt. However, as one probes deeper into Erikson's conceptualization of these recurring crises, it seems evident that each subsequent stage represents a linguistic *transformation of shame.* The negative pole of each crisis is actually an elaboration of shame, given new or wider meaning. Each subsequent crisis involves, at least in part, a reworking of shame.

Consider the poles of each identity crisis more closely: basic trust versus *basic mistrust,* autonomy versus *shame and doubt,* initiative versus *guilt,* industry versus *inferiority,* identity versus *role confusion,* intimacy versus *isolation,* generativity versus *stagnation,* ego integrity versus *despair.* The affect most critical to the development of mistrust, guilt, inferiority, isolation, and so on, is shame. Those cognitive symbols reflect differences not in affect per se but in *coassemblies* of affect with perceived causes, targets, and consequences. Certainly, other affects may become fused along with shame in the formation of these recurring crises, but the one affect central to the sense of identity is shame.

Helen M. Lynd (1958) expands on Erikson's work and conceives of shame as deeply embedded in the individual's search for identity. She describes the shame experience as comprising unexpected exposure, incongruity or inappropriateness, threat to trust, and involvement of the whole self.

Helen B. Lewis (1971, 1981, 1987a, 1987b) explores the relationships among guilt, shame, identification, and the superego, again from a psychoanalytic perspective. She views guilt and shame as different, though equally advanced superego functions (states) that develop along different routes of identification. Differing in their phenomenology, guilt and shame have a common source in internalized aggression. Guilt is generated by identification with the threatening parent, which then creates an internalized threat, whereas "identification with the beloved or admired ego-ideal stirs pride and triumphant feeling; failure to live up to this internalized admired imago stirs shame" (1971, p. 23).

More recently, Leon Wurmser (1981), also working from a psychoanalytic perspective, distinguishes shame anxiety, shame affect proper, and shame attitude. For Wurmser, shame guards the boundary of privacy and intimacy while guilt limits the expansion of power.

Other investigators within the psychoanalytic community continue the inquiry into shame. Broucek (1982) examines shame in relation to narcissistic disorders, calling it the keystone affect. Morrison (1983) also examines shame in relation to narcissism and self-esteem, while Fisher (1985) views shame as central to borderline development. Finally, Nathanson (1987a) synthesizes research data from infant observation, psychoanalytic theory, and Tomkins's affect theory.

Though previously neglected and minimized, shame has finally moved center stage. Knowledge of inner states, however, is ultimately the prisoner of the particular language used to describe those states because language shapes perception. The psychoanalytic language attempts to account for shame with a distinct panoply of constructs already deemed valid. Indeed the failure to attend to shame until quite recently is a direct result of the failure of various psychological linguistic systems to arrange shame into meaningful relationship with other observables. Our psychological languages generally have not adequately described or explained that most elusive of human affects, shame—not psychoanalytic theory, not object-relations theory, not interpersonal theory, and not cognitive-behavioral theory. We must therefore look elsewhere in order to understand the alienating affect, illuminate its impact on the development of both personality and psychopathology, and grasp its dynamic role in human affairs. The foundation for our continuing examination of shame is affect theory.

AFFECT THEORY

Silvan Tomkins (1962, 1963a, 1982, 1984, 1987a) has presented a model for an affect theory of motivation and a precise language to differentiate the innate affects. Tomkins's formulation is summarized in the following chart, where nine innate affects are distinguished. Separate terms for low and high intensity are listed for most of the affects, and each affect is described in terms of the corresponding facial responses:

Positive

1. Interest—Excitement: Eyebrows down, track, look, listen

2. Enjoyment—Joy: Smile, lips widened up and out

3. Surprise—Startle: Eyebrows up, eye blink

Negative

4. Distress—Anguish: Cry, arched eyebrows, mouth down, tears, rhythmic sobbing

5. Fear—Terror: Eyes frozen open, pale, cold, sweaty, facial trembling, with hair erect

6. Anger—Rage: Frown, clenched jaw, red face

7. Shame—Humiliation: Eyes down, head down

8. Dissmell: Upper lip raised

9. Disgust: Lower lip lowered and protruded

Affect is primarily facial behavior, according to Tomkins. Only secondarily is it bodily behavior, encompassing outer skeletal as well as inner visceral responses. Tomkins has reversed the traditional view of the primacy of the viscera by making the face the primary site of the affects:

> In short, affect is primarily facial behavior. Secondarily it is bodily behavior, outer skeletal and inner visceral behavior. When we become aware of these facial and/or visceral responses we are aware of our affects. We may respond with these affects however without becoming aware of the feedback from them. Finally, we learn to generate, from memory, images of these same responses which we can become aware of with or without repetition of facial, skeletal or visceral responses. (1962, pp. 205-206)

In Tomkins's view, the primary blueprints for cognition, decision, and action are provided by the affect system:

> Rather, I see affect or feeling as *the primary innate biological motivating mechanism,* more urgent than drive deprivation and pleasure, and more urgent even than physical pain. Without its amplification, nothing else matters, and with its amplification anything can matter. (1987a, p. 137)

We are urged to explore and also attempt to control whatever conditions evoke positive or negative affect. Four general images, or strategies develop in human beings: maximizing positive affect, minimizing negative affect, minimizing affect inhibition, and maximizing power to accomplish the other three strategies.

Tomkins accounts for the differential activation of affect by three variants of a single principle: the density of neural firing or stimulation. Density refers to the number of neural firings per unit of time. There exist three general classes of affect activators and each class further amplifies the actual source that activated it. These classes are *stimulation increase, stimulation level,* and *stimulation decrease.* The three classes of motives include affects activated by stimulation that is increasing, that is level, and that is decreasing.

The source of neural firing can be either internal or external. When the density of neural firing suddenly increases, human beings will startle, become afraid, or become interested. Which affect becomes activated will depend on the suddenness of the increase in stimulation. However, when neural firing reaches and maintains a high, constant level of stimulation, in excess of the optimal, the human being will respond with anger or distress. The particular affect activated again depends on the actual level of stimulation. Finally, when neural firing suddenly decreases, the human being will laugh or smile with enjoyment; it is the suddenness of the decrease in stimulation that determines which occurs.

The foregoing activation profiles comprise the set of innate activators of the six primary affects, three positive and three negative. These profiles are illustrated in Figure 1.1.

In addition to the six primary affects, Tomkins distinguishes one affect auxiliary, shame, and two drive auxiliaries, dissmell and disgust. Consider the drive auxiliaries first. Dissmell and disgust are innate defensive responses, functioning in an auxiliary manner to the oxygen, thirst, and hunger drives. Coming into contact with a noxious-smelling object may activate dissmell, causing the upper lip and nose to be raised and the head drawn back. A noxious-tasting object may activate disgust and then be spit out, or if swallowed and toxic, may activate nausea and be vomited out. Dissmell and disgust are drive auxiliary responses that have evolved biologically to protect human beings from noxious objects. However, these responses are evolving beyond the status of drive-reducing acts; they are increasingly emitted to biologically neutral stimuli as well. In contrast to these two drive auxiliaries, shame is an affect auxiliary. It functions in an auxiliary manner to two primary affects, interest and enjoyment, by inhibiting them after they have been activated.

Central to Tomkins's affect theory is the conception of affect itself as amplification. Affect amplifies a particular response by being similar to that response—but also different. It is an *analog amplifier.*

One form of affect amplification is produced by the quality of responses from specific affect receptors: sweating in terror, reddening of the face in anger, dilation of blood vessels and accompanying facial warmth in enjoyment. There is a second form of affect amplification that is produced by the similarity of a particular affect's profile, in time, to its activating trigger. By being analogous in its profile of activation, maintenance, and decay, affect both amplifies and extends the duration and impact of whatever activates it. Affect becomes immediately coassembled with its activator, and conjointly simulates its activator in its particular profile of neural firing.

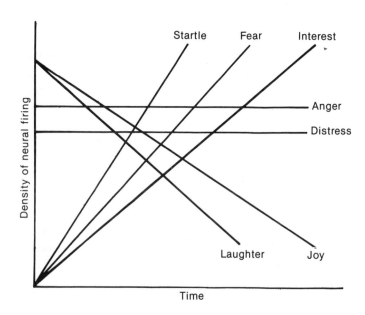

Figure 1.1 Graphic representation of a theory of innate activators of affect. (Reprinted from Tomkins, 1962, p. 251.)

Tomkins considers the face to be the central site of affect responses and their feedback. He regards the skin in general, and the skin of the face in particular, as being of the greatest importance in producing the *feel* of affect. The feedback from the patterned changes in facial muscle responses provides the feel of specific affects. Tomkins further believes that the complex affect displays on the human face evolved primarily as sources of motivating feedback. The communication of affect, then, is a secondary spin-off function rather than the primary function.

Each affect, furthermore, has as part of its innate program a specific cry or vocalization that is subserved by specific patterns of breathing. There has been a universal confusion of the experience of *backed-up affect* with that of biologically and psychologically authentic *innate affect*.

The free and open expression of innate affect is highly contagious. All societies, therefore, exercise varying degrees of control over affect expression, and particularly over the cry of affect. Societies in general neither encourage nor permit their members to cry out in rage or excitement, in distress or terror, whenever or wherever they wish. The open expression of affect is restricted beginning at an early age and strict control is exerted particularly over the voice.

Because the free vocalization of affect is suppressed in all societies, what is actually being experienced as affect is pseudo, or backed-up affect. This phenomenon can be observed in a child trying to suppress laughter by swallowing a snicker, struggling to maintain a stiff upper lip in an effort to keep from crying, or tightening the jaw in order not to cry out in anger. In every case, the technique of suppressing the vocalization of affect involves holding one's breath.

Tomkins conceives of what is commonly called "stress" as backed-up affect, and many of the endocrine changes associated with stress are the consequence of backed-up affect. Psychosomatic illness might thus be one of the prices of the systematic suppression of the innate affects.

Affect is the primary innate biological motivating mechanism. Tomkins's theory views affect in terms of amplification because affect functions as an analog amplifier. The face is the central site of these patterned affect responses and the skin of the face produces the feel of affect. Suppression of the vocalization of affect produces pseudo or backed-up affect, which in turn results in specific endocrine changes. Such suppression also causes ambiguity about what affect feels like, since so much of our affective life as adults represents a transformation of the affective response rather than the simpler, more direct and briefer innate affect. Therefore, it is the affect mechanism that mediates stress: the development of various psychosomatic syndromes is the consequence of backed-up affect and corresponding endocrine changes. Finally, examining the relationship between affect and the responses to affect must include motor responses, retrieved memories, and constructed thoughts.

Affect connects its own activator with the response that follows it, creating a coassembly of activator-affect-response. The affect imprints the responses to it with the same amplification exerted on its own activator. Thus, the increasing rate of stimulation that activates excitement affect results in a further amplification of both its activator and any responses that follow, whether actions or thoughts. These responses are simultaneously amplified by the same profile of increasing density of neural firing, producing accelerated actions or equally rapid thoughts. The creative artist or scientist who awakens in the night excited over a discovery experiences the amplification of excitement affect. The rapid flow of thoughts, or actions, mimics the stimulation profile of the activator of excitement. The significance of the affect mechanism lies in the fact that it is both an amplifier of its activator and of any response it evokes. This connection arises simply from the overlap in time of the activator, affect, and response.

Extensive empirical investigation of affect theory has been in progress. Cross-cultural studies support Tomkins's theory by demonstrating the universality of the innate affects (Ekman, 1971). Studies of five literate cultures, four Western and one Eastern, and of two preliterate cultures from New Guinea prove that, as Tomkins theorizes, there are universal facial expressions of emotion. Ekman postulates both cultural differences in facial expression as well as universals, which he describes as "facial affect program[s], located within the nervous system of all human beings, linking particular facial muscular movements with particular emotions" (1971, pp. 278-279).

More recent research on autonomic nervous system activity demonstrates that different innate affects have different physiological correlates. Ekman, Levenson, and Friesen (1983) find that autonomic activity distinguishes between positive and negative affects as well as among particular negative affects. Their findings challenge theories of emotion that propose autonomic activity to be undifferentiated, providing additional empirical support for Tomkins's affect theory.

PHENOMENOLOGY OF SHAME

Shame is the affect of inferiority. No other affect is more central to the development of identity. None is closer to the experienced self, nor more disturbing. Shame is felt as an inner torment. It is the most poignant experience of the self by the self, whether felt in the humiliation of cowardice, or in the sense of failure to cope successfully with a challenge. Shame is a wound made from the inside, dividing us from both ourselves and others.

> If distress is the affect of suffering, shame is the affect of indignity, of defeat, of transgression and of alienation. Though terror speaks to life and death and distress makes of the world a vale of tears, yet shame strikes deepest into the heart of man. While terror and distress hurt, they are wounds inflicted from outside which penetrate the smooth surface of the

ego; but shame is felt as an inner torment, a sickness of the soul. It does not matter whether the humiliated one has been shamed by derisive laughter or whether he mocks himself. In either event he feels himself naked, defeated, alienated, lacking in dignity or worth. (Tomkins, 1963a, p. 118)

Phenomenologically, to feel shame is to feel *seen* in a painfully diminished sense. Shame reveals the inner self, exposing it to view. The self feels exposed both to itself and to anyone else present. That exposure can be of the self *to* the self alone, or it can be of the self to others. Central to an understanding of the alienating affect is that shame can be an entirely *internal* experience. No one else need be present in order for shame to be felt, but when others are present shame is an impediment to further communication.

Shame is felt as an interruption, and it functions to further impede communication. The very experience of shame itself is communicated. The individual whose head hangs, or whose eyes lower, or whose gaze is averted, however briefly, is directly communicating shame. Shame turns attention to the face, thereby heightening visibility of the face and therefore of the self. Shame is an act that reduces facial communication, but paradoxically also heightens awareness of the face. Blushing, for example, only compounds shame, causing one even to feel ashamed of shame. Tomkins links shame to the taboo on looking directly into the eyes of another and to the equal taboo on looking away too visibly. Because shame inevitably calls attention to the face, shame and self-consciousness are tightly bound.

In the midst of shame, the attention turns inward, thereby generating the torment of self-consciousness. Sudden, unexpected exposure, coupled with binding inner scrutiny, characterize the essential nature of the affect of shame. Whether all eyes are upon us or only our own, we feel fundamentally deficient as individuals, diseased, defective. To live with shame is to experience the very essence or heart of the self as wanting. Shame is inevitably alienating, isolating, and deeply disturbing.

Consider the binding effect of shame more closely. Sustained eye contact with others becomes intolerable. The head is hung, spontaneous movement is interrupted, and speech is silenced. Exposure itself eradicates speech, thereby causing shame to be almost incommunicable to others. Feeling exposed further opens the self to painful inner scrutiny. When the attention turns inward, we are suddenly watching ourselves, scrutinizing critically the minutest detail of our being. The excruciating observation of the self that results, this torment of self-consciousness, becomes so acute as to create a binding, almost paralyzing effect.

This binding effect of shame is central to understanding shame's impact on personality development. The binding effects of exposure, of feeling *seen,* acutely disturb the smooth functioning of the self. Exposure binds movement and speech, paralyzing the self. The urge to hide, to disappear, is a spontaneous reaction to the self's heightened visibility; it can overwhelm the self. To feel shame is to feel inherently bad, fundamentally flawed as a person. A consuming loneliness gradually can envelop the self in the wake of shame, and deepening self-doubt can become one's constant companion. Even so, shame remains an ambivalent affect.

In the midst of shame, there is an ambivalent longing for reunion with whomever shamed us. We feel divided and secretly yearn to feel *one,* whole. The experience of shame feels like a rupture either in self, in a particular relationship, or both. Shame is an affective experience that violates both interpersonal trust and internal security. Intense shame is a sickness within the self, a disease of the spirit.

The experience of apparent transparency, so often referred to in regard to shame, is created precisely by the sense of exposure inherent to shame. Many shame-based individuals, for example, feel as if they are impostors, only waiting to be unmasked. When we are watching ourselves, scrutinizing whatever we see nakedly revealed, it only *seems* that the watching eyes belong to others. This is, of course, heightened when other people are actually present and may, in fact, be watching. Hence, the situation of being in a group will be especially likely to activate shame and intensify further the sense of exposure. Likewise, the exposure inherent in shame creates the sense of nakedness before an audience: it feels *as if* others can see inside us or actually read our thoughts. Shame fuels the growth of such distorted perceptions, one of the key building blocks of paranoia, for example.

The expression of shame is inherently problematic, but is made more so in this culture. Not only does exposure itself interrupt speech, but how is one to express openly what must seem one's inescapable flaw? In this culture people are not encouraged to reveal their failings and inferiorities. They are not taught in the school or family how to tolerate shame, effectively release it, and overcome its sources.

In the early years of life, shame is predominantly a wordless experience irrespective of its duration. Later, shame experiences become transformed by language. Shame increasingly becomes a partially cognitive, self-evaluative experience with the attainment of formal operational thought in the Piagetian sense, but it begins as a largely wordless experience and remains so for some time.

In the experience of shame the self feels exposed. When the attention turns inward the self watches the self, thereby generating the torment of self-consciousness. Sudden, unexpected exposure, coupled with binding inner scrutiny, characterizes the affect of shame. One can feel foolish or bad, deficient or inherently flawed. Exposure binds the self because feeling *seen* acutely disturbs the smooth functioning of the self. Exposure can interrupt movement, bind speech, and make eye contact intolerable. Shame paralyzes the self. In spite of the torment, the self still longs for reunion with the other. Because shame is an ambivalent affect, it is deeply disturbing. The dynamics of shame and honor operate wherever people encounter one another, whether informally or intimately. Even loss of life can be preferable to loss of face because human beings innately resist the lowering of the head or eyes in shame.

FACIAL SIGNS OF SHAME

What do we observe when we view the shame-experiencing self? The facial signs of shame, particularly notable in children, include hanging the head, lowering or averting the eyes, and blushing. Tomkins (1963a, p. 133) theorizes that the face is the primary site for both the registration and communication of affect: "The self lives in the face." The shame response of hanging the head or lowering the eyes is a response that causes an immediate reduction of facial visibility, which is why we have historically referred to shame in terms of *loss of face*. To lose face is to lose honor. Suffering such indignity and defeat is intolerable, whether among boys and girls in a neighborhood playing "King of the Mountain," or among nations similarly gripped by insult. We have only to recall the recent Falkland Islands war or the hostage crisis in Iran to illustrate the dynamics of shame on the international stage. Hanging one's head in shame deeply mortifies the spirit, whether as individuals, families, or nations. Loss of face itself is further cause for shame. Inevitably, there is shame about shame.

It is important to note that there are also a number of characteristic facial defenses against shame. Tomkins (1963a, pp. 145-146) describes three. First is the *frozen face,* in which the facial musculature is chronically frozen, kept under tight control.

Second is the *head-back look,* in which the head is tilted back rather than forward and the chin juts forward. This facial posture is created by such particular parental responses to shame as, "Keep your chin up." Tomkins conceives of the head-back look as an *anti-affect* response produced via the *opposite* of the shame response, in head and chin up, not down. It need not necessarily be taught by someone else, since it can be taught by the self to the self, as in, "I *won't* lower my head—in fact, I'll raise it *more than usual,* not just up."

Finally the *look of contempt* is a third facial defense. This particular look manifests as a sneer, with the upper lip raised. Contempt is a blend of dissmell and anger affects. According to Tomkins, the look of contempt is most often a *recasting* defense, that is, "I will shame you." It is invoked whenever dissmell has been used by the *other* to evoke shame.

SECONDARY REACTIONS TO SHAME

Shame can be followed by any affect, including shame, as when one blushes in shame, becomes aware of blushing, and then becomes further ashamed of blushing. The most typical affects observed to follow shame are *fear, distress* (the crying response, more commonly called sadness), and *rage* (an intensification of anger affect). Fear of further exposure or further occurrences of shame is a prominent consequence of the alienating affect, particularly when any expression of shame itself becomes shamed. Distress frequently accompanies shame, all too often masking it. A young girl, for example, may hang her head after a defeat or scolding and then begin to cry. Usually it is one of the overtly displayed secondary reactions that is more easily seen and attended to by significant others. Too often shame is missed or ignored. The third reaction, rage, serves a vital self-protective function by insulating the self against further exposure. While expressions of rage sometimes do invite contact, rage insulates the wounded self. When rage becomes further magnified as hatred it will function to actively keep others away. These secondary reactions function to mask shame from view.

Consider the following situation. A young boy is attempting to put together a truck with his erector set by making it match the model in the diagram. Suddenly, he gives up, obviously frustrated. Next he momentarily hangs his head, uttering not a word, and then abruptly throws the model and tools across the room, slamming them into the wall. One need simply observe the affect sequence and ask him, "When you feel frustrated, do you feel shame and then get very angry?" This would allow shame conscious expression.

In addition to these varied secondary affective reactions typically observed to follow shame, the facial defenses described previously may also function as secondary reactions. All of these potentially mask shame from view, interfering with its accurate perception.

SHAME COMPLEXES

Language plays a central role in the perception of inner states, and perception is always an active, constructive process. The words used to describe inner states inevitably alter them, shaping perception itself. Language can either sharpen or mask the perception of shame. Through language, particular meanings about the self are created and become differentially attached to distinct shame experiences. Having so many different names for its various manifestations has hindered recognition of the underlying *affect* of shame present in each of these disturbing inner states.

Shame complexes become manifest in a broad range of interpersonal contexts. A variety of inner states have been distinguished, given different labels, and so mistakenly conceived as distinctly different: *discouragement, self-consciousness, embarrassment, shyness, shame,* and *guilt.* In Tomkins's view (1987a, p. 143), these states do not reflect differences in affect per se, but rather, differences in their coassembled activators, targets, and reducers. Because of the differential coassembly of perceived causes and consequences, including perceptions, cognitions, and intentions, these states are actually experienced, overall, as quite different. Yet their core affect is identical.

Inner states are complex coassemblies. The affect organizing a particular state is preceded by an activator or cause and also followed by various targets and consequences. It is the unique coassembly of *activator-affect-consequence* that determines the experience of these states as distinctly different. They are not different with respect to affect, but their coassembled causes and targets create distinctly different phenomenologies. Discouragement feels different from embarrassment, and each feels different still from shyness, though the underlying affect in each is the same. Discouragement is actually shame about temporary defeat. Self-consciousness is the self exposed in shame, the self scrutinizing the self. Embarrassment is shame before any type of audience. Shyness is shame in the presence of a stranger. Shame is loss of face, honor, or dignity, a sense of failure. Guilt is shame about moral transgression, immorality shame. These are the coassembled inner states that become organized around shame as their principal affect.

Discouragement

Shame is experienced as discouragement when defeat is perceived as temporary. The self is not incapable or inferior, yet. Only the self's effort has failed, but temporarily. Here one feels defeated for the time being by a difficult task that one has failed to solve. The exposure is of the self to the self. Or shame may be occasioned by the failure to attain whatever goal has been set on this particular try. Shame in the form of discouragement, for example, is frequently observed during the course of psychotherapy. When clients experience inevitable setbacks in their struggle against ingrained dysfunctional patterns, their perceived defeat, however temporary, inevitably reactivates shame, thereby producing discouragement.

Self-Consciousness

Self-consciousness is usually mistaken for anxiety, which, of course, often *accompanies* it. However, the two are quite different affects. Anxiety is a manifestation of fear affect, while self-consciousness is a manifestation of shame.

The affect of shame calls attention to the self, exposing it to view, and the self lives in the face. We become suddenly aware of being seen, unexpectedly aware of our face. We become *self-conscious,* as if the self suddenly were impaled under a magnifying glass. The shame response of hanging the head or lowering the eyes is one that reduces that agonizing facial visibility.

Since shame is primarily a response of facial communication reduction, awareness of the face by the self is an integral part of the experience of shame. Blushing of the face in shame is a consequence of, as well as a further cause for, heightened self- and face-consciousness. As previously noted, individuals may blush in any part of the body to which attention is directed. The face is the most common locus of blushing because the face is the chief organ of general communication of speech and of affect alike. The self lives where it exposes itself and where it receives similar exposures from others. (Tomkins, 1963a, p. 133)

Embarrassment

Being seen as socially inappropriate is the essence of the state of embarrassment. Behaving clumsily, appearing foolish before one's peers, or being ill-mannered at a social gathering are instances of social incongruity we learn to avoid. While some may seemingly shrug them off with a laugh at the time, these scenes can replay inside the self, producing a deepening mortification. Individuals dread their recurrence. However mild or intense, embarrassment is not a different affect. Feeling socially ill-at-ease, self-conscious, or exposed is simply another form of shame. Embarrassment is shame before an audience.

Shyness

Shyness is shame in yet a different context, either in the presence of *or* at the prospect of approaching strangers. The presence of the stranger activates the feeling of exposure, which then binds the self. This is what commonly has been called shyness: feeling socially awkward, dumb, speechless. By giving it a different name, we have lost sight of the underlying affect, shame, which governs the patterning of shyness.

By viewing only the outward form, and calling shyness a learned behavior, the centrality of affect is missed. And by viewing shyness as some inevitable derivative of oedipal strivings or counter-strivings or other such drive conflicts, the primacy of affect over drives is missed.

Shame

Shame is loss of face, whether at the hands of a bully or a parent. Shame is hanging the head, whether in response to, "You should be ashamed of yourself" or "I'm so disappointed in you." Shame feels like a wound made from the inside. Shame is dishonor, fallen pride, a broken spirit. Even the threat in "castration" is double-edged, as Tomkins (1963a, pp. 526-529) first observed: along with *castration fear* there is *castration shame,* the inevitable humiliation inherent to castration. The beaten, humiliated individual, whether defeated as a child by a brutalizing parent or defeated as an adult by a dead end career or marriage, has been defeated by shame, has endured it until it has broken the self. If unchecked, shame can engulf the self, immersing the individual deeper into despair. To live with shame is to feel alienated and defeated, never quite good enough to belong. And secretly the self feels to blame; the deficiency lies within. Shame is without parallel a sickness of the soul.

The concept of shame unfolding here encompasses meanings beyond what has been traditionally signified by that term. The source of low self-esteem, poor self-concept, or diminished self-image is shame. That is the affective source of later feelings of inadequacy or inferiority. Shame is also the source of what have been referred to as narcissistic wounds or injuries. For all these reasons, it makes sense to consider shame as the central, integrative concept that unites all of the foregoing inner states. Each represents a different face of shame.

Guilt

Distinguishing shame from guilt has occupied psychologists for decades. Most have attempted to describe guilt and shame within the psychoanalytic linguistic system. Piers and Singer, Erik Erikson, Helen B. Lewis, and Leon Wurmser have each framed their observations within psychoanalytic language, a language that does *not* adequately differentiate the affect system from the drive system. Although psychoanalysis has recently embraced object-relations theory, it has nevertheless retained crucial linguistic blind spots, thus failing to make other critically important distinctions within its domain. Psychoanalysis has recognized the importance and psychological impact of relationship experiences, particularly in the family, but it has as yet no phenomenological language for affect in general, let alone for shame in particular, and no developmental language of the self.

From an affect theory perspective, experiences labeled *guilt* must be further examined phenomenologically. We must not stop at the symbol as though it were the inner event itself. Other theoretical perspectives continue the prevalent guilt/shame dichotomy because they lack a precise language to differentiate inner events at the more fundamental level of affect. Tomkins gives us a new and richer glimpse of the underside of human motivation.

In Tomkins's schema (personal communication, 1986) guilt is not a different innate affect, but instead is viewed, as a theoretical concept, as *moral shame.* "The critical thing in what we label guilt is the *ethical judgment of immorality,"* according to Tomkins.

Concepts, however, are not only used theoretically, but for communication purposes as well. In this context the term "guilt" has been widely used to refer to a broad spectrum of inner states. These are affective states organized around different combinations of negative affects, each coassembled with the ethical judgment of immorality. Hence, they are all *labeled* ambiguously as "guilt." Tomkins distinguishes the following:

1. Shame *about* moral matters (not a separate affect per se, but rather a different phenomenological origin and target) which has been labeled with a different word (just as we label shame shyness if it involves reticence whereas we call the *same* affect shame if it is the distance *and* negative feeling of the other which is coassembled with shame).

2. Self-disgust, or self-dissmell or contempt against the self by the self for moral infractions. I now label contempt as *dissmell and anger* combined. Dissmell is the innate smell response to bad odors. Contempt adds anger *toward* a response which innately (dissmell) is *away from* the bad smelling object.

3. Anger at the self for moral infractions.

4. Distress at the self for moral infractions.

5. Fear at the self for moral infractions.

6. Any combination of these affects and judgments against the self by the self.

7. Any one of the above experienced as coming from an "internalized other" toward the self. (Tomkins, personal communication, 1986)

From the perspective of affect theory, guilt is immorality shame. But from the perspective of common usage, guilt reflects a broad spectrum of affective states. The particular face of guilt can be moral shame, and the self hangs its head. Guilt can also be moral distress, and the self grieves in remorse. On the other hand, the face of guilt can be moral disgust or moral dissmell, and one part of the self becomes the judge while another part of the self becomes the offender. Guilt can also take the form of punitive self-blame, recruiting the affect of anger but directing it in a self-accusatory, blaming fashion. Fear of exposure or punishment and moral outrage are other affective states that fall under the ambiguous label, guilt. While the ethical judgment of immorality is present in each of these "guilt" states, they feel and actually are so different because their organizing affects create distinctly different phenomenologies.

A LANGUAGE FOR SHAME

In order to advance as a science, we must return to accurate observation of inner experience. We must fit to inner states words that remain grounded in phenomenology. The language we create to describe the self must be specific in its referents, precise in its definitions, clear about its limits, and simple in its description. We must construct an accurate language of the self and a precise language for shame that are not imposed upon inner experience, but rather illuminate it. Language creates tools and these tools tune inner states further into awareness. In turn, these tools enable us, as scientific observers, to perform inner operations, actual experiments, which either confirm or disconfirm previous observations.

CONCLUSION

This inquiry into the impact of shame on personality has first considered the nature of shame as an affect. In subsequent chapters, respectively, we will consider the human life cycle in order to identify critical sources of shame in various interpersonal settings. Then we will examine the nature of the process of internalization by considering how shame becomes differentially linked with other affects, drives, and interpersonal needs. This will set the stage for next examining the process of psychological magnification specifically in relation to shame. The affect of shame becomes both internalized and magnified, thereby shaping and ultimately dominating the emergent personality. The developmental sources of shame, internalization of shame, and psychological magnification of shame comprise the three critical process dimensions. Finally, we will reexamine psychopathology from the perspectives of affect theory in general and shame theory in particular, resulting in a new formulation of shame-based syndromes.

Two

The Face of Shame Over the Life Cycle

We are all much more simply human than otherwise,
be we happy and successful, contented and detached,
miserable and mentally disordered, or whatever.

HARRY STACK SULLIVAN
Conceptions of Modern Psychiatry

We have been examining shame from the perspective of affect theory and we have considered shame as one of a group of innate affects. Shame is primarily facial behavior, manifesting on three dimensions: facial, phenomenological, and visceral. The facial signs of shame are demonstrable: the head hangs, the eyes are lowered or averted, or the face blushes. Phenomenologically, to feel shame is to feel *seen,* acutely diminished. Exposure is an inherent feature of the inner experience of shame. This affect of shame, thus, is multidimensional.

Our further examination of the role of shame in personality development rests on the formulation of shame as an affect. Consider the nature of the affect mechanism as Tomkins views it:

> It is my view that affects are sets of muscular, glandular, and skin receptor responses located in the face (and also widely distributed throughout the body) that generate sensory feedback to a system that finds them either inherently "acceptable" or "unacceptable." These organized sets of responses are triggered at subcortical centers where specific "programs" for each distinct affect are stored, programs that are innately

endowed and have been genetically inherited. They are capable, when activated of simultaneously capturing such widely distributed structures as the face, the heart, and the endocrine glands and imposing on them a specific pattern of correlated responses. One does not learn to be afraid or to cry or to startle, any more than one learns to feel pain or to gasp for air. (Tomkins, 1987a, p. 137)

If affect is a set of biologically inherited, subcortical "programs" as Tomkins postulates, then each affect has both innate and learned activators. Clarifying the nature of shame's activation, then, will illuminate the vicissitudes of shame over the life cycle. Shame is a life cycle phenomenon, confined neither to childhood nor to the family, nor is it exclusive to mother-infant interactions. The complexities of human development argue for a broader examination of the sources of shame.

INNATE ACTIVATOR OF SHAME

The innate activator of shame is the incomplete reduction of interest or joy. "The experience of shame is inevitable for any human being insofar as desire outruns fulfillment sufficiently to attenuate interest without destroying it," according to Tomkins (1963a, p. 185). Thus, shame is an affect auxiliary because it operates only after the positive affects, interest or enjoyment, have been activated. Shame functions as a specific inhibitor of continuing interest and enjoyment.

Shame is potentially present from birth on. One of the earliest onsets of observed shame dates from the time the infant is able to distinguish the mother's face from the face of the stranger, as early as seven months of age. By then the infant has learned to expect mother's smiling face in response to vocally calling mother from another room. But when the infant is suddenly greeted with the face of a stranger instead of mother's expected face, the incomplete reduction of interest or enjoyment resulting from such disappointed expectations, or imagined scenes, spontaneously activates shame.

Consider the following situation. A man has two sons; his oldest son, along with three friends, requires two more players to complete their basketball teams. They invite the man and his younger son to join. The younger boy begins the game displaying much excitement and joy, but his mood gradually turns to disappointment when he is not given equal opportunity to play; he is a good four years younger than the other boys.

Once the game becomes truly competitive, the younger boy is increasingly excluded. In response he displays a "pouting posture"; pouting is a mixture of deepening shame and anger. The younger boy's tolerance finally evaporates and suddenly he flees into the house, crying. His father follows him in, and finds the boy crying bitterly on the couch. Sitting down beside his son, father places an arm around him, and listens as the boy intermittently cries and voices his feelings: "They aren't giving me the ball. They don't want me out there. They're ignoring me." The boy feels unimportant, little. Mixed with distress and shame is intense rage at his humiliators. His father simply acknowledges how badly his son feels and agrees openly with everything he says, "You're right, son, they don't want you in the game and you feel little." In effect, father is approaching the boy's shame, allowing it expression. His father is validating both the boy's perception of what was actually happening during the game *and* his inner experience of himself, his shame. The boy suddenly dries his tears, gives his father a hug and abruptly darts back outside to rejoin the game, his shame having been released.

This situation illustrates how the sudden, unexpected reduction of positive affect (excitement and enjoyment), as long as it remains a partial reduction, can activate shame. The younger boy was initially excited and joyful to be invited to join the game. I have to assume he was imagining scenes of playing and contributing as an equal team member and that he was also imagining himself playing well, though the *image* he sought to match was one four years older. Children must contend daily with older siblings and adults whom they can never match in skill or accomplishment, guaranteeing a perpetual vulnerability to shame in the earliest years. When the boy's particular expectations concerning his playing on the team—his imagined scenes of positive affect—became repeatedly disappointed in reality even though he still longed for them, shame became activated. Even after running into the house, he had not renounced the scene.

Whenever an individual's fundamental expectations (imagined positive scenes or desired outcomes in relation to people, events, or accomplishments) are suddenly exposed as wrong, shame is activated. Whenever expectations are thwarted or disappointed, shame is also activated. These are all instances of the innate activation of shame, triggered by the partial or incomplete reduction of positive affect or of the imagined scenes thereof.

INTERPERSONAL ACTIVATOR OF SHAME: BREAKING THE INTERPERSONAL BRIDGE

Exploring shame from the perspective of interpersonal relations is just as important as understanding its innate activator. A relationship is a bond between two individuals, whether a parent and child, teacher and student, two siblings, two peers, a therapist and client, or two adults. Each person begins as a stranger to the other. This is as true of mother and child as it is of adults meeting for the first time. The mother must actively reach out to and enter her infant's phenomenological world. Establishing a bond is an ongoing process, never an end state. It requires certain essentials, not the least of which are consistency, stability, and predictability. Tending an infant's requirement for tactile stimulation, for touching and holding, is as crucial to forming a bond as is tending to the requirements of physical safety, warmth, and food. Petting a strange animal begins to establish attachment ties just as fondling a baby does. Cooing and talking, whether to an animal or a human infant, further strengthen the emerging bond.

For human beings, it is the extended gazing into each other's eyes in the midst of suckling that magnifies the bond between infant and mother. The eyes are indeed windows to the soul. The mother's smiling face is like a magnet, drawing the infant into her inviting eyes. Through the eyes we can experientially enter one another. By gazing in mutual enjoyment into one another's eyes, we actually merge into one another and, however briefly, experience ourselves become *one*.

Identification begins as a visual process, but quickly becomes an internal imagery process, encompassing visual, auditory, and kinesthetic scenes. It is that universal scene of communion between mother and infant, accomplished through facial gazing in the midst of holding and rocking during breast or bottle feedings, that creates the infant's sense of oceanic oneness or union. *That* is basic security. The mutual, intense facial gazing in contentment displayed between infant and mother, a pattern sustained well after hunger has been satisfied, provides the necessary experience of identification between them. Each merges with the other through their eyes, and mother and infant feel a sense of *oneness*. It is not oral gratification that is primary, but rather, the visual scene of union— identification—and its accompanying affect—enjoyment—that instead govern development.

The face has central importance in interpersonal relations because the facial gazing between infant and mother is the source of primary identification, the earliest form of communion. That sense of oneness is recaptured later in adolescence and adulthood whenever there is mutual surrender to visual merging. The shared eye-to-eye scene is the most intimate of experiences possible between human beings. The identification scene first experienced in infancy is the source of the emergent bond linking infant with mother, and also with father.

The human bonding process necessarily comprises sufficient and consistent experiences of positive affect, reduction of negative affect, tactile touching, security holding, and identification, especially through recurring smiling facial gazing. These interpersonal scenes are all critical to establishing emotional ties, the vital bonds that span the gulf between a strange infant and mother, and later father, drawing them securely together. An *interpersonal bridge* forms out of reciprocal interest and shared experiences of trust. Trusting must be matched by the parent behaving in a trustworthy fashion. Consistency (not perfection) and predictability (not rigidity) are crucial to building an interpersonal bridge, whether with a child, friend, or client.

The earliest scene of mutual facial gazing must be continually reconfirmed. The child needs to *feel convinced* that each parent truly wants their individual relationship. A distinct, evolving relationship needs to be experienced by each child, separately with father and with mother. It is the distinctive patterning of relationship experiences over time that matters. Each child needs to feel loved, as Fairbairn (1966, pp. 39-40) puts it, as a separate person in his or her own right; Bill Kell (Kell and Burow, 1970) describes children as needing to feel wanted individually by each parent. Such an experience of being in relationship with a parent creates the interpersonal bridge. A relationship must be genuine and honest. It must be genuinely desired by the parent for this particular child, this real, flesh and blood, actual person, and not for some imagined or hoped-for image of a son or daughter. Wanting a relationship must also be overtly expressed in word and in action. It must be verbalized when genuinely felt and it must be lived out consistently. Parents must behave in ways that *convince* a child of being loved as a unique self and truly wanted. It is the impact of parental behavior that counts. When there are two or more children, it becomes all the more essential to cultivate with each child separate relationships that may encompass different activities or interests.

Otherwise, a child may indeed feel some sense of belonging to a family, but without a feeling of individualized, personal relatedness. When everything is done as a family, experiencing distinct relationships separately with each parent is unfortunately precluded.

We have considered the human bonding process at length for a reason: breaking the interpersonal bridge is the critical event that activates shame, the *interpersonal activator*. Barriers to communion with another, to continued shared positive affect with another, will rupture the interpersonal bridge. Any event that ruptures the interpersonal bridge vitally linking infant to mother, father, or anyone else significant, will activate shame. The failure to fully hear, openly validate, and understand another's need by directly communicating its validity can sever the interpersonal bridge and thereby activate shame. Whether or not the parent chooses to actually gratify a child's need, the parent must take time to care, to hear. A child can tolerate disappointment from a parent without lasting shame when the parent has taken time to listen and understand, even if the request must be denied or put off. The child will at least feel heard, with the need understood, and the inner experience validated. Some sadness or grumbling will follow, but any shame will be temporary and eventually released, neither internalized nor magnified.

When one has behaved insensitively or reacted badly, and has thereby activated shame in someone loved or valued, all that is required in reapproaching the other is to openly, honestly acknowledge one's own part. This will release the other's shame. When shame activation is followed directly by actively restoring the interpersonal bridge, internalization and further magnification of shame do not occur.

We have examined the activation of shame from two perspectives: the innate activator and the interpersonal activator. Shame is generated by the incomplete reduction of interest or enjoyment *and* by breaking the interpersonal bridge. Experiencing a need and expecting a response can be viewed as two sides of the same phenomenological event. We experience *expectations* phenomenologically as imagined scenes of positive affect— desired outcomes in relation to people, events, or accomplishments. Individuals depend on those vital interpersonal scenes, those desired outcomes, both expecting and needing them. Shame becomes activated whenever fundamental expectations of a significant other (imagined scenes of interpersonal need) or those equally fundamental expectations of oneself (imagined scenes of accomplishment or purpose) are suddenly exposed as wrong or are thwarted.

When viewed from the perspective of interpersonal relations, breaking the interpersonal bridge emerges as the dynamic event, and it matches phenomenology. When viewed from the perspective of affect, the operation of the innate activator can be observed; it too matches phenomenology. Each viewpoint complements the other by enlarging our vision of the self, thereby illustrating as well the relativity of language in describing inner experience. We will greatly advance our own science if we follow Jacob Bronowski's (1971, pp. 38-39) lead and begin to view science itself as a living, evolving *language* for describing nature. All of our grand models of the psyche, our varied psychological theories along with their competing schools, are only languages for describing the domain of inner experience.

DEVELOPMENTAL SOURCES OF SHAME

In completing our examination of the nature of shame as an affect, we must consider the human life cycle in its entirety to reveal critical sources of shame. The alienating affect is not confined to early childhood; shame is possible at any point in the life cycle. However, there are obviously important differences between early childhood shame experiences and those that occur later, in adolescence and adulthood. The signs of shame particularly evident among children are the external, facial ones: hanging the head, lowering or averting the eyes, and blushing. Only after language as a symbolic function has matured are we able to translate these shame experiences into words, creating particular meanings about the self. Such transformation by language is a later step in the developmental process, one we will examine more closely in due course. As we proceed, we will observe the operation of both the innate and the interpersonal activators of shame.

The human being evolves through a series of distinct *developmental phases:* infancy, childhood, adolescence, adulthood, and old age. Shame is potentially encountered during each developmental epoch; though its specific sources will vary. Human beings also progress through a series of overlapping *interpersonal settings:* family of origin, school, peer group, work, wider culture, and family of procreation. Critical sources of shame exist in each of these settings. Because shame can be experienced and reexperienced during each subsequent developmental phase and throughout the broadening network of interpersonal settings, shame is a life cycle phenomenon.

Preverbal Shame Activation

The first occurrences of parental anger can be potent activators of shame as well as of other negative affects in the earliest years. Initial expressions of anger, inevitable in early childhood, are likely to be experienced by the child as a rupture. Early parental anger can sever the vital interpersonal bridge linking infant with mother and with father. The first experience with parental anger for a young verbal child might be greeted with, "You don't like me anymore?" Shame feels like a rupture in self or in the relationship. However, it is not suggested that anger should be avoided, but that the interpersonal bridge must later be actively restored.

With preverbal children, reaffirming the relationship by restoring the bridge can only be accomplished through touching and holding. Lacking language, the reparative means available is physical contact. Verbal reassurance from parents is insufficient. Reaching to be held in the midst of parental anger is the child's own attempt to reaffirm both self and the ruptured relationship, to feel restored and secure. At such moments, touching and holding communicate protection and security, the foundation of trust.

Failure to respond to the child's spontaneous request for holding, activated by parental anger, confirms shame. Holding a child when the child initiates it by reaching upward, even while the parent is still angry, restores the interpersonal bridge. With older children, the restoration can increasingly be accomplished verbally as well as physically, though some amount of holding may yet be necessary, even essential. Parents need not avoid the expression of anger toward their children. The central idea is that failure to restore the interpersonal bridge following the expression of parental anger will intensify the rupture, leaving the child trapped in shame.

Shame and Abandonment

Either feelings of or fears of abandonment are typically observed in connection with shame. While breaking the interpersonal bridge activates shame, the experience of shame itself, particularly when repetitive or prolonged over time, further severs the bridge, creating a gradually widening gulf. Children will experience shame as abandonment when parents are not reassuring in their responses to shame and instead magnify the rupture even further. Consider the following scenarios. Some parents silently withdraw from a child, refusing to relate, literally freezing out the child. Such tactics can last for hours or even days. Another way in which shame can escalate into abandonment occurs when a parent becomes overtly contemptuous, whether facially, in word, or in deed. Direct threats of leaving the child are an example. The affects of disgust and contempt (anger plus dissmell) communicate complete rejection of the offensive, disgusting child. A final parental pattern is to overtly withdraw love and prolong this unreasonably. The enactment of any of these interpersonal scenes inevitably magnifies shame into abandonment.

Shame in Later Childhood

While the activation of shame is frequently inadvertent, it can also be direct and intentional. Here shame is utilized purposely as a method of control. Such practices are not examples of a rationally conceived strategy of manipulation. Rather, they are intergenerational in nature. Shaming patterns are deeply rooted in analogous scenes from the parent's own childhood, scenes that have become embedded in the parent's memory but are now reactivated and passed directly to the next generation. These patterns of interaction knit together the fabric of the self within the family; they also knit the generations of a family into a miniculture, a shame-based family system.

Shame on You

Two widespread images of shaming in Western culture involve repeatedly pointing and shaking the index finger or crossing and then sliding one index finger repeatedly over the other. Contrast these gestures with those found in the East. In Chinese culture, for example, the shaming gesture involves rubbing the index finger repeatedly on the face in a downward direction.

Even young children will quickly learn the respective gesture from parents and then repeat it openly for one another. Along with this action come verbal accompaniments such as "You should be ashamed of yourself" or "Shame on you." The face of the parent may look angry or disgusted or equally ashamed. Affect, imagery, and language are directly engaged in creating the shaming scene. And it is the *scene* that subsequently becomes stored in memory inside the self.

You Are Embarrassing Me

When the face of the parent is lowered in shame, the head of the child will hang similarly. Communications from a parent such as "You're embarrassing *me*" will inevitably activate shame in the child, causing him or her to stop whatever is making the parent obviously ashamed. Here, the face of the child merges with the face of the parent, the two becoming one. Gradually, the child becomes but an extension of the self of the parent. Imagine the following scene. Father is working at his desk at home. His 14-year-old son walks in, eyes downcast. Father notices his scratched and bruised face. The boy avoids looking into his father's eyes, avoids father's face entirely. He hangs his head, defeated. Father stares silently at his son's face, then comments about the obvious bruises. He had been beaten in a fight, the boy explains hesitantly. Father stares coldly. Then he speaks to his son: "You go back out there and do what you have to do. When *you're* out there, *I'm* out there. When *you* have marks on your face, *I* have marks on my face." The parent's use of the parent's own shame is a powerful though more subtle method of shaming.

I Am Disappointed in You

The expression of deep disappointment in one's own child creates a global accusation, an indictment of deficiency. To be such a disappointment to the loved or needed parent is to be unworthy of belonging. Communications such as "I'm so disappointed in you—how could any child of mine have done this!" can be crushing to a boy or girl so dependent on parental acceptance, approval, and love. Disappointment can be equally communicated facially and, in response to that look, the child will invariably hang the head or lower the eyes. The child will lose face.

Disparagement

Various means produce disparagement. Any action that belittles a child will activate shame. While rage may be the reaction overtly displayed, in all likelihood there will have been a momentary lowering of the head or eyes preceding the expression of rage. Or the self may hang its head *inside* while outwardly displaying defiance. Belittling can occur at the hands of a parent or an older sibling. Name-calling is a prevalent form of disparagement that can wound the self: "Stupid," "Clumsy," "Oaf," "Sissy," "Crybaby," "Fatty," "Beanpole." Such belittling is all too often disguised as humor and teasing can be carried to the extreme or enacted repetitively. There is a vast difference between the good-natured poking fun between friends and the teasing that ridicules another, however its intent may be denied. Many families are organized around such pervasive teasing that then becomes a potent source of shame.

Transfer of Blame

The scene in disparagement is different from the scene in transfers of blame. The activators are different, the facial expressions are different, and the meanings created are equally different. Yet the affect that becomes activated is identical in both situations: shame. The transfer of blame is an action-language-affect pattern of unique qualities and tremendous ramifications. Imagine the following scene. Mother and father have just returned home to discover a minor disaster. Something has gone wrong. Something unfortunate has happened. Someone must be found responsible. Whose fault is it? Who is to blame? The guilty party must be cornered. Simply repairing the mishap is not sufficient in a blaming family; responsibility for the mishap must be placed *somewhere*. Blame must be transferred to *someone*. Blaming is an accusation, an action that recruits the affect of anger but directs it in an accusatory manner. The face of blame is accusatory as well as angry. Blame, in turn, activates intolerable shame, shredding dignity and self-respect, in the face of which one may even be forced to renounce all responsibility for the mishap itself. In the midst of blame, there is no way to keep one's head held high. Permutations of that scene are infinite and equally epidemic in this society. The blaming parent speaks with the voice of the culture as well.

Contempt

If the facial scene in transfers of blame is accusatory anger, the facial scene in contempt is the sneer, which is a learned transformation of dissmell. In disgust the face *spits out,* but in dissmell the face *pulls away.* Contempt, however, is a learned combination of the affect of anger and the drive auxiliary of dissmell. By combining anger with dissmell, contempt functions as a signal and motive to others, as well as to the self, of either negative evaluation or feelings of rejection. The face pulls away in dissmell from the offending, "bad-smelling" other, and in disgust the face spits out the "bad-tasting" other, while the urge to vomit is the affect of disgust experienced directly on the level of the hunger drive. Dissmell and disgust, in Tomkins's view, are drive auxiliary affects that "appear to be evolving from the status of drive-reducing acts to those that have as well a more general motivating and signal function, both to the individual who emits this signal and to the one who receives it" (1987a, p. 143). Just as the infant pulls away from bad-smelling objects or spits out bad-tasting food, the parent similarly rejects the child as if it, too, were bad-smelling or bad-tasting, pulling away in dissmell or spitting out in disgust.

When imagery and language further transform the face of dissmell into an affective scene that is repetitively reenacted, by combining dissmell with anger, we have the origins of vicious teasing and of sarcasm as potent interpersonal activators of shame. Siblings in a family can be merciless to one another. Contempt by one will activate shame in the other, which is then returned in retaliation. Contempt breeds contempt. Parental expressions of contempt either directly toward the child or toward others profoundly shape the family culture into a breeding ground for shame. Considerably older siblings, together with relatives, often can function significantly as activators of shame. As the peer group and school setting become increasingly central in the child's expanding world, new arenas emerge for encounters with the alienating affect. A contemptuous teacher can mortify the spirit of a child. And one of the universal scenes of contempt involves the peer group. Nowhere is contempt matched for severity, pleasure in wounding, and repetitiveness. Imagine the scene when classmates catch a girl wetting her pants and taunt her mercilessly, well into the following year. The class joke (imbecile or jerk) is never allowed to forget it. And how many families function likewise? To be mocked and laughed at by one's peers or family is to be held in such contempt that one is not fit to belong.

Contempt also becomes expressed through critical, condescending, or fault-finding pattens that are the principal interactions in too many families. The self feels elevated in contempt. Others are looked down on, deemed inferior, beneath one's dignity. Contempt affect is the source of that sense of superiority often displayed toward others. Arrogance wears the face of contempt. Cynicism is contempt with the affect greatly diluted. Sarcasm and teasing are the products of contempt edged with humor. The affects of dissmell, disgust, and contempt are the source of prejudice and discrimination, which are always founded in partitioning the superior from the inferior. Contempt is the affect of rejection. To live in an environment of contempt, whether experienced in the family, peer group, or wider culture, guarantees perpetual subjection to shame, self-contempt, and/or counter-contempt for others.

Humiliation

Humiliation is a profound and utter defeat. To be defeated in battle is to be deeply humiliated, whether that defeat is experienced by one nation at the hands of another—as Germany was humiliated at the end of World War I and, more recently, Great Britain was humiliated when Argentina invaded the Falkland Islands—or by a child at the hands of a parent. Breaking the will of a child is perhaps its most extreme form. If the child is defeated by the parent at every turn humiliation becomes complete. Some parents continue to believe that their "wicked" child must be whipped into line, the willful spirit broken. Repetitive beatings are a potent form of direct and recurring humiliation. Smacking a child's face is deeply humiliating in itself, causing an immediate loss of face. Mild, controlled spankings activate mild shame; uncontrolled violent beatings, especially with objects, profoundly wound the self, inducing hatred and revenge-seeking along with shame. For individuals struggling to reassert their dignity, pride, and honor over their shame, and for nations that go to war to avenge their honor, humiliation walks hand-in-hand with seeking revenge.

Humiliation scenes are universal. One young woman recounted how she had been hit repeatedly with a frying pan by her mother, and how her father had hit her with his fists, belt, or a paddle. An older man recalled how his father once took a board and hit him across his back. As a final illustration, imagine the following scene. A young man recounted during the course of therapy how, as a boy, he was hit or beaten every day by either his father or mother. On one occasion he was forced to his knees before his father, who stood towering over him after a beating. His father then demanded of his son, "Repeat after me, 'I am God.'" The young boy, sobbing on his knees and still hanging his head in shame, had to repeat obediently, "You are God." His humiliation had become complete and that scene was seared into his memory.

Performance Expectations

Even the pressure to perform at a skill or activity can activate shame. The skill in question may involve a physical activity such as a particular sport. Or it can involve the use of language, as in being pressured to speak clearly or grammatically. Over-correction of any skill activates shame in the form of self-consciousness or exposure. My hypothesis concerning stuttering, for example, is that this disorder originates in the early fusion of shame with speech. When the stutterer later struggles to regain power over the speech-related shame scene, the listener paradoxically feels powerless and experiences shame in the presence of the stutterer who is struggling to speak.

Pressure to excel at any activity is invariably experienced as performance expectations. Since expectations are, phenomenologically, imagined scenes of positive affect, parental or peer pressure to excel is usually accompanied by the expression of disappointment or disgust upon failure. Imagine the following situation. A young boy is learning to ride a bicycle and his father has little patience for his son's clumsiness and poor coordination. Father pressures his son to learn faster, to perform better. When the lad continues to disappoint father's expectations (father's own scenes) with his clumsy attempts, at last father gives up and walks away in utter disgust. The boy is left there hanging his head in shame; he cannot help but experience his own self as a failure.

Performance expectations invariably activate shame in the form of disabling self-consciousness, because individuals actually are more able to be or do their best when they feel that however they do is good enough. Only then can the self function freely. The pressure of performance expectations is disabling because anticipating success or failure can activate binding self-consciousness. The self becomes immobilized under scrutiny. The watching eyes of the self impale the self under its magnifying gaze.

Parents, peers, and teachers play a central role in the development of performance expectations. Again, it is the pattern of experiences over time that has enduring impact. Binding self-consciousness invariably disrupts the learning of any skill.

Adolescence and Shame

Adolescence is a developmental epoch during which there is a rapid magnification of shame. It is a time of profound, unsettling changes. Formal operational thought, in the Piagetian sense, is attained. Thought itself becomes an object of thought, making symbolizing about symbols possible. Hormonal activity is under way, unleashing a host of physiological and physical changes. Voice tone begins to change, particularly in males. Facial blemishes appear, as do adult bodily characteristics: body hair, breasts for females, genital development. The sexual drive matures. The accustomed self of the young girl or boy is transforming into a young woman's or man's. All of these changes call attention to the self and expose it to view. Comment by even well-intentioned parents and comparison by peers only call further attention to the self and intensify exposure by heightening visibility. Such actions may be greeted with a burst of rage or by silent withdrawal.

Self-consciousness and shyness are present well before adolescence, but inevitably become heightened during this particular developmental phase. The affect of shame accounts for many disturbances of self-functioning that now appear: awkwardness, clumsiness, the retreat inward to reduce visibility, frequent or unexpected rages, and other affective eruptions.

The sense of feeling on-stage before a watching audience, common in adolescence, is a consequence of shame affect. The eyes of the imagined audience belong to the self. It is the self who is watching the self, and it is the self who is judging the self. Formal operational thought can certainly embellish the scene, but self-consciousness is not the product of thought alone. Affect is primary. And the primary affect of adolescence is shame.

Many paranoid-sounding phenomena that begin to appear at this time are actually manifestations of shame. Adolescents feel exposed, *seen,* scrutinized; they feel open to view. Adolescents feel as if others can see inside of them, see their faults or defects, maybe even read their thoughts. This is how shame feels on the inside. Shame is a fertile breeding ground for paranoia, which we will examine more closely in a subsequent chapter.

Male-female relations are a new context for shame during adolescence. Developing men and women begin to establish emotional ties. Intimacy itself invariably activates some degree of shame. Individuals who previously have been shamed around touching and holding now experience intensified inhibitions or disruptions at the prospect of physical closeness. Those who have been shamed around sexuality in earlier years now experience an intensification of that connection. Sexual functioning is disrupted by the slightest onset of shame, along with other negative affects, and sexual identity itself becomes both molded and distorted by shame. Pride in self, in body, in sex, and in gender are crucial for an integrated self-identity to develop. Shame instills doubt, a voice whispering despair. Now shame has taken on wider meaning: *inferiority*.

Attachments among young men, and among young women, are equally shaped by shame. The two most widely shamed expressions of personality in contemporary American culture, especially among men, are crying and touching. The affect of distress, which manifests as sadness or hurt accompanied by crying, is always negatively sanctioned in the peer group and often in the family as well. Contempt is a predominant means used for shaming in both settings. Expressions of affection, tenderness, and touching/holding eventually become taboo among males in American culture. This occurs in the family, when parents shrink back from an adolescent's embrace or become embarrassed. It also happens in the group subculture of early adolescence when peers resort to such derogatory name-calling as "sissy," "queer," and "faggot." Touching between males becomes heavily shamed and taboo, although touching among women remains somewhat more culturally acceptable. While men generally have been shamed both for crying and for touching/holding, women in American culture traditionally have been shamed for expressing anger and asserting power. The way to create a so-called "macho" personality is through shaming any individual for crying and touching/holding, while simultaneously rewarding expressions of anger, contempt, and competitiveness. In a socialization process that continues through adolescence, women learn to define their self-identity through a relationship to a man, and men learn to define their self-identity through future work and career. Failure in either will activate shame.

Adolescence is a time of universal vulnerability to shame. The conditions for magnification of shame scenes are present; in a climate of shame, shame will magnify.

Impact of Culture

Personality becomes profoundly shaped by the patterning of experience first in the family, then in the peer group, and, finally, in the school setting. The child, however, is never a passive recipient of events. The hereditary frame and environmental influences are uniquely organized by each evolving self, to paraphrase Alfred Adler (Ansbacher & Ansbacher, 1956). Perceptions of events and their interpretation are always active, constructive processes. Each individual participates directly in the self-meanings created out of environmental experience, whether beatings at the hands of a parent, peer group ridicule and mockery, or disparagement from a valued teacher in school. Family, peer group, and school are also the instruments of culture through which values and taboos are transmitted. The motives of shame and honor publicly contend wherever individuals encounter one another.

The role of culture in molding personality is no less crucial than the role of the family or peer group; it is only less visible. Consider culture more closely. Culture is the fabric that bonds a people together, the web of meaning created out of national symbols and traditions. An interpersonal bridge stretches through our cultural consciousness, uniting us in common purpose. Our destinies become joined together. The evolution of culture is fueled by the *identification need;* we feel identified with one another, and thereby experience communion. A bond is forged out of experiences of identification, and a sense of belonging grows. The mode through which cultural identification develops (and implicitly national and religious identification as well) is public celebration of holidays, rituals, and heroes. Through retelling their nation's heritage and history in stories read at bedtime, in literature studied at school, in films, and on television, and through participating in its hopes and dreams, its conventions as well as taboos, people feel identified with something larger than themselves. They feel identified with one another.

The web of meaning so created evolves into a *cultural script* to expand on Tomkins's (1979, p. 217) concept. A script consists of rules for predicting, controlling, responding to, and interpreting a magnified set of scenes. Scripts are action-language-affect patterns that are rooted in governing scenes. Scripts create an identity, the particular life-part each individual is expected to enact. Three central cultural scripts in contemporary American society that continue to activate shame, and thereby mold the self, are *to compete for success, to be independent and self-sufficient,* and *to be popular and conform.*

The success script is rooted in mythic American images of the self-made man or woman. These archetypal figures are dominant in the literature of this nation and in the "American Dream," which is handed down from generation to generation: "You can be anything you want to be if you only try hard enough." Competing for success and achieving by external standards of performance are the clarion calls of the culture. From an early age, individuals are stimulated to always seek their advantage over others through competition. Achievement becomes the measure of self-esteem, of one's intrinsic worth or adequacy. All must strive to be successful and success is measured by accomplishments. When external performance becomes the unfortunate measure of self-esteem, the success script generates anxiety in the form of fear of failure because success is always partly out of one's control. When self-validation becomes solidly based on external standards, competition is fostered, further generating hostility and fear. Failure to attain the culture's prize, the American Dream in its various forms, now activates shame. Failure becomes the mark of inferiority. Simply being average must seem a curse. The success script also strangles the capacity for caring and vulnerability because competitors cannot afford to care about each other.

A second cultural script is to be independent and self-sufficient. Deeply embedded in our cultural consciousness are images of the pioneer, cowboy, farmer, and more recently, the detective and astronaut. These archetypal figures mirror the desire to stand proudly alone, never needing anything, never depending on anyone. Instead of being a source of strength, needing becomes a sign of inadequacy. Many individuals would prefer to remain lost for hours rather than ask anyone for directions because doing so would publicly announce their ineptness and acknowledge their shame. Other individuals cannot accept physical assistance, let alone emotional sustenance because, as they would undoubtedly describe it, they would feel "too proud" to do so. They would not feel too proud, but too ashamed. The Appalachian father and mother, for example, who feel *too proud* to accept a handout to help support their family, actually feel *too ashamed* to do so. To need is seen as being inadequate, shameful.

The third cultural script is to be popular and conform. Individuality is neither recognized nor valued because our culture prizes popularity and it also prizes conformity. The consequence is that being *different* from others becomes shameful. To avoid shame, individuals must avoid being different, or *seen* as different. Thus, introverts are traditionally shamed in this culture for being quieter, less social, less outgoing. Any ethnic, racial, or religious subgroup is similarly vulnerable to shame because it is different. Individuals who adopt an alternate lifestyle for whatever reason are equally susceptible to shame because they are different from the cultural norm. The awareness of difference itself translates into feeling deficient, lesser.

These are competing cultural scripts. Accomplishing all three simultaneously is virtually impossible. Furthermore, men and women have been differentially scripted: men to compete for success *and* to be independent and self-sufficient, women to be popular and conform. Crossovers are inevitable since all three scripts are deeply embedded in American culture, and they have molded our national character. These cultural scripts inevitably generate shame, through which culture shapes personality.

American society is a shame-based culture, but here shame remains hidden. Since there is shame about shame, it remains under taboo. Even our language denies shame or masks it from view. We speak about feeling "too proud" to do this or that, whereas doing this or that would actually cause us too much shame. It is not pride that binds us, it is shame. The taboo on shame is so strict in this culture that we behave as if shame does not exist. That taboo must be lifted.

Other cultures are organized more openly around shame and its counterpart, honor. In traditional Japanese culture, to bring shame upon oneself also brought shame and dishonor upon one's family and upon one's ancestors as well. The traditional response to shame was ritual suicide. Mediterranean cultures continue to reflect the central role of shame in private relations as well as in political relations among the various nations and cultural subgroups of that region.

Shame in Adulthood

Other theorists have largely concentrated on shame experienced in childhood and predominantly at the hands of a parent, almost always the mother. Such a narrow focus misses the dynamic complexity of self-development, its continuities as well as its discontinuities. The father and siblings play equally central roles in the genesis of shame. The peer group, the epoch of adolescence, and the wider culture likewise function as potent generators of shame. Development, however, does not stop with adulthood. Significant sources of shame follow, and individuals who have seemingly managed to avoid serious crippling from shame during childhood and adolescence may become unexpectedly faced with shame, and subsequently defeated by shame, later in adulthood. Four general classes of shame activators emerge in adulthood.

Powerlessness

The condition of powerlessness is a psychological phenomenon with profound consequences. Powerlessness, the perception of lack of control, begins as the state of helplessness into which all individuals are thrust at birth. One of the most primitive organized scenes is that initial scene of primary powerlessness. That scene, endured over an extended time frame, conditions the need for power—to be able to predict and control; the feeling of power is fundamentally a sense of inner control. Maturation gradually shrinks the condition of powerlessness and extends the child's experience of power and his or her perception of inner control. But the vicissitudes of life are always beyond any individual's full control. Life is always uncertain. Any life event or situation that wrenches away that sense of inner control renders one potentially powerless.

Powerlessness experienced anew during adulthood reactivates that earlier governing scene of initial primary helplessness. The adult is then immediately transported back into that original scene and relives it in the present with all its affect reawakened. Imagination is a telescope in time to echo Jacob Bronowski (1973, p. 56). Powerlessness is not an affect per se but an *activator* of affect; it is experienced with any of the negative affects or combinations thereof. Defeat, failure, rejection, and loss thus guarantee a perpetual vulnerability to shame, which is likely to be experienced either singly or in conjunction with other negative affects.

To illustrate this phenomenon, let us examine the *affect dynamics* of powerlessness more closely by considering a contemporary issue of widespread concern: AIDS. Ambiguity about the disease has decreased but not enough to quell a growing national hysteria. In the face of science's unsuccessful attempts to predict and control AIDS, contemporary society has been reduced to reenacting the Black Plague panic of the Middle Ages.

Consider the affect dynamics involved. AIDS activates a sense of acute powerlessness and uncertainty. Whether actually receiving the diagnosis itself or only imagining oneself contracting the dreaded disease, the consequence is real or imagined catastrophe. AIDS can neither be predicted nor controlled. Not enough is known to determine exactly what precursors are necessary to leave the body sufficiently weakened and thus susceptible, and how to predict the course of the disease, and how to cure it. That life-threatening uncertainty renders all individuals potentially powerless and seemingly trapped, itself a regressive experience. Powerlessness in any significant sphere of life (vocation, family, health) causes an intrusion of early experience by returning one experientially to that original primary helplessness of infancy. When that governing scene is reactivated, one is instantly transported, as if through an airlock, back in time.

Any person suffering from AIDS is likely to experience powerlessness with any negative affect or combination thereof: fear, anger, distress, shame, dissmell, disgust. The most toxic for the self are fear and shame. AIDS is a stigma. An AIDS diagnosis is not only a sign of shame but a source of further humiliation through public revulsion. More than that, many experience an AIDS diagnosis as a sentence of death.

These conditions create rapid magnification of conjoined terror and humiliation. Affect magnification, according to Tomkins (1963a, pp. 282-283), refers to any systematic increase in intensity and/or duration of affect, with or without suppression of the overt expression of affect. Such magnified negative affects are likely to exert a further suppressive effect on the already weakened immune system of the individual with AIDS.

The prior state of the individual's self-identity is another important consideration in assessing the psychological impact of AIDS. The resulting affect magnification unleashed by AIDS may reactivate and recruit old scenes, long since seemingly resolved, causing even further magnification and accompanying regression.

The person with AIDS lives in a social group. Society in general is experiencing equally rapid magnification of affect with AIDS as the source and the AIDS individual as the target. It is not unlike the hostage crisis in Iran some years back, during which a group of Americans were both powerless and trapped over quite an extended time period while an entire nation experienced an analogous powerlessness, activating conjoint rage and shame. Regarding AIDS, however, a growing number of individuals are reacting with terror, with humiliation, and with extreme disgust. Many are responding, not only to people diagnosed with AIDS but to entire at-risk populations, especially homosexuals, with even more violent contempt. This is the identical blend of punitive anger with distancing dissmell that occurs in a lynching. Individuals with AIDS, as well as homosexuals in general, are experiencing accelerating humiliation and terror in response. They are being treated as a truly persecuted minority whose humiliation is imposed with a reign of terror.

These are potentially psychotic-making conditions. Terror and shame activated by AIDS itself are being further magnified by fear, humiliation, disgust, and rage activated by societal response. The reality of AIDS is magnetizing a cultural shame that is still under strict taboo. Shame about sexuality in general, and more specifically about homosexuality, is now being displaced onto AIDS. Cultural disgust and shame about homosexuality are being transferred to AIDS and people with AIDS—who are equally repudiated whether or not they are homosexual—and further reinforced by terror.

The powerlessness of AIDS individuals parallels that of Michigan automobile workers in 1980 and middle-American family farmers in 1985. Powerlessness has affected all three groups. Each feels robbed of a sense of inner power. Their ability to predict and control their own lives suddenly, unexpectedly, is taken away. Each, however, experiences powerlessness differently. Consider each group more closely. The person with AIDS feels powerless most immediately in the area of health/life prospect, but with significant accompanying losses or threats of losses in the areas of friendship, home, and employment. AIDS means loss of life, but also loss of support. The automobile worker who experiences a job layoff feels acutely powerless primarily in the area of career/work and secondarily in other areas. Job layoff means loss of employment, but also loss of dignity. The family farmer simultaneously feels powerless in the areas of career/work, home, and identity/purpose. Farm foreclosure means loss of home as well as loss of work. More than that, it means loss of identity, of one's central purpose for living.

Now consider the reactions of these three groups more closely. For the automobile worker and family farmer, shame and rage are the two negative affects magnified to the greatest degree, in contrast to the person with AIDS, for whom shame and terror are the principal affects conjointly magnified. These are the critical affects that become differentially magnified for each group, but other negative affects can be prominent as well. Automobile workers and family farmers, for example, also experience heightened fear and distress, while the person with AIDS also experiences heightened rage and distress. The central idea is that particular negative affects or combinations thereof become magnified differentially in response to powerlessness depending on the various factors involved.

The consequences of rapidly magnified affect and its systematic suppression are profound. One result is *backed-up affect.* According to Tomkins (1979), endocrine changes are a further consequence of backed-up affect. It is the experience of backed-up affect along with its resulting endocrine changes, such as the elevation of blood pressure in suppressed rage, that actually produces the effects somewhat ambiguously referred to as "stress." The systematic suppression of affect causes backed-up affect, the consequences of which are endocrine changes. What is commonly called stress is actually backed-up affect and its resulting endocrine changes. Backed-up affect, therefore, can eventuate in substantial psychosomatic illness. From an affect theory perspective, then, stress is invariably mediated by affect.

Figure 2.1 illustrates this *powerlessness-affect-stress* cycle. Powerlessness experienced in any *security area* (defined by the need to predict and control) will activate a negative affect or a combination of negative affects, the eventual suppression of which results in backed-up affect and accompanying endocrine changes—stress. The consequences of rapidly magnified and/or backed-up affect are varied: violence, suicide, psychosomatic illness, sexual abuse, physical abuse, and addiction.

Vocation

Failure in vocation appears in many forms. It can occur through actual loss of a job, which activates grief, a manifestation of distress affect, and also activates shame, feeling seen as lesser. Failure translates into exposure of the self in a diminished sense. Loss initially activates powerlessness, which in turn can be experienced with any combination of negative affects. The association between shame and inferiority becomes particularly amplified in a success-oriented culture.

Loss of promotion, or the perception that one's career advancement has been consistently thwarted, also activates powerlessness, followed by shame. Each individual has a *dream,* and that inner vision, imagined off in the future, directs one's path, pulls one toward it, shaping itself into being through imagination. Human beings construct their dreams out of images, which collect, coalesce, then explode into a future scene, a governing vision of what they imagine themselves becoming. First, the scene is imagined. Then if it begins to govern, if it becomes experienced with enduring and recurring positive affect, the dream is actualized. As Tomkins observes, "What is consciously perceived is *imagery* which is created by the organism itself. . . . The world we perceive is a dream we learn to have from a script we have not written." (1962, p. 13).

The dream can take any form: becoming a scientist, physician, or lawyer; becoming an administrator or executive; owning one's own farm or business; becoming rich, famous, or powerful; owning a home; having a family; becoming a star; becoming an artist or musician, tradesman or craftsman, athlete or academic. One's guiding dream is a scene of purpose. The human being is motivated by these future *purposes,* and these purposes invariably are conscious ones. Our lives are constructed around a dream, but when our dream is thwarted, powerlessness and shame are activated.

The dream can be thwarted by actual failure in career, loss of job, loss of the dream itself—the realization that "I'll never attain it"—and also by retirement. These are specific activators of shame throughout adulthood, as witnessed by the fate of the family farmer today. Loss of the family farm also means loss of the dream, their essential purpose for living, that had become an essential part of their identity. Retirement is especially amplified in this culture because of its *compete for success* script. When achievement is the principal source and measure of self-esteem, retirement inevitably creates a vacuum within the self.

Relationships

We have typically associated relationship loss exclusively with grief, the distress affect, and have largely missed the prevalence of shame as an entirely separate affective response to loss. Both affects are likely to be present together and in combination with other negative affects. Shame is the source of "feelings of rejection." It is the affect of shame that is described as rejection when the activator is an interpersonal one. Failure in relationships generally, especially when repetitive, will also activate shame. Feeling disappointed or discouraged in a relationship can likewise be a source of shame.

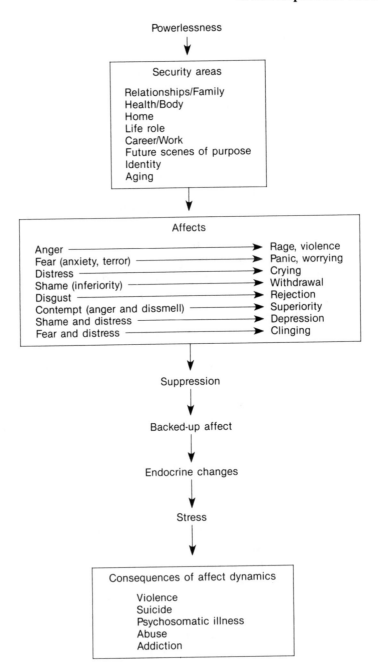

Figure 2.1 Powerlessness-affect-stress cycle.

Loss of the dream can activate shame in the sphere of relationships as well as vocation. The dream may be one of marriage, family, or a particular lifestyle. Any life event that thwarts an individual's dream has the potential to activate powerlessness and then shame.

The actual loss of a relationship also means loss of the dream, which is why failure in marriage is such a potent source of shame. Even the word "divorce" itself is still stigmatized. Shame is rooted partially in the actual failure of the marriage, but also in the breaking up of the family— inevitably a profound loss and disappointment for children.

An additional source of shame is the public acknowledgment of the failure. The actual process of divorce in contemporary society guarantees increasingly public exposure of the self.

Feelings of shame, which are both certain and natural in response to divorce, must be assimilated. Unassimilated shame is insidious and psychologically toxic to the self.

Aging

The aging process remains a universal source of shame, one that is rooted in the body. Just as adolescence is a potent activator of shame—of *body shame*—human aging continues to activate shame. Decline of appearance, bodily function, and vitality become increasing sources of shame as aging progresses. When the surrounding culture overvalues youth, that shame is magnified. Bodily decline is experienced as a loss, and loss activates distress affect as well as shame affect.

Death is another potential activator of distress and shame. As with relationship loss, we have typically viewed death principally in the context of grief. Although grief is obviously present, shame is no less so, only more hidden from view. Fear and anger are other principal affects activated by death. These affects occur in definite combinations or characteristic sequences, and all have to be experienced, differentiated, expressed, and assimilated. The various phases of the grief process as typically conceived are actually a direct function of affect dynamics.

The universal symbol of ultimate human powerlessness is death. Powerlessness is the critical intervening step in the sequence of affects that follow in the wake of death. How any particular individual characteristically responds to powerlessness is a function of prior affect socialization, the relative dominance of one or more affects within the personality, the prevalence of shame itself, and emergent strategies of avoidance and escape from shame.

With a consideration of death, we have rounded out the sources of shame in the human life cycle. Far from being confined to childhood, renewed encounters with the alienating affect are always possible.

SUMMARY

Briefly recapitulating what we have been considering, the sources of shame span the life cycle. Preverbal shame activation stems from the earliest experiences with parental anger, which sever the interpersonal bridge. It also stems from failure to reaffirm the relationship by providing physical touching and holding when the child reaches to be held by the angry parent. Furthermore, shame can be experienced as abandonment when the parent becomes emotionally unavailable, freezes out the child in silent withdrawal, overtly withdraws love, or becomes overtly contemptuous. The offensive, disgusting child is now completely rejected.

Shaming may be unintentional, may be resorted to in an effort to control the child, or may be used to break its will. *Shame on you* is a direct and familiar scene. *You're embarrassing me* burdens the child with the parent's shame; the face of the child now merges with the face of the parent. The two become one and the child becomes but an extension of the self of the parent. *I'm disappointed in you* is another scene that creates a global accusation. More direct shaming strategies include open *disparagement* or belittling, direct *transfers of blame* for mishaps, *contempt,* and total *humiliation* and defeat (as in physical beatings). *Performance expectations* comprise a further source of shame.

Adolescence is a developmental epoch critical for the genesis of shame because adolescence is a universal source of shame. The inevitable bodily changes call attention to the self, exposing it to view. Many paranoid-sounding phenomena, which begin to appear at this time, are actually manifestations of shame.

In addition to the family setting, the peer group and school setting are arenas in which the motive of shame plays out. Culture is a further source of shame. Three cultural scripts in contemporary American society continue to generate shame: compete for success, be independent and self-sufficient, and be popular and conform.

Throughout adulthood, avenues exist to renewed encounters with shame. *Powerlessness* in any sphere of life, because it is an impediment and therefore thwarts positive affect, can activate shame. Failure or loss in *vocation,* to the degree to which vocation has been invested with positive affect, also activates shame. Failure also simply may involve loss of one's dream. Likewise, failure or loss in *relationships* is another general source of shame in adulthood. Loss of a loved one activates grief and distress affect, but it also activates shame. Loss of a relationship may also mean loss of one's dream, which is why failure in marriage is such a potent source of shame. Inevitably, there is shame about divorce. *Aging* also is a universal source of shame. Bodily decline can feel deeply humiliating. Finally, shame may be experienced in the face of *death,* that universal symbol of ultimate human powerlessness.

FROM SHAME AS AFFECT TO A SHAME-BOUND SELF

We have been examining shame from the perspective of affect theory. Other theoretical perspectives, including psychoanalytic, object-relational, interpersonal, family systems, and cognitive behavioral, have largely missed the primacy of affect over all other sub-systems within the self. We do not mean to exclude these other perspectives, but simply to rearrange the observed phenomena within the domain of our science. Affect theory partitions the domain of inner experience in a decidedly new manner. From the perspective of affect theory, shame is an innate affect. More precisely, shame is an affect auxiliary because it only becomes activated following the activation of one of the positive affects, interest or enjoyment. All affects function as amplifiers. Shame amplifies our experience, giving texture and meaning to the experienced self.

The developmental process by which shame dynamically impacts the self involves a progression in two ways. First, the intensity, duration, and frequency of shame increases systematically, which Tomkins (1963a, pp. 282-283; 1979; 1987a) refers to as *affect magnification* in contrast to affect amplification. Magnified shame is more toxic to the self, just as chronic shyness is more disturbing than momentary shyness and enduring inferiority is more crippling than momentary shame over failure. Second, shame becomes *internalized* so that the self is now entirely capable of reproducing shame. Not only does the shame response itself become internalized, but internalization spreads shame throughout the self. Shame becomes like a cancer, malignant.

Three

Internalization of Shame

The imaginary people of preadolescent fantasy may seem to us insubstantial; the imaginary play of the preadolescent may seem but old, romantic folklore crudely adjusted to the spirit of the times. The illusions that transmute his companions—if they be illusions—may seem to us but certain of an early end, a disillusionment. But whatever his people, real, illusory or frankly imagined, may be, they are not mean. Whatever his daydreams with his chum, whatever his private fantasies, they are not base. And as to his valuations of others, here we may take pause and reflect that it may be we who see "as through a glass, darkly."

HARRY STACK SULLIVAN
Conceptions of Modern Psychiatry

The process by which the self internalizes, and so reproduces, its own experience is central to how the self actually functions and develops. The self unfolds, evolves, and becomes shaped through ongoing interaction with the interpersonal environment, and through the ways it stores, reproduces, elaborates, and transcends that experience. Although it is a complex and multifaceted process, *internalization* is actually a simple idea. It is through *imagery* (encompassing visual, auditory, and kinesthetic dimensions) that the self internalizes experience. What is internalized are images or scenes that have become imprinted with affect.

We are constructing a developmental theory or language of the self that remains solidly grounded in phenomenology. The centrality of affect in the development of personality and psychopathology is the foundation of this developmental self theory. Both the physiological drives, such as hunger and sexuality, and the primary interpersonal needs require *amplification* by affect. The excitement affect displayed at a football game, for example, is fundamentally no different than the excitement present in sexuality. The sexual drive requires fusion with excitement and enjoyment, the positive affects, for potency and integration to occur. At the first sign of negative affect, particularly shame or disgust, sexuality is immediately disrupted.

Interpersonal needs are experienced as critical *scenes* focused around recurring patterns of fundamental human interactions. These needs are imagined scenes of positive affect; to need is to expect something from another. Phenomenologically, these needs/expectations are experienced as *images* of events desired: a trip to the circus, a bedtime story, a warm embrace. The desired scene is first imagined with anticipation of enjoyment and communion, then it is actualized. One of the primary vehicles for the actualization of scenes, for the communication of needs and expectations, is language.

A beginning conception of interpersonal needs has been articulated by Harry S. Sullivan (1953b) and Bill Kell (1970) of the interpersonal school, as well as by W. Ronald D. Fairbairn (1966) and Harry Guntrip (1961, 1969, 1971) of the object-relations school. However, these first formulations of interpersonal relations lack precise definition of the broad relationship requirements for optimal development and also fail to partition affect and therefore to recognize its primacy. My theory of interpersonal development defines these relationship requirements and takes affect theory as its foundation.

What are the primary interpersonal needs? I have distinguished the following interpersonal needs, which I conceive to be innate and universal: need for relationship, need for touching/holding, need for identification, need for differentiation, need to nurture, need for affirmation, and need for power. To need is to imagine a scene involving another person who is central in one's world. To expect something is to imagine a scene amplified by excitement affect and by enjoyment affect. Needs may be openly acknowledged, understood by the other, and thereby fused with positive affect. Or they may act as pathways to relationship deprivation and to shame.

The scene is the event as it is lived, experienced; affect fuses with and amplifies the scene. Scenes focused around *interpersonal needs* and relationships, expression of *affect,* expression of the sexual and hunger *drives,* and around *competence* become imprinted with affect and stored in memory.

These scenes are the building blocks of personality. According to Tomkins (1979) scenes are also able to fuse together directly, thereby magnifying one another, ultimately creating families of scenes. Language gives particular meaning to these original scenes or *governing scenes,* and then continually remakes their images, synthesizing ever-new repetitions.

We now have a triad: *affect, imagery,* and *language,* which are the central processes shaping the self and identity. Affect amplifies and imprints scenes, and the presence of the identical affect in two different scenes increases the likelihood of the scenes becoming interconnected, directly fused together. Such *psychological magnification* of scenes creates families of scenes. Our thinking language continually remakes images of those crucial, ever-to-be relived, governing scenes. Language further evolves into distinct action language patterns, or *scripts,* for predicting and controlling a magnified set of scenes. A script is not *identical* with language because it may or may not include language. For example, in a motor script there are minimal language components. Governing scenes of shame undergo magnification by imagery and further transformation by language. These processes are central to the development of personality as well as of various pathological distortions of the self. They are equally central to psychotherapy.

Conceptions of human motivation have been evolving. A self motivated by sexuality and aggression is vastly different in conception from a self motivated by affect and by scene. Freud's original concept of libido subsumed both affect and drive without distinguishing either. Libido subsequently gave way to the drive concept, but affect remained obscured. Personality and psychopathology still were conceived as determined by the innate patterning of "instinctual drives"—sexuality and aggression. Later came an inquiry into the impact of relationship experiences, predominantly within the family. Working an ocean apart, Harry S. Sullivan (1953a, 1953b, 1956) and W. R. D. Fairbairn (1966) reversed the primacy of the drives. Each argued that the pursuit of satisfying, secure relationships mattered more than the gratification of drives. While Fairbairn framed his observations within the psychoanalytic linguistic system,

Sullivan sought to create a new, more operational language. Thus were born *interpersonal theory* and *object-relations theory*. However, all psychodynamic theories remain caught in a fundamental dualism: drive versus relationship. Either personality is conceived as organized and structured around innately unfolding drives or it is viewed as organized and structured around interpersonal relationships. Some attempts at resolution simply mix the two perspectives.

The partitioning of affect and drive is the contribution of Silvan S. Tomkins. Neither relationships nor drives are primary; affect is primary. Tomkins (1962, 1963a, 1979, 1981, 1982, 1984, 1987a & b) conceives of affect as the *primary innate biological motivating mechanism*. It is affect that gives texture to experience, urgency to drives, satisfaction to relationships, and motivating power to purposes envisioned in the future. The affect system and drive system are distinct, interrelated motivators. They empower and direct both behavior and personality, but the drives must borrow their power from affect. The interpersonal need system reflects a third motivational construct usefully distinguished from the first two. Developmental self theory synthesizes these perspectives by positing multiple motivational systems. Experiencing shame in connection with other affects, physiological drives, or interpersonal needs becomes a significant contributing source of internalization.

AFFECT SHAME BINDS

Tomkins has distinguished nine innate affects, and the expression of any affect, positive or negative, can be responded to with shaming. Sufficient and necessary repetitions of the particular affect shame sequence will create an internalized linkage, or *bind*. This can be true for any set of affect sequences. When the expression of anger, distress, fear, or excitement (any affect) becomes associated with shame, later experiences of those affects will activate shame spontaneously by triggering the entire scene. Shame need no longer be directly activated. The particular affect itself becomes bound by shame, its expression constricted.

Through the creation of specific or multiple binds, shame is able to exercise a powerful, indirect control over the self. As a result of shame's unique binding effects, expression of the shamed, hence forbidden, affect may become completely silenced, disguised, replaced by a more acceptable affect, or entirely hidden from view. When all affects meet with shaming, a total affect-shame bind results, and affect per se becomes shameful.

Fear-shame binds result when children are shamed for being afraid or otherwise expressing fear. This can occur in response to nightmares, imagined "monsters," or running away from the neighborhood bully. These individuals will feel there is something wrong with them whenever they are afraid later in life. They will experience shame, spontaneously and unexpectedly.

Distress-shame binds result when children are shamed for crying either in the family or in the peer group. Later experiences of distress affect, which are naturally activated by loss or death, will spontaneously activate shame as well. This is why so many individuals feel ashamed or embarrassed by crying, especially in front of others. It is the presence of shame that causes distress to be experienced as *breaking down* in front of others. A distress-shame bind will cause the self to feel deficient as well as sad. This is the source of the widespread discomfort with openly acknowledging death and dying in this culture.

Anger-shame binds function analogously. Shaming any expressions of anger affect, whether verbal or behavioral, will cause anger to be experienced as shameful. That affect may become either partially or completely inhibited. When parents react with either shame or distress (crying) to their children's natural expressions of anger toward them, the resulting anger-shame bind takes on the distinctive feel of guilt. As one example of this socialization pattern, consider parents who communicate that they feel "hurt" by their children's expression of anger. Harming others violates a moral code. The ethical judgment of transgression produces guilt, though affectively anger has been associated with and thereafter bound by shame. The guilty aggressive act may either mask or accompany shame about self. Even when shame remains localized in the aggressive act itself, not in the self, the ethical judgment of immorality will make shame moral shame. Aggression is nothing more than the extension of affect into action, and guilt over aggression is not a drive derivative. It is an affect derivative.

Finally, enjoyment-shame and excitement-shame binds develop when the expression of positive affect in whatever context meets with shaming. Consider a young girl who returns home excited and joyful over an accomplishment at school. She is greeted by her mother with, "Well, don't get a swelled head over it!" The girl's head immediately hangs in shame. Following sufficient repetitions of enjoyment-shame sequences, future experiences of enjoyment over accomplishments will activate shame spontaneously. Enjoyment thereby becomes bound by shame. Individuals who experience shame in response to either compliments received from others or to their own accomplishments have internalized such binds. Receiving a compliment will then spontaneously activate shame, leaving these individuals feeling unworthy or undeserving. And instead of experiencing true pride in accomplishment, they will experience their work with shame, as insufficient or not good enough.

Experiential Erasure: The Hypothesized Mechanism of Repression

The binding effects of shame are rooted in exposure itself. Sudden or unexpected exposure acutely disturbs the natural flow of self-functioning: freezing movement, silencing speech, immobilizing the self. The binding effects of shame may stop at the boundary of expression of affect, allowing conscious awareness of the shame-bound affect, with only its outward expression altered or silenced.

When the binding effects of exposure, however, spread inward to the conscious awareness of the shame-bound affect, a form of *experiental erasure* may occur. Particularly intense or prolonged experiences of shame literally can erase the contents of consciousness. It is the sense of exposure inherent in shame that causes this experiential erasure. My hypothesis is that this is the principal mechanism of repression proper, which would mean that the origin of repression lies in the process of shame internalization.

The degree of repression produced by experiential erasure is qualitatively different from that of other so-called repressive phenomena such as the actual disavowal of self. It is useful to distinguish these more active efforts to silence or sever particular aspects of self-experience from the effects of shame per se. We will examine mechanisms of "psychic surgery" when we consider the development of identity scripts and their attendant effects: disowning and splitting.

DRIVE-SHAME BINDS

The specific affect-shame linkages, or binds, are stored in the form of scenes. Particular scenes around affect expression take on distinct patterns, and so are given special meaning. Scenes around sexuality and hunger satiation also are imprinted with affect and stored. Drive-shame binds are created analogously to affect-shame binds.

The socialization of sexuality begins with the infant's discovery of its genitals. Masturbatory activities, from infancy through adolescence, become ready targets for shaming. Sexual curiosity and sexual play are additional avenues to shaming, and nudity is yet another potential source of sex-shame binds. Analogous to affect-shame binds, when the expression of sexual behavior or sexual urges (drive signals) is sufficiently or consistently shamed and therefore bound by shame, sexuality itself spontaneously activates shame. All later sexual dysfunctions have their origins in sex-shame binds, or in sex-disgust binds that develop analogously and frequently appear in conjunction with sex-shame binds.

Experiences with the hunger drive are similarly amplified by and imprinted with affect, through differential patterning with positive affect versus negative affect—most notably shame and disgust. Hunger satiation becomes associated with shame and disgust in many families when mealtimes turn into power struggles or battle zones; when children are force-fed, sometimes to the point of vomiting; when children are overly criticized during meals; when parents simply call too much attention to eating behavior or weight gain; and when direct shaming occurs around eating, weight, or bodily appearance. socialization patterns in which the hunger drive is very early associated with shame and disgust leave the individual particularly vulnerable to the development, much later, of an eating disorder.

Instead of remaining a source of enjoyment, of positive affect, eating becomes fused with shame and disgust. These patterns are additionally magnified in this culture because it especially prizes thinness and youth.

As different clusters of self-experience become increasingly bound by shame, the self gradually loses freedom of movement. Its freedom of expression is restricted and the self becomes ever more constricted, bound.

INTERPERSONAL NEED-SHAME BINDS

Affect-shame binds and drive-shame binds are stored in memory in the form of scenes. These scenes, which are focused around affect expression and drive expression, profoundly shape the experienced self over time. *Affect scenes* and *drive scenes* are two general classes of scenes that are differentiated and organized around shame. Affect-shame scenes evolve out of direct affect-shame sequences or binds, become organized around the unifying affect of shame, and then control later expression of the shame-bound affect. Drive-shame scenes develop and function identically in relation to the sexual and hunger drives.

There is a third general class of scenes: *interpersonal need scenes.* These relationship scenes, which are focused around expression of primary interpersonal needs, are heavily imprinted with affect, thus blurring their distinction. However, there is a discernible patterning to these relationship scenes that argues for further inquiry and closer examination. Just as there are distinguishable, though limited numbers of primary innate affects and primary drives, there is an equally distinguishable set of primary needs, that is equally limited in number. Interpersonal needs are focused around fundamental human interactions that are both innate and critically tied to the very progress of the self in living. Optimal development depends directly upon their satisfaction. Their association with shame will create analogous need-shame binds and need-shame scenes.

This conception of primary interpersonal needs is based on Tomkins's (1979, p. 211) concept of scene. Each of these primary needs manifests directly as a particular scene. Each is expressed in the form of specific governing scenes that are imagined as well as experienced interpersonally. These scenes are conceived to be both universal and particular and they become amplified by affect, positive as well as negative. Their fusion with positive affect encourages further interpersonal expression and integration within the self, while their amplification by negative affect, most notably shame, produces relationship deprivation and disruptive shame binds. Certainly, in each case it will be the balance of negative over positive affect amplification, or positive over negative, that is decisive in the development of the self. Interpersonal needs constitute one general class of scenes. Within that class, the following are discernible: relationship scenes, holding scenes, identification scenes, differentiation scenes, nurturing scenes, affirmation scenes, and power scenes.

What does it mean to say that certain relationship experiences are *needed*? By calling something a need we are singling out a fundamental patterning of interpersonal interaction that becomes amplified by and fused with affect, positive or negative, and that becomes stored within the self as an interpersonal scene. Its further role in personality is a direct function of its further magnification. There are a limited number of these innate primary needs or interpersonal scenes, but these are usefully distinguished from both affect and drive scenes. The specific interpersonal needs that I have distinguished to date can be observed to occur consistently; they also match phenomenology. This formulation significantly expands the concept of the interpersonal bridge by examining both the specific relationship requirements for maintaining it and the multiple pathways for breaking it.

Need for Relationship

Forming and maintaining a mutually satisfying relationship with a significant other is a fundamental interpersonal need central to human maturation. Biological birth does not guarantee a relationship between infant and parent—mother or father. The reality of the infant's dependence upon its parents for survival does not in itself win over its emotional loyalties; an interpersonal bond must also be formed. This trusting bond evolves directly from the establishment of emotional ties between infant and parent.

Both parent and child experience feelings, needs, and expectations in relation to the other. What conveys the parent's desire to have a relationship is expressed *interest* in entering the child's experiential world, which the child will eventually reciprocate. The infant *is* socially responsive to and interactive with its caregivers from the earliest months, as Stern (1985) demonstrates. The condition of mutuality—mutual interest and enjoyment—conveys to each that the relationship is genuine and valued. More important, the child experiences that the relationship is actually wanted by the parent. Birth alone does not satisfy the need for relationship. The evolving bond between child and parent must be genuinely desired, expressed in word and action, and also lived out consistently over time. These conditions create the interpersonal bridge.

Through such a relationship, the growing child feels secure in the knowledge of being loved as a separate person, as Fairbairn (1966) expresses it, and genuinely wanted, as Kell (1970) describes it. This is an experience of being in relationship to another significant individual; it communicates that one is special to the other. Each child needs to feel wanted and thereby experientially know with certainty that he or she is special. Each child, furthermore, experiences this need in relation to each parent. The growing child requires a distinct relationship with each parent, a relationship enabling the child to feel *wanted* by that parent.

When a child consistently fails to experience this distinct, individualized relationship, shame is generated because the interpersonal bridge is ruptured. The impact of parental actions *convinces* the child that he or she either counts as a person or instead is not wanted. Consider more closely how shame is generated in a dysfunctional parent-child relationship. There are a number of critical patterns. One arises when either or both parents do not actually want the child or instead desire a child of the opposite sex. Such rejection can be clear and open, ambivalent and hidden, entirely unconscious, or defended against by overpossessiveness and overprotectiveness. Resentment toward the child will inevitably find expression, however secret, leaving the child feeling responsible for not belonging.

Another pattern in which shame is rooted involves the parent expecting the child to make up for the parent's deficiencies or to live out the parent's unfulfilled dreams. In these instances the child is seen as an extension of the self of the parent, not as a separate individual. A third pattern occurs when the parent looks to the child for parenting, thereby reversing the natural flow of the parent being present for the child; the child must tend the parent's needs instead. A final pattern involves the parent repeatedly conveying to the child that he or she is never to need anything emotionally from the parent; this communicates that the child should have been born an adult and therefore must relinquish childhood without ever having had it. Each of the foregoing relationship patterns is a potent source of shame. Each ruptures the interpersonal bridge.

In order for a genuine and mutual relationship between child and parent to evolve, certain conditions are necessary. The child must be consciously wanted and the parent must be able to be emotionally present for the child, available to satisfy the child's core needs and not the reverse. The child must be enabled to relinquish center stage and also enabled to respect and care about the needs and feelings of the parent. That is the essence of mutuality. Nevertheless, the relationship flow of the parent being present for the child, not perfectly but humanly, must remain intact. When these fundamental conditions are missing and dysfunctional relationship patterns predominate, the child becomes entangled in a web of profound uncertainty. The conditions essential for basic security are absent, leaving the child feeling unwanted. If the pattern of rejection persists, the child will eventually feel lacking in some essential way, deficient. This is shame.

Need for Touching/Holding

The human infant's requirement for tactile as well as other forms of sensory stimulation is well known. The tactile sense refers to the human skin as a sensory organ. While the requirement for human touching is biologically based, it has broader interpersonal meaning as well. The purely physiological component of tactile stimulation, touching, does not adequately convey its developmental significance. Tactile stimulation during the first years of life is necessary for the infant to thrive. The quality of holding is the foundation for the earliest sense of self.

With maturation, the need for holding differentiates; it is required less often and in response to increasingly specific activators. Physical touching is one of the principal ways of expressing affection or tenderness. At certain times the need for a direct experience of bodily contact or bodily warmth motivates a child's desire to be held. At other times, physical holding is the child's natural desire in response to emotional distress, as occasioned, for example, by physical injury. Hurting oneself, crying in distress, and then requiring physical contact with a parent is a typically observed pattern. As development progresses, the source of distress shifts from the physical domain to the intrapsychic and interpersonal domains. When emotional hurts, in addition to physical ones, motivate the child to seek out *physical* comforting, verbally expressed reassurance is not likely to be sufficient to reaffirm the child's inner well-being. On these occassions, holding communicates protection and security—the basis for trust. These special embraces at significant moments when the self is experiencing distress, shame, or pain carry enduring impact. These are the moments in one's emotional life that represent the *need for holding*.

On those occasions when anger is expressed toward a child, particularly a preverbal child, shame may be generated through severing the interpersonal bridge. Parental failure to restore that bridge following expressions of anger intensifies the rupture, leaving the child trapped in shame. Furthermore, parental failure to respond directly to the child's request for holding, even in the midst of parental anger, will lead to direct association of shame with the need for touching, and to eventual repression or experiential erasure of that need.

Physical touching can become inadvertently shame-bound through a parents' unintended impact. In the earliest years, a child is typically provided opportunities for physical touching and holding, though unfortunately this is later withdrawn. Too often parents fail to sense their child's need for reaffirmation of the ruptured relationship or the child's own inner security, and therefore fail to provide that reaffirmation through a spontaneous and needed embrace. Here the principal impediment is parental shame about touching; parents cannot perceive in a child what they cannot allow in themselves. The recognition that a child needs to be held occurs through active, though not necessarily verbal, transmission of the need; it is probably an imagery process. All too often, however, that ambivalent yearning to be held remains entirely unspoken, even to the self that needs it. Although that need may never be directly communicated, parents will at times understand their child's need and provide appropriately for it. On many other occasions, the parent fails to recognize that need, vaguely experienced within the child.

When the need for holding fails to be understood, however it happens, shame is generated. The child feels that either the self is deficient or the need is fundamentally bad. The need for holding becomes bound and eventually controlled by shame.

Typically in American culture, males are particularly admonished not to touch one another, and are heavily sanctioned when they do so. An adolescent boy, accustomed to embracing his father, will feel betrayed when his father suddenly shies away from his touch, feeling him too old to embrace. No less a wound is experienced by an adolescent girl when her father unexpectedly communicates that something is wrong with their embracing or with her continued sitting on his lap. In each case the need for physical holding becomes bound by shame. Such a shame-bind also develops when parental holding continues to occur, but in response to the parent's need rather than the child's. Shame is also generated when parental touching becomes inappropriately sexualized. Finally, parental embarrassment with physical contact itself will transfer directly to a child or adolescent, causing the discomfitting behavior eventually to cease and the child's inner need for holding to become bound and silenced. Each of these patterns constitutes a rupture of the interpersonal bridge, and a significant source of shame.

Even when the need for touching is responded to positively and appropriately within the family, there continue to be critical avenues to shame within the peer group. The need for touching remains— along with the cry of distress—one of the most severely shamed interpersonal expressions within contemporary American culture.

Because of its developmental significance and multiplicity of meaning, human touching/holding is a fundamental interpersonal need. Furthermore, physical contact in the form of touching or holding, while pleasurable, is *not* inherently sexual. The widespread cultural confusion of sexuality with physical holding has created one of the most significant sources of shame about a natural, universally experienced human need. Touching is a sensory experience, and therefore a pleasurable one. But so are *listening* to music, *seeing* a captivating sunset, *tasting* an exquisite meal, and *smelling* flowers. The need for physical contact must be clearly distinguished from sexuality, which encompasses the physiological sexual drive, genital contact, and genital activities (drive amplified by excitement affect). The two motivators certainly may merge or even become permanently confused. But touching that serves distinctly sexual ends must be distinguished, both theoretically and behaviorally, from touching that communicates affection and from holding that is vital to restoring trust and security and to reaffirming the self's well-being. Nonsexual touching/holding must be distinguished, understood, and embraced as an inherent part of the self. Shaming distorts it.

Need for Identification

The phenomenological experience of identification is one of *merging* with another. Identification begins as an observational process, largely visual, but quickly becomes an imagery process. What is observed outside the self is transferred inside through imagery, which serves as a bridge from outer to inner, thereby enabling the child to experience being an actual part of mother or father. Open, close communication between parent and child facilitates identification as does modeling, by enabling the child to join the parent experientially through imagery, and so feel identified with that parent. Individuals identify in order to emulate those they admire, to feel *at-oneness* or belonging with these special ones, and to enhance their sense of inner power from so doing. The identification process is mediated by sustained mutual looking, extended facial gazing. Visual merging takes place principally through the eyes. Looking directly into the eyes of another person, and holding that gaze, is an intense form of interpersonal communication. Because the eyes are indeed windows to the soul, one can experientially enter another through the eyes, the two momentarily becoming fused as one. Generally, the intensity of mutual looking activates the feeling of exposure (shame) and the self turns away from visual merging, focusing attention upon itself instead. Therefore, the phenomena of merging and fusion, typically associated with borderline pathology, are an expression of a developmentally based interpersonal need, however exaggerated or blended with shame.

Consider the nature of the phenomenon in terms of the parent-child relationship. The need to identify is the wish to be like the valued parent. It is the motive that enables the parent to transmit, and the child to acquire, a personal culture. Parental mannerisms, patterns of speech, styles of behaving, and even ways of standing or walking may be admired by a child and unconsciously adopted as though the child were acquiring a part of the parent or practicing to be like the parent. Anyone admired, including siblings, relatives, and friends, arouses the need to identify.

Observation is the first step in the identification process. The child has to be able to observe what will later be adopted. Observation is critical to identification, however unconscious the entire process may be. But visual communication from one person to another is typically a problematic situation. Observation frequently involves facial gazing, and sustained eye contact is the most intense form of interpersonal communication, according to Tomkins (1963a, pp. 179-183; 1982, pp. 385-386). Instances of visual observation of others and the sustained meeting of eyes, of extended facial gazing, represent an important manifestation of the need for identification.

Through the eyes one individual can see into another, thereby experientially entering the other and coming to know the other from the inside. The eyes bid one enter and when the eyes meet, the bidding is a mutual one.

The earliest form of this identification scene is the shared experience of extended facial gazing between infant and mother in mutual enjoyment. It is the affect of enjoyment that particularly amplifies the identification scene, thereby creating a need for that scene.

After infancy, the meeting of eyes usually is brief; only rarely does one sustain that mutual gaze for longer than a moment because the intensity of the eye-to-eye scene becomes intolerable. When the duration of eye contact passes beyond a critical point, the intensity of the experience activates the feeling of exposure, or shame. Briefer instances of mutual gazing allow for some degree of affective communication and visual merging or identification. However, there comes a point when the self turns away from that merging with the other and focuses attention upon itself instead. That point is a function of the critical density of the affective experience and is highly individual. Shyness, or shame in the presence of strangers, will influence an individual's capacity for sustaining eye contact. The same individual will avoid the direct meeting of eyes under certain circumstances, while encouraging facial gazing at other times.

Looking into the eyes of another person who is simultaneously looking into one's own eyes is a powerful nonverbal experience. Mutual facial gazing becomes bound by shame, according to Tomkins (1963a, p. 171), when the child is shamed both for looking too directly into the eyes of a stranger *and* for being shy in the presence of a stranger. Associating shame with the visual process, particularly with mutual facial gazing, is one important way in which identification itself is interfered with. The need to identify itself eventually may become bound by shame.

While identification is rooted in mutual facial gazing, the need to identify is broader in meaning. Identification is the source of belonging, of rootedness, of connectedness, and of a sense of communality with others.

Childhood and adolescence, as preparation for adulthood, are times when preparedness and direction are especially urgent. Knowing how another human being functions on the inside—handling the vicissitudes of life, coping with joys and frustrations, facing critical choices, meeting failure and defeat as well as challenge and success—enables the child or adolescent to feel prepared for life. Through such close communication with a parent or significant other, a sense of belonging grows. Whenever the self is in need of direction or preparedness for coping with uncertain or threatening situations, the presence of an identification figure maintains inner security while enabling an evolving self to navigate the unknown. At each critical turn in development, from adolescence to old age and death, the need for an external model that serves as an internal guide for the self reemerges with renewed vigor.

The interpersonal environment must support the identification need. Appropriate individuals with whom the child or adolescent can identify must be available. These potential identification figures also must actually permit identification to occur. By directly providing support for the self, identification encourages growth, returning the evolving self into the world feeling restored and able to cope more effectively. Identification is one vital source from which identity evolves.

The principal models for the development of the gender component of identity, masculinity and femininity, are the parents. A boy learns what it means to be a man from his father and a girl learns what it means to be a woman from her mother. Close and open communication between child and same-sex parent fosters that identification. Talking openly with a child about what is truly important to the parent, including hopes and dreams, enables the child to join the parent experientially through the child's own imagery and thereby feel identified with that parent.

Parental identification occurs in any event, and more so if the parent is rewarding. In spite of initial, positive identification with a parent, events can interfere with or block identification entirely. Critical situations in the course of a particular child's life shape the future. Consider the situation of a father who beats his son. One consequence is that the boy slowly begins to reject his father as someone with whom to identify. While a certain amount of identification still occurs, this involves ways in which the boy learns to shame and humiliate himself. He no longer seeks out his father at those crucial times when he needs preparedness, direction, or comfort.

When a child adopts an unwelcome parental mannerism, but is told, "Don't do that," from either parent, the child is thrown into a dilemma. Either parent can interfere with the child's identification efforts through admonitions not to be like the admired parent. When the child responds with, "But you do it," the typical forthcoming reply is, "Do what I say, not what I do." The child's identification efforts thereby become associated with shame.

In another scenario, a particular child may not even be permitted to identify with one or the other parent. Either the child is kept at a distance, or close communication occurs only for the parent's need and never in response to the child's.

In another scenario, the child enjoys imitating the parent and is frequently observed doing so. However, the child's identification efforts directly activate shame in the admired parent. Either the parent feels ashamed of the particular behaviors being adopted by the child, or the parent had been previously shamed for identification itself. The parent responds by directly shaming the child or by simply displaying shame in response to the child's identification behavior. In either case, the child will internalize shame about identifying with that parent.

Consider one final scenario, in which the child is able to identify but learns quickly that occasions of experiential merging are followed by the parent's attempts to hold onto or control the child. Identification always is a fluctuating need, followed by needing to separate. When separation is resisted or shamed, the child may have to renounce identification altogether in order to avoid being engulfed and trapped. The need becomes intensely ambivalent; part of the self desperately longs for it while another part just as strongly avoids it. In such an insoluble dilemma lie the seeds of later distorted relationships with others.

Identification is a human process. The identification need continues throughout the life cycle; it is by no means confined to childhood. To the degree that the need is responded to sufficiently, and differentiation is equally supported, the emerging adult is able to navigate life autonomously while discovering others with whom to identify, such as mentors when entering a trade, career, or profession.

The need to identify will press for expression periodically throughout life, whether in relation to specific individuals or particular groups. Individuals gravitate to one another, creating the kind of bonding implied in identification. A sense of kindred spirit, of common purpose, brings people together who can identify with one another through whatever medium unites them. Loyalties to various groups evolve. People identify with a religion, a way of life, or a social cause. It may be a political party that wins their loyalty, or a football team. Loyalties evolve into allegiances. The need to belong to something or someone, to feel identified with something larger than oneself, can shape the course of one's life.

Need for Differentiation

The need for separateness, differentness, and mastery is the interpersonal motive empowering individuation; it is amplified by excitement affect and contempt affect. The self differentiates as it develops by coalescing certain identifications while discarding others, defining itself through action. Becoming a differentiated, separate self is its dynamic expression.

Examining the differentiation motive will illuminate another critical source of shame internalization and a further means of breaking the interpersonal bridge. While identification expresses the need for fusion, oneness, and belonging, differentiation embraces an equally vital striving for separateness and mastery, the instrument of individuation. Each individual differentiates his or her unique self by discarding those attitudes and practices acquired from others that are no longer desired and by further developing those qualities congruent with the inner self. To differentiate is to say, "This is me—I am different." Strivings for autonomy and independence emerge from this fundamental need, which begins to manifest itself with the dawn of the locomotive capacity. When an infant initiates movement away from its mother, separation has already begun. Separation from the mother is followed by establishing separate relationships with each parent and then by separation from the family. When development proceeds on course, separation culminates in attaining a separate identity.

The active discovery of his or her uniqueness and differentness as a person enables each evolving self to know with certainty, "This is who I am." An open recognition and acceptance of who one is, and who one is not, is essential to experiencing oneself as a fully separate individual, a distinctly different and valuable self.

Separation is as central to the progress of human development as identification. These universal, often conflicting needs oscillate throughout the life cycle. They represent the twin poles of human nature. Andras Angyal (1965) conceptualizes them as *autonomy* and *homonomy,* one trend functioning in two directions. Referring to the human being, Angyl writes, "His striving for mastery is embedded in his longing for participation" (p. 29). The quest for separateness takes many forms. When parents teach a child a task, the child frequently performs it differently. This change occurs because each self strives to find its own unique way, to discover its differentness. Holding ideas or beliefs that are at variance with a parent's is another expression of separation. Choosing different careers or life styles, as well as departing from parental values or religion, represent other variants of the motive. Departing from parental religion, values, or practices is a continuing expression of the need to differentiate, to become a separate person in one's own right. Separation from the family occurs on multiple levels. Fully taking the reins in one's own life is the central and governing scene.

The striving to separate does not occur in isolation; competence is necessary to support separation. This is where separation and mastery interface. A child who has not learned how to be a competent worker will not feel secure enough to separate. Similarly, a child who has not learned how to relate effectively to peers through developing interpersonal competence will likely retreat from separation. In order for separation from the family to proceed according to its developmental timetable, the emerging adult has to feel secure as well as competent. That knowledge is gained through taking increasing responsibility for oneself, particularly during adolescence, when the striving to differentiate, both to separate and acquire mastery, reaches peak intensity.

Increasing mastery walks hand-in-hand with becoming a fully separate person. Mastery initially manifests itself through the young child's desire to exercise new functions, explore the environment, acquire language, and gain control over bodily functions. The acquisition of mastery occurs in two channels: developing mastery over bodily and psychic functioning and developing competence in the environment.

Consider shame's disruptive impact upon both separation and mastery strivings. Overprotectiveness and overpossessiveness are two means by which separation can be resisted. A child's moving away from the mother or family is frequently resisted by parents. A child may be shamed for having certain values, ideas, or preferences if these are perceived as threatening. When legal adulthood is attained, parents may still forget to relinquish their power. Excessive parental control produces a climate in which children feel powerless as well as trapped; this is a seedbed for shame.

Interference with the child's natural and spontaneous efforts to differentiate engenders shame. If separation is resisted or forbidden by a parent, the child will either become openly defiant in order to preserve autonomy, hide differentiation efforts from the disapproving parent, or outwardly submit to enforced dependence on the parent yet inwardly withdraw into a secret world, to a place the parent cannot follow. What the child has learned is that something is wrong, shameful, about wanting to be separate or different.

Whether it is in regard to exercising new functions, exploring the environment, acquiring language, or gaining control over bodily functions, shame can become a barrier to gaining mastery. One of the most pronounced arenas for the genesis of shame is "toilet training," over which the battle of wills inevitably ends in humiliation for the child, who is often responded to with contempt or disparagement when bladder or bowel control fails. Likewise, if a parent continually corrects a child's speech, that child may become acutely self-conscious about talking and then retreat from verbal interaction. This is one source of stuttering. Overcorrection activates self-consciousness which disrupts the learning of any skill. While much depends on the particular child's native resources and temperament, shame can obstruct the child's early efforts to develop mastery.

The central idea is that differentiation, whether expressed through separation or mastery, is vulnerable to shame. Any given individual may emerge feeling either strong or weak, autonomous or dependent, competent or inadequate. The failure to actively encourage and support differentiation, along with punishing, shaming, or interfering with it, fosters a dependent adaptation to life.

Need to Nurture

The need to nurture is the need to help, give to, and comfort others. Children can be frequently observed to respond sympathetically to distress affect from peers, other siblings, or a parent. Unless interfered with, thwarted, or shamed, *affection-giving* is an innate need or interpersonal scene that becomes fused with the positive affects, enjoyment and excitement. The need to nurture represents an interpersonal interaction in which the child is not in need of receiving emotionally but of giving to another. Children *want* to give to their parents, whether in the form of affection or gifts. Their need is for mutuality—shared enjoyment in the very act of giving. How that embrace or gift is received by the significant other involved, parent or relative, determines whether the child feels that his or her love is accepted as good. This is the other critical observation made by Fairbairn (1966): not only must the child feel loved as a separate person (need for relationship), but the child must also *feel* that his or her love is accepted as good.

How the child is received furthermore determines whether the need to nurture is validated and integrated or becomes bound by shame. Consider a father who may be feeling badly one day. His daughter, sensing her father's distress, comes over to offer a hug or some comforting words. All the father need do is receive the girl's offering respectfully. However, if he feels ashamed of appearing so weak in front of his own child and rejects his daughter's approach, the girl will learn to feel shameful about wanting to give comfort to him. This is the inevitable outcome unless the father later openly and honestly acknowledges his own discomfort, thereby taking responsibility for his part in what occurred between them and restoring the interpersonal bridge.

Need for Affirmation

The need for affirmation is the need for valuing, recognition, and admiration. Children need to feel singled out and openly valued. To feel recognized as a unique self is central to self development. A parent's open pride in a son or daughter is one example. When a child is admired, that child feels affirmed. To be admired by another is to be gazed upon with deepening enjoyment, to be openly smiled upon. It is the gleam in the parent's eyes along with the smile on the parent's face. Admiration from a parent also mirrors back to the self the self's own joy. Affirmation of self is a recurring need, observed in adulthood no less than in childhood. It is not a sign of deficit, but an expression of a fundamental need central to human maturation and to the optimal functioning of the self.

Internal security is never entirely beyond the reach of threat. Throughout life, individuals experience moments of self-doubt. Effectively navigating such crises is vital because each individual needs to continue feeling that the person within, the inner self, is still worthwhile and valued. Through having someone significant directly provide that affirmation of self one is enabled to give it to oneself. A self-affirming capacity thereby emerges. Through developing this inner source of valuing, individuals cease being entirely dependent on the evaluations of others for their own sense of self-worth and esteem.

Another dimension of affirmation involves a basic valuing of one's uniqueness and differentness. These inherent qualities, which set one child apart from another, must be recognized, acknowledged, and valued openly. Through having one's own unique differences valued by significant others, one begins to value them in oneself. Each evolving person must be valued for his or her unique configuration of temperament, talents, and interests.

Shame may develop in a child from a failure to affirm any inherent aspect of the self. In terms of parental expectations, a particular child may have been born the wrong temperament for the sex. Although cultural expectations have broadened, quiet, introverted boys and aggressive, extroverted girls traditionally have been shamed in this culture. When a child's native temperament disappoints anyone significant, the ground is laid for the genesis of shame. That child cannot avoid the experience of being a disappointment, and will feel deficient because of it. Parental behavior, however unintended, can have rejecting impact upon the child by communicating failure to meet parental expectations, even when parental attitudes are not inherently rejecting.

While affirmation of self is vital, equally central is affirmation of a relationship. When a rupture in a relationship is perceived, whether it has actually occurred or only been imagined, a spontaneous attempt to reaffirm or restore that relationship naturally follows. However, if that attempt either fails to be understood or is resisted by the significant other concerned, then affirmation is not experienced; instead one feels emotionally isolated in the relationship and shame inevitably is confirmed.

When affirmation is not forthcoming at various critical moments, an awareness of difference between self and other translates into a comparison. Tomkins (1963a, pp. 238-240, 435-438) refers to this as the "invidious comparison." The comparison usually is one of good versus bad, better versus worse, and so on. Rather than valuing the difference between self and other, individuals feel obliged to wipe it out. Beliefs, values, and practices appropriate for one person will transfer to the other without their appropriateness for the self ever being considered. Interpersonal transfer occurs through a sequence of internal thought processes like, "She has many friends. I don't have lots of friends. Maybe I *should*. What's wrong with me?" There are infinite permutations of that process.

Affirmation of emerging sexuality by the opposite-sex parent is equally important as identification with the same-sex parent. Puberty unleashes both physiological and psychological changes. In order to develop relationships that eventually integrate sexuality, each adolescent first needs to "practice," that is, flirt, with the opposite-sex parent. This enables the adolescent to develop a complete relationship with a member of the opposite sex with confidence of satisfaction. The opposite-sex parent needs to *accept* the adolescent's flirting behavior and also to openly *admire* the emerging femininity or masculinity without, however, sexualizing the relationship. When that parent fails to accept and admire— through either open disparagement, shrinking back from the adolescent's practicing efforts, or inappropriate sexualizing of their relationship— shame may generate swiftly and disrupt the integration of sexuality and the capacity for sexual enjoyment and excitement.

Need for Power

The need for power is fundamentally a need for inner control over one's own life. A sense of inner control is the felt experience of power. It is a need to be able to influence one's environment, to feel consulted, to have an impact, to feel heard. To experience choice is to know power, being able to predict and control what happens. Any life even that wrenches away that vital sense of inner control activates powerlessness.

The long childhood of human helplessness, the *powerlessness scene,* conditions the need for power. Extending the experience of power diminishes the condition of powerlessness. Helplessness is one of the most primitive of the organized scenes, along with the equally recurring scene of extended facial gazing between infant and mother during suckling, the *identification scene.* Later experiences of powerlessness, particularly extended ones in significant spheres of life, are psychologically regressive. By reactivating that original governing scene of infant helplessness, recurrences of powerlessness return us experientially to that state. The dialectic between power and powerlessness itself is innate.

Consider more closely the nature and source of that dynamic. The roots of the power motive are embedded in the human infant's condition of helplessness experienced at birth and thereafter. The human being is born powerless, entirely dependent upon the goodwill and benevolent care of human caretakers. Months must pass before the infant is able to reach for an object seen and desired. Infants also frequently display a powerless rage in response to their state of helplessness. That state of powerlessness, the wellspring of the need for power, must be endured over an extended period of time, conditioning the emergent need for power as human development unfolds.

As each bodily function matures, the infant exercises it over and over precisely in order to gain control over it, displaying enjoyment at every success. Controlling the hand to reach for an object that has fallen, then grasping it and finally bringing it close is a developmental accomplishment, and an experience of power. As each bodily function comes under conscious control, from walking to language to bladder and bowel regulation, the experience of power expands and the condition of powerlessness diminishes.

The power motive is a direct outgrowth of the extensive epoch of helplessness that human infants must endure. Powerlessness is the experiential ground from which emerges the earliest sense of self. It is powerlessness that gives rise to the need for power—to control one's hands, to make one's legs move as willed, to control one's body and its functions, to speak one's thoughts and have them listened to, to go wherever one wills to go, to chart one's own direction according to inner promptings, to control one's life. It is that profound and lengthy condition of helplessness during infancy that shapes the destiny of human beings to become shapers of the landscape, not merely figures in the landscape, to echo Jacob Bronowski (1973, p. 19).

Powerlessness that is rooted in biological helplessness recedes through maturation. There is, however, a second dimension to power and powerlessness. Children can be granted either too little power over matters affecting them or too much power too early in life. Power is given to another individual through offering a choice, and having a choice in any situation enables the self to experience a degree of inner control, thereby diminishing helplessness. Experiencing choice in a powerless situation becomes an important route to restoring power.

Perception is critical to interpreting a situation as producing powerlessness. A sudden unexpected sense of uncertainty externally imposed, coupled with no control, creates the experience of powerlessness. When one feels powerless, one feels that nothing can be done, that something vital has been wrenched away, and that one is powerless to stop it: powerless is helpless is impotent. When a loved one dies, one's home is threatened by disaster, or job layoffs hit, what is being taken away in each of these instances is a sense of control, of power. Human beings are psychologically motivated by a need for power, a need for a measure of personal control.

The human need for power is *not* inherently a need for power over others, but instead a need to feel in command of one's own life. It is a need to command one's scenes. While power-seeking can certainly grow to monopolize a particular individual's life, it is most likely to become so as a result of powerlessness and shame that have been excessive or prolonged. In such cases power is likely to be relied upon exclusively to protect the self, compensate, or reverse roles, culminating in striving for power over others as a way of life. Initially, however, power functions as a central human need that is not always interpersonally directed. It is as essential to the development of the self as the other primary needs—for relationship, touching/holding, identification, differentiation, affirmation, and nurturing others.

The need for power is also closely related to the need for differentiation, although the phenomenological experience of the two motives is distinctive. Differentiation is the instrument through which individuation occurs. To differentiate is to say, "I am different." Differentiation involves striving to separate from significant others, coupled with striving to acquire mastery aimed at supporting those separation efforts. Here is where the two needs are related: acquiring mastery over bodily and psychic functioning, along with interpersonal and environmental competence, enhances the inner sense of power and the need to differentiate. What distinguishes these two motives, however, is the meaning behind the mastery efforts, the specific governing scene impelling mastery. This distinction is as subtle, and as essential, as the distinction between touching that serves sexual ends and touching that expresses affection or holding that restores trust and security. Just as specific sexual scenes are different from holding and touching scenes, power scenes are different from differentiation scenes. In a sexual scene, the sexual drive is primary, while affection or security are the principal motives in holding scenes. In a governing power scene, gaining control is the central motive whereas becoming different and separate as a person is the motive in a differentiation scene.

Power is a central human need that must be recognized, acknowledged, and responded to positively by parents as well as other significant adults. Individuals must learn how to maintain power in relation to others. Children and adolescents must learn how to regain power in situations that render them powerless.

Power is also the fulcrum upon which hope and despair delicately balance. When one is rendered powerless in any significant area of life, one becomes susceptible to depression, hopelessness, and, eventually, despair. Death of a spouse, loss of a job, and loss of health are threats to security because they activate powerlessness, itself a regressive experience. If prolonged, powerlessness threatens one's ability to sustain courage and hope. The combination of helplessness and hopelessness is psychologically toxic for the self.

The source of power, then, is the long childhood of human helplessness into which the neonate is thrust at birth and from which the infant ever so gradually emerges. That enduring experience, itself shrinking through maturation, conditions the need for power. The adult is later experientially returned to that primary state of helplessness by any life event that thwarts his or her ability to predict and control.

INTERNALIZATION OF SHAME SCENES: AN INTEGRATION

We have examined three principal sources of shame internalization. Scenes of shame become organized around distinct clusters of the self: affect, drive, and interpersonal need. The development of specific or multiple affect-shame binds, drive-shame binds, and interpersonal need-shame binds profoundly shapes the evolving self. These various binds become stored in memory in the form of analogous *affect scenes, drive scenes,* and *interpersonal need scenes,* which, in turn, govern further development of the self.

Furthermore, these internalized scenes have three distinguishable though interrelated aspects. First, the scene has an *affect-belief* component. This component comprises a cognitive label that the self reexperiences along with recurring shame. But this apparent cognitive self-appraisal originated in a specific scene or set of scenes. The affects activated in the original interpersonal event, along with any verbal messages communicated—for example, "Stupid"—become directly fused together in the scene. A girl hearing herself called "stupid" by her mother will internalize the entire scene: mother's disgusted look, angry voice, and the verbal message. She will grow up hearing a voice inside of her calling her "stupid," just as mother did before. That voice belongs to a face, but the visual scene gradually disappears, typically leaving the individual conscious only of the shaming voice.

Second, the scene comprises an *image of interaction patterns,* for example, blame for mistakes. These patterns are not simply cognitive self-appraisals as "worthless," "stupid," or "deficient." Rather, they embody a specific relational dimension analogous to the actual interpersonal relations encountered within the family. It is the image of these interactions that becomes stored as a scene. The scene is imprinted with both affect and language. All of the people present, together with the perceived activator and consequences, are also fused into the scene. The interaction itself is the scene as it is stored. These images of interaction patterns form the basis of the self's evolving inner relationship. A boy, for example, who is repeatedly blamed for errors of judgment will internalize an image of the blaming parent. He will grow up learning to blame himself whenever things go wrong. The internal image of the blaming interaction determines how he will behave toward himself in similar situations.

A third aspect of the scene is the "internalized other," which is a more specific coalescing of the various scenes internalized. At times the self experiences a voice inside either admonishing or disparaging the self, while at other times a distinct interaction pattern, such as blame for mistakes, is experienced. Each is rooted in a scene and these scenes gradually coalesce to form one or more *identification images* based primarily on either one or both parents. Usually the scene itself recedes from conscious awareness, though often hovering at its periphery. What typically remains conscious is an auditory voice inside that, though often confused with the self's own voice, is nevertheless distinct. The voice represents the auditory or language component of the scene. The imagery component is either lost or suppressed, but the voice remains conscious. These inner voices were originally linked to faces. As Tomkins reminds us, "The voice of conscience. . . is the voice of a particular face who, in addition to speaking, is angry or shocked or disgusted or disappointed" (1962, p. 220). Identification images are phenomenologically experienced in the form of auditory voices, though their imagery component is definitely retrievable.

My concept of the *identification image* parallels Fairbairn's *internal bad object* (1966), though important differences exist between these formulations. Describing the "internalized other" as an identification image more closely matches phenomenology. It also reflects the mediating role of imagery in the internalization process. There is one central difference between these two formulations. Fairbairn posits that only bad objects become internalized in an effort to control them, allowing the actual parental figure to remain idealized as good. In contrast, I contend that both positive and negative identification images become internalized. The child internalizes images that derive from fundamentally loving and respecting interactions just as the child internalizes images based on shaming interactions. Furthermore, I do not view internalization as an effort to control anything. It is simply a natural outgrowth of identification, which is itself a human process.

The internalization of shame is accomplished through imagery: scenes of shame become a principal source of identity. These scenes become directly imprinted with shame when the expression of any affect, drive, or interpersonal need is followed by shaming. Sufficient and necessary repetitions of the particular affect-shame, drive-shame, or interpersonal need-shame sequences create the internalized shame linkage or bind. When the expression of any affect, drive, or need becomes associated with shame, then later experiences of these affects, drives, or needs spontaneously activate shame by triggering the entire scene. Shame need no longer be directly activated. The particular affect, drive, or interpersonal need itself becomes bound by shame, its expression thereby constricted.

Through the specific or multiple *affect-shame binds, drive-shame binds,* or *interpersonal need-shame binds,* shame exercises a powerful, indirect control over the self. These three classes of shame binds are stored in memory in the form of scenes. Scenes focused around affect, drive, and interpersonal need expression profoundly shape the experienced self over time. *Affect scenes, drive scenes,* and *interpersonal need scenes* are three general classes of scenes that become differentiated and organized around shame. Affect-shame scenes evolve out of direct affect-shame sequences, become organized around the unifying affect of shame, and control later expression of the shame-bound affect. Drive-shame scenes and interpersonal need-shame scenes develop and function identically.

To recapitulate, these affect, drive, and interpersonal need scenes, which govern the self, have three distinguishable features: (I) an *affect-belief* component, for example, "Stupid"; (2) an *image of interaction patterns,* for example, blame for mistakes; and (3) the "internalized other" or *identification image,* usually manifesting as an inner voice.

Four

Psychological Magnification of Shame Scenes

I have called the unique faculty in which [science and art] both begin the imagination, that is, the human faculty of operating in the mind with images of things which are not present to the senses. The largest hoard of images that we create, and the most powerful method that we have for using them, is language. For human language is not confined to communication as that of animals is. The language of animals consists of signals—perhaps forty sounds and gestures to command action or attention (including attention to the emotions of the signaler). The human gift is to possess a second language in which a man converses with himself.

JACOB BRONOWSKI
The Identity of Man

Imagination, according to Jacob Bronowski, is a specifically human capacity. It is the capacity to anticipate the future, to imagine ourselves into the future, and to operate in the mind with images of things not yet present to the senses. This imaginative faculty is the source of both science and art, and civilization is the achievement of imagination.

The influence of the future on the present is not observable in the realm of colliding billiard balls or splitting atoms, but it is observable in the realms of human action and inner experience. Teleology is an idea already old in the human mind. Carl Jung (1923, 1965, 1968) theorizes that the future partially influences, even shapes present experience; Alfred Adler (1930, 1933, 1959) shares parallel conceptions with respect to human motivation, though he dresses them in different language. Viktor Frankl (1962, 1968, 1969, 1975) makes the motivating power of future goals central to his psychological framework: future goals pull one through life, providing direction and purpose, thereby creating a sense of meaning. For Frankl, the will to meaning replaces the will to power and the will to pleasure. The need for meaning becomes translated into values projected into the future that guide one in the present toward their realization.

Values, as Frankl describes them, are purposes. Lawrence LeShan and Henry Margenau (1982) argue that purpose is present as an essential "observable" in the realms of human behavior and inner experience. Future purposes—what one intends to be, do, or become—direct one forward, shaping the course of life.

Where and how does *purpose,* as a motivator, arise? Silvan Tomkins provides an answer as well as a glimpse of the underside of conscious experience. The scenes imagined with deep, enduring, and ever-recurring affect become these purposes, central to one's sense of self. Tomkins's *script theory* (1979) defines the *scene* "as the basic element in life as it is lived" (p. 211). A scene includes at least one affect and one object of that affect. An event must be "amplified in its urgency by affect" in order for any scene to be experienced. "The perception of a scene, at its simplest, involves a partitioning of the scene into figure and ground" (Tomkins, 1979, p. 221). Affect imprints and amplifies scenes that then become interconnected with and magnified by other affect-laden scenes.

Affect, imagery, and language are the central processes shaping the self and identity. Affect imprints scenes, and the presence of the identical affect in two different scenes increases the likelihood of the scenes becoming interconnected, directly fused together. This process of *psychological magnification* results in the emergence of families of scenes. Furthermore, our thinking language continually remakes images of these crucial, ever-to-be relived governing scenes.

> Psychological magnification begins, then, in earliest infancy when the infant imagines, via co-assembly, a possible improvement in what is already a rewarding scene, attempts to do what may be necessary to bring it about, and so produces and connects a set of scenes which continue to reward him with food, and its excitement and enjoyment, and also with the excitement and enjoyment of remaking the world closer to

the heart's desire. He is doing what he will continue to try to do all his life—to command the scenes he wishes to play. Like Charlie Chaplin, he will try to write, direct, produce, criticize, and promote the scenes in which he casts himself as hero. (Tomkins, 1979, pp. 214-215)

Distinct action patterns, or *scripts,* evolve for predicting and controlling a magnified set of scenes. In Tomkins's script theory, the scene is a happening perceived with a beginning and an end. The script, however, encompasses the individual's "rules for predicting, interpreting, responding to, and controlling a magnified set of scenes" (Tomkins, 1979, p. 217). These rules, first evolving directly out of scenes, become mediated by language, one of the most powerful methods for making images, according to Jacob Bronowski (1971, p. 82). Psychological magnification of particular sets of scenes is the source of both personality integration and disruption.

GOVERNING SCENES

Scenes that one is able to command, or still believes possible to actualize, become guiding purposes. These are the enduring scenes experienced or imagined with deepening enjoyment and excitement. These scenes direct one forward, creating purpose, thereby enhancing psychological integration of the self. But when one is thwarted from commanding these scenes, when even their possibility is suddenly, unexpectedly prevented through, for example, a loved one's death, job loss, or loss of health, then one is rendered powerless. And when prevailing scenes become fused with shame, one's sense of self is inevitably called into question. These evolving *scenes of purpose* expand the previous conception of affect scenes, drive scenes, and interpersonal need scenes. Now we have four general classes of scenes, each of which can become fused either with positive affect or negative affect. Together, these are the roots of identity.

Governing scenes of shame first undergo magnification by imagery and then further transformation by language. These processes are central to the development of personality, to the development of various pathological distortions of the self, and equally to psychotherapy.

Scenes of Purpose

A sense of purpose is central to the lives and actions of human beings. Their purposes, what they imagine for themselves and anticipate in the future, pull them forward in different, often changing directions. Purpose is experienced through envisioned scenes, these heroic dreams. An enjoyable or exciting eventuality that is anticipated through imagination produces a discrete scene that is actually experienced through visualization. Scenes are envisioned in the telescope of human imagination, as Jacob Bronowski (1973, p. 56) conceived it. Then one commands into being those scenes in which one casts oneself as hero. The scene functions as a motivator. Scenes imagined with deep, enduring affect motivate the self to enact them. The self is both player and scriptwriter: hero, writer, and director all in one. These prevailing scenes are like dramas one first "writes" by imagining oneself playing them over and over, and they shape the contours of life. Each imagined "life part" is a constructed scene.

Just as affect-shame scenes develop around particular affect-shame sequences or linkages, *purpose-shame scenes* arise in an analogous fashion. Scenes of purpose become fused with shame when children are ridiculed for the various daydreams, fantasies, or imagined vocations that are voiced to adults. When children are ridiculed for imagining creatures or monsters, imagination itself can become shamed and eventually bound by shame. When imaginative play, which is always accompanied by internal imagery, is continually disparaged or demeaned, scenes imagined in the future become associated with shame. Children are forever asked, "What do you want to be when you grow up?" This is an invitation to shame. Imagine the following response to a child: "What? You want to be a musician! You can't make a living at that. Pick something more practical." Recurring shaming can create a "learned helplessness," the incapacity to imagine a different scene, a new future, a way out.

Scenes of Affect

Families of shame scenes gradually emerge developmentally. Affect scenes, drive scenes, and interpersonal need scenes begin to differentiate. They adhere in distinguishable clusters. Scenes subsequently magnify one another. Affect scenes fuse together and begin to govern affect expression as the self continues to develop. Affect-shame scenes cluster in differential profiles both across individuals and between sexes.

Distress affect and fear affect in males, for example, typically are shamed in this culture and anger affect in females is similarly shamed. Hence, affect expression becomes molded differentially by shame according to the particular affect-shame binds that develop.

Scenes of Drive

Three interrelated clusters of scenes emerge directly from drive-affect interactions. The first comprises *sexual scenes.* These are scenes of positive or negative affect focused around expressions of the sexual drive. The second cluster is *hunger scenes.* Hunger-shame scenes, particularly in combination with hunger-disgust scenes, become enduring images of the self. Sexual scenes and hunger scenes further contribute to the development of a third cluster, *body scenes,* and to body shame. These scene clusters govern drive expression.

Scenes of Interpersonal Need

A group of scenes becomes organized around fundamental interpersonal interactions, rather than around drive, affect, or purpose per se. The patterning of these interactions is hypothesized to be innate, though outward expression is shaped by culture and by shame. Universal and recurring primary *relational needs* are readily observable, identifiable, and distinguishable. Whereas scenes of purpose become organized around a future goal, scenes of affect become organized around affect, or a particular affect, as their focus. Affect expression itself organizes the scene. Scenes of drive become analogously organized around a particular drive, sexual or hunger, as their prime focus. Finally, scenes of interpersonal need have an altogether separate focus: the human relationship itself. These scenes govern need expression and the evolving patterning of relationships.

From Families of Scenes to a Shame Profile

The four primary classes of motivational scenes magnetize other related scenes. The presence of the identical affect, such as shame, increases the likelihood of interconnection between scenes. In Tomkins's view (1979, 1987a & b), the fusion of different affects about the same scene directly increases the potential for magnification. This fusion and interconnection of different scenes defines the process of psychological magnification.

The phenomenology of the *internal shame spiral* illustrates the fusion and interconnection of scenes. When an individual suddenly is enmeshed in shame, the focus turns inward and the experience becomes totally internal, frequently with visual imagery present. Shame feelings and their accompanying thoughts flow in a circle, endlessly triggering each other. The event that activated shame is typically relived over and over internally through imagery, causing the sense of shame to deepen and to absorb other neutral experiences that happened before as well as those that may come later, until finally the self is engulfed. Shame becomes paralyzing.

Phenomenologically, this internal shame spiral is experienced and described variously as "tail-spinning," "spiraling downward," or "snowballing." Furthermore, each recurrence of the shame spiral is likely to recruit previous and even unrelated shame scenes, causing them to be relived and fused together. This process inevitably entrenches shame within the personality, spreading shame throughout the self. Shame becomes malignant, growing like a cancer within the self.

The four general classes of shame scenes continue to govern personality development. Magnification of scenes is an ongoing process and these coalescing scenes of shame create shame nuclei within the self. In my conceptualization of shame, these nuclei crystallize in a Shame Profile.

Affect-shame, drive-shame, interpersonal need-shame, and *purpose-shame* are the four primary scene dimensions in this Shame Profile. They represent the first stage of psychological magnification. Three higher-order scene dimensions later emerge from specific purpose-shame, affect-shame, drive-shame, and interpersonal need-shame interactions. These comprise *body-shame, competence-shame,* and *relationship-shame.* Finally, *identity-shame* or a shame-based identity represents the third stage of psychological magnification. Figure 4.1 illustrates the foregoing interrelationships and stages of magnification that create the Shame Profile.

Tomkins conceptualizes this progression from clusters of scenes to character shame as a *one-many* compression. "In any instrumental relation, it is seen in transforming *one* means into a one-many magnification, as for example, in money. In any end state, the same compression is capable of taking *many instances* and compressing and magnifying them into *one* which stands for all, as for example, the idea of God" (personal communication, 1986).

The stages of magnification expand the depth and scope of shame. Through this process of psychological magnification, imagery profoundly transforms earlier specific, isolated scenes of shame. Furthermore, the Shame Profile illustrates the developmental principle of increasing differentiation followed by hierarchical integration. Scenes of feeling unlovable or inherently defective, for example, are related to, though qualitatively different from, scenes of peer rejection. One is a further magnification of the other.

SHAME PROFILE: A DIAGNOSTIC TOOL

The developmental process through which shame becomes internalized produces a distinctive Shame Profile for each individual. This Profile illuminates the particular affects, drives, interpersonal needs, and purposes that have become bound by shame. That is how shame internalization originates. But when shame-based individuals enter psychotherapy, the picture they present reflects Stage II or Stage III of shame magnification: body shame, relationship shame, competence shame, or identity shame. The Shame Profile can be utilized as a diagnostic tool, a psychological tuning fork for distinguishing and illuminating the specific developmental pathways along which shame has evolved. By utilizing the Shame Profile, we can trace any current manifestation of shame back to its formative influences, to its actual governing scenes. The schematic diagram in Figure 4.1 illustrates the entire developmental process that we have been examining.

Using the Shame Profile, we can observe the progression from specific or multiple affect-shame binds to affect shame scenes that then govern the expression of affect. Similarly, we can observe how particular drive-shame binds develop and culminate in analogous scenes governing the patterning of drive expression. The various interpersonal need-shame binds become stored in memory in the form of scenes governing interpersonal need expression. Finally, purpose-shame binds are entirely variable and unique to the individual, resulting in an analogous cluster of scenes.

An individual displaying inordinate shame associated with body, relationships, or competence can be aided in discovering his or her unique developmental pathways or shame history, thereby returning internalized/magnified shame to its governing scenes. By exploring the socialization of affect expression, of drive expression, of interpersonal

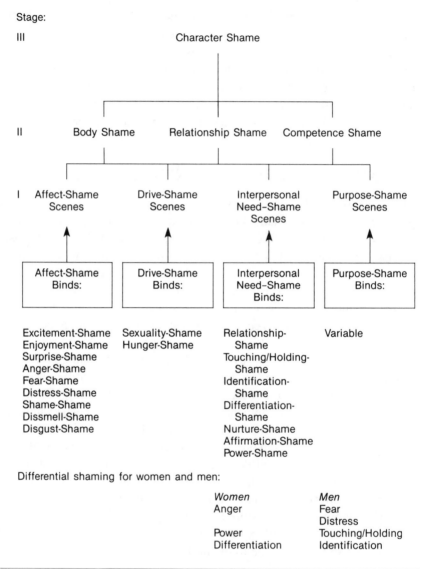

Figure 4.1 Shame profile: stages in psychological magnification.

need expression, and of the expression of imagined purposes, we have an important tool for guiding the recovery of early shaming scenes.

With the Shame Profile we can also observe the predominant patterns of gender socialization within a culture, the differential shaming that men and women typically have received. In American culture, as we have seen, men traditionally have been shamed for expressing distress affect (crying), fear affect, and shame affect. Men also have been shamed for expressing their need for affirmation, for touching/holding, and for identification, to feel merged with another. In contrast, women in this culture traditionally have been shamed for expressing anger affect and excitement affect, for asserting power, and for expressing their need to differentiate from significant others—to define themselves as distinctly different and separate while placing their own desires ahead of others' desires. The new conception of women's development offered by Gilligan (1982) thus can be viewed from the perspective of affect theory. It is the differential shaming that women receive in comparison to men that produces the apparent differences in their development.

Gender-related experiences, including roles, stereotypes, and predispositions, are a direct consequence of affect dynamics. Shame exerts a powerful shaping influence over the development of gender-specific behavior, and that patterning is equally culture-specific. Differential shaming produces the differential patterning of personality expression both within and across cultures. Examining this process offers a new perspective on the development of national character.

TRANSFORMATION BY LANGUAGE: VERBAL AMPLIFICATION

To complete the triad unveiled in chapter 3, language further transforms scenes of shame. Affect amplifies scenes, imagery magnifies them, and language imprints scenes with personal and particular meaning. Different shame scenes become attached to different linguistic signifiers—words—and become coassembled with different activators, targets, and remedies, thereby creating distinguishable shame states: *self-doubt, alienation, rejection, loneliness, worthlessness,* and *inferiority.* These are examples of prominent shame language-feeling states or affect-beliefs, that become organized around the expression of affect, drive, interpersonal need, and future purpose. Higher-order scenes focused around competence, body, and relationships become similarly attached to one or more shame signifiers, creating distinct language feeling states. Finally, identity shame takes on one of the following linguistic signifiers: believing oneself *unlovable, deficient, defective* or a *failure.*

These recurring verbal amplifiers remain as conscious or semiconscious expressions of internalized/magnified shame. Language gives personal meaning to recurring shame scenes, but also directly links scenes together or even reactivates an entire scene. Language is one of our most powerful methods for making images, for continually resynthesizing ever-new repetitions of governing scenes.

We have examined affect, imagery, and language as interactive processes central to the development of the self. Affect imprints scenes and scenes fuse together, magnifying one another into governing scenes. Language evolves into scripts, which then synthesize new repetitions of governing scenes. We will reexamine these processes when we consider the identity construct.

TRANSFORMATION BY INNATE FACTORS

Before we examine the individual's developing rules for responding to, predicting, and controlling a magnified set of shame scenes, we have yet to consider one last set of factors that influences how shame becomes both experienced and expressed. Genetically based factors can be partitioned into three general classes or spheres: *innate temperament, innate intensity of affect, drive, and need,* and *innate sexual orientation.* The general premise is that heredity provides the limiting frame, a propensity toward a particular disposition or orientation, while environment provides the critical shaping influences. But the individual responds to both heredity and environment with creative self-definition rooted in how experience becomes uniquely organized into governing scenes—to echo Alfred Adler (Ansbacher & Ansbacher, 1956).

Innate Temperament: Introversion—Extroversion

Innate temperament, such as a tendency to be either introverted or extroverted, is conceived as biologically given. Mixtures are certainly the rule, and temperament always remains open to considerable modification by learning and the environment. In the introvert, interest is focused inside the self; the opposite is true in the extrovert. The introverted temperament is predominantly, although not exclusively, focused inwardly. The introvert also naturally withdraws deeper inside in response to shame. The introvert is comfortable with inwardness.

In contrast, the extroverted temperament is predominantly, but not exclusively, focused outwardly. In the extrovert, affect itself is more externalized, openly expressed, more visible. Certain extroverts externalize their thinking processes by verbalizing inner experience to others. Because the extrovert tends to externalize affect, he or she is given to naturally occurring oscillations of mood—the extrovert's counterpart to the introvert's profound inwardness.

The introvert moves, psychologically speaking, "in and out" while the extrovert cycles "up and down." This is the phenomenological feel of these particular innate temperaments. In the extrovert, shame manifests as an externally visible mood; in the introvert, it manifests in withdrawal deeper inside the self. Generally, we have failed to distinguish innate temperament from learned temperament, just as, in Tomkins's view (1979), we have failed to distinguish innate affect from backed-up affect, as discussed in chapters 1 and 2.

Innate Affect-Drive-Need Intensity

The distribution of affect intensity, drive intensity, and interpersonal need intensity is not uniform across individuals. The intensity of particular affects, drives, and needs varies widely because heredity endows each individual differently. Anger may be strongest in one child and fear strongest in another. The affect threshold itself also varies. The affect threshold refers to the critical density of neural firing required to activate a particular innate affect. One child therefore may be quick to anger, while another may be much slower to anger, having a higher threshold for activating that affect. The same principle holds for the drives and interpersonal needs. For one particular child, holding scenes and identification scenes may be strongest, while power scenes and differentiation scenes may be the most intense for another. Finally, the tolerance for negative affect in general, and shame in particular, also varies widely.

Innate Sexual Orientation

As they do in the evolution of temperament, heredity and environmental experience interact in the evolution of sexual orientation. Thus, it is my hypothesis that homosexuality and bisexuality each have an inherited predisposition that is one among many contributing factors shaping development. This predisposing factor reflects a *tendency* to invest one's own sex with sexual or erotic excitement (drive amplified by affect), with the mutual enjoyment of touching and holding (need amplified by affect), and with the enjoyment of mutual facial gazing, communion felt as oneness (need amplified by affect). Identification scenes and touching/holding scenes, along with specifically sexual scenes, accumulate in some women around images of other women, just as they accumulate in some men around images of other men. The critical imprinting of these scenes is a complex interaction of genetic factors, prenatal factors, environmental influences, and the individual's active, constructive participation in how experience becomes organized and subsequently rearranged.

> Logically, there is a possibility that the postnatal determinants may need no facilitation from prenatal ones. Defense of this proposition precipitates, yet once again, the obsolete nature-nurture debate, with no resolution. On the issue of the determinants of sexual orientation as homosexual, bisexual, or heterosexual, the only scholarly position is to allow that prenatal and postnatal determinants are not mutually exclusive. When nature and nurture interact at critical developmental periods, the residual products may persist immutably. (Money, 1987, p. 398)

Ambiguity obviously remains. How to separate the effects of an *inherited orientation* from those of *early imprinting* remains a mystery in science. But ambiguity does not preclude hypothesis. It is likely that there are multiple paths directed toward any particular orientation, sexual or otherwise. However, just as a tendency to be either introverted or extroverted is conceived as biologically given, sexual orientation is partially biologically given, though each predisposition remains open to further rearrangement by experience.

DEFENDING SCRIPTS

Examining the individual's developing rules for responding to, predicting, controlling, and interpreting a magnified set of shame scenes will illuminate the particular strategies of defense that develop to protect the self against further encounters with shame. Initially, they are externally directed and forward looking, designed to escape from and avoid future encounters with shame. Rooted in governing scenes, these defending strategies, or *defending scripts,* have affect-imagery-language features.

They comprise distinctive rules for action and cognition. The following general classes of defending scripts become organized around shame.

Rage

Whether in the form of generalized hostility, fomenting bitterness, chronic hatred, or explosive eruptions, rage protects the self against exposure. Rage functions as a defense against shame. The cyclical fueling and inflation of rage insulates the self, actively keeping others away while creating a protective cover. As a defending script, rage organizes and interprets new experiences in order to control magnified scenes of shame, and to predict and respond to future ones.

Contempt

A blend of dissmell and anger, contempt distances the self from others while elevating the self above others. To the degree that others are looked down upon, found lacking or seen as lesser or inferior beings, a once wounded self becomes more securely insulated against further shame. Contempt is the source of conceit, arrogance and superiority, of judgmental, fault-finding or condescending attitudes toward others. Contempt scripts reinterpret new experiences in order to avoid or escape from shame.

Striving for Perfection

Perfection scripts organize the self in order to erase every perceived blemish. The self must excel in an ever-widening circle of activities, while nothing done is ever seen as good enough. Perfecting the self comprises a set of rules for responding to magnified scenes of shame. In predicting and controlling shame scenes, perfectionism is an attempt to compensate for feeling inherently defective, never quite good enough as a person. Hence, the perception that nothing done is ever good enough—it could always have been better. The inevitable result is that one is plunged back into shame. Perfection scripts are therefore both self-limiting and self-validating.

Striving for Power

Scripts that aim at maximizing power over others and maintaining control either in relationships or situations encountered constitute another strategy for protecting the self against shame. Power scripts are rooted in magnified scenes of shame. The rule that develops is precise: take control whenever possible. Taking the power becomes the single-minded rule governing behavior. Gaining power over others and in interpersonal situations, jockeying for position in social groups, and keeping control in relationships are particular manifestations of power scripts. A power script may also grow to dominate the self, eclipsing all other scripts and becoming a way of life. Then power becomes the principal means for maintaining security and enhancing self-esteem. Power becomes the only desired goal.

When power scripts combine with rage and/or contempt scripts, the seeking of revenge is a likely outcome. This is a *recasting* defense, according to Tomkins (1987b, p. 205), because its aim is to reverse roles with the perceived humiliator. Now the humiliated one, at long last, will humiliate the other.

Transfer of Blame

Blaming focuses attention upon who can be found responsible for any mishap or misdeed that occurs. Blaming is a strategy that recruits the affect of anger, but directs it in an accusatory, fault-finding manner. When fault can be clearly fixed somewhere, and responsibility transferred to another, the self is freed of any suggestion of culpability. The self has done nothing wrong because someone else is to blame. The self remains pure, often righteous, in the face of mishap.

The blaming script neutralizes shame by transferring shame away from the self: when things go wrong, find fault somewhere else. Encounters with the alienating affect have grown so intolerable that shame must be transferred to another. The transfer of blame *is* fundamentally a transfer of shame; they are functionally and phenomenologically equivalent. It only *appears* as righteous indignation because the blaming script recruits and directs anger in an accusatory manner. It is this transferring of blame/shame that underlies so-called projection.

Although blaming often develops in this manner, not all blaming is shame-derivative, according to Tomkins (personal communication,

1986). Some blaming is normative, that is, right-wrong, disgust-diss-mell related.

When blaming parents become overidentified with their children, inevitably the child becomes viewed as an extension of the parent. If the child is blemished so must the parent be, for the two are one. The child's natural mistakes, failings, or mishaps become acute threats to the parent's self, and blaming is directed at the child as if he or she were an offending part of the self of the blaming parent.

To recapitulate, blaming scripts defend against shame by transfer-ring that affect elsewhere. Blame-transfer scripts operate by secondar-ily recruiting the affect of anger and then directing that anger in a way that is accusatory, fault-finding. When someone else is blamed, and thereby found responsible, the self remains pure, freed of the contam-ination of culpability.

Internal Withdrawal

Withdrawing deeper inside the self is another strategic alternative. This script reduces exposure and avoids further shame by withdrawing the self deeper inside, allowing escape from the torment of shame. The agony of exposure is thereby reduced, and the loss of the possibility of reunion is also neutralized. The self in effect hides from shame by hiding deeper inside. Only a superficial social mask remains visible, knowable by oth-ers. The real self—the needing, feeling, imagining self—has shut itself in. In response, the individual increasingly becomes a shut-in personality.

Humor

Scripts that recruit enjoyment affect to reduce negative affect, particu-larly shame, constitute an additional strategy of defense. Humor atten-uates the self-consciousness and exposure inherent in shame. The self's momentary estrangement—feeling strange, ill-at-ease, discom-fort, or alienation—is alleviated by the shared enjoyment experienced through humor.

Laughter and humor, shared human activities that recruit enjoyment affect (smiling), are effective means of reducing intense negative affect, particularly shame. They can be utilized in a wide range of universal shame situations or scenes. Telling a joke is well known, for example, as a way of "breaking the ice" at a social gathering or before giving a speech. The inevitable self-consciousness and sense of exposure—shame affect proper—activated by the presence of strangers in these settings is attenuated immediately by humor. Enjoyment experienced in communion with others reduces shame. In addition, the self gains command of the scene, making others laugh instead of being laughed at by others (mocked, ridiculed).

As a defending script, humor takes on many faces, remaining either flexible and adaptive or becoming rigidly relied upon, so entrenched that everything important must be treated lightly and any potential source of shame quickly minimized through humor before it strikes. Furthermore, humor may combine with contempt scripts, producing mockery, sarcasm, cynicism, or even self-deprecatory humor as particular variants of this defending script.

Denial

Denial scripts operate directly at the level of perception. When all attempts to escape from or avoid shame become blocked, thwarted, or defeated, the next line of defense is denial at the level of perception itself. Denial is a final line of defense when action strategies fail. Denial functions just like other scripts, guarding the boundary between self and environment. Denial scripts attempt to exclude shame from awareness by denying its perception, or by denying the perception of anything that might arouse shame.

Summary

Defending scripts are rooted in, and become organized around, the affect of shame. Their function is to predict and control scenes of shame, whether externally encountered or produced from within. Interpreting through language and responding to future scenes of shame are additional functions of these scripts. Defending scripts comprise the essential rules for accomplishing all of these aims. Initially, they are forward looking and externally directed in operation.

IDENTITY SCRIPTS

The self is the feeling and thinking, imagining and judging, and willing and directing center within the personality. It embraces conscious and unconscious dimensions. Identity, in contrast, is the *conscious* experience of that self together with the active, living relationship the self comes to have with the self. According to Tomkins, no decision made by any science is more important than the most general assumption about the nature of that science's domain. Tomkins conceives of the human being as an information-duplicating organism.

> We will direct our attention to the more obviously analogic and symbolic informational phenomena of duplication in the human being. We conceive of man in this respect as an inter- and intra-communication system, utilizing feedback networks which transmit, match and transform, information in analogical form and in the form of messages in a language. By a communication system we mean a mechanism capable of regular and systematic duplication of something in space and time. (1962, p. 9)

The self becomes organized around scenes it later reproduces, and identity becomes organized around scripts. Identity is the highest order class of scripts. All scripts first evolve from scenes, but then scripts increasingly produce or determine scenes. Multiple and competing identity scripts coexist within the self in either a fragmented, patched-together, or integrated manner.

Individuals internalize interpersonally based scenes of shame and later reproduce them internally. The bridge linking outer experience with inner development is imagery, which encompasses visual, auditory, and kinesthetic dimensions. For example, in the case of sexual or physical abuse, the skin itself is directly involved and so becomes imprinted in the scene. What is stored is a kinesthetic scene.

Internalized scenes of shame, or shame coassembled with other negative affects, become the models that shape distinct patterns of inner relating. Affect-laden scenes are recreated in the present by language action patterns and also reactivated by new scenes that are sufficiently similar to old scenes. These original scenes are reenacted and relived, reproducing shame along with other negative affects.

Affects experienced toward other people create distinct relationships. These evolving relational patterns are based on positive affect, on negative affect, or, more frequently, on affect mixtures, affect ambivalence. In an analogous vein, each individual experiences, actually cocreates, a distinctive *inner relationship*. Characteristic patterns of action evolve within the self, operating to either affirm or undermine it, just as characteristic patterns of reaction evolve interpersonally.

Divisions within the self become manifest through the self's active inner relationship. External relationships with others are more visible, but the inner relationship is no less real, no less vital to security. Nothing is so precious to the self as its own integrity. Inherent parts of the self, these clusters of self-experience, can be *owned*—valued and embraced, actually integrated. Or they can be *disowned;* inner peace is then replaced by internal strife. Actively disowning any inherent self cluster creates and then maintains insecurity.

The scenes recreated and relived inside the self are rooted in earlier, largely interpersonal interactions with the environment in key settings, most notably that of the family. The peer group and school setting are also important sources of governing scenes, but interpersonal learning in the family is the principal model for the self's evolving and distinctive inner relationship. Individuals typically learn to treat themselves precisely the way they were treated growing up, because no wish of the child is greater than to be like the loved or needed parent. Internalization is a direct outgrowth of identification.

Scenes of shame are internalized through imagery. They are later reproduced through silent analog construction, according to Tomkins (1979), or through auditory analog construction mediated by distinctive and observable scripts. Governing scenes are reactivated in the present and thereby relived through either of these modes.

Identity evolves out of complex affect-imagery-language interactions. It is neither simply a coalescing of scenes nor a strictly cognitive process. Just as *defending scripts* develop to help escape from or avoid further shame, *identity scripts* emerge to organize the self uniquely. They are like defending scripts, but turned against the self. Like other scripts, identity scripts encompass the rules for predicting, controlling, interpreting, and responding to a magnified set of scenes. In contrast to defending scripts, which are forward looking and externally directed, identity scripts are directed internally and look backward as well as forward. New experience is reinterpreted in the light of prior experience. Defending scripts predict and control future, externally based scenes of shame. They guard the boundary between self and world, but identity scripts invade the self. The enemy is now within. While defending scripts aim to avoid or escape from shame, identity scripts inevitably reproduce shame.

Self-Blame

Three distinctive identity scripts develop in response to shame and become organized around prior scenes of shame. Their activators and organizing affects are typically different. In a *self-blame* script, the activator is usually some kind of mishap, mistake, or failure. Self-blame recruits the affect of anger, but directs it in a self-accusatory manner. The self accuses the self, angrily blaming the self for whatever mishap has occurred. Analogous to blame-transfer defending scripts, self-blame identity scripts involve a fixing of responsibility, an accusation in this case against the self. Both the self-blame identity script and the blame-transfer defending script develop in a blame-oriented family, where attention is repeatedly focused not on repairing mishaps, but on determining fault, on who is to blame. In these families, as in the wider culture in general, interest is directed solely at locating someone who can be held accountable for the mishap—other adults, one's spouse, even one's child. Although a child in a blaming family will tend to learn similarly to transfer blame away from the self, that child may in addition, or instead, learn to direct blame inward.

The essence of the self-blame identity script is the repeated accusation of the self for real or imagined mishaps or misdeeds, angry denouncement of the self, and humiliation of the self with accusations of fault. There is no way to maintain dignity and self-respect; a self-blame script remorselessly calls these into question.

Comparison Making

A pattern of invidious comparison will undermine the self. This culture teaches everyone to compare themselves to one another, so *comparison making* within a family becomes all the more toxic. Individuals learn to compare their differences and find themselves lacking, because this culture neither recognizes nor values individual differences. Comparison-making parents speak not only with their own voice, but with the voice of the culture as well.

In a culture that generally fails to recognize and value individual differences, the awareness of difference between self and other inevitably translates into an invidious comparison. Awareness of difference is the unique activator of this particular identity script, which then functions to reproduce shame. Internal comparison making evolves either from directly *experiencing* oneself being actively compared by significant others (including parents, siblings, teachers, peers, and the media), or from indirectly *observing* comparison making modeled by others. Internalization is always a direct outgrowth of identification. Parents and other family members frequently model comparison making through the devaluation of others. Likewise, peers in school, for whom the pressure to conform to widely held images of popularity is most insistent, repeatedly engage in comparison making at the expense of someone's good feelings about self.

As is the case with the self-blame script, the comparison-making script becomes an actual way of relating to oneself, a specific way to actively maintain and spread shame by reproducing, and thereby further magnifying, original scenes of shame. Comparison making is a second source of negative identity, another internalized script for relating to the self that encompasses affect, imagery, and language components. Through either comparison making or self-blame those earliest scenes of shame are relived, thereby magnifying their power to shape identity.

Self-Contempt

While comparison making actively devalues the self by translating differences into deficiencies, the *self-contempt* script actually rejects the self. Contempt, a blend of dissmell and anger, is the communicator of and is also experienced as rejection. By distancing the self from whatever arouses that contempt, it also elevates the self above others. The object of contempt, be it self or other, is found offensive, something to be repudiated. Contempt adds punishing anger to distancing dissmell, as symbolized by a lynching. The most extreme expression of contempt is a lynching. This image combines an intense punitive quality (via anger) with a total and permanent repudiation of the offending other (via dissmell). The severity of the image of lynching matches the severity of the affect of contempt. Such lynching-like contempt can be directed at others, and it can be turned with equal severity against the self.

Contempt manifests interpersonally through overly critical attitudes toward others. Contemptuous individuals become perpetual critics, always finding something wrong, some fault with people or things. A visibly contemptuous parent will enable a child to acquire through identification a similar posture toward the world. When contempt is directed interpersonally, judgmental, fault-finding, or condescending attitudes infiltrate human relationships through defending scripts: others are looked down upon, found lacking, or seen as lesser, inferior beings.

Contempt turned against the self in the form of an identity script, however, creates an actual split within the self: one part becomes the offender while the other becomes judgmental, punitive, or persecutory. A self-contempt script can reactivate an individual's original scenes of shame as well as reproduce them.

Whenever scenes are reexperienced, all of the affect imprinted in those scenes is relived as well. Although these scenes typically remain in the background of awareness, they are always capable of reactivation through language, affect, or imagery channels.

Self-blame, comparison making and self-contempt are three affect imagery-language action patterns that critically shape negative identity. By reproducing shame, these scripts become the source of enduring self-hatred, pervasive inferiority, and consuming worthlessness.

Inner Voices

The inner voice script generally has been misunderstood as a cognitive process. Consider the script more closely. It is mediated by the *identification image* of the blaming, comparison making, or contemptuous parent, that alien "internalized other" now located within the self. Identification images are internalized out of interactions with parents and become deeply embedded in those critical governing scenes. The internal *image* of the parent typically manifests as an inner voice, and so is mistaken as a purely cognitive phenomenon. The imagery aspect gradually recedes from consciousness or hovers at its periphery. The inner voice of the parent is distinct from the self's own voice, but is mistaken as actually belonging to the self. That inner voice once belonged to another, and to a particular face. Since only the voice has remained conscious, it *appears* that these voices reflect strictly cognitive self-talk or inner dialogue.

This is not a dichotomous phenomenon, however. In some cases, the parental voice actually merges with the self's own voice, partially or completely, while in others the two voices remain separate and distinct. These outcomes represent two poles of a continuum. The process by which the parental voice merges with the self's voice, whether positive or negative, is continuous. No matter how integrated it actually becomes, that inner voice always originates from a scene.

Cognition or language is only one dimension of the phenomenon; imagery is the more fundamental dimension. Inner voices are manifestations of the self's distinctive inner relationship. These voices reflect complex action patterns, coassemblies of affect-imagery-language that then reproduce scenes and, hence, shame.

Reenactment of Scenes

We have examined three identity scripts—three specific patterns of inner action that perpetuate insecurity, three observable ways in which the self actively relates to the self. Each identity script continues within the self a pattern first encountered interpersonally. Though originating in the past, each script is actively maintained in the present, undermining even the most positive of new experiences by reinterpreting them. These scripts are further mediated by the *identification image* of the blaming, comparison-making, or contemptuous parent, that alien "internalized other" installed within the self.

Affect-laden scenes are recreated in the present by these specific identity scripts. In this case, analog construction is auditory, mediated by a voice, through which governing scenes are reenacted and relived. They also are recreated when new scenes, sufficiently similar to old scenes, directly stimulate silent analog construction. No apparent "voice" actually need be experienced inside the self for the reproduction of shame or other negative affects to occur.

Negative identity scripts turn the self against the self, undermining security, valuing, and wholeness. Consider a boy whose father is overtly contemptuous whenever the boy needs anything, causing him to experience acute shame about needing. The boy grows up to hate the needing child inside of him, seeking to purge himself of needs. He learns to reenact toward himself the analogous scene experienced at the hands of his father.

Disowning of Self

Owning and disowning are potential action outcomes or by-products of identity scripts, positive and negative, respectively. Through negative identity scripts, distinct parts of the self previously associated with shame become the targets of further strife, now experienced internally. The reenactment of scenes generated by any of these identity scripts creates further magnification of shame. Disowning results directly from the additional magnification produced by identity scripts. Shame-bound parts of the self now become actively disowned. Disowning is an action performed by one part of the self against another. It reflects a second stage of magnification beyond that produced by identity scripts: further magnification of actual parts of the self into autonomous clusters or coexisting configurations. The *needing self* and *feeling self* are self-clusters; the *child self* and *adolescent self* are self-configurations, or developmental phases of the self.

The self is actually a coalescing of different selves, a process that evolves through distinct phases. These developmental phases include the earliest child self or selves, the adolescent self, and the later, increasingly mature selves. These self-phases are always demarked by *identity script magnification,* whether positive or negative. Each subsequent self-phase encompasses all preceding self-configurations, much as a tree adds rings of growth. Each earlier phase of self remains potentially within awareness, capable of sudden or unexpected intrusion into consciousness. The developmental process is one of increasing differentiation of these various self-configurations, followed by their hierarchical integration.

When identity scripts are predominantly positive, then actively *owning* and embracing these distinct self-configurations is the eventual outcome. The self is oriented toward integration. However, when identity scripts are negative, active *disowning* emerges as the prominent reenactment inside the self. Disowning is the action process through which dissociation or disavowal actually occurs and dissociative phenomena develop, a process that Harry S. Sullivan (1956) originally described. Disowning positions the self toward disintegration or fragmentation.

Splitting of the Self

Internal strife waged relentlessly against disowned parts of the self results in an actual *splitting of the self* into two or more partial selves or caricatures of the self. Splitting reflects a third stage of magnification, a final reenactment within the self. Identity scripts, disowning, and splitting fall along a definite continuum; each is a further magnification of the former.

Splitting is not a defense as typically conceived, but a final step in a magnification continuum. Figure 4.2 illustrates the process.

Contempt turned against the self is the principal means by which splitting occurs. Splitting is actively maintained by negative identity scripts that have become so magnified that autonomous partial selves split off and then coexist within the same individual. Multiple selves, or so-called multiple personalities, are a definite developmental possibility. What distinguishes schizoid selves, multiple selves, borderline selves, and narcissistic selves will be explored at length in the next chapter.

Splitting of the self is an outgrowth of a broader, more widely observable process, the disowning of self. Disowning is itself an elaboration, a further magnification of distinctive, negative identity scripts. All later pathological distortions of the self have their origin in this process.

Shame-Based Identity

The final step in the developmental sequence occurs when one's essential identity becomes based on shame. Defeats, failures, or rejections need no longer be actual, only perceived as such. The internal shame process has become magnified beyond what the basic affect of shame itself might produce as an amplifier, whether in the form of shyness, embarrassment, or guilt. The internalization and further magnification of shame have created an identity, a distinctive pattern of relating to oneself, that continuously absorbs, maintains, and spreads shame. The self has become shame-bound. Furthermore, the internal relationship between owned and disowned parts of the self directly recreates within the self the identical shame-activating qualities initially encountered interpersonally.

This concludes our examination of the development of the self in the context of shame. Development, however, does not cease here. Distinctive clinical syndromes emerge and must also be examined if theory is to have explanatory power. Affect theory in general and shame theory in particular provide the foundation for reformulating psychopathology.

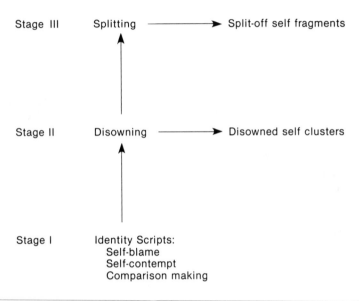

Figure 4.2 Stages in magnification.

Five

Reformulating Psychopathology

*Never forget that in psychology the means by which
you judge and observe the psyche is the psyche
itself. Have you ever heard of a hammer beating
itself? In psychology the observer is the observed.
The psyche is not only the object but also the subject
of our science.*

C. G. JUNG
Analytical Psychology

The developmental theory of shame, identity, and the self is based on the
critical interplay of affect, imagery, and language. Developmental self
theory synthesizes the object-relations theory of W. R. D. Fairbairn
(1966) and Harry Guntrip (1961, 1969, 1971), the interpersonal theory of
Harry S. Sullivan (1953a, 1953b, 1956) and Bill Kell (1970) and Silvan
Tomkins's (1962, 1963a, 1979, 1982, 1987a, 1987b) affect theory. The
alienating affect so disturbs the functioning of the self that eventually distinct syndromes of shame arise. Each is rooted in significant interpersonal failure, displays a characteristic patttern reproducing shame, and further distorts the self, creating varied disorders of self-esteem. Shame
becomes internalized through imagery and these scenes govern syndrome
development.

Governing scenes of negative affect lie at the heart of addictive, compulsive, and narcissistic disorders. While other negative affects play a
vital role in many cases, the role of shame is central. Disorders of self-
esteem and disorders of mood have resisted effective therapeutic intervention as well as precise theoretical conceptualization, because we have

110

largely failed to grasp the primary role of affect and its primacy over other subsystems within the self. Compulsive, addictive, borderline, and narcissistic syndromes, which continue to elude effective intervention, are rooted in *affect dynamics* in general and *shame dynamics* in particular.

Psychopathology must be reexamined in the light of affect theory, and then reformulated. Syndromes must also be examined from the perspective of shame. While shame is central to the development of many disorders, not all psychopathology is rooted in shame; shame alone does not produce all forms of psychological disturbance. The magnification of any affect is potentially toxic to the self, according to Tomkins (1987a, p. 150), and this is as true of fear affect as it is of excitement affect. The following formulation of shame-based syndromes, however, is a first step in the direction of reformulating psychopathology. It is the natural extension of Tomkins's conceptualization of affect, scene, and script, which were applied to self-development in the previous chapters, into the domain of pathological development.

SYNDROME DEVELOPMENT: GENERAL CLASSES

Affect theory illuminates the normal functioning of the self along with its various pathological distortions. Distinct classes of syndromes develop in response to affect dynamics and become organized around an individual's predominant affect(s). In certain individuals, the affects of fear and anger become magnified, and thereby emerge as the dominant forces within the self. For others, distress is paramount. All individuals encounter shame to some extent, but shame becomes coassembled differentially with various negative affects and also differentially magnified. The extent and prevalence of shame in relation to other negative affects across different syndromes is an empirical question. Different ethnic groups, for example, vary in the prevalence of shame and differ as well in their respective targets of shame. Syndromes generally become organized around shame in conjunction with other critical affects. Shame nevertheless plays a vital role, because no other affect is more central to the sense of identity and none is more disturbing to the self.

Six general classes of shame-based syndromes can be observed. The first is a group of *compulsive syndromes,* in which repetitive reenactment has become magnified. Here, I subsume addictive disorders, eating disorders, sexual abuse, and physical abuse. It might, however, be argued that addiction is sufficiently different from the others to warrant a separate classification.

The second general class comprises *schizoid, depressive,* and *paranoid syndromes,* which become organized around shame in conjunction with other key negative affects. From this perspective, paranoid schizophrenia is viewed as a further magnification of the paranoid posture.

Phobic syndromes constitute the third general class. Here, fear is widely observed as the manifest affect, overtly displayed, while shame is frequently the latent affect; the phobia guards against further encounters with shame. Agoraphobia is one example of accelerating phobic reactions, but not all phobic syndromes are focused necessarily around shame.

Sexual dysfunction syndromes are the fourth general class. In these instances, the sexual drive has become fused with shame, either by itself or in combination with disgust and fear. Examples of specific sexual dysfunctions are impotence, lack of orgasm, and premature ejaculation. The disruption of sexuality is neither a drive derivative nor a relationship derivative. It is an affect derivative.

Fifth is a group of *splitting syndromes,* including multiple personality, borderline, and narcissistic personality disorders. These are all syndromes in which the phenomenon of splitting has become further magnified. Splitting is itself a magnification of a much more widely occurring process that I label *disowning,* as discussed in chapter 4. Self-contempt and self-blame, which are internalized and directed against the self, actually mediate the disowning process, and therefore the splitting phenomenon as well. Distinctive splits within the self organize the self in a unique fashion. Splitting of the self may result in two or more partial selves, or multiple selves (multiple personalities) within the same individual. Borderline and narcissistic syndromes represent distinctive variations on the dynamic of splitting.

Sixth is a group of *sociopathic* and *psychopathic syndromes.* These syndromes essentially involve a misfiring of conscience and must be examined in terms of shame in order to delineate the necessary and sufficient determinants of antisocial behavior. Failures of human attachment invariably become sources of shame. The vicissitudes of shame illuminate the origins of these syndromes.

These six general classes of shame syndromes are by no means mutually exclusive. Mixtures are likely and particular syndromes may develop sequentially because of the human being's "marvelous plasticity of mind," to echo Jacob Bronowski (1973).

DETERMINANTS OF SYNDROME DEVELOPMENT

In further delineating these evolving syndromes, five factors must be distinguished and viewed as interactive. First, the *organizing affects* of various syndromes may be distinctly different. The conjoined magnification of shame-humiliation and fear-terror, for example, produces a different clinical picture than the conjoint magnification of shame and distress. Likewise, the internalization of contempt—contempt turned against the self—together with shame produces yet a third distinctive syndrome. Different clinical syndromes initially can be ordered in terms of their principal organizing affects. When shame is present, it typically is coassembled differently with other negative affects. A careful examination of the particular affect dynamics of each syndrome, and of each unique individual case, will illuminate one of the important determinants of syndrome development.

Second, each syndrome is rooted in qualitatively different *governing scenes.* The scenes in phobic syndromes are different from the scenes in splitting syndromes. While the organizing affects in phobias—fear, or shame conjoined with fear—are identical to those in paranoid schizophrenic syndromes, where shame and terror are conjointly magnified, the governing scenes in which these affects are rooted are different. Examining the particular affect-shame, drive-shame, interpersonal need-shame, and purpose-shame binds by utilizing the Shame Profile will illuminate these important governing scenes. The Shame Profile illuminates for each individual the critical developmental pathways along which shame has evolved, thereby pointing to specific governing scenes and enabling their recovery. Likewise, the experienced "internalized other" images, or identification images, are phenomenologically different in the various syndromes, and also function differently.

Third, evolving defending strategies further distinguish different syndromes. Particular *defending scripts* emerge and then become differentially magnified, propelling the self further in distinct directions. Just as the face actually looks different in response to different affects, the "face of the self" looks different according to its competing scripts. Rage, contempt, power, perfection, blame transfer, withdrawal, humor, and denial scripts evolve to enable the self to escape from and avoid intolerable shame, to protect the self from such external threat, and to predict, control, interpret, and respond to the critical organizing affects that have become magnified into the individual's governing scenes.

The self is in the process of adaptation, gripped inexorably by its scenes, creating either caricature selves, partial or multiple selves, a patchwork self, an easily fragmented self, a self divided and at war inside, a shut-in self, a defiant or compulsive self, or a magnified posture—schizoid, depressive, or paranoid—toward the world. Organizing affects, governing scenes, and defending scripts are three factors that shape these evolving syndromes. The particular *identity scripts* that also develop comprise a fourth critical factor in syndrome development. A self-blame script, for example, gives the self a qualitatively different face than does a self-contempt script. To the degree that *ethical judgments of immorality* are further compounded with these negative affects directed against the self, these syndromes, or particular instances of them, take on the distinctive feel of so-called guilt states. An essentially shame-based individual, then, can give the appearance of being guilt ridden. Theoretically, guilt is more accurately understood as *immorality shame,* according to Tomkins (1987a). Shame, either singly or in combination with other negative affects, most notably anger, dissmell, and disgust, takes on the distinctive *feel* of guilt when the shame becomes moral shame or immorality shame. Furthermore, moral shame, moral dissmell, moral disgust, and moral outrage generate a broad range of "guilt" scripts. They are different from general self-blame or self-contempt (dissmell plus anger) scripts in that the ethical judgment of immorality must be added to them in order to produce "guilt."

Different negative identity scripts organize the self differently. We have identified three: self-blame, self-contempt, and comparison making. Any of the defending scripts (externally directed) can transfer inside the self and generate identity scripts (internally directed). We thus would expect to see identity analogs of power scripts and perfection scripts just as we saw identity analogs of blame-transfer scripts and contempt scripts—self-blame and self-contempt, respectively. Subjugation of certain abhorred parts of the self and inner overcontrol are identity analogs of power scripts, and forever erasing blemishes of the self is an identity analog of perfection scripts. Humor, coupled with contempt, produces self-deprecatory humor, another identity script analog. Denial and internal withdrawal also have identity analogs. Denial at the level of perception can extend increasingly inward, and withdrawal can isolate any part of itself deeper inside. Different syndromes emerge depending on the particular identity scripts and their varying stages of magnification (disowning and splitting, for example).

Finally, *innate temperament,* along with other innate factors and predispositions, comprises the fifth determinant of syndrome development. Innate introversion-extroversion, innate affect-drive-need intensity, and innate sexual orientation constitute the distinctive inner frame for each unique self. Just as innate affect is different from backed-up affect, innate temperament is different from learned or environmentally modified temperament. The introverted child assimilates experience differently than the extrovert while invariably being changed by that experience. Introversion-extroversion represents a continuum, not a dichotomous variable, just as affect distribution and sexual orientation are continua. Temperament and sexual orientation are neither fixed nor immutable at birth, nor are they entirely the result of experience, imprinting, or early learning.

In one sense, what we are looking at is the direction of investment of affect. In introverts, interest and affect generally are focused predominantly inward; in extroverts, the reverse is true. Affect likewise may be primarily oriented toward, or invested in, opposite sex *or* same sex. One becomes sexually *excited* (drive amplified by affect) by members of the opposite sex, by members of one's own sex, or by both. Similarly, one *enjoys* communion (need amplified by affect) with members of the opposite sex, same sex, or both. Sexuality is always amplified by affect. The integration of innate affect orientation (introverted-extroverted) and innate sexual orientation (same sex-opposite sex) is inherent dimensions of the self. Innate factors influence shame and are influenced equally in return. Shame about temperament and shame about same-sex sexual orientation are important additional determinants of syndrome development.

NUCLEAR SCENES AND SCRIPTS: CLASSIC PARADIGMS

We have considered a number of critical determinants of syndrome development: organizing affects, governing scenes, defending scripts, identity scripts, and innate temperament. These are general determinants. So far we have not distinguished among various types of scenes. According to Tomkins (1979, 1987b), people are characteristically governed by a multiplicity of scripts generated to deal with particular sets of scenes. These classes of scenes vary widely in their degree of magnification. The set of scenes first determines the script in the early stages of magnification. However, as magnification increases, the script increasingly determines the scenes.

In Tomkins's view, *nuclear scenes* are defined by their rate and continuity of growth. Their underlying nuclear scripts continue to grow in intensity of affect, in duration of affect, and in the interconnectedness of scenes. Nuclear scenes can never be achieved totally or possessed permanently. Good scenes can never be good enough and must be endlessly perfected; bad scenes can never be entirely avoided or renounced. Nuclear scenes never stop seizing the individual. The conditions that produce nuclear scenes are the conditions of unlimited magnification.

> What is it which guarantees that human beings will *neither* master the threats to which they are exposed nor avoid situations which they cannot deal with effectively? Mortality and death is one paradigm for such a state of affairs—because it cannot be mastered, nor can it be avoided. Another paradigm is the classic triangular scene (either due to the arrival of a sib, or the presence of the father) in the family romance. The male child who loves his mother excessively can neither totally possess her (given an unwanted rival) nor totally renounce her. He is often destined, however, to keep trying and characteristically to keep failing. Why does he not learn then that he would be happier to make peace with both his mother and with his rival? Many human beings do just this, but to the extent to which the male child can neither possess nor renounce, he remains a perpetual victim. (Tomkins, 1979, p. 229)

Classic paradigms for nuclear scenes include *death/mortality* and *triangular* scenes. Death is an inevitability and therefore constitutes a paradigm. It can be neither mastered nor avoided. Religion has evolved partially in response to that nuclear scene, promising a solution in the next life that is unavailable in this one. The solace of religion is the balm for death fear and death shame. Death humbles all. Since mortality cannot be avoided or mastered, belief in an afterlife is one attempt at solution of the insoluble.

The presence of an unwanted rival constitutes the triangular scene. That rival can be either the other parent or another sibling. The classic oedipal situation dissolves into one nuclear scene among others, and the oedipal scene involves shame every bit as much as it involves fear. As Tomkins (1963a, pp. 526-529) observes, shame invariably accompanies castration fear; castration is thus a double-edged danger. Whether or not the triangular scene becomes radically magnified for any given individual remains an open question. Its magnification is not predetermined, since it depends on the affective amplification of that scene and on its interconnection with other related scenes.

Certain children may see the other parent as the unwanted rival; others may see another sibling in that role. Each individual participates actively and directly in how these scenes become organized. Consider a young boy commenting at dinner how he is going to marry his mother when he grows up. When his father asks what his son will do with *him,* the boy eyes his father curiously, then smiles and responds, "Oh, I'll just marry you too." An ingenious solution. This same boy one day observes another family approaching as he and his father walk down the street. Approaching them is a mother and father walking with a young child between them. "Do all families have two children?" he asks. "No," his father answers, "some families only want one child." Without breaking his stride and without looking up, the boy responds, "I wish our family only had one child." And it is quite apparent who is to be gotten rid of.

To the foregoing classic scenes I add *powerlessness* scenes. The primitive scene of primary powerlessness is one that human beings encounter over and over throughout life. We can never entirely master it, nor altogether avoid it. Ultimate human powerlessness in vocation, in relationships, in health, over safety of one's home, over aging, over *any* good scene, returns one experientially to that earliest scene of primary powerlessness experienced during infancy. The wish for possession of the good scene becomes radically magnified along with the inability to renounce the wish. The human being is caught between having possessed the scene however briefly, only to have lost it once again. Powerlessness is another classic paradigm for nuclear scenes.

Nuclear scenes constitute an important class of governing scenes that profoundly shape the experienced self. Identifying any of these paradigms in particular cases further illuminates the operation of governing scenes in syndrome development.

COMPULSIVE SYNDROMES

Syndromes become organized around shame along with certain other negative affects. In some syndromes it may be shame plus fear or shame conjoined with distress that is central, while in other syndromes the prominent affect combination may be shame plus rage plus distress. Different cases displaying the same syndrome may also differ in their organizing affects. Examining the group of compulsive syndromes will illustrate the point.

Physical Abuse

One important class of shame-based syndromes is *physical abuse.* These disorders are rooted in the conjoint states of powerlessness and intense humiliation (shame), two inevitable consequences of parental abuse. Repetitive beatings are a recurring source of shame for children whose parents cannot control and otherwise safely discharge their own mounting rage. Parental rage triggers the reenactment of a scenario culminating in physical abuse, but that parental rage itself has earlier origins. Parents who physically abuse their own children were typically abused themselves while they were growing up. They felt equally humiliated, and continue to live with unresolved shame in their own lives. Children of shame-based parents will inevitably activate their parents' shame, causing the cycle to repeat itself with shame passed from generation to generation.

Shame-based syndromes that develop within individuals cause *shame-based family systems* to form. There is, however, a critical intervening step in the development of such syndromes and systems. Parental shame is embedded in a series of *governing scenes.* It is these original childhood scenes of the parents that later become reactivated by their own children.

Like magnets, scenes compel reenactment. Phenomenologically, a scene is an entrance, a psychological "black hole" drawing the conscious adult self inward. It is a portal in time. The mature self is immediately transported back into these original scenes, which then are reexperienced fully. Once a governing scene has been reactivated the original experience is relived in the present with all its affect reawakened.

To illustrate the process of *recasting* abusive scenes, consider the following situation. Margaret grew up in an abusive family and entered psychotherapy because she found herself occasionally beating her own daughter. She was also experiencing considerable shame about this behavior. Once her shame began to be released, we were able to explore what precipitated the reenactment. Margaret described her experience as feeling like something "snapped" inside of her and then she was taken over, lost in the act of repeatedly beating the girl. At times she would have no awareness of what was happening until the beating was over; at other times she would "awaken" in the midst of beating her daughter, as if she had temporarily lost consciousness. I asked Margaret to describe every detail concerning the onset of both the beatings she herself had received as a child and the beatings she now delivered to her daughter.

During one session, Margaret mentioned that she heard a growling sound just before she "snapped" and began beating her daughter. I asked her to show me what she was describing, to behave it for me. She was silent for a few moments; then she began to growl, louder and louder. Suddenly, she began shouting at me in German. Instantly, her entire face changed before my eyes, becoming contorted. She almost looked like a different person. She pounded the desk over and over and seemed about to leap at me. I simply waited, sitting on my own anxiety, allowing the scenario to play itself. Finally, I called her name distinctly several times and asked her to look directly into my face. When our eyes met, I asked her to continue looking into my eyes; then I said it was time to come out of the scene, to return to the present. Gradually, she quieted and recomposed herself.

As we reflected together on what had just occurred, Margaret mentioned that her father came from Germany. She recalled that he used to beat her as a child, he would begin shouting at her in German. That always had preceded the beatings she received. The growling sound that Margaret was able to recall hearing at the moment she reenacted that scene with her own daughter was the sound of her father's voice in the original scene. But Margaret had recast the original scene; now she was playing her father's role. She literally became her father, both facially and behaviorally.

Parents who are about to abuse their own children are simultaneously reliving scenes in which they also were beaten, but they relive the scene with a difference: they relive it from the perspective of their own parent as well. Now they actually play their parent's role. In Tomkins's (1987b, p. 205) schema, they *recast* the original scene. The internal image of the abusive parent mediates the process, and the governing scene maintains it, compelling reenactment and thereby also reproducing shame.

Governing scenes of physical abuse may lead to a compulsive reenactment of abuse, creating a shame-based family system. Abuse may be reenacted, however, in various forms and with varying targets: repetitive abuse may be directed toward self, toward spouse or toward one's own children. Invariably, there is also intense secondary shame about being an abusive parent or spouse, which further fuels the cycle.

Other abused individuals may reenact their governing scenes by entering new relationships that then repeat the original pattern of abuse. For example, many women who were abused as children cocreate an analogous relationship with a man who is abusive toward them. Rather than either recasting the governing scene or abusing themselves directly, they reenact it by recreating an analogous relationship in which they are treated in the present virtually identically to the way they were treated in the past. Abused women seek out such a relationship because they feel compelled to reenact their original governing scene. And it is that governing scene that compels them to return again and again to the abusive relationship.

The organizing affects in physical abuse syndromes are shame and rage, conjointly magnified into explosive scenes, the reenactment of which governs the self. To understand the abusive parent or spouse, we must first discover their specific governing scenes. Defending scripts and identity scripts are rooted in these scenes, and vary across particular cases. Different syndrome profiles are likely, though repetitive reenactment of shame scenes emerges as their unifying factor.

To recapitulate, the physical abuse syndrome is rooted in powerlessness and humiliation (shame), two consequences of repetitive beatings. Typically, the abusive parent was similarly abused as a child. Parents who are about to abuse their own children simultaneously reexperience, and therefore reenact, analogous scenes from their own childhood. But they relive the scene with a difference: now they play their parent's role. The scene has been *recast*. Scenes compel reenactment, transporting one back into these governing scenes as though into a psychological "black hole." The original experience is relived with all its affect present.

Sexual Abuse

Compulsive disorders are rooted in affect dynamics. These disorders inevitably reproduce shame and at the same time attempt to reduce it. Hence they are shame-based. *Sexual abuse* is a second class of compulsive syndromes. Incest and rape are two distinct types of sexual abuse that activate intense inner states of powerlessness, bodily violation, and humiliation. In the midst of shame, one feels to blame. Childhood incest generates poignant, often crippling shame, along with other negative affects. When the experience of violation, helplessness, and betrayal is disowned, the self withdraws deeper inside to escape the agony of exposure. Alternatively, the self torments the self brutally with disgust and contempt turned against the self, thereby causing the actual splitting of the self.

The scene of violation is seared into the victim's imagination. That scene may hover at the periphery of awareness or instead repetitively replay itself in consciousness, fantasy, or night terrors. The scene also may be banished from awareness, fully disowned, resulting in the self becoming frozen, statuelike. That scene of forcible violation, as experienced by the victim, is itself a reenactment, a transformation of a scene of equal powerlessness and humiliation experienced by the perpetrator of the assault at the hands of a different tormentor.

It is not only the victim of incest or rape who responds with a shame reaction or becomes shame-based as a person. The perpetrator of the assault or violation is equally shame-based. Such acts are acts of power and revenge, born of impotence and fueled by shame. The rapist is haunted by scenes of torment and is driven to reenact them, this time in the role of tormentor. The roles are reversed, thereby recasting the scene. The victim, the target of revenge, is confused with the source of the perpetrator's shame. By defeating and humiliating the victim, the perpetrator momentarily becomes freed of shame. Fundamentally, theirs is a shame-based relationship.

The incestuous parent or adult is similarly shame-based, equally gripped by governing scenes and driven to reenact them. The reproduction of shame for both child and parent creates not only a shame syndrome for each but a shame-based family system as well. Each member is scripted to play a particular role. For example, some women who experienced incest during childhood reenact that scene by cocreating a relationship with a man who will later sexually molest their child. Men who are incestuous with their children are also reenacting governing scenes of shame, though not necessarily of incest, but they recast the original scene. Governing scenes first generate scripts, and the scripts both create and subsequently maintain the family system as shame-based.

To summarize briefly, in sexual abuse syndromes, intense shame (humiliation) is the predominant affect and is accompanied by fear, distress (sadness, crying), and rage. In the midst of shame the victim feels to blame—an inevitable result of shame. The violation scene replays itself in consciousness or night terrors, or hovers at the periphery of awareness. If instead the scene is banished from awareness, disowned, the self emerges frozen, statuelike. The perpetrator of the assault is equally driven by scenes of powerlessness and humiliation, but experienced at the hands of a different tormentor. The rapist is haunted by scenes of torment and is driven to reenact them, this time in the role of tormentor, thus reversing roles and recasting the original scene.

Addictive Disorders

In examining the third class of compulsive syndromes, *addictive disorders,* addiction must be viewed broadly. Although there are specific substance addictions to alcohol and various chemicals, addiction itself can spread. Any object potentially has the power to become compulsively desired. Addiction to relationships, addiction to gambling or to work, as in the familial "workaholic" syndrome, and sexual addiction are further extensions of the addictive process. The objects of addiction must be distinguished from the process by which addiction develops and is maintained. The addictive process is distinctive: repetition, resistance to change, compulsion.

Central to an understanding of the addictive process is the profound, often discouraging sense of powerlessness over the addiction itself. This particular feature is true of every addiction, whatever the object. The tail increasingly wags the dog, engendering secondary shame about the addiction. Any individual feels humiliated when controlled by an addiction to anything, and additionally humiliated when attempts to renounce it and regain power over it fail. The addict then feels defeated by the addiction. Therefore, addicts grow to hate themselves, becoming increasingly disgusted at their helplessness and their lack of resolve and inner strength. The addictive process repetitively reenacts a scene that creates intense shame, disappointment in self. Addictions are rooted in internalized scenes of shame, or shame conjoined with other negative affects. The objects are repetitively longed for, causing repetitive disappointment in self.

Addiction can function partially as a substitute for shame-bound interpersonal needs when it develops in response to failed or disturbed relationships. For example, the alcoholic who has a relationship with his or her bottle originally may have learned to substitute something else for a human relationship. Dependence on a *sedative for intense negative affect* was that substitute. Critical failures in the human environment caused those vital needs to become bound by shame, resulting in overwhelming negative affect.

Children with addictive parents invitably internalize images of those parents. These scenes continue to shape the self, propelling it along one or another line of development. Governing scenes of intense negative affect lie at the heart of addictive disorders, but addiction itself does not necessarily require disturbed relationships in order to develop.

The addiction functions primarily as an escape from intense or overwhelming negative affect—shame alone, same conjoined with other negative affects, or any negative affect. Whenever feelings of shame are encountered, they can be reduced by becoming addicted to something. Addiction sedates intense negative affect, and originates from sedative scripts that develop into addictive scripts, according to Tomkins (1987b). The addiction also reproduces shame, thereby reactivating the entire cycle. This cyclical reactivation of shame, as well as of other negative affects, ensures that governing scenes are reactivated as well.

Sedative Scripts and Addictive Scripts

In general, scripts refer to the rules for predicting, interpreting, responding to, and controlling a magnified set of scenes. Tomkins defines a *sedative script* as one "that addresses any problematic scene primarily as though the first order of business was to attenuate or to reduce entirely the negative affect which that scene has evoked" (1987b, p. 185). Sedation refers not to overcorning the source of the negative affect, but rather to the intention to reduce the negative affect itself, whether or not that intention proves successful. Reaching for a cigarette is one type of sedative act. Other types of self-sedation include alcohol, drugs, eating, sex, travel, driving, walking, running, television, conversation, reading, and music.

Sedative scripts, which in Tomkins's view are used *only* to sedate experienced negative affect, vary in frequency and duration of activation according to the experienced frequency and duration of negative affect. The frequency of sedative acts is a function of both *source affect,* the affect generated by the scene itself (not by the outcomes of responses to the scene), and the relative *effectiveness* of the scripted sedative act. When attempted sedation proves effective, the sedative act is terminated and its general frequency is reduced. However, when the sedative act proves ineffective, it will instead be repeated and its general frequency will increase. Paradoxically, the use of sedative acts increases "as a conjoint function of the density of source affect and of the *ineffectiveness* of the sedative affect" (1987b, p. 188). Psychological sedation mimics biochemically based drug habituation; in each case, the individual requires more and more of the drug or sedative act as they become less effective as sedatives.

The following factors favor the development of sedative scripts, according to Tomkins. Negative affect itself must be the primary target for attenuation. This means that the density of the ratio of positive to negative affect must be neither so positive as to reduce the need for sedation nor so negative as to prompt an addictive script. The individual must additionally believe in the *possibility* of reducing negative affect and in the *desirability* of doing so without being constrained by ideological norms against sedation. Finally, the self must favor itself as the agent of sedation in contrast to seeking assistance from others to reduce negative affect.

Critical to the shift from sedation to addiction, according to Tomkins, is the degree of magnification of the absence of the sedative. However temporary, the absence of any particular sedative (pacifier, cigarette, alcohol) itself produces intense negative affect—panic. The resulting urgency experienced about obtaining the sedative further increases magnification of the awareness of its absence. There is an important second factor equally critical to the shift from sedation to addiction: the degree of magnification of the necessity and desirability of the sedative for relief of its own absence. The absence of the sedative results in intolerable negative affect and *only* the absent sedative (pacifier, cigarette, alcohol) can, and will, provide relief. The absence of the sedative is greatly magnified in awareness and the necessity and desirability of the sedative for relief of its absence is equally magnified. The urgency felt now is unconditional. The necessary and sufficient condition for addiction, then, is the combination of (a) high density of negative affect only *partially* reduced by the sedative act and (b) critical experiences of panic-inducing deprivation of the sedative act. "One has then begun the critical transformation of dreading the absence of the sedative more than the original . . . negative affect source" (1987b, p. 195).

The *preaddictive* script represents a critical step in the transformation of sedative to addictive dependency. In this script, sedation itself is further magnified by a substantial increase in urgency. Furthermore, sedation is required as a *necessary* condition to remain in the scene or to act in it. In a preaddictive alcohol script, the individual believes he or she cannot meet others without the soothing drink *before* entering the threatening scene. "This increased urgency, and its moving forward in time, is the hallmark of part of the difference between sedation and what will later be transformed into the *unconditional urgency* of the addictive script" (1987b, p. 189).

The *intention to renounce* the sedative act has the consequence of increasing negative affect in a very specific way. The *ineffective* attempt to renounce is one way in which sedative scripts become transformed into *addictive scripts*. "An addictive script is one in which a sedative has been transformed into an end in itself such that the individual is perpetually vigilant toward the absence or presence of the distinctive feature whose absence is punishing and whose presence briefly provides relief, but whose continuing presence becomes sufficiently skilled that it provides minimal awareness and affect" (1987b, p. 191).

As a precondition, addictive scripts require a sedative script that has validated, according to Tomkins, an act as a reliable means of reducing negative affect. Addictive scripts require, furthermore, a considerable magnification of the instrumental efficacy of the power of the sedative. "The sedative act must become a one-many relationship, such that the *same* means is a means to an increasing *variety* of sedations as ends" (1987b, p. 193). To become addicted, then, the sedative act— alcohol, drugs, food, or sex—must have been comforting in many different negative scenes. "Whether these scenes make one afraid, angry, distressed, ashamed, or disgusted, the [sedative] must have proven to be equally capable of neutralizing such differently troubling scenes. . . . Not only is a one-many magnification of sedation required, but the one sedation must *also* thereby have been magnified as the *unique* means to those many ends" (1987b, p. 193).

A third condition necessary for the formation of an addictive script is a transformation of the unique one-many means into an equally unique end in itself. This entails a critical "shift from original negative affect as source to *sedative deprivation affect* as *new source affect*. One cannot become addicted until one has learned that to be without the sedative is much worse than any other negative affect that the sedative might reduce" (1987b, p. 193).

Affect Inhibition and Affect Hunger

Two specific forms of addiction, alcohol addiction and sexual addiction, illustrate several distinct affect dynamics. In Tomkins's view, when the expression of affect is chronically inhibited, a condition of *affect hunger* is created.

> The inhibition of the overt expression of any affect can be punitive. To feel excited but not to be able to show it, to feel like smiling but to be unable to smile, to feel like crying but to be unable to cry, to feel enraged but to swallow it, to feel terrified but to have to hide it, to feel ashamed but have to pretend that all is well, to feel disgust but have to smile— any and all of these are punitive experiences which produce affect hunger, the wish to express openly the incompletely suppressed affects. Alcohol has for centuries provided therapy for affect hunger of all kinds, releasing the smile of intimacy and tenderness, the look of excitement, sexual and otherwise, the unashamed crying of distress, the explosion of hostility, the intrusion of long-suppressed terror, the open confession of shame, and the avowal of self-contempt. (Tomkins, 1963a, p. 268)

Alcohol is initially resorted to in order to release suppressed affects, particularly shame. At "the time of intoxication the promise of relief from the communication of shame overwhelms the impulse to hide it" (Tomkins, 1963a, p. 269). However, the morning after, the alcoholic becomes seized with shame at his or her alcoholic shamelessness. Thus, alcoholic intoxication functions as a *de-inhibitor* of suppressed affect. It minimizes the inhibition of shame and self-contempt as well as other affects, permitting the emergence of suppressed affect.

Affect Promiscuity

When we examine the phenomenon of sexual addiction in the light of affect dynamics, two prominent factors emerge. First, sexuality also can function as a *de-inhibitor* of suppressed affect. "For many, the intensity and intimacy of sexuality provides an isolated island for the free avowal of affects otherwise over-controlled" (Tomkins, 1963a, p. 270). A second affect dynamic in sexual addiction is *affect promiscuity*, which means that objects for affect investment are sought indiscriminately.

Affect promiscuity is a result of two principal strategies: minimizing the inhibition of affect expression and maximizing positive affect. The individual who has become addicted to an intense level of excitement requires varied and changing objects that will "pay off" in perpetual thrills. Whenever there is satiation or a lull, such people are compelled to find new challenges that will rekindle excitement: continually solving crossword puzzles, reading detective stories, skiing, mountain climbing, gambling, or seeking new sexual partners.

In every case what governs the pursuit of objects is the affect payoff involved; the objects do not govern the affects. In excitement promiscuity, excitement governs the search for new objects that will provide the requisite intensity of that affect. Thrills must be sought continually, and when the object no longer provides them, the incessant quest after excitement is renewed. When excitement promiscuity enters the sexual sphere of life, the individual is forced into sexual promiscuity in the search for excitement. The endless striving for affect payoff overshadows even strong ties of enjoyment in more enduring love relationships. The quest after excitement dominates the personality.

> By affect promiscuity we mean such an intensification of any affect that objects for affect investment are sought indiscriminately. If I must cry, then I will seek out tragic objects. If I must experience terror, I will court danger. If I must express anger, I will pick fights. If I must feel ashamed, I will expose myself to certain defeat. If I must feel self-contempt, I will seek humiliators, provoke contempt or do what is disgusting. Sexual promiscuity is but one vehicle of affect promiscuity. Nor is affect promiscuity restricted to negative affects and their open display. I may be as indiscriminate in the avowal of tenderness and excitement, e.g., in sexuality, as I am in the avowal of self-contempt, if joy and excitement are affects which I must suppress in my everyday world. . . . (Tomkins, 1963a, p. 270)

Affect dynamics account for the development of both sexual addiction and alcohol addiction. These syndromes become organized around particular affects and their inhibition or suppression. We have examined alcoholic intoxication and sexuality as two de-inhibitors of suppressed affect. They are vehicles for minimizing the inhibition of shame and other affects, positive as well as negative. We also have considered sexual promiscuity as a consequence of affect promiscuity. In the next section we examine an affect dynamic that is a factor in both forms of addiction.

Displacement of Affect

Tomkins theorizes "that whenever any affect, positive or negative, must be suppressed, for whatever reason, and whenever such overt suppression produces an intolerable intensification of this affect . . . appropriate objects will be sought upon which the suppressed affect can be displaced and overtly expressed" (1963a, p. 272). Let us examine this dynamic in relation to alcohol and sexuality by considering the displacement of the oppressor and the vicarious overt show of humiliation this displacement permits.

> The resort to alcohol, which permits either the open avowal of self-contempt and/or the picking of a fight with a strange adversary who will defeat and humiliate one, vicariously, is one way in which such displacement operates. The channeling of a humiliating defeat into sexual experience which degrades and humiliates is another instance of displaced, vicarious humiliation. Alcohol and sex, though both permit the emergence of suppressed affect, are not, however, necessarily restricted to the function of enabling specific displacement in which a substitute object is sought as a vehicle for affect which had to be suppressed in a particular situation. (Tomkins, 1963a, p. 273)

Summary

Addictive disorders comprise a third class of syndromes in which shame, either singly or in combination with other negative affects, plays a central role. The addiction functions as an escape from or sedation of these intolerable negative affects. Feelings of shame, for example, can be reduced through becoming addicted to something. Addiction sedates intense negative affect, but the addiction also reproduces shame, thereby reactivating the cycle. The addictive process repetitively reenacts a scene that recreates and intensifies shame. The objects are longed for repetitively, causing repetitive disappointment in self; the self feels powerless, defeated by its own addiction. Furthermore, the addiction functions by substituting sedation of intense negative affect for shame-bound interpersonal needs. Critical failures in the human environment have resulted in deep shame surrounding these vital human needs. The progression from sedative scripts to preaddictive scripts and then to addictive scripts is central to an understanding of the nature of addiction. Finally, affect hunger, affect promiscuity, and affect displacement are three additional affect dynamics that shape the addictive process.

Eating Disorders

In *eating disorders,* as with all of the compulsive syndromes, there exists a sense of powerlessness over the process as well as intense secondary shame about it. Eating disorders such as bulimia, anorexia, and bulimarexia are largely disorders of shame. Individuals suffering from these disorders typically experience themselves as inherently deficient, worthless, or disgusting—as failures.

Let us consider bulimia in order to illustrate its governing affect dynamics. This syndrome comprises two phases that recycle: bingeing and purging. Shame is present during each, though differently experienced and coassembled; the scenes motivating behavior during bingeing and purging are different. Bingeing on food is a substitute for shame-bound interpersonal needs. When one feels empty inside; hungry to feel a part of someone; desperate to be held close; craving to be wanted and admired, respected and loved—but these have become taboo through shame—one turns instead to food. But food can never satisfy the inner need. Longing becomes shame, or shame along with fear and distress, and so one eats more to anesthetize the longing.

The shame about eating—eating that remains hidden, secret—represents a *displacement of affect* (shame) away from the original source (self). The shame about bingeing on food is a displacement of the deeper, internalized shame about self.

During the bingeing cycle, shame gradually intensifies. The purge cycle adds something crucial to the process: the affect of *disgust.* Tomkins views dissmell and disgust as innate defensive responses, auxiliary to the oxygen, thirst, and hunger drives. "The early warning response via the nose is dissmell; the next level of response, from mouth or stomach, is disgust" (1987, p. 142). Disgust, dissmell, and nausea function as signals and motives to the self, as well as to others, of feelings of rejection. Dissmell and disgust are evolving from the status of drive-reducing acts to that of motivating affects.

The vomiting to which bulimics frequently resort in order to purge themselves of the shameful food they so shamelessly devoured is, from an affect theory perspective, the disgust reaction experienced on the drive level. Everyone has on occasion reacted with an urge to vomit in response to an emotional situation. The purge cycle, vomiting, represents the affect of disgust experienced directly on the level of the hunger drive and experienced overtly in action.

Why vomiting? Why such an intense form of purging? There is a kind of emotional cleansing that occurs if one literally bathes in shame. Magnifying the intensity of shame, according to Tomkins, rapidly brings it to peak intensity, causing an explosive eruption of affect and thereby automatically reducing shame. This is Tomkins's concept of *affect magnification* applied to bulimia. Bingeing gradually accelerates shame, but purging quickly magnifies it, bringing it to peak intensity through self-disgust. When shame peaks, there is a "bursting effect," leaving the individual feeling purged, cleansed, even purified. Self-purging through vomiting continues until defeat and humiliation are complete. The bulimic emerges, not only purged of food, but temporarily of shame as well. Shame can be reduced only by first magnifying it until it reaches peak intensity. By magnifying shame in intensity and duration, its fire is burned out, which creates the sense of cleansing. The bulimic behaves so as to guarantee complete humiliation, acting to magnify and accelerate humiliation because this affect has become intolerable.

This is a masochistic strategy of reduction through magnification. Tomkins defines this strategy as "a species of masochistic behavior the aim of which is to increase negative affect to such a point that it produces an explosive overt eruption of affect which ultimately thereby reduces itself" (1963a, p. 283).

Tomkins's concept of affect magnification is central to an understanding of bulimia, a disorder rooted in shame and in the masochistic strategy of reduction through magnification. By affect magnification, Tomkins refers to any systematic increase in intensity and/or duration of affect, with or without suppression of the overt expression of affect. Affect magnification can feed equally well on expression and suppression, and affects also can be minimized and reduced either through overt expression or through suppression. There is not necessarily a relationship between expression and intensity or duration of affects, or between suppression and intensity or duration of affects.

> Magnification is one of the prime reasons for the vicarious expression of humiliation. After insult and incomplete suppression of humiliation, the inability to suppress self-contempt or shame can be reinforced by a circular intensification of humiliation and the nature of the insult as this is re-experienced again and again upon review. The smouldering ashes of humiliation recruit images and re-interpretations of the antagonist so that he grows more and more offensive. As this happens, the embers of shame and self-contempt are fanned into hot flames which in turn recruit cognitive reappraisals that provide fresh fuel for the magnification of the negative affect. Just as individuals fall in love at a distance, so may they fall in hate with one who has humiliated them. The mutual, circular magnification of humiliation and insult following humble withdrawal from insult is a prime condition for producing a level of humiliation such that the individual is forced into the vicarious avowal of his feelings. It, of course, also happens that the individual fortified by righteous indignation and incensed by the monster of his own imagination now returns to vanquish his original antagonist. (Tomkins, 1963a, pp. 282-283)

The internal imagery of the bulimic reflects the internalized relationships with internal parental identification images. These internal relationships mirror the original parental ones in which shame and self-contempt first generated. Relationships with identification images recreate the shame process. They reproduce shame. These inner relationships mirror the sources of shame and the interpersonal needs that became bound by shame.

Anorexia displays a different pattern of scripts for responding to shame. Instead of craving food, the anorexic actually rejects food via dissmell, distancing the self from vital nourishment. It is the affect of *dissmell* that is recruited and directed against food and eating. By distancing the self from food, the anorexic seeks to control food, eating behavior, and, by implication, weight gain. But the apparent control exerted over food is, on closer inspection, an attempt to control the perceived sources of shame. The deeper internalized shame about self is displaced directly onto food. Not only does the anorexic struggle to control food, but, more important, to *distance* the self via dissmell from the perceived source of shame, which has become equated with food. Instead of being nourishing, food seems to have become noxious in the extreme. Additional strategies that develop in the anorexic in response to internalized shame are perfectionism and control. Although perfection scripts (perfecting the self) and power scripts (controlling food intake) are the overtly displayed defending strategies, it is the recruitment of dissmell affect specifically in response to food that determines the distinctive patterning of anorexia.

There are certain precursors that favor the development of an eating disorder. Typically, there is an early fusion of shame and/or disgust with hunger drive satiation. A variety of patterns have been observed in which this fusion has occurred. In some families, meal-times are battlegrounds. Forcing children to sit at the table until everything is eaten most likely will generate a power struggle and result in intensified shame-humiliation. Some children are actually force-fed, even to the point of vomiting. A third pattern involves overattention, coupled with criticism (contempt affect), which is directed toward table behavior, eating behavior, bodily appearance, and/or weight. Rather than becoming fused with positive affect, the hunger drive is instead fused with shame and disgust. Such patterns favor the later development of an eating disorder. Culture also plays a role in influencing the course of syndrome development. Cultural attitudes toward the body, weight, and appearance are significant factors to be considered. Yet culture works on the self through affect, particularly shame.

Syndrome Analysis

Examining the particular affect dynamics of each syndrome will illuminate the centrality of shame, as it will the role of the other negative affects that have become conjoined with shame. We must attend first to affect and its vicissitudes, and doing so is a very different way of organizing clinical data.

Table 5.1 summarizes the preceding syndromes by ordering them along certain common dimensions.

SCHIZOID, PARANOID, AND DEPRESSIVE SYNDROMES

When we consider *schizoid, paranoid,* and *depressive* syndromes, we must begin our analysis with an examination of the affect dynamics of each syndrome. Shame has become differentially coassembled with other negative affects in creating a distinct posture toward the world. The organizing affects, defending scripts, and innate temperament, along with identity scripts and governing scenes, are the principal factors influencing syndrome development.

Individuals who are innately predisposed toward introversion defend against shame by internal withdrawal. Relationships are either avoided or abandoned, and the individuals may display an oscillating in-and-out pattern with respect to relationships. Ambivalence characterizes their interpersonal relations, resulting in a *schizoid posture.* Introverts behave in this way in response to excessive shame because their innate temperament already is focused predominantly inward. Shame, though deeply disruptive, manifests in withdrawal deeper inside the self. A social mask convincingly disguises the inner turmoil.

Shame has become excessive either because of repeated failure of the supporting interpersonal environment or as a result of experiencing a degree of shame well beyond the individual's capacity to tolerate or neutralize. When an introvert is forced to contend with excessive shame, the typical response is to hide deeper inside. While some innate introverts develop "learned extroversion" in response to shame, usually the self becomes more hidden, shut in, further isolated, increasingly detached from others.

Because interest is focused primarily outside the self, the extrovert cannot so easily abandon human interaction. The extroverted temperament is also predisposed toward overtly displaying affect. Natural oscillations of mood occur, creating a tendency toward cycloid mood swings; just as the introvert moves in and out, phenomenologically, the extrovert cycles up and down. These are tendencies, predispositions that always remain open to modification and recombination. In response to excessive shame, the innate extrovert is likely to develop a *depressive posture.* Tomkins views depression as a syndrome of shame and distress.

We conceive depression to be a syndrome of shame and distress, which also reduces the general amplification of all impulses. This reduction of amplification is both neurological and humoral. In relative hypoglycemia we noted the failure of normal adrenal support when the zest for life is impaired. In depression there is a more general reduction in amplification probably mediated through the reticular formation and other amplifier structures. The observed hypotonia, therefore, is a consequence of that reduction in amplification which is characteristic of intense and enduring shame which has been accompanied by equally intense and enduring distress, which together constitute depression. (1963a, pp. 126-127)

Table 5.1 Determinants of Compulsive Syndromes

	Physical Abuse	Sexual Abuse	Addictive Disorders	Eating Disorders
Organizing Affects	Shame Anger	Shame Fear Distress	Shame Other negative affects	Shame Dissmell Disgust Fear
Governing Scenes	Powerless Violation Need-shame scenes	Powerless Violation Need-shame scenes	Powerless Need-shame scenes	Powerless Need-shame scenes
Defending Scripts	Power Blame transfer	Power (abuser) Withdrawal (victim)	Denial Sedative Addictive	Perfection Power (food)
Identity Scripts	Self-blame	Self-blame Self-contempt Disowning Splitting	Self-blame Self-contempt	Self-contempt
Innate Temperament	Introvert or extrovert	Introvert or extrovert	Introvert or extrovert	Introvert or extrovert

The internalized process for reproducing shame, which is the individual's set of internal activities that eventuates in depression, varies across different types of depression. The addition of self-blame or self-contempt identity scripts gives depression a further distinctive mark. The commonly accepted view of depression as anger directed inward misses the central and prior role of conjoined shame and distress. The anger accompanying shame can indeed be directed against others, against the self, or alternatively against both. However, although directing anger inward is a secondary means of reproducing shame, it is not itself the source of depression. Furthermore, the anger observed in depression is *disgusted* anger, according to Tomkins (personal communication, 1987).

The depressive episode is a condition in which shame and distress have become sufficiently prolonged as to be experienced as a continuing mood. The self's internal activities that perpetuate depression constitute the individual's internalized process for reproducing shame. That process will continue because it has become an integral part of that individual's identity.

In the following passage, Tomkins compares depressives and paranoids from the perspective of affect theory:

> Both depressives and paranoids have been shamed by their parents, but depressives have been loved as well as shamed, whereas paranoids have not been loved but have been terrorized as well as humiliated. For the depressive there is always a way back from the despair of shame to communion with the loving parent who ultimately feels as distressed as does the child at the breach in their relationship. For the paranoid there is no way back. Like the member of a truly persecuted minority group, his shame is imposed with a reign of terror. If he resists his inferior status, he does so at a threat to his life. Shame is reinforced by terror. (Tomkins, 1962, pp. 436-437)

Either temperament type, introvert or extrovert, can furthermore develop a *paranoid posture* in response to excessive shame. All three of these postures fall along a magnification continuum. The earliest form of the paranoid posture is a *paranoid script* through which all experience is reinterpreted.

Tomkins originally conceived of this development in terms of a monopolistic affect theory, an ideo-affective posture toward the world (1963a, pp. 454-455). In his most recent formulation of script theory (1979, 1987b), the concept of the script encompasses the earlier formulation. In any event, the paranoid script becomes monopolistic in the sense that perception, cognition, and action come under increasing domination by the script. The interpretation of events is seized by it and increasingly dominated. Even evidence that contradicts the script is twisted into supporting evidence. The interpretation of even apparent trivialities is radically magnified, producing an intolerable burden of humiliation. Extreme action strategies include complete withdrawal, mutism, and complete immobility, as in catatonic stupor. These represent terminal phases in the sense that the individual has been totally defeated. Prior to this phase, however, there is unrelenting warfare; the individual under the grip of a monopolistic humiliation theory or script first generates and tests every conceivable strategy to avoid and escape total defeat at the hands of the humiliating other. This is the paranoid posture.

Increasingly, shame captures the personality in such a fashion that unrelenting opposition results. In the paranoid posture, a theory forms; it is a theory both about self and about the world. The self is never completely relieved of its burden of humiliation. According to Tomkins, "the over-interpretation of the malevolent contempt of the other results in frequent misfiring of over-avoidance and over-escape strategies which expose the self to humiliation from the over-inflated insult, which add fuel to further over-interpretation and more desperate strategies of defense" (1963a, p. 455). The paranoid's humiliation theory is a generic one; it refers to shame, disgust, contempt, self-contempt, and self-disgust, as well as to amalgams of these affects with other negative affects, most notably fear. It is truly a monopolistic affect theory.

By a monopolistic affect theory, Tomkins is referring to the complete domination of the self by the affect of shame conjoined with fear. Shame holds a monopoly over the personality in the sense of monopolizing the interpretation of life events, current as well as past and future. In terms of Tomkins's later script theory, a paranoid script has evolved through which all experience is reinterpreted and over-interpreted. In that sense, interpretation itself has become monopolistic because shame has become monopolistic relative to other affects and in its effects over the self.

The paranoid posture becomes organized around affect—shame (humiliation) and fear (terror) conjointly—with each affect experienced at increasingly extreme levels of intensity. The individual then becomes vigilant, forever on guard, always scanning the environment for signs of expected humiliation, betrayal, or blaming. For the developing paranoid, experience becomes excessively personalized with innocent events misinterpreted as personally malevolent. And blame is always transferred away from the self.

To continue our analysis, consider Harry S. Sullivan's views, on the dynamics of paranoia. Although Sullivan lacked both an accurate affect theory and a precise language for shame, his conception nevertheless closely parallels Tomkins's formulation.

> The paranoid dynamism is rooted in (1) an awareness of inferiority of some kind, which then necessitates (2) a transfer of blame onto others. But before I discuss these two processes, I want to make it clear that these alone constitute merely a paranoid slant on life; for a full-blown paranoid state, something else is necessary—the misinterpretation of events to constitute an explanation, usually rather transcendental in nature, of what is troublesome.
> The awareness of inferiority means that one is unable to keep out of consciousness the formulation of some chronic feeling of the worst sort of insecurity, and this means that one suffers anxiety and perhaps even something worse, if jealousy is really worse than anxiety. The fear that others can disrespect a person because of something he shows means that he is always insecure in his contact with other people; and this insecurity arises, not from mysterious and somewhat disguised sources, as a great deal of our anxiety does, but from something which he knows he cannot fix. Now that represents an almost fatal deficiency of the self-system, since the self is unable to disguise or exclude a definite formulation that reads, "I am inferior. Therefore people will dislike me and I cannot be secure with them."
> . . . And the great thing is that finally a happy hypothesis has been received into awareness: It is not that *I* have something wrong with me, but that *he* does something to me. One is the victim, not of one's own defects, but of a devilish environment. One is not to blame; the environment is to blame. Thus we can say that the essence of the paranoid dynamism is the transference of blame. (Sullivan, 1956, pp. 145-146)

It is utilization of the transfer of blame as a generalized strategy for adaptation to the human world that is the heart of the paranoid posture. Transfer of blame is the predominant defending script utilized by the developing paranoid. When it becomes radically magnified, the paranoid posture emerges. Wrongdoings, mistakes, and failures must be disowned but then transferred away from the self to others. When the source of

one's own shame can be located elsewhere, and shame itself transferred
to another, the self becomes temporarily cleansed. Transfers of blame create a break, not only with reality but with sincerity as well. Furthermore,
the paranoid invents a malevolent belief system through the misinterpre-
tation of events, as Sullivan describes it, or through monopolistic interpretation, as Tomkins describes it. This emerging belief system provides
confirmatory "proof" for the paranoid's original posture, thereby creating
a fully self-sustaining system. The paranoid's belief system may further
culminate in a self-righteous "holy war" if the decision is made to perse-
cute the perceived persecutors.

From an affect theory perspective, *paranoid schizophrenia* emerges as
a special case of the paranoid posture:

> Paranoid schizophrenia is that special case of the paranoid posture in
> which the individual is both terrorized and humiliated at the same time,
> and in which the only level on which the individual can respond is in his
> beliefs and fantasies, delusions of persecution and grandeur. There are
> those who have also been terrorized and humiliated who do not develop
> paranoid schizophrenia, because anger is strong enough and fear is suf-
> ficiently weaker, so that although direct counteraction is blocked fan-
> tasies of revenge are more open and delusions of persecution and
> grandeur do not develop. (Tomkins, 1963a, p. 480)

Syndrome Analysis

While the paranoid relies on the transfer of blame as a predominant
defending script, the schizoid is usually an innately introverted individual
who utilizes internal withdrawal as his or her principal defending script.
Mixtures of these postures are inevitable, and individuals also vary considerably in the degree to which either posture develops and how
entrenched it eventually becomes. Temperamentally cycloid, extroverted
individuals encountering excessive shame conjoined with distress develop a depressive posture. When that individual's governing scenes include
the transfer of blame experienced at the hands of a parent, then a paranoid
script develops along with the depressive posture.

Table 5.2 illustrates the interrelationships among the various factors
influencing syndrome development.

PHOBIC SYNDROMES

When fear affect becomes radically magnified, a variety of "anxiety neuroses" may arise. Phobias constitute syndromes in which fear has become so magnified that it has seemingly engulfed the self. Fear of open public places, fear of crowds, fear of small enclosed rooms, fear of elevators, fear of heights, fear of driving on bridges, and fear of particular animals, such as spiders or snakes, are examples of typical phobic reactions. Although fear is the predominant organizing affect in many instances, creating a true anxiety syndrome, the manifest fear may be masking something deeper.

The phobia can function as a defense. Against what? In many apparent phobias, it is an encounter with shame that is being warded off. The phobia is a fear of a particular scene, whether an open space or a closed-in room. That dreaded scene is defended against by avoidance. Avoidance thus characterizes the phobic reaction, creating its distinctive patterning over time. The phobia is an avoidance or escape from a scene in which fear is magnified radically, either singly or conjointly with shame. What we are actually observing in phobias is the operation of *phobic scripts,* which are sets of rules for predicting and controlling any magnified set of scenes. These scenes involve either fear affect or fear conjoined with shame. Phobic scripts control shame by avoidance; paranoid scripts control shame by the transfer of blame and subsequent monopolistic interpretation. The phobia itself also generates secondary shame—shame about being phobic. Phobic scripts and scenes must be further examined in order to differentiate their organizing affects.

Many individuals who "appear" phobic are avoiding, dreading, and fearing a renewed encounter with the alienating affect. Some who consciously fear open places or crowds, when pressed to imagine themselves actually present in the dreaded scene, report feeling the terror of being *exposed.* The manifest fear, though itself noxious, is actually secondary to the much more disturbing sense of exposure inherent in shame. A woman once described her shame as seeming as though she were a hare in a field with barking dogs closing in, leaving her feeling frozen upright, paralyzed.

Table 5.2 Determinants of Schizoid, Depressive, and Paranoid Syndromes

	Schizoid	Depressive	Paranoid
Organizing Affects	Shame	Shame Distress	Shame Fear
Governing Scenes	Need-shame Scenes (variable)	Need-shame Scenes (variable)	Need-shame Scenes (variable)
Defending Scripts	Internal withdrawal	Variable	Blame transfer
Identity Scripts	Disowning Splitting	Self-blame Self-contempt	Disowning Splitting
Innate Temperament	Introvert	Extrovert	Introvert or extrovert

Others who feel phobic about closed-in places, including small rooms and other confined areas, dread feeling trapped, suffocated, paralyzed, unable to escape. The sense of suffocation is created by the binding effects of shame, causing the peculiar sensation of the room closing in. Whenever I have pressed individuals who were seemingly claustrophobic to vividly imagine and reexperience their dreaded scene, they became aware first of fear and then of shame. Fear had masked the deeper affect of shame. Imagining the scene and thereby vividly reentering it evoked the feeling of exposure— feeling naked, revealed, seen. Shame manifests as exposure, compelling immediate exit from the scene, even an imagined one. It is the affect of shame that acutely disturbs the self, binding and paralyzing the self.

Following repeated or intolerable shame encountered in any setting, fear and then avoidance are likely secondary reactions. When fear of an external scene is radically magnified together with avoidance of that specific scene, a phobia develops. When the feared event in that scene is shame, shame is embedded directly in the developing phobia. Even when shame is not thus embedded, there typically is secondary shame about being phobic.

SEXUAL DYSFUNCTION SYNDROMES

Affect theory also illuminates the origin of disturbances in the sexual sphere. Sexuality requires fusion with the positive affects, excitement and enjoyment, for potency. The sexual drive must be assisted by affect as an amplifier if it is to function at all. The natural, smooth flow of sexuality is in reality a direct consequence of affect dynamics, not drive dynamics alone.

When the sexual drive becomes fused with shame, dissmell, disgust, or fear, either singly or in combination, then the natural flow of sexuality is disrupted. The affects most critical to the development of sexual dysfunction are shame, dissmell, and disgust; fear, though manifest and seemingly of paramount importance, actually plays a secondary role.

So-called "performance anxiety" is more accurately described as fear of exposure, actually fear of a new shame experience in the sexual sphere of life. The anticipation of sexual failure, however defined by the self, is an anticipation of shame, the dread of renewed humiliation. When sexual failure occurs, and recurs, whether through premature ejaculation, impotence, or lack of orgasm, a radical magnification of shame results, further binding the self.

That frequently reported sense of feeling on-stage or watched, which is so disruptive to the flow of sexual enjoyment and excitement, is a direct consequence of shame. When the self feels exposed, the self watches the self. Self-consciousness invariably binds the self.

Consider a 35-year-old man who sought therapy because he had never been able to experience orgasm through either masturbation or intercourse. After several sessions, we began to explore his inner experience during intercourse. At the time, he was in a relationship with a woman who was happy to assist him. I invited my client first to imagine himself in a sexual encounter and then to describe his own experience as he observed it. Later, I suggested that he similarly observe his inner state during intercourse throughout the following week. In keeping with my suggestions, he began to observe more accurately his own inner reactions and gradually was able to recognize and subsequently identify a peculiar sensation: feeling *watched*. It was as if he were on stage. His description of feeling watched now oriented us toward exploring shame. We began to discuss shame, how it operates and how it binds the self, creating paralysis. We also examined self-consciousness, which is a direct by-product of shame, and this clearly matched his inner experience during sex. We had uncovered the affective source of his dysfunction.

Then I taught him how to release shame by *refocusing attention* back outside. The essence of this technique is to consciously stop focusing attention inwardly upon oneself and to effortfully refocus attention back outside. Since the attention turns inward when shame generates, the key to releasing shame is to literally force the attention outward. Becoming immersed in external sensory experience, particularly when it is visual and physical experience combined, accomplishes that critical refocusing of attention.

My client returned the next week and excitedly announced that he had done it. "Done what?" I asked. He reported that he had had intercourse that week and actually had experienced orgasm for the first time in his life. Naturally, I shared his joy. Clearly, it was shame that had been paralyzing him all those years.

Early fusion of sexuality with shame, with dissmell, and/or with disgust is a developmental precursor of adult sexual dysfunction. The patterning of affect with drive is a process spanning years. Sex-shame binds create the nuclei of eventual dysfunction in the sexual life.

SPLITTING SYNDROMES: BORDERLINE, NARCISSISTIC, AND MULTIPLE PERSONALITY DISORDERS

Individuals who manifest extreme splitting can be classified in terms of the perceived target of splitting and its degree of magnification. Negative identity scripts and their accompanying inner voices represent one pole of that continuum. Disowning falls in the middle of the range, and splitting lies at the opposite pole. The varying degrees and targets of splitting widely observed in borderline, narcissistic, and multiple personality disorders are the direct consequence of affect dynamics.

Borderline and Narcissistic Disorders

The degree to which *disgust, dissmell,* and *contempt* become directed inward or outward is a central factor in so-called borderline and narcissistic development. The magnification of disgust, dissmell, and contempt (hence, their internalization as well) is the principal means by which splitting occurs. When disgust, dissmell, and contempt remain directed outward, employed largely as defending scripts (strategies of external protection and reaction), an exaggeration of the self's importance can occur. The self becomes inflated over others, potentially leading to the development of a grandiose self that appears egotistical, even shameless.

But when disgust, dissmell, and contempt are turned against the self of the defending individual, one part of the self performs "psychic surgery on another part of itself, so that the self which feels ashamed is totally and permanently split off and rejected by a judging self" (Tomkins, 1987a, p. 152). In this case, the so-called dissociative type of narcissistic disturbance results.

A second important factor in borderline development is *rage,* an inflation or magnification of anger affect. Borderline development typically is associated with damaged self-esteem or damaged narcissism. This is shame. The overtly displayed rage is the shame-based individual's secondary reaction to shame that has become magnified to the point of intolerability. Other defending scripts have not developed to either guard the self or mask shame from view. We therefore are likely to observe directly these intense, often eruptive shame-rage reactions in individuals who have become pervasively crippled by shame.

Another central dynamic of the borderline is the susceptibility to, or proclivity for, *fusion* or *merging.* These are manifestations of the interpersonal need for identification. The need for fusion or merging, which occurs principally through the eyes, has not become pathological, simply exaggerated, itself radically magnified. The shame-based individual ambivalently longs for a return to mutual communion, for oneness.

So-called "ego boundaries" are a direct function of affect dynamics. Defending scripts that develop against shame can so insulate the self that impermeable boundaries arise. These defending strategies may operate against the primary interpersonal needs as well, particularly the identification need. The seemingly autonomous, separate individual, with strong and impermeable boundaries, has erected barriers to ward off shame and/or experiences of merging, identification. Although this is a much more tolerable and culturally adaptive stance, it is *not* necessarily psychologically "healthier." It only appears to be because we traditionally have approved of and valued, both in Western culture and in our science, separateness over identification, anger over distress, and disgust over shame. The affects of disgust and anger together empower separateness, fueling eventual differentiation, and their conjoined magnification produces the impermeable boundaries that are viewed as signs of "ego strength."

Individuals who remain open to fusion or merging with others, which is amplified by enjoyment affect, are also more vulnerable to shame via identification. Their boundaries appear more permeable because the distinction between self and other is lost at the moment of merging. What is described on the one hand by the concept of ego boundaries, whether permeable or impermeable, strong or weak, can be equally well described on the other by affect dynamics.

Identification must be examined from developmental and interpersonal perspectives, and ultimately from cultural perspectives as well. When experiences of identification with a parent are followed by the parent's attempts to hold onto or control the child, then the need for identification itself is experienced as engulfment or enmeshment. In this context, merging with the parent becomes dangerous—desperately desired and equally desperately feared, hence magnified. The need itself now is ambivalently experienced. When the parent interferes with the child's subsequent, natural attempts to separate, the child learns to equate separation with abandonment. This association is heightened when the parent's affective response toward the child is dissmell or disgust. Interference with either identification or individuation through shaming creates the *fusion-abandonment dynamic* typically observed among borderlines.

Consider more closely the phenomenon of *splitting,* which is commonly associated with borderline development. The splitting of "good" versus "bad," meaning bad self and good other, is itself a direct consequence of shame magnification. In the midst of shame, the self feels to blame, deficient, bad. It is the magnification and internalization of shame that creates the bad self. Furthermore, since parents typically are viewed as infallible by children, and all too often behave in ways that perpetuate such a belief, the parent invariably becomes equated with being good, and is so idealized. This aspect of "splitting," however, stands in marked contrast to the actual psychic surgery produced by contempt, disgust, or dissmell turned against the self. The splitting of bad self and good other results from internalized/magnified shame, but the splitting of the whole self into a shameful self and a judging/persecuting self results from the addition of dissmell, disgust, or contempt turned against the self.

Multiple Personality Disorders

The disowning process can be pursued relentlessly by the self to erase whatever has created the awareness of intolerable defect. Since parents are seen to be infallible, defect must then reside within the self. A harsh, punitive internalized identification image (internalized other) mediates the disowning process. Disowning is a direct consequence of the further magnification produced by negative identity scripts. When disowning is relentless or begins at too early an age, and positive counterbalancing experience with significant others is lacking, then disowning can eventuate in such a profound splitting of the self that independent, split-off selves emerge.

Consider Sally, who grew up in a climate of contempt. Whenever Sally expressed her feelings or needed anything emotionally, her mother invariably responded with contempt. Gradually, Sally learned to behave analogously toward herself. She internalized this relationship and began to feel similar loathing and disgust for the needy little girl locked away inside of her. As a woman, Sally felt a measure of inner calm only when that weak, disgusting part of her remained hidden. Whenever the needing and feeling part of her awakened, Sally instantly became vicious and brutal toward herself. She meted out swift punishment to herself in the form of self-contempt and occasional physical self-abuse. This was Sally's way of attempting to destroy the needy little girl hidden inside of her, the part of her so painfully disowned by her mother.

The splitting in Sally was pronounced. Within her existed a weak, insecure, shameful little girl self that had been disowned and split off. Coexisting along with it, however, was a persecutory partial self, functioning quite independently, that sought to destroy the little girl partial self. In Sally, no intact self developed. Instead, her inner life was comprised of two infantile partial selves, each a distinct personality. One was childlike and needy, shameful, while the other was harsh, punitive, and often persecutory.

As a second example of multiple personality syndromes, consider Rita. She lived with a blaming, fault-finding, intrusive, domineering father. Her mother, by contrast, was no more than an extension of her husband—not a real person in her own right, separate from her husband. Her mother could offer neither solace, comfort, nor protection to Rita, who felt abandoned by her mother. To compound matters, when Rita was a child, her father sexually molested her repeatedly. No integrated whole self ever developed. Instead, Rita's self fractured and then became increasingly fragmented over time. Her child self withdrew deeper inside to escape shame. It was deeply hidden within her, locked away and frozen. Another part of Rita became disgusted and angry. It turned against her in a vicious and brutal manner, thereby reenacting the analogous scene with her father. Still another part of Rita became identified with her mother and appeared whiny, confused, and listless. Each of these three partial selves, or infantile personalities, had a different name. Rita referred to each by name and was never without their presence.

Disowning and splitting can eventuate in distinct, split-off partial selves. These multiple personalities then function independently within the person, arresting development. This is an unfortunate turn of events because nothing is so precious to the self as its own integrity, its essential wholeness.

Splitting Revisited

The usefulness of any language is determined by its precision, its accuracy, and its ability to organize existing observables into meaningful relationship. Jacob Bronowski wrote:

> My view is that knowledge is a rearrangement of experience, in which we put together those experiences that seem to us to belong together, and put them apart from those that do not. And the control of nature depends on just this separation, between actions that have been shown to be relevant to a given end, and those that appear irrelevant. A scientific theory, and the whole scientific picture of the world, is an imaginative grouping of all these experiences. (1971, pp. 26-27)

The distinctions currently being drawn between borderline, narcissistic, multiple personality, and schizoid phenomena are actually less useful than would at first appear. The individuals described by Harry S. Sullivan (1953a, 1953b, 1956, 1972) as *schizophrenic* (but not psychotic) were not unlike those W. Ronald D. Fairbairn (1966) described as *schizoid.* Individuals who were described as schizoid or schizophrenic 40 years ago increasingly are being described as *borderline* or *narcissistic* by Kohut (1971, 1972, 1977), Kernberg (1975, 1976) and others today. Certainly, not all instances of borderline or narcissistic disorders are schizophrenic or even schizoid, but these are nevertheless overlapping syndromes. While all manifest splitting, there is greater ambiguity and confusion remaining than these descriptive categories actually account for.

Borderline is apparently the disorder of the day. Individuals labeled borderline today would in all likelihood have been labeled schizoid or even schizophrenic in years past. These same individuals would probably be described as evidencing multiple personality disorders by still other clinical observers. Diagnostic assessment is an illustration of Bronowski's thesis within the domain of our particular science. Clinical diagnosis is an imaginative grouping of clinical facts, itself a rearrangement.

The central question pertains to the utility of clinical language: how useful is any particular language, any given conceptual arrangement, for partitioning and organizing clinical phenomena? The language presented here is a new rearrangement of experience. Its usefulness will depend on its demonstrated precision and accuracy, on its implications for action in child rearing, interpersonal relations, and psychotherapy, and on its general expansion of knowledge.

SOCIOPATHIC AND PSYCHOPATHIC SYNDROMES

The syndromes we have examined in this chapter are all syndromes in which the affect of shame has become magnified, whether singly or conjointly with other negative affects. Many of these syndromes reflect the development of an overburdened, harsh, or exceedingly punitive conscience. This is a direct outgrowth of excessive shame experienced in childhood—excessive in duration, intensity, and/or frequency. The optimal development of conscience depends on adequate and appropriately graded doses of shame that do not overwhelm the child, but instead are effectively neutralized and counteracted. Conscience misfires because of either too little or too much shame.

The individual who engages in antisocial behavior, who behaves in ways that are sociopathic or psychopathic, behaves *as if* without shame. Obviously, these syndromes reflect a misfiring of conscience, but equating that with an absence of shame is a mistake.

Developmentally, these are individuals who experienced deep failures, and corresponding shame, in their early significant relationships. That impediment resulted in a failure to attach to, and so identify with, their parents. Therefore, their capacity for empathy, which grows directly out of identification, also failed to develop. Other people are viewed by them solely as objects to manipulate, because identification has been blocked or impaired.

The antisocial or psychopathic individual is not without shame, however. Shame is experienced, but only in the presence of others. The capacity to respond with shame has not been *internalized,* and internalization is what causes the child to be ashamed of norm violation whether or not the parent is aware of it. Instead, because the shame response remains *externalized,* the child is ashamed of norm violation only when the parent discovers what has been done. When the crime goes undetected, the self feels no shame.

The failure of conscience to become internalized is a result of the prior failure to attach to and identify with the parents. Identification is a necessary developmental precursor that causes one to *want* to care about the feelings of others; it also causes the shame response itself to become internalized.

PERSPECTIVES ON PSYCHOPATHOLOGY: SHAME-BASED SYNDROMES VERSUS SHAME-BASED FAMILY SYSTEMS

We have examined the development of psychopathology principally from the perspective of syndromes that become organized around particular affects. Syndromes develop within individuals in response to their governing scenes and scripts. Each emerging syndrome is a constellation of affect, scene, and script. Affect, imagery, and language are the principal determinants of development, optimal as well as pathological.

Governing scenes and scripts generate these various syndromes within individuals. However, individuals also live within a social group, the family. When viewed from the perspective of that social group, a distinct family system can be observed. That family system will be either functional or dysfunctional. The varying family rules and injunctions existing within a family system constitute its particular rules for predicting, interpreting, controlling, and responding to a magnified set of scenes. They comprise *family scripts.* These family scripts are analogous to the individual's scripts for managing distinct affect-laden scenes.

The two adults who join together to form a family are already governed by their individual scenes and scripts, however parallel or analogous. Their separate, individual scripts later recombine, generating a family script or even a set of family scripts. The family system that can be observed is a direct consequence of these evolving family scripts. We can observe distinctive family scripts in dysfunctional families; as those governing scripts become further magnified, the family will in turn become increasingly dysfunctional in response. We can therefore expect to observe abusive family scripts, addictive family scripts, bulimic family scripts, alcoholic family scripts, and so on.

Insofar as shame is a prominent feature in these families, their corresponding family scripts will be analogs of the various defending scripts and identity scripts considered earlier in connection with self-development. A woman who grows up in a shame-based family will internalize scenes of shame, from which her defending scripts and identity scripts later evolve. When she marries a man who has grown up in a different, though equally shame-based family, then their individual and separate scripts recombine. That recombination generates a new family script that then mediates the reenactment of governing scenes from one generation to the next.

Furthermore, each family member is scripted to play a distinct part or specific role. The family system is a family drama that has been fully scripted. The various family members constitute its cast of players. Increasingly, the family script determines the scenes within the family, and its hold over the players is enormous.

The emergent family script is a reenactment of the original, individual scripts and becomes the vehicle for generating new governing scenes. The drama is reenacted, passed from generation to generation. The dynamics of affect, scene, and script account for the development of family systems, whether shame-based or not. The family system is a product of family scripts just as culture is a product of cultural scripts.

FROM SHAME-BASED SYNDROMES TO AFFECT-BASED SYNDROMES

Solving the problem of shame does not entirely solve the problem of psychopathology because not all syndromes are shame-based. In particular cases, shame itself may play a minor role relative to other affects. Rather

than arguing for shame as the singular source of all psychological dysfunction, I am arguing, first, for a reformulation of psychopathology
based on affect theory and script theory and, second, for an expanded
awareness of shame as a central dynamic in the development of psychopathology as well as personality. Understanding shame in particular
and affect in general are equally vital to the process of psychotherapy.
Reformulating theory regarding the development of personality, the genesis of psychopathology, and the determinants of psychotherapeutic
change is essential in order to construct a general science of the self.

This book is a necessary first step in the direction of reformulating psychological theory. We have examined various syndromes that become
organized specifically around shame, or shame conjoined with other negative affects, and the next step is to extend this paradigm to include a general reformulation of all psychological disorders. If affect is primary, then
affect must be our starting point in reexamining the nature and development of clinical syndromes. By focusing specifically on the affect of
shame, I have shown not only how such an endeavor might proceed, but
why such reformulation of accepted theory has become imperative. The
constructs of *affect, scene,* and *script* constitute a radical rearrangement
of experience, a new imaginative grouping within the domain of inner
experience, a new scientific theory.

FROM A SCIENCE OF THE SELF TO A SCIENCE OF PSYCHOTHERAPY

The foregoing reformulation of psychopathology, together with the developmental self-theory presented earlier, leaves us on the threshold of constructing a science of the self. That endeavor necessarily is an evolving
one because all of the factors influencing syndrome development have
not been identified. However, affect theory and script theory provide a
more precise, accurate conceptual map for organizing psychological
facts, developmental as well as pathological.

Examining the critical roles of shame and identification has illuminated their interplay in the unfolding of self-identity. The developmental theory of the self is based on three central interactive processes: affect,
imagery, and language. Extending developmental self-theory into the
domain of psychopathology in order to account for the origins and per-
petuation of psychological disorder has further illustrated the direct appli-

cation of the paradigm and gives it explanatory power. But theory must also have direct implications for action. Translating theory into action will lead to more effective psychotherapies for specifically shame-based syndromes as well as clinical syndromes in general.

Part II

Psychotherapeutic Intervention

I think that the power that we see expressed [in primitive cave paintings] for the first time is the power of anticipation: the forward looking imagination. In these paintings the hunter was made familiar with dangers which he knew he had to face but to which he had not yet come. When the hunter was brought here into the secret dark and the light was suddenly flashed on the pictures, he saw the bison as he would have to face him, he saw the running deer, he saw the turning boar. And he felt alone with them as he would in the hunt. The moment of fear was made present to him; his spear-arm flexed with an experience which he would have and which he needed not to be afraid of. The painter had frozen the moment of fear, and the hunter entered it through the painting as if through an air-lock.

JACOB BRONOWSKI
The Ascent of Man

Six

Restoring the Interpersonal Bridge

*For the only therapy is real life. The patient must
learn to live, to live with his split, his conflict. his
ambivalence, which no therapy can take away, for if
it could, it would take with it the actual spring of life.*

OTTO RANK
Will Therapy

Psychotherapy is a recent invention when viewed from the perspective
of human evolution. It is barely a century old. Consider the various
assumptions and beliefs that undergird the practice. We think of psychotherapy in the context of treatment: someone is sick and must be
cured, something is broken and must be fixed. Illness and cure are
metaphors that condition how we think about what we do. They cannot
be gotten rid of because they are intertwined in the very language that
we use. Even the word *psychotherapy* reminds us of them, though the
original Greek words from which it derives, *therapeia* and *psyche,* meant
healing and *soul,* respectively.

Psychotherapy stands at the juncture of art and science. It is the modern version of primitive man's cave painting: we too have frozen the
moment of fear, and our client enters it, in the safety of the consulting
room, through imagination. Like those early cave paintings, psychotherapy is preparation for action, for living. Both take advantage of imagination, both work through imagination. If science has sought knowledge of

155

nature and art has sought knowledge of self, then psychotherapy is both science and art.

Human evolution has proceeded through distinct stages. The early hunter-gatherer stage eventually gave way to a settled agricultural stage. The industrial age that later followed has been all but absorbed by the modern age of technology, which must never be equated with science. They are not equivalent. Although technology derives from science, if we are to survive on this planet we must become a scientific civilization and not remain simply a technological society. The space shuttle disaster so graphically witnessed live on television, must mean, if anything, the death of technology as a god.

It is the technological vision, however, that continues to hold psychotherapy prisoner. We believe the answers inevitably lie in the direction of *technique*. In the rush toward technical sophistication or expansion, what is unfortunately lost is the human relationship. We conceive of psychotherapy more as technique or stratagem than as relatedness or connectedness, essential belonging. And that is what increasingly is being lost today on a much wider scale: the loss of community, of communion with others. We feel it in our bureaucratic society, students feel it in our impersonal educational institutions, and children feel it in their alienated families. That loss is what invariably brings clients into psychotherapy in the first place. So what do we offer them? More of the same.

Illness versus cure, art versus science, and technique versus relationship are three fundamental assumptions that, however subtly, profoundly shape the psychotherapeutic process. When these assumptions remain unconscious in the therapist, their effects are only less visible.

Psychotherapy must mirror development by actively engaging the identical processes that shape the self. It must be rooted in precise and accurate knowledge of how the self develops, functions, and changes. A conception of psychotherapy emerges directly from such an evolving vision of the self. If affect, imagery, and language are the central processes shaping the self, then these identical processes must equally be engaged in order to effect therapeutic change. Continuing to create and recreate new therapeutic techniques and technologies, without first reexamining the nature and actual functioning of the self and thereby grounding technique more solidly in developmental self-theory, will result only in a babel of technical approaches that are particular, confusing, conflicting, and limiting. Nature is neither so complicated nor so unreachable.

When syndromes resist therapeutic intervention, what happens? We generate new techniques. It is as if the only answer lay in the direction of technical expansion, rather than in the phenomena themselves. When we turn to consider the not unrelated question of child development, it is not technique but parenting that emerges into focus. And parenting is a better model for psychotherapy than any technique could ever be.

Psychotherapy must attend to the full range of the primary affects. Each of the affects must be made conscious, made fully aware to the conscious self inside each individual. All affects must be distinguished, experienced, and labeled accurately. Anger must be distinguished from dissmell, disgust, and contempt, the latter being a compound of anger and dissmell. Shame must be distinguished from fear and distress (the crying response), just as self-consciousness, which is a manifestation of shame, must be distinguished from anxiety, which is a manifestation of fear. The widespread lack of precision in our scientific language has seriously hindered both theoretical and therapeutic progress in psychology. To borrow an analogy from a sister science, if an electron were interchangeably called a neutron or a positron by physicists adhering to different schools of thought, imagine the confusion that would result. In psychology, such confusion is common fare and, what is worse, taken for fact. Without precision in our language, our concepts, and their definitions and phenomenological referents, we cannot advance as a science, and our clients cannot progress in psychotherapy.

Psychotherapy must provide a reparative, security-giving relationship, one that heals shame through new experiences of identification. Above all, psychotherapy is a relationship, not a technique or stratagem. Techniques and stratagems are certainly useful and often utilized, but always within a specific context, a human relationship. And relationships are never equivalent to technical sophistication. One can be quite proficient technically, yet quite impoverished at human relating. A reparative relationship is a relationship that repairs developmental deficits. These deficits are both relational and intrapsychic. Just as children require a security-giving relationship for optimal growth, so do clients. The conditions for growth do not change upon becoming an adult or entering into a therapeutic alliance. A therapeutic relationship is not identical to a parenting relationship, but they are functionally equivalent. The process is analogous. Shame is not something to be fixed—it must be healed. And shame becomes healed through experiences of identification between client and therapist. The kind of therapeutic relationship needed to transcend shame, to overcome its crippling effects, and to restore the self, is an identification relationship. How identification heals shame and what an identification relationship is are examined in this chapter.

Finally, psychotherapy must directly engage imagery—not only language—in order to make conscious and reshape governing scenes. Therapy is by no means entirely a cognitive process. The "talking cure" put forth by Freud is neither precisely "talking" nor exactly a "cure." Healing is a better metaphor than cure for psychotherapy. The therapeutic value of language is not to be minimized, but if only language or cognition were activated, personality change would not occur. Because maladaptive patterns are rooted in governing scenes, these actual scenes must be reactivated directly within the therapeutic process. They must be made fully conscious, actually reexperienced in the present with all their imprinted affect fully released. Reshaping these governing scenes is a conscious process, not strictly a cognitive one. Therapy by metaphor works because any therapy that activates imagery as well as language will be effective.

Psychotherapy, then, must be solidly grounded in knowledge of how the self develops and actually functions. That is the only sound basis for constructing effective psychotherapies. Knowledge is always an expanding enterprise, neither fixed nor final, and is never immutable.

In working with shame-based clients there is one serious dilemma. In order for these clients to fully enter and actually reexperience their shame, which is a necessary therapeutic task, psychotherapists have to be willing to do likewise. There are several important reasons for this. First, because effective therapy cannot remain an intellectual exercise, a distant, emotionally unavailable, unknowable therapist will only recreate the original traumatic scene. Such a therapeutic posture will fail to enable individuals crippled by shame to feel restored and whole. In order to effectively tolerate and master shame, clients require therapists who already are able to do so.

Second, shame activates shame. A client's shame can and will spontaneously activate shame in a therapist. Therapists who avoid or otherwise defend against their own shame, however activated, unfortunately recreate their client's familial patterns. This can, however, be turned to therapeutic advantage, provided therapists openly, honestly acknowledge their part, and thereby own it. That is always therapeutic. Third, therapists cannot enable clients to experience feelings or needs they do not allow in themselves. This is a therapeutic reality. Shame needs to be experienced and better tolerated. In order for clients to learn how to withstand the affect of shame while understanding its varied sources, past as well as current and internal as well as interpersonal, psychotherapists must do likewise. Psychotherapy is a reciprocal relationship. Psychotherapists become affected and changed by their clients even as clients become enlarged through the encounter.

In considering the question of therapeutic modality, there is a fundamental need for an individual relationship to repair early shame and relationship deprivation. In this sense, therapy can provide significant reparenting that is aimed at building a secure, self-affirming identity, a competent self able to live with increasing autonomy. However, there is also a need for therapeutic group experiences, but only within a security-giving environment, in order to complete the healing process. The resolution of shame is greatly aided when it occurs in group settings, but timing is critical. Not everyone is ready for a group, or even the same kind of group, at the shame time. There is no one general format or sequencing that all clients can be moved through.

Psychotherapy must be designed to fit each client, not the reverse. If we are concerned with quality treatment and, above all, effective treatment, then each client must be approached as a unique individual with particular needs.

The value of therapeutic group experiences as a complement to individual therapy partially accounts for the effectiveness of Alcoholics Anonymous groups for alcoholics and eating disorder groups for bulimics. Support groups and treatment groups resolve the inevitable secondary shame about the syndrome itself.

I view the combined use of individual and group therapy, either contemporaneously or sequentially, as the treatment of choice with shame-based syndromes. This is not to be routinely applied, however, to every case. Individual clients need to proceed through the therapy process in their own way, not necessarily ours.

Translating knowledge of affect, imagery, language, shame, and identification into effective strategies for healing shame will result in a competent self emerging in clients, a self that feels whole, more integrated, and both valued and affirmed from within. I view psychotherapy as an evolving integration of four central process dimensions. The therapeutic process must actively restore the interpersonal bridge by creating a reciprocal therapeutic relationship. By adopting a developmental focus, internalized shame is returned to its interpersonal origins, its governing scenes. Similarly, a focus on making conscious and then reshaping how the self actually functions as a self, in the present, results in regrowth of identity and healing of shame. Finally, interpersonal relations must be changed to directly foster equal power in current relationships and, particularly, the family of origin. Each process dimension is examined in a separate chapter.

SECURITY-GIVING RELATIONSHIP

Shame-based clients require the kind of *security-giving relationship* that has been so lacking in their lives. For the therapist, this translates into being genuine and honest with clients. Because trust is a reciprocal process, therapists must actually earn their client's trust. How? By first openly acknowledging and validating their mistrust. By enabling their sense of inner competence. By offering them tools for more effective living. By being models—allowing them to know an actual person from the inside.

A security-giving relationship directly fosters security. It allows dependence as well as independence, identification as well as separation/individuation. It means communicating honest caring and respect, not in words alone, but by living them out over time within the therapeutic relationship. A security relationship is mutually wanted.

Consider Ben, who initially came into therapy because of a fear of "going crazy" like his mother. When he was 5 years old Ben's mother was hospitalized, and he went to live with an aunt and uncle. Because they never adopted him and repeatedly reminded him he did not belong there, Ben continued to feel different from others, defective. He never really had a family and that was the root of his shame. He grew up feeling unwanted and uncared for. Therapy offered him an opportunity to repair his deprivation through experiencing the kind of relationship with an older male that he had needed with a father. He came to feel valued and cared about, and to understand that the people who raised him were incapable of providing what he needed. The failing was not his. In some of our sessions, we simply talked about various matters of mutual interest, much as a father might with a son.

IDENTIFICATION RELATIONSHIP

The kind of therapeutic relationship essential for healing and regrowth is an *identification relationship*. Becoming known to our clients invites their identification with us. There is one important guideline to follow. In my therapeutic relationships, I share only relevant and appropriate aspects from my own life that are already resolved, and only for the client's need, never my own. When a therapist shares current, unresolved conflicts, it burdens the client and misdirects the flow of the relationship. Therapists need to be emotionally available for their clients and not the reverse, just as parents need to be freely giving and genuinely responsive to their children and not the reverse.

Seeing how another human being actually functions as a self repairs one of the recurring failures in development, the failure of identification. So many clients have been deprived of that experience. Letting oneself become known when a client is experiencing shame, just like a parent with a child, is a healing experience.

THERAPY BY METAPHOR

Therapy can be viewed as constructing a mutual language. *Therapy by metaphor* is an essential feature of the interpersonal bridging process. While language is the principal vehicle for building the relationship bridge between strangers, between two separate experiential worlds, the use of metaphor directly engages imagery. Therapy by metaphor not only communicates understanding but also illuminates governing scenes.

Consider Laura, a young woman who came into therapy to see if she was "crazy," as her father had always told her. Well, no, she certainly was not crazy, but she seemed frozen inside, the needing and feeling part of her locked deeply away. Therapy proceeded slowly, intellectually, until the fourth session. I sensed she was feeling shame, a prisoner of exposure. She appeared to be feeling acutely self-conscious during our meetings. After she agreed with my observation, I asked her if she was willing to try something. Looking at me quizzically, she nodded. I invited her to relax in the chair and close her eyes, adding that I would close mine and I would not peek.

She laughed. Then we closed our eyes and simply verbalized whatever images came to mind.

Immediately, her entire manner changed. Her voice deepened, her speech slowed. Images of the past began to surface. Then she remembered a time "when the shadows came out at night." They came from the closet. At first they were friendly, but then they turned on her.

We gave that part of her a name: *Laura of the Shadows*. Other images surfaced. Many times she remembered being treated by her parents like a doll, as if she were something to be taken down to play with or to be put away. I called that part of her *Laura Doll*. Now we had a metaphor for the real self, disowned and split off inside, and also the false self, her superficial mask. In later sessions, whenever I wanted to bring Laura back to either of these scenes, I had only to remind her of Laura Doll or Laura of the Shadows.

As another example, consider Jenny who entered therapy because of her fear of a heart attack. She described her life as perpetually frantic. This struck me as a metaphor for her relationship with her dead mother. When Jenny was two months old, her mother became sick and died. As an adult Jenny was afraid of "causing a scene" and so would avoid confrontations or asserting herself. Deep inside she felt not good enough. I gave her tools to cope with her manifest fears and perplexing reactions. I suggested she *observe* them consciously and then write about her reactions in order to *detach* from them while gaining a clearer picture.

This gave Jenny more inner control, which also increased her sense of competence. Then she pulled back and cancelled a session. She was clearly ambivalent about depending on me. At our next meeting we talked about all the "dirty linen" inside of her. She remembered a scene with her stepmother saying how her long hair was so dirty. Her stepmother told Jenny that she had to have her hair braided or else have it cut short, but she wanted it long. The theme of powerlessness continued to resurface.

Regarding her fear of a heart attack, I asked her, "Did they tell you your real mommy was in heaven?"

"Yes, they did."

"Then it's natural to want to see her, which translates into dying as the connection," I thought out loud.

Jenny now realized she needed to know more about her real mother. She thought about confronting her father for that information. During a later imagery experience Jenny opened up to her deep shame and deprivation, her profound inner loneliness.

REPARENTING

Another essential feature of the therapeutic relationship required to repair shame is *reparenting*. This is not conceived as a technique, but an actual mirroring of development. Given the sources of shame, and the relationship failures from which it stems, therapy must create an analog of parenting. I have told many clients that it is only to the degree to which they experience our relationship as real that they will become healed. Clients have asked if they could actually imagine me as their father. This is not technique, but a human relationship.

There is no road map for reparenting. Once, a young man I was working with recalled that he had never had a birthday party while growing up. His parents were too busy and considered it frivolous. I surprised him with a party the evening of his birthday. To another client, who had never had a stuffed animal as a child and felt too ashamed to buy one, I gave a teddy bear. Both situations produced an eruption of affect from governing scenes, which was then assimilated by reliving those deprivation scenes while integrating the new positive scenes.

Reparenting essentially translates into providing for a client's needs when appropriate and genuinely felt. Therapists must never give what they do not have to give, or what feels uncomfortable or wrong. Honesty is always therapeutic. Therapists must know their limits as well as what they actually feel for each particular client.

A reparenting conception of therapy naturally involves regression. Governing scenes of shame must be recontacted and fully reexperienced. They must be relived completely, thereby releasing all affect. Only then can new scenes of love and respect for self be created. Internalizing new scenes and new positive identification images derived from the therapeutic relationship, are the beginning foundation of a self-affirming identity, a competent self.

Reliving governing scenes *is* regression. Experiencing a therapist as an actual parent makes the entire therapeutic process an actual rebirth of self. Those individuals who have the courage to suffer, thereby completely reliving their governing scenes while experiencing therapy as a real relationship, also experience the deepest healing and regrowth.

TRANSFERENCE: DIFFERENTIATING THE REAL RELATIONSHIP FROM THE TRANSFERENCE RELATIONSHIP

This particular conception of the therapeutic relationship, which is considered essential for healing shame and regrowth of identity, is not the traditional view espoused within the context of accepted psychodynamic theory. Psychotherapy involves providing a reconstructive relationship that entails living out a corrective emotional experience. Completing developmental tasks or failures is an inherent feature of the therapeutic process. Growth begins in, and requires, a distinct personal relationship. It cannot occur in a vacuum of relatedness. Individuals who have been deprived of adequate parenting will not thrive in renewed isolation. They must experience the missing relationship with a new mother, a new father. They desperately need to feel identified with *someone*. The therapeutic environment must recreate the conditions for growth, reawakening the developmental process itself.

Being-in-relationship is an evolutionary imperative. Traditional psychodynamic/psychoanalytic views of the therapeutic alliance violate that imperative. Therapist distance and neutrality, the so-called "blank screen," damage client self-esteem by reproducing shame. That is an inevitability. Psychotherapy is not a neutral activity, but a human one, and it must create an analog of parenting to be effective.

The therapeutic process requires a genuine human relationship between client and therapist, a security-giving relationship, an identification relationship. What of *transference*? The concept of transference bears reexamination particularly in the light of Tomkins's script theory (1979, 1987b). The reenactment of governing scenes is the mechanism of transference. When governing scenes are reactivated and subsequently imported into current new relationships, transference occurs. With respect to the psychotherapy relationship, then, transference is a special case of the operation of scenes. The particular reactions transferred to the therapist are always mediated by the client's governing scenes. Similarly, clients who do not express or verbalize their reactions but instead "act them out" are actually living out their scenes. The so-called *acting out* phenomenon is simply the overt or behavioral reenactment of scenes.

Transference is by no means a singular phenomenon. Certain clients transfer reactions experienced toward mother or father directly to the therapist. Their transference takes the form of direct *scene reenactment,* whether verbalized or acted out. The client is reenacting toward the therapist the analogous scene as it was originally experienced; the client now plays the identical part or role originally played toward the parent. In this instance, therapist and parent become one. Feelings or attitudes originally directed toward the parent now are directed toward the therapist, and feelings or attitudes originally experienced from the parent are now experienced as emanating from the therapist. Transference has indeed occurred; a governing scene has been imported into the current situation, the therapeutic relationship.

In a second form of transference the client *recasts* the scene. Here the client still reenacts the scene with the therapist, but instead plays the identical part that the parent actually played in the original scene. In this latter case, the client behaves toward the therapist the way the parent previously behaved toward the client. Feelings and attitudes experienced as emanating from the parent are now aimed and directed toward the therapist *as if* the therapist were the client in the original scene. The *internalized other* within the client, which is embedded in the client's governing scenes, mediates this reversed scene reenactment. Recasting the scene produces a reversed transference.

The process of transference, whether direct or reversed, verbalized or reenacted behaviorally, is a direct function of the operation of governing scenes. It occurs when the necessary and sufficient activators of governing scenes are present. That typically involves the perception of similarity, but with a difference. The client is responding to imagined relationships between shared dimensions of two different situations. The current interaction with the therapist activates the client's governing scene, and an analog of that scene is then constructed and imported into the present situation.

Consider the following example. In the form of therapy I have been developing, I allow my attention to cycle, to flow both toward and away from my client. In order to deepen contact with my own imagery, which I consider essential to my being therapeutic, I often look out of the window or even close my eyes. Clients typically have feelings about my behavior that we can then explore.

On one occasion, I did not have any inkling that anything was wrong until I received a letter from a female client. In it she expressed her intention to end therapy, saying that one day she might have the courage to find another therapist, one who *really* cared. I was perplexed. When I reflected over our months of working together, I could not identify any clues to what had gone wrong. Carefully, I considered how to respond: Do I consider the matter concluded by her letter? Do I wait a while longer? Do I write a letter back? Do I have the secretary call? Since we had had a relationship, however brief, I decided to call her myself and I called the very day I received her letter. She was surprised to hear from me, thinking I would not bother. I simply expressed my sorrow at her decision and wished her well. Gradually, she softened toward me and I inquired about what had gone wrong. She did not know. I invited her to come in, even for one last session if that still remained her wish. At least we could try to fathom what had happened between us. She agreed to come in.

During this next session, I again expressed my sadness at how badly she was feeling toward me. She experienced me as uncaring. As I sat with her, I searched inside to ascertain whether she was accurate. I allowed my attention to flow between us. No, I did not dislike her.

I did not feel angry or resentful toward her, nor especially distant from her either. My reactions toward her did not match her reactions toward me, nor how she *experienced* me feeling toward her.

She decided to resume working together following that session. Somehow, her feelings of mistrust had lifted sufficiently, leaving her feeling better about our relationship. I still had no idea what had happened. Our very next session began fine, but halfway through it again she started talking about ending therapy. Immediately, I began attending to the sequence of events between us. As we examined the interaction backwards in time, suddenly she realized when the change had come about. It was prompted moments before when I was looking out of the window. First she had felt abandoned, then she had felt an acute sense of shame, and rage had quickly followed. That sequence of events happened in rapid succession, obscuring precise discrimination. As we searched further, it became apparent that this identical pattern was responsible for her initial intention to end therapy. Now we had discovered the source of her perplexing reaction.

Having done so, the next step was differentiating the *real relationship* between us from the *transference relationship*. I explained to her that, yes, I do like to look out of the window, and sometimes I even close my eyes. That was true and an essential aspect of who I was, both as a person and as a therapist. However, I had no intention of abandoning her. I both validated her perception and owned my part of the process.

Experiencing me as abandoning her and not caring for her were transferred reactions. Inadvertently, I had activated a governing scene. At the conclusion of that session, I further suggested that somehow what I had done also must have happened before.

She came in the very next session having recalled similar scenes involving her father. The memories had unexpectedly returned during the intervening week. These were scenes in which her father sat reading in a chair, hidden behind a newspaper. She remembered numerous occasions when she attempted to get his attention, but was always shut out by his newspaper. He was truly uninterested in her. She felt abandoned by him, profoundly uncared for. Those scenes were the source of her transferred reactions and actually mediated the process of transference.

The psychotherapy relationship is a reciprocal one. If the therapist behaves in ways that are sufficiently similar to but also different from the client's parent, and thereby activates the client's governing scene, causing its importation into their present relationship, then an analogous process can happen for the therapist. The client invariably will activate governing scenes in the therapist that are then, potentially, capable of being imported into their relationship. The name given to that phenomenon is *counter-transference.*

Not all feelings or reactions on the part of therapists, however, represent counter-transference. Many are indeed real. In particular cases, certainly, there may be a mixture of both real and transferred reactions, but equating all therapist feelings and attitudes with counter-transference is as ludicrous as equating all parental reactions toward children with unresolved neurotic strivings. Parents have real and appropriate feelings toward their children, just as therapists experience genuine feelings toward their clients, who also have honest and real feelings in return. Too often the judgment of counter-transference is wielded by senior clinicians in order to shame novice therapists.

Offering a genuine relationship to clients, one that is security-giving and directly fosters identification, does *not* preclude transference. The actual transferring of affective reactions from earlier significant relationships will still occur. It is indeed more difficult to distinguish the transferred from the real and current reactions of clients within the context of a therapeutic relationship fostering security and identification. However, this particular form of therapeutic relationship does not prevent transference. Similarly, a therapeutic relationship based on the principles of fostering security, identification, and reparenting does not make either the therapeutic relationship or process impure. The widely held belief that the traditional "blank screen" form of therapeutic relationship is more pure is mistaken. The latter therapeutic posture inherently "pulls" more hostility from clients because it inevitably generates more shame. Traditional psychoanalytic forms of therapy constitute a shame-based system.

Frustration and deprivation can facilitate growth, but only when in moderation. This is as true for clients as it is for children. Graded and appropriately timed frustrations often stimulate positive change. The central questions remaining are *when* to frustrate and *what* to frustrate. If the aim is to mobilize and make conscious a client's earlier deprivation, this can be accomplished by actually providing some of what was missed just as well as by continuing to deprive the client. Frustrating a client's need to feel understood or cared about, to feel important or special to the therapist, to feel identified with the therapist, to feel respected and admired, is never therapeutic.

TOUCHING AND HOLDING: CLIENT NEED VERSUS THERAPIST DILEMMA

The principles of fostering security, identification, and reparenting constitute a unique form of psychotherapy that, to be implemented effectively, further requires that therapists be fully conscious and differentiated within themselves. Therapists must know their particular needs, both healthy and neurotic, as well as their talents and limits. They must know their actual feelings toward individual clients along with the sources of their reactions. They must know enough about themselves to distinguish what is real about them from what is transferred to them. They must know the meaning of their behavior toward specific clients as well as the meaning particular clients have for them. In the absence of such differentiated knowledge about themselves, therapy will misfire.

Psychotherapy is not a neutral activity. It can certainly enhance growth for both participants in the relationship, or for all participating when the modality is group or family therapy. However, psychotherapy can also restrict growth. It can further damage self-esteem. Therapists can abuse clients just as parents abuse children in the family and teachers abuse students in educational institutions. In all three cases, what occurs is an abuse of power.

Preventing such abuse is paramount. Prevention begins in accurate self-knowledge, coupled with an understanding of power dynamics in any relationship. Trust depends on the appropriate uses of power, and the abuse of power inevitably violates trust. Abuse activates shame. The abuse of power subverts any relationship, whether between parent and child, teacher and student, or therapist and client.

What has all this to do with the question of touching and holding? There are few more compelling dilemmas for therapists than this very question. Whether to physically touch or hold a client inevitably raises the specter of abuse. Many accepted Rules of Practice were designed to prevent the possibility of subverting the therapeutic relationship by therapists who act out their own unresolved or unconscious needs. Rules, however, never guarantee ethical behavior. The question remains as to whether the Rule itself is a therapeutic necessity.

Some forms of psychodynamic psychotherapy advocate creating a *holding environment* for clients. This is presumably to be accomplished through a combination of verbal, interpersonal, and emotional means, but not through actual physical contact between client and therapist. Other forms of therapy are directly touch oriented. Some even utilize holding as a technique. However, the science of psychotherapy, along with its practice, must be solidly grounded in theory. Therapeutic decisions must have a sound basis in self-development. Whether, when, and how to touch and to hold remain therapeutic dilemmas.

The need for touching and holding must be clearly distinguished from sexuality. Not all touching is sexual. Touching certainly expresses tenderness and affection. Often the need is simply for an experience of bodily contact, which is indeed *enjoyable,* but not necessarily sexual. Holding, particularly at times of distress or shame, communicates not so much affection as protection and security, the basis for trust. Obviously, the shared experience of physical touching reflects a range of meanings, only one of which is sexual.

Shame-based clients typically have been seriously deprived of adequate or consistent touching and holding. That need has become acutely bound by shame. For those who have been either sexually abused or physically abused, the skin itself has become associated with bodily violation. Exploring the nature and quality of touching/holding as it was experienced directly in the family will illuminate the affective patterning of the client's need. Touching may have become fused with shame, with fear, or with disgust instead of with enjoyment. The need may also be experienced ambivalently. It may have become confused with sexuality, so that all touching now means something sexual. The meaning of touching/holding to the client must be carefully examined in order to know how best to proceed.

At times, I ask clients how they would feel if I offered them a fatherly hug. I may even ask their permission to do so. Or I might simply suggest my offering a hug and then observe how they respond. At other times, I will spontaneously place an arm around a client's shoulder as we walk to the door, or instead give a client a pat on the back. Always, I observe how clients react, and later we process the event together in order to examine its meaning for the client. With still other clients, particularly when in the midst of acute distress or shame, I may reach out and touch their hand.

If I experience any hesitation, doubt, or ambivalence within me about doing any of the above, then I wait. Instead, I explore with them their prior experiences of touching and holding. Finally, I always let clients know that the best way to obtain something they need is to be clear in asking for it. I usually prefer it when clients are able to ask directly for holding.

When I am working with a client who was sexually abused, I am extremely cautious so as not to confuse matters further. Even though I may make it quite clear that my touching is purely affectionate and fatherly, my client may nevertheless misinterpret my actions. Thus, a sexually abused female client may have an easier time acknowledging the need for holding, and then accepting touching, from a female therapist than from a male therapist.

Consider the following case. During our first session, a young woman struggled to reveal her secret: she had been repeatedly molested sexually by her father as a child. Her pain and shame were profound, and still she felt to blame. With my encouragement she recovered the scene and reexperienced all of the feelings embedded in it. One day, she came in and announced to me that she had discovered something else.

"Then I came to the worst thing of all," she said.

"What was that?" I asked.

"It's not what he did to me, it's what he *didn't* do. "

I was puzzled.

"It's that never, not once did he ever hold me, just hold me. He didn't have to do nothing, just hold me and hold me and hold me and not let me go."

Several moments passed in silence as she gazed at the floor. I simply waited.

"Now I'm gonna ask you to do something, but only if you want to." She asked with much embarrassment, asked by casting down her eyes and stammering over words. "Would you . . . please . . . hold me," she continued, "but only if you really want to . . . 'cause you don't have to . . . and remember, you don't need to do nothin' . . . just hold me."

Her eyes remained downcast. I quietly pulled my chair over next to hers and placed my arm around her shoulder and simply held her. Not a word was spoken for some time. A short while later, I asked her if she had ever had bedtime stories read to her. She said she hadn't because no one had time for her. So I picked out a favorite children's book from the shelf and proceeded to read her a story. Her eyes went big and round and she listened intently as I read to her. When the story ended, she gave me a great big hug and we were done for that day.

Touching and holding are not a technique. They must not be employed artificially either. Touching, however it may manifest, must grow directly out of the evolving relationship bond between client and therapist. It must be experienced as real for both. Touching must feel comfortable and natural to the therapist or it will never feel right to the client. Its mode of expression must fit both participants in the relationship. And it must be offered for the client's need, not the therapist's. Touching and holding must be offered when honestly, genuinely felt, never as a strategem.

Seven

Returning Internalized Shame to Its Interpersonal Origins

But through a variety of adverse influences, a child may not be permitted to grow according to his individual needs and possibilities. Such unfavorable conditions are too manifold to list here. But, when summarized, they all boil down to the fact that the people in the environment are too wrapped up in their own neuroses to be able to love the child, or even to conceive of him as the particular individual he is; their attitudes toward him are determined by their own neurotic needs and responses. . . . As a result, the child does not develop a feeling of belonging, of "we," but instead a profound insecurity and vague apprehensiveness, for which I use the term basic anxiety. It is his feeling of being isolated and helpless in a world conceived as potentially hostile.

KAREN HORNEY
Neurosis and Human Growth

The developmental dimension of the psychotherapy process essentially involves a reversal: internalized shame must be returned to its interpersonal origins, its governing scenes. In order to accomplish that, shame must be made fully conscious, along with its current sources and originating scenes. Accurate naming is vital to this endeavor. Differentiating shame from other affects is itself an important, though frequently difficult therapeutic task.

IDENTIFYING SHAME IN THE CLINICAL INTERVIEW

There are four classes of shame indicators that are clinically useful. The affect of shame is multidimensional. It operates facially, affectively, cognitively, and interpersonally. The accurate perception and identification of shame depends on observing these four modal dimensions for its presence.

Facial Signs

Paying attention to the external, *facial signs* of shame, its nonverbal indicators, is vital to recognizing shame. Initially, certain clients manifest shame overtly and directly, through either avoidance of eye contact, averting their eyes, or staring at the floor. Eyes or head down, eyes averted, and blushing are characteristic signs of shame. Some clients suddenly become ill-at-ease when they are looked at directly or when they become aware that eyes are upon them. Then they look away. Avoidance of mutual facial gazing and direct eye-to-eye contact is a definite sign of shame. Alternatively, others will instead adopt a staring posture, and actually stare directly into the therapist's eyes; this is essentially a counter-shame defense, masking their own deeper shame. One young man commented that he learned as a child how to stare directly into his parents' eyes in order to make them uncomfortable, ashamed, when they attempted to discipline him. Other facial defenses against shame that are observable in the interview are the head-back look, frozen face, and look of contempt.

During the first interview with a young woman, initially she was rather carefree. She laughed freely and seemed relaxed, at times even giggling. Suddenly, her entire manner changed and she appeared younger, more frightened, even helpless. She grabbed hold of her sides and held herself tightly, looking down at the floor. Then she rocked back and forth. She began to mumble, seemingly oblivious to my presence. All at once she turned upside down in the chair, her feet straight up in the air; the rest of her curled up as a ball. I let her know I was still present. At times she responded to me, but at other times I could not reach her. Periodically, she resumed her gesturing, holding herself and rocking. During these periods, she was unable to look at me. If our eyes met for an instant, she immediately covered her face with her hands. Occasionally, she even buried her face under her arms. As I observed her behavior, I began to wonder about shame. I realized I was witnessing an intense shame reaction that was being repetitively reactivated. Shame had engulfed her. Then I knew that if I became impatient, intellectual, too detached, helpless, or threatened, the entire drama now beginning to unfold could abruptly hide once again. I told us both that we would see it out together and understand it. Eventually we did: she had been sexually molested by her father as a child.

Affective Signs

In addition to the facial signs of shame, careful attention to the phenomenological experience of shame is necessary. Shame feels like unexpected exposure, suddenly being revealed as lesser. The self feels exposed to view, as if impaled under a magnifying gaze, but the watching eyes belong to the self. Because language is imprecise, the inner experience of shame is typically misidentified as anxiety, even as paranoid thoughts.

A sense of exposure is inherent in shame. The various forms in which the alienating affect becomes manifest, the range of shame complexes, provide direction for further therapeutic exploration. Shyness, embarrassment, discouragement, self-consciousness, and guilt comprise critical *affective signs* of shame. Depression is similarly comprised of shame along with distress. Observing any of these affective states, then, indicates the presence of shame as an underlying dynamic.

Shame as affect must be further distinguished from internalized shame. This is akin to the distinction Tomkins draws between affect as an amplifier and magnified affect. As affect amplification, the nature of shame is partial and temporary, as in momentary embarrassment or shyness. But as affect magnification, shame is radically increased in toxicity, as in chronic shyness or enduring inferiority. Affect magnification refers to any systematic increase in frequency, intensity, and duration of affect. Magnification of shame results, according to Tomkins (1979, 1987a & b), from combining multiple affects about the same scene and also from combining multiple sources of shame about the same scene. Psychological magnification is the process by which isolated scenes become interconnected, directly fused together, thereby creating families of scenes.

The therapeutic task is finding an *entrance* to a client's shame. A particular young woman once described how she had always felt left out in her family; she was an artist in a family of mathematicians and felt devalued.

"You must have felt like the ugly duckling," I said to her.

She lit up and immediately replied, "That's right, that's exactly how I felt!"

Cognitive Signs

Another woman began talking about her self-defeating ways in an early session. She said she always feels like a fraud, an impostor about to be found out. She *knew* the truth: she is not the competent, intelligent professional everyone thinks she is. Instead, she is really stupid, inferior. That was her shame, and the impostor syndrome was how it manifested cognitively.

The impostor syndrome is one of the important *cognitive signs* of shame affect. Low self-esteem, diminished self-concept, and deficient body image are other ways in which shame manifests cognitively. Shame can also take the form of worthlessness or feeling oneself unloveable. It can appear as a vague sense of feeling insubstantial, not whole, or even empty inside. Some clients actually believe that no real self is present within them. Others feel acutely inferior, deeply inadequate, or like inherent failures. Some just feel "crazy. " For others, there is a sense of inner deficiency, of something vitally wrong within. They speak of always feeling different from others; when I ask, "Different, or defective?" they resonate to the latter. As a way to access shame sometimes I ask a client, "Have you ever felt that there was something wrong with you inside?" The challenge is discovering a linguistic entrance. Whatever its cognitive form, each of these descriptions embodies a wound made by shame.

Interpersonal Signs

The final class of shame indicators operates interpersonally, either directly in relation to the therapist or in interaction with others as described to the therapist. The general *interpersonal signs* of shame can be observed through the operation of the various defending scripts that generate in response to governing scenes of shame. Rage, contempt, and power scripts are readily observable in the interview because they frequently are directed at the therapist. Certain individuals attempt to control the interview or interaction as a way of maintaining power. Others become overtly contemptuous of the therapist; for instance, one woman said to me, "You're nothing more than hired help." Rage can manifest in various ways, including stormy interchanges whenever shame is activated or approached.

Perfection, transfer of blame, and internal withdrawal scripts can operate subtly; they may be activated in response to the self, to others, or to the therapist. Perfection is generally focused on the self; it is the self that must incessantly strive to excel, improve, or become more perfect. Transfer of blame operates defensively in order to find fault somewhere else; shame must be transferred away from the self onto others, even the therapist. Internal withdrawal results in a shut-in personality; the individual remains hidden from view.

Humor scripts can be either flexible and adaptive or rigidly relied upon. A relaxed sense of humor is not necessarily a sign of disturbance. Humor can indeed facilitate the emergence of the interpersonal bridge. Sarcastic humor or self-deprecatory humor, however, are quite another matter. When humor is inflexible as a shield against shame, the interpersonal encounter does not deepen.

Denial can be the most entrenched of all the scripts. It is a generalized strategy of defense that always distorts perception as well as the quality of interpersonal interactions. Its effect is to neutralize the impact of others. Denial scripts literally deny access to the self, potentially leaving therapists frustrated.

The operation of any of these interpersonal patterns points significantly to the presence of shame.

APPROACHING AND VALIDATING SHAME

In order to reverse the developmental sequence, shame must be approached actively and validated openly. Shame needs to be given direct expression. Clients have to become fully conscious of their shame, able to recognize when they are actually experiencing shame and able to identify its sources. They must also learn how to master this disturbing affect.

Consider Joe, who entered therapy because of recurring depression. His depressive bouts were activated, as we began to understand, whenever he allowed himself to feel close to someone. Then he immediately drew back and later felt depressed. When we examined the sequence of his reactions, it became clear that Joe felt intense shame about his relationship needs. Gradually, he realized he actually hated and wanted to purge the needing boy hidden within him. In exploring the roots of his self-hatred, we discovered that his father was overtly contemptuous whenever Joe expressed a need for anything from him. That was the model for Joe's turning contempt against his own self, thereby becoming split.

Another example. Jeff felt intense longing triggered by a particular face. He recently had met a woman whose face was the exact face he always had been searching for. In her presence, his longing reawakened. This was followed immediately by his feeling unattractive: "She couldn't possibly be interested in me—I'm so ugly." His longing had turned to shame. Jeff had approached this new relationship differently than his previous relationships; this time he was clear and direct about his feelings for the woman and also about his expectations of the relationship. By openly expressing his feelings and needs, Jeff discovered that they were looking for a different kind of relationship. The woman became distant on their subsequent meeting and Jeff came away feeling he always does something wrong. At our next session he commented, "I always destroy the relationship."

"No," I answered. "You did it *differently* this time. Every relationship is an experiment; it doesn't have to work out. Besides, look at what you've learned: you discovered the particular *face* that calls to you, and saw your inner ugliness. That's why it hurt so much. Her drawing back only confirmed what you already felt."

"That's right!" Jeff exclaimed, feeling greatly relieved, though realizing there was still more therapeutic work to be done.

REFOCUSING ATTENTION: A TOOL FOR MASTERING SHAME

In order to enable clients to better *tolerate* the affect of shame, I teach them a specific tool for releasing that affect at the moment shame is generating. This will neither heal nor resolve internalize or magnified shame, but it will enable clients to let go of shame whenever it becomes reactivated in the present. When shame generates, the attention turns inward, as if impaling the self under a magnifying gaze. The tool for releasing shame is *refocusing attention*. By consciously, effortfully, refocusing attention back *outside* the self through sheer effort of will, shame is immediately released. This can be accomplished through becoming immersed in external sensory experience, particularly visual and physical. Refocusing attention is especially useful for interrupting *internal shame spirals*. Clients must be enabled to recognize, intervene consciously in, and terminate their shame spirals. Attempts to understand the experience while it is spiraling or snowballing only embroil one deeper in shame. Deliberately refocusing all of one's attention outside oneself by becoming visually and physically involved in the sensory world surrounding the self breaks the shame spiral and allows shame feelings and thoughts to subside. Turning the attention outward effectively interrupts shame spirals, thereby allowing the individual previously held prisoner by shame to enjoy various solitary or relational activities, from public speaking, dancing and sports, to sexual pairing. Enjoyment creates new scenes of positive affect where previously there had only been shame.

Refocusing attention is neither a precisely cognitive nor a strictly behavioral technique. Instead it is an *affect tool*. By utilizing it, we are working directly with affect. Refocusing attention is a specific tool for releasing affect, in this case, the affect of shame. It is a tool for managing affect and, hence, it enhances mastery of shame.

To understand the operation of this tool, let us review the phenomenology of shame. The essence of shame involves turning the attention inward upon the self. In the midst of shame, the self feels excruciatingly exposed, revealed as lesser. Suddenly, we are watching ourselves. It is this inner scrutiny, this torment of self-consciousness, that creates shame's binding, paralyzing effect upon the self.

Once I understood the essential phenomenology of shame, I immediately began experimenting with techniques for releasing shame. I remember walking in the gardens near my office. I attempted to refocus my eyes back outside and accomplishing this reversal required considerable effort. I focused my attention outward by focusing directly onto the environment surrounding me. I noticed the texture of the trees, the color of the flowers, the shapes of the clouds above me. I even talked to myself about what I was seeing and hearing in order to refocus all attention back outside. It worked because the feeling of shame had passed; shame had been released.

I began experimenting further with this technique by using it with clients directly during therapy sessions; I also taught it to them for later use. The principle is a simple one, but mastering it can prove quite difficult. Practice is required. And this further requires one to reenter the shame scene, the situation that directly activates shame.

For some individuals, public speaking activates shame. In this setting, refocusing attention outward can be implemented by counting the people present, looking to see who is actually there, or focusing on who might be interesting enough to get to know. As long as the focus of attention remains directed outward, one remains free of shame.

A particular client felt paralyzed by shame at the mere thought of dancing. He would not even dance in the privacy of his own home—with the lights out. He first had to decide he wanted to overcome this obstacle. He had to be determined to be satisfied with nothing less than full recovery. Then I instructed him, after considerable therapeutic work with shame, to reenter the dreaded shame scene: he had to go dancing in public. He and his wife arranged to go out that Saturday evening. After agonizing with himself, he finally braved the dance floor. Immediately, he felt exposed: everyone was watching him, laughing at him, mocking him. In reality, he was watching himself, he was mocking himself. It only seemed that the watching eyes belonged to others. I had instructed him to focus his attention entirely on his partner, to look only at her and talk to himself only about how well she was dancing. He was to notice only his partner and to admire her as well. Within moments, he felt surprisingly free of disabling shame and his body even resonated naturally to the music. To his amazement, he was dancing.

Of course, self-consciousness just as quickly returned and he became stiff, awkward, and clumsy once more. Suddenly, he found himself quite literally standing still on the dance floor. But he remembered my instructions and persevered. Once more he refocused his attention back outside, directly onto his dancing partner. And he continued this procedure throughout that entire evening, feeling increasing joy where previously there had only been shame.

The recovery process entailed six months of reentering the scene while actively refocusing attention. He even began to look forward to dancing. Eventually, he felt only a twinge of shame upon stepping onto the dance floor, and later in the process, a twinge immediately before doing so. Later, his anticipatory shame occurred only at the thought of dancing. And finally, shame became completely disconnected from the activity of dancing. Critical to this process is the creation of new, positive affect scenes; enjoyment and excitement must become associated with the specific scene that previously had been fused with shame.

Earlier, we considered how to apply this particular affect release technique in the sexual life. Application of both the principle and the tool itself is identical in these two situations. However, refocusing attention may require adaptation depending on the context involved. Some modification may be necessary given the unique situation at hand. For example, another individual, an older woman, felt acute self-consciousness upon entering the steam room at her health club. When I explained the technique of refocusing attention outwards, she thought about it and then told me, "That would never do." Directly focusing her attention on the other women in the steam room would never enhance her comfort. So I suggested a variation: upon entering the steam room and sitting down, she was simply to *close her eyes.*

I instructed my client to return to her health club and reenter the dreaded scene, the steam room. She was to find a comfortable place to sit down and then close her eyes. The next week she reported to me that this technique had worked very well, surprisingly so. She had felt completely comfortable for the first time in a steam room. My client experienced no shame.

Why had I suggested closing her eyes? Closing the eyes is another way of working with the focus of attention in order to reduce shame.

Refocusing attention is an affect tool for releasing shame. It directly enhances the capacity to tolerate the affect of shame in particular situations previously disturbing to the self. By feeling armed with a specific tool for releasing shame, individuals need no longer dread the alienating affect.

Another client and his oldest son were returning from karate practice and decided to stop for ice cream, but the boy wanted his father to go in alone and bring it out to him. The reason, he said, was that he would feel embarrassed being seen there while in his karate uniform. His father mentioned there was a simple way to overcome his discomfort. "Oh yeah?" he answered, his curiosity having been piqued. Then the boy's father explained the technique of refocusing attention. As they were getting out of the car, the boy looked at his father and said, "This better work." It did, according to my client.

RECOVERING INTERPERSONALLY BASED SCENES OF SHAME

In order to return internalized or magnified shame to its interpersonal origins, governing scenes must become conscious. These scenes can involve the family, peer group, or school setting. Reshaping those governing scenes requires courage and determination, which cannot be taught. Clients must find these essential resources within themselves. Change is never immediate and must be lived out over time. Governing scenes cannot be erased or entirely disconnected either, nor can the psyche be reprogrammed. Governing scenes, those psychological "black holes," certainly can be recognized with increasing efficiency, but they are always capable of reactivation. Individuals are forever caught by their ability to synthesize new repetitions of governing scenes. The client "is victimized by his own high-powered ability to synthesize ever-new repetitions of the same scene without knowing that he is doing so" (Tomkins, 1979, p. 231). No amount of understanding the past will enable clients to become aware of new analogs *before* they are constructed. The process can happen silently or be mediated by an inner voice. It can occur suddenly and unexpectedly, without apparent reason, or envelop one with the force of a tornado.

Consider a young man who came into therapy because of difficulties relating to women. Early during the course of therapy, he happened to mention how he had been hit or beaten every day while growing up. He mentioned this in passing, thinking such treatment at the hands of parents to be natural. My outrage on his behalf gave him the courage to look more closely. Months into therapy, he called me at about four o'clock in the morning. A governing scene suddenly had become conscious. Prompted by our deepening therapeutic inquiry, a memory came back unexpectedly that night and it left him terrified. When he was about 14, he remembered being beaten into wakefulness. He had been asleep at the time and apparently his father had come home late in the evening, entered his bedroom, and began beating him as he slept. He recalled waking up abruptly in the midst of that beating, feeling confused, disoriented, humiliated, and terrified. Upon recovery of the scene, he was once again disoriented, terrified, and paralyzed with shame. His deep rage and disgust for his father surfaced later.

Another example. Shame can also result directly from one's own actions. In the course of therapy, Ruth, a woman in her mid-40s, revealed how she had been arrested many years ago for selling marijuana. The police had offered her a deal: in exchange for identifying her sources, they would let her go. Therein lay her conflict: to protect her friends and go to prison or make the deal and spare herself. Her choice was between the unknown terror of prison, along with the accompanying stigma of a criminal record, and the certain humiliation of cowardice. She chose the deal. Only later did she discover that, in fact, the police required her to be present at each of the subsequent police raids, thereby personally betraying her own friends. The look on each of their faces as they realized her betrayal haunted her from that point on; she could look no one in the face, least of all herself. Ruth considered herself a coward, weak and spineless, utterly contemptible. For years, she continued to torture herself for her cowardice. Reliving the scenes of betrayal, especially imagining the faces of her friends as they were being handcuffed, caused her shame to deepen through magnification. Over the ensuing years, Ruth continued to blame herself mercilessly for betraying her friends. Contempt for herself was unrelenting.

Imagery is one important tool that facilitates the recovery of governing scenes. Another is writing. By observing their inner experience and then writing in a journal about it, certain clients are able to retrieve early memories. We will consider these avenues further in the next chapter.

CONSTRUCTING A SHAME PROFILE: MAKING SHAME BINDS CONSCIOUS

Therapists must guide clients toward discovering early relationship failures in order to understand how their shame was caused. Using the affect, drive, interpersonal need, and purpose systems as a conceptual map, a *Shame Profile* can be constructed for each client. Therapist and client actually can begin to visualize those specific interpersonal scenes as well as their internalized analogs, and then observe clusters of shame nuclei, for example, affect-shame binds or interpersonal need-shame binds. By searching out how specific affects and interpersonal needs became bound by shame, those particular affects and needs now can be validated and the binding effects of shame eventually dissolved. When clients experience those affects and interpersonal needs directly within the therapeutic relationship, the deepest and most enduring new scenes of positive affect are created.

Consider Judy, who sought therapy because she was bulimic. In the course of therapy a shaming history in her family clearly emerged, experienced particularly at the hands of her father. He was an extremely critical individual; nothing she did was ever good enough. She recalled once helping him with a household repair; when she brought him the tool she thought he asked for, he became angry and critical: "Why didn't you realize I meant something else, you should have known better." Her father also would make disparaging comments about her appearance, body, and weight, disguising these remarks as, "I was only joking." Judy felt deeply wounded inside, but her pain and shame were ignored or minimized. Meal-times became a particular battleground because her father turned eating into a power struggle. At times, she was even force-fed to the point of vomiting.

As we worked together, I invited Judy to *observe* her reactions immediately preceding bingeing and also purging. Next she learned consciously to *delay* first her bingeing, and subsequently her purging, by recording her observations. Keeping a journal to record those observations enabled her to consciously mediate and delay what had always been a repetitive, automatic process.

Months later when Judy became involved in a new relationship with a man who excited her expectations but equally disappointed them, her governing scenes became magnetized and reactivated. After several disappointments, Judy found herself becoming furious at the man. First, I validated her rage. This enabled her to express her anger to him directly. Immediately after this, she became seized with scenes of their next meeting: she imagined herself running up to him, throwing her arms around him and apologizing profusely. In response to these imagined scenes, Judy called me; she was afraid she would give up her anger.

I responded by suggesting that an old scene was being reactivated. After a few moments the memories came, along with an eruption of affect—distress and shame. Three distinct scenes emerged. The first was a scene of abandonment stimulated by her mother. Judy remembered fighting with her brother as a child on one particular day and her mother suddenly, unexpectedly, threatened to leave them. That night she had a disturbing dream in which her mother did in fact leave. The second scene involved her father and his never holding her or sitting her on his lap. Her anguish and shame were deep. The third scene involved fights with her father. She always felt like it was her fault and she had to apologize. She had to be the one to say, "I'm sorry." Her father would never admit to mistakes or say that he was sorry. This last scene was one in which her anger at her father became converted into feeling to blame, feeling guilty. Judy now had recovered three critical governing scenes.

Then I said to her, "You feel *young* to me in those scenes."

"I'm feeling young right now," she answered through her tears.

"You can be as young as you need to be with me," I replied gently. "Bring that young little girl inside of you to me. I'm a safe person."

That night Judy experienced the full depth of her rage: rage at the man who had been exciting but disappointing her needs, not unlike her father, and rage directly at her father as well. She allowed herself to slam doors, bang things in her room, and she even smashed the wall, leaving a gaping hole in it. When her rage was finally spent, Judy felt much more integrated.

LEARNING A LANGUAGE

The process of dissolving shame binds involves learning a language for how the self actually functions. Such a language is never imposed upon inner experience, but rather illuminates it from within. Clients must be taught how to distinguish and accurately name their specific affects and interpersonal needs, as well as how to distinguish both from their physiological drives. The evolving language of the self, which partitions affect, drive, interpersonal need, and purpose, functions as a psychological tuning fork. Language illuminates inner states as if with a spotlight. The process is one of *differentiation* of inner states followed by *owning* them, all accomplished consciously. Clients must be taught how to *experience, name,* and finally *own* each affect, interpersonal need, and drive. This enables shame-bound affects, drives, and interpersonal needs to become validated, actively embraced, and eventually integrated as distinguishable parts of a coherent self.

Learning a precise language of the self is a vital tool for dissolving shame binds. Learning a language for how the self functions, as a self, creates inner mastery and competence, thereby enhancing overall effectiveness in living. Having an accurate language equally fosters the increasing differentiation of the self. This is an essential developmental task.

DEFENDING SCRIPTS

Defending scripts must be focused on directly in order to be made fully conscious. Clients then can begin to regain the choice over engaging or releasing them. Defending scripts, as armor for the self, will be let go only gradually, once trust is more firmly established.

Consider Ann, who would talk in our sessions about how she "vented" and "stored" her feelings. She "vented" them into a particular place so she did not have to experience them. Ann felt as if she was squeezing her feelings into a can, actually squeezing her own self shut. This is what she meant by "venting" her feelings away somewhere. When we explored the source of this defending script, Ann remembered locking herself in the bathroom or into her bedroom as a child whenever she felt upset. At the same time she would squeeze her fists tight and also hold her breath. This was how she learned to suppress crying, initially, and then all affect.

Another example. Marty's main defense was simply to *talk about* his feelings without actually *feeling* them. When I remarked upon this during our fourth session, he readily agreed, but quickly rambled on. He said he wanted to please me.

"You don't ever have to get healthier; you can even stay neurotic," I answered.

This surprised him.

"I didn't expect that." Then he said he had run out of things to say.

"That's good," I countered. "Now we can get somewhere."

Then he wanted me to ask him questions, but I said I would not. We spent about 15 anxious minutes with Marty remaining silent and feeling uncomfortable because he had no more words to hide behind. He felt acutely self-conscious and then he began to cry. Later, he said that he felt he had discovered a part of himself he had never seen before.

One final example. Robert presented a curious posture in therapy: he always wore a smile. His smile had the distinct appearance of a mask. Whenever he expressed anything the least bit painful or distressing, his mask-like smile instantly appeared. I never commented about the smile, since doing so very likely would have made him too self-conscious, but I continued to observe it carefully. Robert also had great difficulty with eye contact. Rarely would he look me in the eyes, and he appeared visibly uncomfortable whenever he did so. Usually, he just averted his eyes and stared at the floor. His shame was too great.

Robert was aware of his inability to sustain eye contact. He had even been criticized for it by others. After he raised the topic with me, we began to explore its meaning over the course of the next several sessions. And we began to explore how he felt when he was with me.

During that session, I moved my chair closer and looked directly into his eyes. Immediately, Robert looked away. Then I invited him to look into my face.

"There's nothing inside of you that I will feel ashamed of," I said to him.

"It's like . . . I have to wear this mask all the time," he answered, still avoiding my eyes.

"I've noticed the mask, this smile of yours," I replied. "Do you remember when you first put on the mask?"

He pondered silently. Then the memory returned.

"It happened when I was 6 years old. I was home with my grandmother, waiting for my mother to return from work. That afternoon my dog ran outside and was hit by a car. My dog died and I cried and cried. I had lost my best friend. That dog was everything to me. I must have cried for hours. But I knew I had to stop crying before my mother returned. "

"Why was that?"

"I knew I couldn't ever *look* sad or upset. It always made her very tense and annoyed with me. That was when I first put on my smile— and I never again took it off. I always wear it, like a mask."

ILLUSTRATING THE DEVELOPMENTAL PROCESS: A CASE STUDY INVOLVING AN ADDICTION SYNDROME

The following case illustrates essential features of the developmental process we have been considering. Michael sought therapy following an acute anxiety attack. At our first interview, he was able to identify the following triggers: he recently turned 35; he had just moved back to the United States in order to begin work at a new firm after spending several years in Europe; he felt acutely self-conscious in his first business meeting; finally, he had always known there was something missing inside of him and now he wanted to learn how to care.

Michael described a profoundly painful, shaming history. His father was very critical of him and was physically abusive as well. One day his father actually had told Michael he never loved him; Michael was an adolescent at the time. His father was also an alcoholic, and Michael remembered always feeling deeply ashamed of his father because of his alcoholism. He also felt ashamed of both parents because of their lower-class manners. For years he had been living a lie to mask his shameful past.

At our first session, I gave him specific tools to enable his competence: I invited him to *observe* consciously his disabling "anxiety attacks.'"Michael was feeling so overwhelmed by terror that he was unable to function. His prior image of himself as strong, capable, and always "on top of things" had been shattered. Now he was reduced to panic. His terror had to be brought under inner conscious control. That was our first priority. He needed to feel he was able to do something between our sessions, to act, and not feel helpless. The tool I offered him, *consciously observing* his anxiety, would enable him to detach from his terror and thereby let go of it. His fear would be reduced by observing it. I also told him I would be available to him between sessions; he could call me whenever he needed to.

After two months of therapy, he called one night in crisis and came over later that evening. He had quit alcohol, cigarettes, and tranquilizers all at once. Michael went cold turkey. The focus of his anxiety was again a fear of having a heart attack. His deep emotional pain, which had been suppressed for years, now manifested as tension and pain experienced in his left chest. I pressed him to experience consciously his inner pain, but he was afraid he would die or go crazy if he did. Then he began to cry, and he cried almost hysterically, burying his head in his hands.

Michael felt lost inside, imagining a wall or curtain as he later described it. Behind it were scenes, faces, his father, and all his shameful acts and lies. I simply sat beside him, held him close, with an arm around him, as he cried and gradually released his pain.

Later, he felt like a weight had lifted and he knew that I had been right. I told him about how it had been for me once when I was turned down for promotion years before. But the pain in his chest suddenly returned. Intuitively, I placed my hand over his heart and the pain instantly went away.

Michael said, "I need to be touched," as he pressed his hand over mine.

I told him it was a human need and when no one was around he could imagine me there, my hand on his chest. I told him I felt honored to share his pain, but he could not believe this.

"I'm passing on what was given to me," I countered. Then he was able to accept it.

Michael called the next night. Now the pain was no longer localized over his heart. He felt it in his feet or abdomen or head, but as a pressure, not a pain. He needed to know I was there, to touch base with me. I told him to feel into the pain whenever it resurfaced. Now he knew that the pain was emotional: his affect had been suppressed and this produced backed-up affect, as discussed earlier, which subsequently became converted into somatic expression.

Michael gradually started allowing himself to need me and depend on me more and more. He also was able to remain dry, not having taken valium or alcohol for some time.

Several weeks later, Michael called and again asked to see me. I arranged to meet him at my office. He had been feeling agitated because of a realization he had had the previous day that terrified him. Michael had tried to phone me earlier, but when there was no answer he was afraid I had left town.

Michael had been home for a visit and while there had tried to talk honestly with his mother. Maybe it was a mistake, but he had to try, he said. His mother was unable to understand him and he felt acutely disappointed by her response. He even cried with her, but felt there was no one at home to depend on, no one anywhere, except me. He said he was scared by how much he needed me now.

"Don't let me down," he whispered to me, tears in his eyes.

"I am in this too. I *will* go with you and I *won't* abandon you," I answered gently.

He relaxed, seeming reassured for the moment.

His entire way of being as a person in the world had cracked. Now he needed to depend on another human being for his emotional life and this terrified him.

"When have you allowed yourself to *need* another human being as you now need me?" I asked him.

"Not in over 20 years," he answered, looking off into another time, another place inside.

While at home, he also spent time with his father. Michael knew before he went that he would end up drinking with him, though he had remained alcohol-free for several weeks. After he had left his parents' home, and was alone again, the realization hit him: *I'm just like my father!*

He began to see his father in himself. That "internalized other," that identification image based on his father, at last became conscious. Then he realized when it had happened. He was 12 years old when he began to realize he was no longer a boy but a man.

Michael's body was developing and he had his first ejaculation. That was when he began modeling himself directly after his father, copying his mannerisms, internalizing his attitudes, calling himself "Mike," instead of using his boyhood name "Micky," because it seemed more grown up. At this point he actually became *Mike* and actively persecuted the part of him that experienced feelings and needs. He locked little *Micky* away deep inside. One part of Michael was now beginning to treat other parts of him exactly the way his father had always behaved toward him.

Now Michael was able to actually see this pattern enacted in his family, and the analogous pattern reenacted within him. This was the source of his self-hatred: contempt, first at the hands of his father, now from the enemy within.

I told him about the *internal saboteur* [Fairbairn's (1966, p. 101) original term], an effective metaphor for the splitting process. I named his saboteur *Mike,* the part of him allied with his father, the part of him he has unfortunately mistaken for his real self. This was the part that became split-off as *Mike* when he was 12 years old.

Michael initially felt even more confused at the thought of different partial selves coexisting within him. "If I'm not *Mike* or little *Micky,* then who am I? Oh, God, now there are three of me!" We laughed.

Later, he was able to see the hope of it—a vision of moving beyond feeling trapped by his present identity, even as little *Micky* felt trapped by *Mike.*

He realized that *Mike,* the part of him identified with his father, would not let little *Micky* come out.

"Men aren't supposed to cry or to need," he added.

Michael had internalized many crippling injunctions about being a person and particularly about being a man. These scripts reproduced his shame. Then I gave him a tool. I asked him to observe the part of him inside that feels like his father, that he long ago named *Mike.*

"Neither agree with the *voice* nor disagree with it: simply observe it consciously," I explained. "Hold a part of yourself back inside as a friendly observer. And keep a journal to record your observations, and whatever those injunctions are. Then try to recall the original scenes in your family where you first experienced them."

Over the next three months, various turbulent conflicts surfaced. Michael would periodically resort to alcohol or cocaine and then become consumed by shame and self-contempt. Expression of pain struggled against suppression of pain. His distress-shame bind resurfaced over and over, as did his intense need for me, which oscillated with his equally intense terror of needing. Contempt for me became a defense against needing. Trust fluctuated with mistrust.

Michael then missed a session, having become drunk the night before, which caused him to oversleep. He called to apologize. Several days later he felt consumed once more by shame and self-contempt and the old fear of having a heart attack. He called, finally, feeling overwhelmed by his distress and need. I arranged to see him that evening. Michael knew he needed to cry, struggled with it, then asked me to assist. I moved closer and sat beside him and held him close. Slowly, he went into his pain.

To create an *entrance,* I named his wounds: "Your father called you sissy. Your father would trip you and make you fall. And he once told you he never loved you." I voiced these out loud for him.

Spontaneously, Michael went into active imagery. Suddenly, he saw little *Micky* hiding under something, afraid to come out. He clung tight to me for some time.

Michael said he was too afraid to cry by himself. He feared the dreaded consequences of crying, the humiliation scenes with his father.

"When you hold me," he added, "the fear goes away. Then it's safe to cry."

We were able to release some of his backed-up distress affect and the shame bound to it. He cried once more when I later spontaneously drew him close. This time he let go deeper, his whole body cried, actually heaving in sobs.

Later, I offered him observations about his addiction cycle. I explained how the buildup of incompletely suppressed distress and shame increased both his anxiety, which manifested as a fear of dying or having a heart attack, and his fear of the dreaded consequences of expression of need and affect, the humiliation embedded in earlier scenes with his father. Intense inner conflict then raged. He drank alcohol in order to release the inhibition of affect. While he did experience partial release, later he was overwhelmed by shame and self-contempt, often lasting several days. His reexperiencing of shame and self-contempt then further fueled the process.

Michael called me that day in the midst of the latest of these reenacted patterns, enabling me to observe his entire addiction cycle.

I also observed to Michael that he was teaching himself to *need* alcohol in order to reduce negative affect, particularly shame and distress. I suggested that he may have been feeling too good lately, having allowed himself to feel closer to me. His fear of dying had also disappeared. Michael's internal conflict over letting go into his inner pain had raged to the critical point.

After I offered him the above observations, we examined his last few binges. Michael recalled a prior *urge* experienced just before bingeing on alcohol that so far had eluded further differentiation. I told him that he needed to say "no" to the addiction in order to make that vague urge more conscious. Then he needed to observe it.

At a later session, Michael hinted about needing to be held. He said he had had his cry the previous Saturday, as if that were all he was entitled to. I simply held him and his body convulsed. He felt both pain and shame, and also intense shame about being held.

"It feels both strange and good," he later told me.

Michael said he needed me to hold him in order for him to experience the pain. I answered, "That's fine, but you can also learn to ask."

He cringed, whispering, "I'd feel too ashamed."

I held him again, answering, "I'm a better fix than alcohol." He laughed.

Michael relaxed into the pain, went deeper the second time. And he held me tight.

At another session, Michael recounted a recent visit home where he had a confrontation with his father. He finally was able to express to his father what he actually thought of him. They threatened one another physically and he left. Then Michael wrote his father a letter in which he voiced more about what he had missed from him. He also told his father he no longer looked to him as a father. For Michael this was an important developmental task: differentiation from father.

At the very next session, Michael pulled back emotionally and cut off from both himself and me. Then he told me he planned to drink that night; he was eyeing me for my reaction. I observed out loud about the cycle from needing and feeling to suppressing to drinking as a release.

"When you cut off inside, you also cut off from me," I reminded him. He was ambivalent but struggled to remain open.

What surfaced next was shame about his appearance, his intelligence, and his sexuality. At the end of that session, I told him I wanted him not to drink until our next meeting—to consciously resist it. This would make the process more conscious and break the pattern of his addiction cycle. He denied drinking was a problem, but then agreed that it was. Michael left that day having agreed to do as I had suggested.

Over the subsequent month, Michael became increasingly distant from me. He was resistant to further historical exploration and equally resistant to active imagery. He became more autonomous and independent. His drinking recurred and his use of cocaine increased, but these fluctuated with periods of abstinence. We were at an impasse.

I responded to our changed relationship in the fashion I have developed over the years: I became *detached* in order to observe both his patterns and our interactions. Finally, it occurred to me that I had taken sides against his addiction. This meant that I had become too invested in his not drinking, thereby reenacting his familial conflicts directly in our relationship.

At the following session I refocused in order for us to reconsider together what we had accomplished and where we were heading; and I openly acknowledged his real growth. I sided *with* his resistance and said I had been late in recognizing his independence. Only then were we able to reconnect. Once more, Michael felt me allied with him.

We continued on an as-need basis during the following summer. We had one or two sessions along with several telephone conversations, triggered by occasional anxiety reactions. Michael also became involved in a relationship with a woman. Now he was once again more anxious. There was also considerable pressure from his mother to visit home more often.

"What's wrong?" she would demand of him. Michael felt helpless to respond.

"The message you need to give is this," I answered. "Say, 'I will come home when *I* want to.' Be clear and direct." This relieved him greatly.

Michael's anxiety resurfaced that fall. Again, his inner conflict was increasing. I said to him, "There's a particular *scene* connected with it." I also acknowledged directly his actual "identity loss": loss of old patterns of behaving, loss of old defenses, loss of biological family. "Inevitably this creates confusion," I continued, "a sense of no longer knowing who one is." I pressed Michael about the scene and he began to open to it.

"I feel like something's covering me or holding me down," he answered. "It looks bloody, but there's no blood. It's all *red* somehow."

Michael repeated this once more, then added a further image. "I just saw something, and it terrified me. Like when I thought I was having a heart attack."

Then he ran from the vision, saying, "I can't see it!"

"Yes you can!" I insisted. "You pick yourself up and get right back on that horse!"

"All right, I will." Michael tried again, but could not focus the scene any clearer.

Later, he spontaneously said, "I feel like he's trying to kill me." That image terrified him and he asked me if it could have been true.

"Yes, in many different ways. He could have actually said it, or just facially *looked* it, or he could really have been out of control."

"It's my father," Michael finally admitted to himself.

Later, he described the scene as follows: "There's someone in it, and I'm in it." The rest remained shadowy.

Then, he had another spontaneous image: "I just felt like sucking my thumb."

"That's little *Micky*. Let yourself do it."

"I'm not ready for that. . . . Now I don't feel comfortable talking."

"Of course not. You feel ashamed of wanting to suck your thumb."

We ended it there. I told Michael to feel into the scene whenever it resurfaced, to visualize the scene vividly and reexperience all of the feelings embedded in the scene. I also reviewed for him how we first entered the scene: the *entrance* was the knot of tension in his chest; then feeling something covering him or holding him down; then the bloody sense, and finally, the color red. Michael remembered the entrance.

"We need to nurture ourselves," I added, "at all levels in order to heal shame. That means little *Micky* too."

Then, Michael asked me if I thought it was a good idea for him to join the Big Brother Program. He had been assigned a young boy to work with. I asked him if he thought he could manage the time.

"I can do it."

"Then, if you want to be a Big Brother, go ahead."

"I'll be able to do all the things I could never do as a child, like go to the circus." He laughed to cover his shame.

"There won't be just one little kid at the circus," I mused. He laughed again.

"I've done the same thing," I added. "Sometimes, I take the little boy still inside of me to the movies. When my two sons come along, I'll even say there are 'three kids' going today. And you can take little *Micky* places whether or not you take on the Big Brother role."

Michael's shame was on the path toward healing. His inner self was moving toward regrowth and reintegration. In the next chapter we will examine specific aspects of that process in depth.

HANDLING RESISTANCE IN THERAPY

There are various forms of resistance. One form is directed against exploration of the quality of early significant relationships. In order to overcome this, I attempt to interest clients in discovering exactly how their maladaptive patterns developed. I will comment offhandedly, "Either you just happened to get born this way, in which case we cannot do anything about it, or else they were learned somewhere, and usually not from strangers either." Eventually, curiosity wins out.

Silence during sessions typically has been viewed as resistance to therapeutic work. Generally, the affective source of silence is shame, which is the affect that causes the self to hide. Shame itself is an impediment to speech. In response to client silence, therapists must be prepared to approach directly, to actively engage their client not with questions but with speech. This is the case except when clients use words to distance themselves from their affect and to hide behind; then silence can be therapeutic. It is the therapist's task to build a bridge, and words can be its building blocks. Client silence is not a response to anxiety but to shame, and therapist silence will only intensify shame for the client. Shame additionally may be mixed with rage and so produce an angry silence, analogous to a shamed child who withdraws behind a closed door, refusing to relate.

Another form of resistance operates against experiencing the therapeutic relationship as genuine. I have said to many clients, "Only to the degree to which you experience our relationship as real will healing come about." Clients typically attempt to neutralize the therapeutic relationship in order to protect themselves against another disappointment, another failure. Those clients who are seen in private practice, and therefore pay a fee for psychotherapy, can neutralize the relationship because of its fee-for-service basis. Others who are seen through a clinic where services are free or at reduced cost also can neutralize the relationship by perceiving it as the therapist's job. Trusting a relationship again is that dangerous.

Unwillingness to relinquish old patterns, old scripts, is another form of resistance. Those scripted patterns of action and reaction have become a principal component of identity. Clients cling to old scripts, however unsatisfying, because giving them up is equivalent to a loss of identity. Only reliance on the therapeutic relationship enables a client to relinquish the old while struggling to embrace the new.

After a period of therapeutic engagement, when some resolution has occurred, inner harmony may set in for awhile. Clinicians call it a flight into health, a sign of resistance to deeper therapeutic work. Indeed it may be that. Following intensive confrontation with one's inner conflicts, there comes a time to rest from further struggle. A measure of inner peace has been won, the quality of life has improved just enough, and resistance to further pain increases. My usual response to this particular form of resistance is to suggest to my client that we stop therapy for the time being. Rather than confront their resistance head-on, I have found it much more effective to sidestep it. By suggesting that we take a break from therapy, we part as allies, not as adversaries. The break itself allows any resistance to evaporate, since there is nothing opposing it. Once their resistance vanishes and inner conflict resurfaces, clients are willing, and ready, to resume therapy. Since we parted with the idea of resuming active therapy at a later time, clients do not typically experience their return as a loss of face, a personal failure. Instead their return was expected. I find this approach to handling this particular form of resistance more efficient and also considerably more effective.

TERMINATION OF THE THERAPY RELATIONSHIP VERSUS SEPARATION FROM THE THERAPIST

My practice of handling resistance brings us to the question of termination. The form of therapy I have been developing involves a commitment of availability. That means being available to clients between our appointed sessions, since crises do not typically conform to schedule. Such open availability also is a more suitable analog of parenting. When clients have regressed, they are analogous to young children who might awaken in the night from a nightmare; the client's nightmare, however, is typically a conscious one. My offer of availability means that clients are free to call me any time of the day or night. The only thing I guarantee is that I will be honest with them: I will only talk with them when I am able to do so. I will never give ambivalently, never say yes when I really mean no. Hence, I will not permit them to impose on me, which is one of their deepest fears based on prior experience. I do not become resentful, because I am able to set clear and firm limits without anger. If I am unable to talk when they call, I first inquire as to the nature of their distress, and then I indicate when I can return their call. What I offer is to try to be available for them to the best of my human ability, I fully expect to occasionally be a disappointment, to make mistakes, to misjudge their needs. And if I can make mistakes, while our relationship survives, then they can make mistakes as well without feeling lesser for them.

Being available to clients between sessions, particularly in the evenings or during the night, is often essential for shame-based individuals, whether presumed borderline or not. It is important to allow them to depend, to permit them to identify, which will actually foster their increasing differentiation as a self and their eventual separation from the therapist.

On occasion it may be necessary to lend some weight to the process, however. One young man with whom I had been working for six months came from a family with a mother who had been intrusive and close-binding, critical and demanding. His father had been distant and emotionally unavailable. Every independent action or decision of his was questioned or criticized by them, leading him to internalize the identical pattern. He was approaching the end of his freshman year at college and began to agonize over his summer plans. I intended for us to take a break from therapy for the summer and had told him so. In fact, he had known that when we began therapy six months earlier. His struggle was over whether he should return home for the summer as his parents wished or remain on campus and work, living on his own. I told him I thought that returning to his home environment, which invariably reproduced his shame, was not desirable from my point of view. I encouraged him to consider every alternative, including working in his home town, if that was his decision, but not living at home. He agonized for weeks over what to do, wanting desperately to make the break, but equally fearing the separation. Then he asked me if I would continue to see him regularly if he decided to stay on campus. I thought about it carefully. After it occurred to me three times, which is my usual guideline for timing observations, I said to him that I would not see him regularly, but that I would be around if he needed something; he was certainly free to call, but summer was mine. He became enraged at me, and extremely demanding. He tried every argument to convince me to change my mind: I was abandoning him when he needed me the most; he would literally die if left on his own. That was his deepest fear: he was terrified that he would actually die if he separated. My response was clear, "You need to find out if that is true."

His conflict raged through the final days of the academic year. Until the very last I still had no idea what he would decide. When he called me the next week to tell me he had found a summer job and an apartment to share, and was remaining on campus in spite of tremendous opposition from his parents, I was truly delighted. His will to health had won out. My belief in him had apparently given him the courage to separate. And my having stood firm against all his demands gave him a model for behaving similarly with his parents, who told him they would disown him if he moved onto campus for the summer.

Not only had he separated from his parents that summer, but he grew in confidence and inner security. He remained in contact with me throughout the summer, calling about once a week. He discovered, as he later put it, that not only did he not die, but he grew measurably stronger. When we resumed active therapy that fall, he was a changed young man.

Separation is a developmental task that is directly embedded in the nature of the therapeutic process. Identification and differentiation (encompassing separation and mastery) are equally embedded. But termination is quite a different matter. Separation and termination are by no means equivalent. Separation from the client's family is an important therapeutic goal. Within the therapeutic relationship, eventual separation also is a necessary outcome. However, separation from the therapist does not necessarily translate into termination of the relationship between client and therapist. While their relationship will change, it need not end in some fixed and final sense.

The form of psychotherapy I have been developing is one that includes periods of intensive work alternating with appropriately timed breaks. When I sense the time for such a break approaching, I usually suggest to clients that we stop therapy for awhile, knowing we can resume when they experience further need. When clients voice their readiness to take a break, I typically agree with them because doing otherwise would interfere with their differentiating from me. Questioning their decision to break off therapy, or interpreting it as resistance, would communicate that I doubted their ability to function independently. It would shame them for wanting to be separate. When we consider taking a break from therapy, it is always in the context of continuing on an as-need basis. Clients will often recontact me when issues resurface, when they need to resume active therapeutic work, when an immediate crisis occurs, when good news happens, or when they want to reexperience interpersonal connection with me.

There are times when particular clients actually move away. Then termination in the usual sense applies. Even in those cases, however, there need not be a final end to the relationship. I have remained in contact with certain clients over both time and distance, if that has been *their* wish.

Termination is a flexible concept, and it is more accurately understood as separation. How the process actually occurs varies markedly from client to client. Some leave feeling grateful, expressing what they have received. Some leave saddened, aware of their impending loss. Others bring gifts, openly expressing their appreciation, and how those gifts are received is important. Certain clients leave matter-of-factly, as if nothing consequential had occurred. And some inevitably leave angry. I have learned to allow clients to leave therapy, to separate, in whatever ways *they* need to.

Individuals proceed through therapy in their own unique way. How they separate and eventually conclude therapy is equally unique. Separation is a process, and is essential to the broader developmental process that psychotherapy must be designed to mobilize.

Eight

Identity Regrowth and Healing Shame

Frustration of his desire to be loved as a person and to have his love accepted is the greatest trauma that a child can experience; and it is this trauma above all that creates fixations in the various forms of infantile sexuality to which a child is driven to resort in an attempt to compensate by substitutive satisfactions for the failure of his emotional relationships with his outer objects. Fundamentally these substitutive satisfactions. . . all represent relationships with internalized objects, to which the individual is compelled to turn in default of a satisfactory relationship with objects in the outer world.

W. R. D. FAIRBAIRN
Psychoanalytic Studies of the Personality

How the self actually functions in the present must be made fully conscious. Here we are concerned not with historical exploration per se, not with the developmental roots of dysfunction, not with the therapeutic relationship itself, not even with other relationships outside of therapy. Instead, the focus is on the *self's relationship with the self.* How the self actively, currently relates to the self must be attended to. That is a direct therapeutic task. Internalized patterns that undermine the self must become fully conscious and then actively relinquished or replaced. The specific focus here is on identity scripts, disowning, and splitting. The

199

therapeutic aim is to facilitate identity regrowth and healing shame, the eventual reintegration of the self. To accomplish that end, the required therapeutic process includes a number of vital dimensions.

CONSCIOUS DIFFERENTIATION OF IDENTITY SCRIPTS

Increasing differentiation of the self is a developmental task. It is also a therapeutic objective. *Conscious differentiation* must be worked for actively by the client and must be guided by the therapist. In order to make any pattern conscious, we begin by observing it. I invite clients to pay attention to how they treat themselves, how they behave inside. Observing *inner voices* becomes an important entrance to the scene. I ask clients to imagine holding back a part inside as a friendly observer, which creates a conscious *center.* By observing the impact of inner voices, how they make the client feel, we can begin to name them. Naming patterns accurately is important because names create tools, enhance inner power, and illuminate inner states. They provide clues to the past as well as gateways to release and change. Therapists must recognize and distinguish *self-blame, comparison making,* and *self-contempt,* and also teach clients how to do so. These governing negative identity scripts, which are embedded in governing scenes, are then enabled to become conscious.

Consider Steve. During one session he offhandedly mentioned the things he should be doing or was supposed to do. This clued me in to the presence of his inner voices. Steve agreed that he heard a voice inside always admonishing him to do or be something. I suggested that he observe the voice over the next week, neither agreeing with it nor disagreeing with it. He was simply to observe it consciously and then record in his journal whatever the voice said.

At our next session, Steve came in visibly agitated. He brought in a notebook and immediately began describing the voice. It repeatedly accused him of things he had done in the past. Steve was obviously uncomfortable and was experiencing acute shame about these past deeds. It took him some 15 minutes before he actually was able to recount any of them. I moved my chair closer to his and actively encouraged him to face his shame. He could not look at me while he spoke and often stammered, struggling against his shame to speak the forbidden words.

What finally emerged was a series of sexual scenes involving peers, all infused with shame. The first involved mutual touching with a girl at age 7. The next occurred at age 8 when he was engaged in sexual play with an 8-year-old girl who was visiting. They were fondling each other and made some attempts at intercourse, but what happened next was critical; their 16-year-old male babysitter walked in and said, "I'll show you how it's really done." He took them into the parents' bedroom and forced the young girl to have intercourse with him. It was extremely painful for her and Steve remembers simply standing there helpless, watching the entire scene. The babysitter made them both promise not to tell anyone. Afterwards, Steve remembers comforting the girl in his arms, feeling that it was all his fault.

The next scene occurred when Steve was 11. This one involved a 14-year-old female babysitter who encouraged Steve to masturbate her, which he did. This left him feeling guilty.

When Steve was 12, he began engaging in sexual play with a boy his own age. This behavior continued over a period of several months until one day they kissed each other. Then abruptly they stopped all sexual activities because of fear and shame. From that point on Steve began defending against his same-sex sexual fantasies. He responded to such images by telling himself he was not supposed to feel that way about other males.

The next scene occurred when Steve was 14 and involved the older brother of a friend, a man some 30 years of age. The older man seduced Steve. Their sexual activities left Steve feeling acutely disgusted with himself. That was his last scene involving another male.

When Steve was 18, a woman wanted to have sex with him, but he refused. His first attempt at intercourse with a woman occurred two years later. This time he was impotent.

These scenes revealed a consistent pairing of sexuality with shame and disgust. The scenes became reactivated by Steve's *inner voice,* which continued in the present to blame his current disappointments or failings on his past "sins." These scenes were also the source of his continuing feelings of sexual inadequacy. Making love with a woman invariably reactivated the old scene of the babysitter forcing himself on the little girl while he stood by helplessly watching. Recovering Steve's governing scenes was the first step in a lengthy process and observing his contemptuous and blaming inner voices created the vital entrance to those scenes.

RECOVERING GOVERNING SCENES

Therapist and client must work together actively in order to *recover governing scenes.* Self-observation of inner voices is an important means to that end. This process involves the client asking whose voice is speaking inside or who the voice feels like. I will suggest to clients that it is not their own voice they hear speaking, or, if it feels like theirs, that it once belonged to a different face. In order to directly engage imagery I ask clients to imagine putting a face to the voice. I invite clients to attempt to recall situations when something similar might have been experienced. It is considerably easier to let go of an old pattern once its origins are known. Furthermore, the affect embedded in those original scenes is released when the scene becomes conscious, and this release of affect is central to the healing process necessary for resolving shame.

A young man in therapy began observing his inner voices in the above manner. He came in one session and said, "The voices are always blaming me or judging me for my past sins. They tell me that's why I'm such a miserable person now. " After further probing, he recounted a series of childhood and adolescent aggressive scenes with peers, teachers, and parents that left his angry feelings fused with shame, fear, and disgust. Observing his inner voices became an unexpected entrance to these governing scenes.

THERAPY AS AN IDENTIFICATION RELATIONSHIP: CREATING NEW SCRIPTS AND SCENES

Psychotherapy, as parenting, proceeds by identification. Offering an *identification relationship* translates into offering a model for a new way of relating to oneself, one that is active in promoting inner security. We do this through offering a genuine and honest human relationship that provides for some of our client's deepest needs, caring and respect above all. Because maladaptive patterns became internalized through identification, new experiences of identification between client and therapist heal shame, instill hope, and free our client from the shackles of the past. Identification experiences also provide essential models for new patterns of inner relating, and an effective model for change. When a client is experiencing shame, identification provides healing for the self. These are critical moments in the course of therapy when clients *need* to know their therapists on the inside, to feel identified with them, to feel *one*.

Not only are we engaging the identification process, but, more important, we are directing it for the specific purpose of creating new scenes. Another way to accomplish this is by encouraging clients, when appropriate, to imagine their therapist actually inside with them. By "taking inside" their therapist, clients are enabled to experience the therapeutic relationship as actually present within the self. Through imagery clients are actively internalizing their therapist as a new inner ally, a strong and positive "internalized other." Because imagery is directly engaged, this process generates new scenes of positive affect derived from the therapeutic relationship.

In order to replace the dialogue component of negative identity scripts, clients must create new self-affirming dialogues to replace old ones, and therapists can offer actual words and phrases to substitute. A self-blame script can be replaced with giving oneself the inalienable human right to make mistakes, for example, four times every day. A self-contempt script can be replaced with active respect for self. And a comparison-making script can be replaced with openly valuing the particular attributes one was about to devalue. By further imagining their therapist inside actually speaking these new, self-affirming dialogues, imagery becomes activated in addition to language.

Engaging language is only one dimension of the process; the more fundamental dimensions are imagery and affect. Clients must have new words to say to themselves; they must experience new, positive feelings toward themselves; and they must create new scenes to gradually replace their old scenes. This process creates new scenes of caring and respect for self, positive affect invested in self, by actively engaging affect, imagery, and language. All three processes must be directly engaged in the change process, not just language. Therapists must enable clients to behave toward themselves as worthy and adequate beyond question.

REOWNING DISOWNED PARTS OF THE SELF

Psychotherapy must aim toward *reowning disowned parts of the self.* Earlier developmental phases of the self, for example, the child self or adolescent self, can be recontacted directly through *active imagery.* The boy or girl locked away in shame can be comforted and grown up through imagery. Therapists must teach clients how to actively nurture their inner child self or adolescent self. Teaching and modeling self-forgiveness are equally vital. For clients who have difficulty with imagery, I suggest using an old photograph with a full-face view to deepen contact with their inner child self; gazing at the photograph before employing imagery creates an entrance to the scene.

Letting go of dysfunctional scripts and replacing them with self-affirming ones must be an active, daily process. It requires commitment and conscious effort. Clients must continue to *consciously monitor* their old scripts, keeping alert for the situations most likely to activate them. Replacing the old inner voice with a new voice must continually engage affect, imagery, and language.

The way to heal inner strife and division is through consciously reowning disowned parts of the self. Reowning is also a way of directly reparenting the self. There are both interpersonal and intrapsychic dimensions to the reowning process, which the following case illustrates.

A Case of Shyness

Consider Ron, who becomes shy whenever he is interested in a woman. One evening, we were exploring his shyness. He mentioned a woman in his dance class, where the assignment was to pair up to choreograph a routine. He wanted to ask her, but felt too shy to approach. He joked about hinting when he saw her next.

"No, ask her directly," I said. "Say to her, 'I want to work with you.'"
Ron sprang up from his chair.
"I can't do that!" he exclaimed. "I'd feel too ashamed."

I asked him to imagine himself actually living out the dreaded scene. He went into active imagery, imagining himself approaching the woman of interest. After several quiet moments, he said, "You know, it's not *her* reaction I'm afraid of. It's the reaction of *other* people watching." Much later he said, when he had imagined doing it, he heard the sound of laughter from behind.

I followed up with, "Were there scenes of approaching girls during adolescence with peers laughing?" That was my hypothesis, but I was wrong.

As he entered imagery once more, the memory finally came. One day when he was about 12, he was at home and the girl next door had been over visiting, but had just gone outside.

"You really like her," his mother said to him.

"Yes, better than the girls at school," Ron answered.

Just at that moment, Ron's father walked past, *behind* Ron. "I don't believe it!" he muttered. Walking down the hallway, his father then called out in a mocking, sing-song voice, "Ronny has a girlfriend! Ronny has a girlfriend! Ronny has a girlfriend!"

Over and over, his father chanted. Ron never again asked out a girl.

All that had remained with him was the auditory, or language, component of the scene: *father's laughter.* Whenever he wanted to approach a woman, he heard the sound of laughter *behind* him. This reactivated the scene, which then paralyzed him with shame.

Along with the memory came a flood of affect: shame, distress, wracking pain, as well as rage fused with disgust at his father. He sobbed and I held him close as we put words to his rage, shame, and pain. When we were through, Ron said to me, "Thanks, Dad." The full spectrum of affects that have been defended against by shame need to be recovered, consciously reexperienced, and fully released in order for the scene to be assimilated.

Then I asked him to go into active imagery once more. I wanted him to relive the scene, but this time repair it, heal it somehow. I suggested he talk to that adolescent boy immediately following the ridiculing and actually become the loving and respecting father to himself that he had missed. He was to visualize that adolescent self inside and then talk to him, *father* him.

Ron emerged from the reparenting imagery feeling more whole. Since he was heading for dance class immediately following our therapy session, I gave him a further assignment. I invited him to approach several women in class about pairing up. After each attempt, he was to imagine this new scene of reparenting his adolescent self. He later called it his "Ronny boy fantasy." I reminded him to be sure to engage imagery as well as affect and language. My client continued actively with reparenting imagery for the next year whenever he felt powerless, disappointed, discouraged, or depressed. Though shame eventually became healed for Ron, the process was a lengthy one.

A week after we retrieved the shyness scene, a suicidal depression hit. Continuing to contact and reparent the 12-year-old boy inside helped Ron endure it. He now had a tool, a way of healing those feelings of alienation and worthlessness. He also reached out to two friends and they responded to his need. The depression was triggered by seeing a movie that prompted the realization: "I am alone and I'll always be alone because there's something wrong with *me.*" Ron's deeper internalized/magnified shame had now become fully conscious.

Several weeks later, a situation at a party with a girl he was becoming interested in triggered off another depressive episode. He watched her kissing another man and immediately went into a shame spiral though he had never let her know he had deep feelings for her.

I sensed a pattern with his mother, not just his father, a pattern involving emotional betrayal.

"Who had your mother preferred over you?" I asked him.

This oriented us to further investigative work. I also told him I thought the depressions were coming more frequently now and were more intensely felt as well. That meant he was getting *healthier,* I told him. Ron grimaced, and we laughed.

Another depressive slide came, this one after he spoke to the woman directly about his feelings for her and she reacted with reluctance to their becoming involved. The depression returned two days later and this time he felt intense pain.

"It hurts! It hurts!" he screamed. "When will it ever stop hurting!"

Ron had screamed this the previous night while at home and he screamed it once more in my office.

Then his depression began to lift and Ron once again became reintegrated. But several other depressive episodes recurred shortly thereafter, each triggered by an infatuation-rejection cycle in relation to different women he desired romantically. The most recent episode was triggered by discovering that he was sterile. This news shattered his dream of having children. And each dip into shame also brought up new scenes involving Ron and his mother.

Then Ron called in crisis one night. He needed to see me, still in pain over his sterility. He asked me to hold him, saying, "I need to be held." He came over and sat beside me, crying bitterly as I held him close.

The next situation occurred when he was standing in the foyer of a restaurant. He glanced around and noticed a woman he was interested in. He observed her laughing and talking to someone else. Immediately, Ron began to spiral into shame. We carefully examined the various scenes that had triggered his depressive spirals. The scenes typically involved a woman he liked but did not have, a woman he observed laughing and talking with another man, both of whom were at some distance from him.

At our next session, Ron was feeling very depressed, hopeless, and lethargic. I asked him to go into active imagery and imagine interacting with the woman in question. Immediately, Ron experienced pain and shame, which he resisted. I urged him to feel into it. With my active encouragement his feelings deepened. Then I held him while he sobbed. He said he could not see it.

"You can," I answered, "and it'll hurt until you *see* it."

Ron reentered active imagery. Suddenly, he was transported back in childhood to a particular scene with his parents. He saw himself crying while his mother stood by, laughing at him for crying. She was about to leave and his father was standing further down the hallway. His mother went up to his father and then they were both laughing and talking together. They were ridiculing *him*.

"That's when I learned to bottle it all up." Ron finally said, after his tears subsided.

Ron emerged from the imagery experience feeling reintegrated.

"It feels like being abandoned or betrayed," he whispered. "It's like she's agreeing with my Dad about me; they're making fun of me, mocking me. How cruel."

Ron had finally recovered another governing scene at the root of his depressions. He was able to reexperience and assimilate his shame and distress as well as his intense rage and disgust at his parents. Throughout this entire period, Ron actively utilized inner child imagery on a daily basis. It became a vital tool for coping with his depressive bouts. And he utilized our relationship as well whenever he needed to feel secure.

DISINTERNALIZING IDENTIFICATION IMAGES

In addition to reowning disowned parts of the self, the overly severe, internalized parental image must be actively *disinternalized.* Our client may have to learn to *reject* (via disgust, dissmell, or nausea) both the actual bad parent and the internalized representation of that bad parent. When I invite clients to *imagine* me inside of them or to hear my *voice* inside, I am directing the identification process in order for them to internalize a new, positive identification image. At times, I will invite them to listen to my voice instead of their old critical, blaming, or otherwise negative voices. I encourage clients by letting them know that we can kick out their parental voices and images because together we are stronger. Imagery and affect are directly engaged in this process as well as language in order to dislodge their old poisonous, internalized parental images.

HEALING SHAME: THE PROCESS IN REVIEW

Shame becomes stored in memory in the form of scenes. All of the affect embedded in the original experience becomes imprinted directly in the scene. It is those scenes that then govern the self's further development as well as future behavior. Scenes of shame become impediments to self-esteem and to intimacy.

In order to heal shame, those scenes must first be recovered and made fully conscious. Often scenes operate at the periphery of awareness or remain completely obscured. The challenge is regaining access to the scene, discovering an entrance.

Next the scene must be relived as completely as possible, thereby fully releasing all of the affect embedded in the scene. This means reexperiencing not only shame but all other affects as well. Through this process the affects become assimilated consciously.

Governing scenes then must be reshaped or repaired by actively engaging the identical processes that produced them: affect, imagery, and language. Governing scenes cannot be eliminated. They cannot be disconnected or erased, nor can the mind be reprogrammed like a computer. But governing scenes can be reshaped by creating new scenes with positive affect.

When clients remain in shame-based relationships *in the present,* they also need to take back the power directly in those relationships. This is not historical exploration, but action in the present. The aim is to change those relationships in order for clients to maintain their rightful half of the power. We will return to this dimension of therapy in chapter 9.

Finally, clients may also need to face the actual situation once more and overcome shame directly in the scene. Accomplishing that through imagery may not suffice. When shame is consistently activated in or by a specific situation, that situation itself has to be faced. Enduring the scene while overcoming shame is central to gaining eventual mastery.

In addition to working with scenes, it is critical to actively reown disowned parts of the self, as already discussed. Earlier developmental phases of the self can be directly recontacted through active imagery. The self is an evolving integration, a collection of selves beginning with the earliest child self and progressing through the adolescent self, on to the maturing phases. Each phase must be made fully conscious and then actively embraced, owned as an inherent part of an integrated self.

Central to this process are self-nurturance and self-forgiveness. Clients must be aided to make peace with themselves. They must be taught how to be tender and loving and always forgiving toward themselves. These are essential elements of the reowning process.

The way to heal shame is through consciously reowning and actively embracing—actually reparenting—those rejected orphans within the self. Reowning and reparenting need to be experienced *interpersonally* through restoring the interpersonal bridge directly in the therapeutic relationship. Reowning and reparenting must also be experienced *from within* in order to complete the healing process. This is accomplished through reparenting imagery, which is considered further below.

There is considerable therapeutic value in physical contact, touching, and holding. This is true in regard to the relationship between client and therapist, but it is equally true in regard to reparenting imagery. Both the actual therapeutic relationship and the self's inner relationship must create an analog of parenting.

In addition to touching and holding, new experiences of identification are essential. Therapeutic healing is a direct outgrowth of identification. Through identification shame is transcended. This must be experienced directly in the relationship between client and therapist, and it must also be experienced directly within the self.

Reparenting Imagery

Imagery has received extensive examination in the psychological literature both directly and as it relates to hypnosis. I have neither studied nor been trained in hypnosis. I do not conceive of my particular use of imagery, whether free imagery or guided imagery, as a form of hypnosis. However, the *reparenting imagery* process I have developed has been occasionally likened to hypnosis or to hypnotic regression by individuals either observing or experiencing it.

Theoretically, I do not require the concept of hypnosis in order to account for the phenomena observed. I prefer to describe the process that I am directly activating more simply: it is *imagery*. The concept of imagery is both a necessary and sufficient explanation of the phenomenon. I am working directly with imagery in the sense that Jacob Bronowski (1971, 1973) uses the term and in the sense that Silvan Tomkins (1962, 1979) conceives of it.

Certainly, there are parallels between my use of imagery and Milton Erickson's (1954a, 1964, 1979, 1983) hypnotic techniques. There are obvious parallels between my approach and that of other clinicians. Rather than extensively discuss imagery or hypnosis per se, I intend to illuminate the application of imagery specifically to the process of healing shame. This is a direct application of the identical process through which governing scenes of shame first become internalized. Imagery is engaged in order to repair or reshape those governing scenes.

Experiencing identification within the self is accomplished directly through imagery. This process is not employed as a technique, but instead grows out of the therapeutic relationship itself. In order to make imagery a shared experience between client and therapist, it is useful for the therapist to participate directly. Mutuality maintains the relationship bridge. Therefore, I always tell my clients that I will close my eyes too and that I will not peek while their eyes are closed. To illustrate reparenting imagery, I have developed the following pattern, which is adapted for each individual client.

> Close your eyes and I will close mine. And I won't peek. Imagine you are descending a staircase. It's dark and quiet. When you reach the bottom, you find yourself standing at the end of a hallway. At the other end is a light. Walk toward the light. When you reach it, you are standing in a doorway looking into a room. Walk into the room. It's your bedroom, the room you slept in and played in as a child around age five or six. If you moved often as a child, pick one room that is clear and vivid and stay with it. If you did not have a bedroom, pick the room or closet or place that you went to in order to be alone. Look around the room. Let it surround you. It's just as it was. Everything's the same: the color of the walls, the arrangement of the bed and furniture, even the smell of the room. Walk around the room. Touch everything. Run your fingers along the cracks in the walls. Remember the places you used to doodle or draw? Remember how you used to hide under the bed or under the covers or in the closet? Remember what it was like being a child in this room? Remember your favorite song or game? Look, there's your favorite toy. Pick it up and play with it. It's all here for you to remember.

Now lie down on the floor on your back and look up at the room surrounding you. Remember how huge everything was back then? How
high the ceiling seemed? How tall the dresser was? Everything was
huge, gigantic, and you were so small, tiny in such a big world.
Remember the first day of school in first grade? Remember Sunday
mornings? Remember your sixth birthday? Remember your favorite
food?

Now stand up again and take a long look around the room. You are
your adult self once more standing there in that room. You are grown up,
looking in on your past through a window, a window you have created.

As you scan the room slowly one last time, suddenly you realize you
are not alone. Someone is in the room with you. Look around. Off in the
corner of the room someone is sitting on the floor. Walk over. As you
approach, you can see who it is.

It's a young child, about five or six years old, sitting looking away,
with head bent and eyes downcast. It's the child you were back then. The
child still inside of you is sitting on the floor beside you. Sit down next
to your child and say hello. Recall an old photograph of yourself, and
study it, in order to deepen the contact. Remember your favorite clothes?
Remember the way your hair was combed? When you have a clear, vivid
image of yourself as a child, ask your child to hold your hand. Be the
older friend to your child that you always needed back then. Place an
arm around your child's shoulder or pat your child's hair. Get to know
each other. Ask what your child is feeling deep inside. Ask what your
child is needing from you right now, and freely give it.

Now relive an old shame scene. Ask your child to take you through it
once more. Reexperience it as fully as you are able. Feel every feeling in
the scene. When it concludes, imagine being the loving, compassionate
mother or father to that child you needed back then. Say the things to your
child now that your child needed to hear then. Hold your child on your lap
for as long as your child needs. Be an ally to your child and change that
old scene or simply continue it, creating a new scene.

Imagine taking your child outside to play. Go to the park together and
run through the grass or bushes or simply sit quietly under a tree together. Or go to the beach and jump waves, splashing and laughing. Or sit on
a bench in the backyard and just silently be with one another.

It's getting late now. Time to come in. Bring your child to a new, safe
place that you are creating deep within you. Give your child a great big
hug. Be the good, loving parent to that child you always needed. Now
tuck your child into bed in that safe place deep inside you. Sit on the
edge of the bed and sing a song to your child or tell a story. Gaze into
each other's eyes for as long as you want to and say, "Child, I'm pleased
and proud to have you. I will be with you always." One last hug, one last

kiss good night. You'll be back whenever needed, whenever called. It's safe now. Tiptoe from your child, walk back down the hallway, and up the staircase. Whenever you are ready, open your eyes and return.

In order to illustrate the process of healing shame, both directly in the therapeutic relationship and through reparenting imagery, we will consider another case at some length. It captures essential features of the healing process, though somewhat differently expressed than in the case previously considered. Psychotherapy is not a technique, but a relationship. Similarly, reparenting imagery is not simply a technique, but a cocreated experience between two phenomenal selves, client and therapist.

The Case of the Elephant Man

Jonathan was a gifted poet. He entered therapy because his work had been blocked for some time, blocked by self-doubt and self-hatred. At one point I asked him if he was feeling shame. That word illuminated his inner experience. He had indeed known shame. To begin with, his father was an exceedingly contemptuous man. He criticized Jonathan's enthusiasm and humor, the way he walked or spoke, even the way he fixed sandwiches for himself. Disparagement characterized their relationship, and Jonathan learned to feel never quite good enough as a person. Recurring experiences with his father engendered intense shame, creating a sense of inherent inner deficiency.

Exacerbating these shame experiences was a birth defect, causing Jonathan to suffer repeated derision, ridicule, and humiliation from peers. This continued through junior high school. Each humiliation by peers left him more defeated, alienated, and intolerably alone. He had no one to turn to. With each subsequent shame experience, earlier ones became reactivated, causing his sense of shame to magnify.

Internally, Jonathan began to reproduce shame. Whenever he looked in a mirror, he called himself ugly or fat. This distorted image of himself, rooted in the contempt for his body previously learned from his father and his peers, filled him with so much disgust that at times he felt paralyzed. Jonathan was learning to treat himself with contempt and disgust, much as others earlier in life had done. He directed contempt and disgust inward, and these became inevitable scripts for reproducing shame.

In addition to a self-contempt script, Jonathan also developed a comparison-making script. His father always compared him unfavorably to his older brother and his mother often compared him directly to his father in a fit of anger and disgust. Jonathan learned to compare himself to everyone, finding himself not as popular, not as intelligent, not as competent, not as handsome, not as masculine, not as creative, not as valued. Jonathan's deepening sense of inner deficiency poisoned everything.

Through these evolving identity scripts, encompassing contempt, disparagement, and devaluation, Jonathan continued internally the identical pattern first experienced externally. Just as his father had done, Jonathan devalued his own accomplishments; nothing was ever good enough. Over time, he continued to actively disown, *in the present,* his competence, his intelligence, his masculinity, his body, and his essential value as a human being.

Jonathan was also well acquainted with blame. His father was unable to admit having made a mistake and invariably blamed others. Whenever something was either broken, missing, or misplaced, his father presumed Jonathan was responsible and would not believe his denials. Rather than directing blame outward, like his father, he turned blame against himself. For example, when a relationship with a woman ended, Jonathan felt completely to blame. He called himself unattractive, unmasculine, hopelessly incapable of relating to anyone. His self-blame script was relentless. After a breakup Jonathan invariably felt depressed and utterly deficient.

I invited Jonathan to begin observing how he behaved toward himself at such times. He reported hearing an inner voice saying, "You've never been a success with a woman. You're not a real man. You're no good in bed. Why do you even bother dating when you always screw it up? You'll never be happy—failures like you don't deserve to live."

Jonathan seized upon both real and imagined failings in the relationship, but then magnified them into a complete condemnation of himself. He treated himself just as cruelly whenever he was late for a meeting, misplaced his keys or wallet, or broke something. Jonathan was merciless in blaming himself for mistakes or mishaps, however trivial. After I encouraged him to observe it, he reported hearing an inner voice saying: "You're so stupid. What's wrong with you? Why are you always so disorganized? You never know where anything is. You're so damn clumsy. You don't know how to do anything right. Why don't you think straight?

You should've known better!" Jonathan showed himself neither mercy nor compassion.

Therapy proceeded over several months until Jonathan called me unexpectedly in the midst of crisis. It was a Sunday morning. He had attended a summer stock production of *Elephant Man* the night before, totally unprepared for the savage impact the play would have on him. The Elephant Man's painful deformities, isolation, and anguish both captured and magnified Jonathan's own feelings of freakishness because of his own birth defect, a deformed foot. Jonathan was overwhelmed by his identification with the Elephant Man and by a terrible sense of shame and exposure to the audience, as if all the experiences in which he had been publicly humiliated as a boy were now being dragged across the stage. Too disturbed to stay, he left his friends during intermission and walked home.

That night he had a dream. He dreamt that he was swimming in the ocean, alone. Then sharks appeared. They were circling around him and he became terrified. Now they were closing in for the kill. Jonathan awoke in terror. He could not fall back asleep and so stayed awake until morning.

He decided he would let me sleep a while longer. When he finally called me, he felt torn open and sobbed over and over, "It *hurts,* it *hurts,"* lost in the pain and shame he had closed off for so many years. He could barely speak, but managed to recount what had happened at the play the night before. And he told me about his dream, the nightmare he had had.

I was fully aware of the urgency. This was not one that could conveniently wait until our next appointed session. Fortunately, I had time available and I asked Jonathan if he wanted to see me. He said he did, so I arranged to see him immediately. Since he had no automobile, I offered to pick him up where he lived and we drove over to my office. It was now about nine o'clock in the morning.

When we walked into my office, Jonathan collapsed on the floor, sobbing wildly. I sat down beside him and simply held him. For much of the next three hours we spent together, I held Jonathan through his anguished sobbing. For the first hour all he could do was cry; his whole body heaved. Then I asked Jonathan to put words to his pain. Slowly, Jonathan recounted numerous occasions in which peers would gather to ridicule his deformity. Each scene brought an onrush of pain.

Then he came to the critical scene, the one that had suddenly erupted into consciousness, unexpectedly in response to the play the night before. It occurred during junior high school on a particular day when the teacher left the room for some 15 minutes. On that day, his entire class turned on him, led by his supposedly best friend. In unison, the class began chanting "Club foot! Club foot! *Club foot!*" Over and over they chanted. His desk was in the middle of the room; they surrounded him as they chanted. These were the sharks in his dream closing in for the kill. Jonathan could only sit dumbly at his desk, silently enduring his public shame and anguish.

Compounding all of those humiliating experiences was his parents' total inability to deal with his defect in a helpful, comforting way. Jonathan was unable to share his anguish with his family because his parents did not have the emotional resources to understand, comfort, or aid him in coping effectively with his reality. It activated too much shame in them, and his deformity was almost completely ignored.

Through reliving these painful experiences together with me, Jonathan recontacted the terrified and humiliated boy locked away inside. But we were not done with it. I knew that we needed to find a way to heal his inner wound. All of the shame experiences I had worked with until that point had been activated by others. This was the first time I had been confronted by a shame experience that was partially the result of a birth defect. As I sat pondering what to do next, I began imagining how *I* would have handled the situation had Jonathan been my own son. Therapy must create an analog of parenting. Understanding that oriented me as to how to proceed.

I explained to Jonathan that we had to relive the scene once more. He was to imagine himself back in that junior high class as vividly as he was able and then imagine the class turn on him, chanting as they had done. I said he needed to experience all of the feelings in the scene one more time, but this time he was to *continue* the scene further. I wanted him to imagine coming home immediately following that traumatic scene and then imagine being the good, loving father to that boy he had needed back then. He agreed to do what I had suggested.

I then asked him to close his eyes and picture that traumatic class incident. I also asked Jonathan to verbalize his experience as we proceeded so that I could participate. Next I asked him to picture that boy immediately following the traumatic scene, and imagine talking to him like a loving father: "Say to him what you would've wanted a father to say to you." I waited while Jonathan spontaneously created his own reparenting imagery. "Now," I continued, "I want you to put him to bed inside you, tuck him in, and kiss him goodnight. That boy needs all the love and respect you can offer him. He's been lonely for a very long time. Be the father you needed back then."

Jonathan was able to experience through active imagery the process of reowning and reparenting a part of himself previously shamed and disowned. He told me later, "You know, it was like giving an orphan a home." For Jonathan those words were the most powerful of all. Healing a profound inner wound had begun.

Weeks later, Jonathan happened to mention that he had stopped to admire a teddy bear in a store window. "Why didn't you buy it for yourself?" I asked. He would have felt too ashamed, he answered. As a child he was never allowed to have a teddy bear. During one session, I surprised Jonathan with a teddy bear. He was overwhelmed, and he sat cuddling and conversing with his new friend much as a child would. Every night he took his teddy bear to sleep with him. This became a vital way of nurturing the child within him, in addition to utilizing reparenting imagery. Eventually, Jonathan bought a second teddy bear, then a third, and he gave each a name.

Jonathan experienced reparenting and reowning in several ways. He was able to do so directly through our relationship, for I became the father he never had. Experiences with me became a vital source of new positive scenes. Through reparenting imagery, Jonathan was able to reshape traumatic scenes as well as actively embrace the rejected orphan within him. Finally, his teddy bears provided a means to nurture the child within him directly in action as well. For Jonathan, shame eventually became healed.

SELF-AFFIRMATION: FROM SHAME TO PRIDE

Central to the resolution of shame is the development of a *self-affirming* capacity within the client. The self must learn how to affirm the self from within. This capacity to affirm oneself translates into having esteem for self, valuing of self, respect for self, pride in self. From an affect perspective, as Nathanson also observes (1987b), pride is the experience of enjoyment affect and/or excitement affect focused directly in the self or in the self's actual accomplishments. Pride is enjoyment/excitement invested in self, or in accomplishment by self. But pride has always been suspect. Individuals are generally socialized to avoid the appearance of conceit, arrogance, or superiority. In an effort to banish these particular qualities from children and adults, pride itself has become bound by shame.

If pride is enjoyment over accomplishment, what is conceit? The source of conceit is contempt, not pride. Contempt is an affect blend, comprised of dissmell plus anger. Contempt affect elevates the self above others, who are now perceived as beneath one, as lesser. Contempt is the affective source not only of conceit, but of arrogance and superiority as well. Contempt prejudices the self against others because it invariably partitions the inferior from the superior. The failure to distinguish between pride and contempt has resulted in universal shaming of expressions of necessary pride.

Therapists can enable their clients' sense of pride by teaching them how to develop an inner source of pride in self. One way of collecting pride on a daily basis is by remembering to be proud of oneself five times every day. Often I have instructed clients to keep an "adequacy" or "pride" list by writing down the "small" events in any day that make them genuinely proud. By so doing I am validating their experience of pride. The events noted and recorded can be tangible accomplishments or simply situations handled well enough. Clients must learn that being good enough *is* enough. They must be enabled to be proud, not just of actual achievements, but of who they are and how they live their lives. They must be proud to be the self they truly are. Keeping an adequacy/pride list is one tangible tool for cultivating not just a sense of pride, but an *inner* source of pride.

The capacity to affirm oneself has multiple sources, and pride is one. But it also derives from actively embracing all of the disparate aspects of one's being. Owning these as inherent parts of an integrated self is the only route to self-acceptance. Nurturance of self and forgiveness of self walk hand-in-hand with genuine pride in self. Together, these form a new, self-affirming identity.

Nine

Developing Equal Power in Current Relationships and the Family of Origin

From the disappointments in the very early stages of life outside the womb—in which all things were given—comes the beginning of this vast development of actions, thoughts, foresights, and so on, which are calculated to protect one from a feeling of insecurity and helplessness in the situation which confronts one. This accultural evolution begins thus, and when it succeeds, when one evolves successfully along this line, then one respects oneself, and as one respects oneself so one can respect others.

HARRY STACK SULLIVAN
Conceptions of Modern Psychiatry

The resolution of shame is a multifaceted process. Inevitably it begins in the therapeutic relationship, which recreates the necessary conditions of security. New experiences of identification transcend shame, providing healing for a wounded self. Reparenting must be experienced within the therapeutic relationship as well as directly within the self. Either alone is insufficient. Reparenting imagery is a therapeutic tool for the recovery of governing scenes of shame. Returning internalized shame to its interpersonal origins is the foundation for identity regrowth and the eventual reintegration of the self. Restoring the interpersonal bridge creates hope, an eventual pathway out of the prison of shame.

The psychotherapy relationship is the source of therapeutic healing, the wellspring from which all other processes flow. It equally serves as a vital model for interpersonal relations. If eventual separation from the therapist is a goal of therapy, then clients must develop interpersonal competence. Otherwise they will lack the psychological skills and tools necessary to support separation. Building competence, then, must be a principal goal of psychotherapy. Competence is founded on two fundamental principles: coping effectively with the sources of shame and developing equal power. We will examine three interpersonal arenas in this context: the existing relationship between client and therapist, current interpersonal relationships generally, and relationships within the family of origin in particular.

RESOLVING SHAME IN THE THERAPIST-CLIENT RELATIONSHIP

Resolving shame requires an understanding of the sources of shame in any context. The therapist-client relationship is no exception. There are two broad classes of shame activators to which psychotherapists are uniquely vulnerable: universal and particular. Universal activators are embedded directly in the nature of the psychotherapeutic process and are universal across all therapists, at least potentially. Particular activators, however, are specific to individual therapists, unique to the person of the therapist.

Universal Activators of Shame in Therapists

Self-disclosure by the therapist is one universal activator. Owing to the Rules of Practice embedded in the discipline, therapist self-disclosure is often viewed as a violation of the Rules. Typically, considerable inner turmoil or conflict surrounds this issue for therapists. Self-disclosure often activates shame in therapists, particularly in the absence of appropriate guidelines. Without them, therapists remain confused as to *when* to self-disclose, *how* to self-disclose, and *what* to self-disclose. Uncertainty itself can activate shame. Rigid adherence to a rule—such as remaining unknowable, never answering questions, never revealing oneself—is not a guaranteed solution to the conflict, nor an absolute safeguard against shame. The inner conflict remains. Therapists will eventually deviate from the Rule somehow, thereby potentially activating shame. When the Rule remains steadfast, the inner wish to depart from it still may activate shame. And when the Rule itself is adjusted to flexibly incorporate therapist self-disclosure, in appropriately timed and measured ways, the therapist then becomes open to shame by the very action of becoming known and, hence, more vulnerable. Shame is a potentiality for psychotherapists with *or* without the Rule. Shame is possible however one proceeds on the issue of self-disclosure.

The issue of touching and holding between client and therapist is another universal activator of shame. Once again, the Rules of Practice advocate abstinence from any touching. Violation of that Rule is equivalent to transgression, and so will likely be experienced as moral shame, the sense of having done something wrong. Adherence to the Rule functions as a safeguard against that shame. Even in the face of unwavering adherence, clients frequently present therapists with unique challenges and crises. They invariably confront their therapists with unexpected requests or needs that then rekindle the struggle with previously accepted Rules. Clients who initiate touching or ask directly for holding will inevitably activate shame in therapists. The Rule is not a permanent shield. Distinguishing between touching and holding that are therapeutic in both intention and impact, and touching that is sexual in either intention or impact, is of central significance. Sexual touching must remain off-limits in the therapeutic relationship just as it must remain off-limits in the parenting relationship.

Client demandingness or neediness is another and altogether different universal activator of shame in therapists. Clients who are overly demanding or needy may be experienced as overwhelming by their therapists. Demandingness often masks deprivation. Understanding that connection enables a therapist to sidestep those seemingly insatiable demands. Deprivation itself can take various forms: deprivation of primary needs for, say, relationship or touching/holding; deprivation of honest feedback concerning their impact on others; deprivation of necessary and appropriate limits; deprivation through being granted too much power too early in life; and deprivation through parents acceding directly to their demands. The impact of client demandingness is clear. Therapists end up feeling: *whatever I give, it is never enough; whatever I do, it is never good enough.* The result is shame.

Still another potent, universal activator of shame in therapists is client discouragement. When clients become discouraged about their progress, they are experiencing a variant of shame. Discouragement is shame about temporary defeat, and client discouragement transfers, as all feelings do. Therapists often become discouraged in response to their clients being discouraged. The failure on the part of therapists to attend to client shame in the form of discouragement accounts for many clients dropping out of therapy. Therapists have to be willing to experience their own shame before they will be able to recognize and validate their clients' shame. The failure to acknowledge one's shame as a therapist, whether in the form of discouragement or some form of internalized shame, can result in blaming clients for not progressing adequately in therapy. In so doing, therapists very likely reenact their client's original familial pattern, a pattern in which failure activated shame followed by parental blame. Defeat or failure invariably activates shame, in therapists as well as in clients. Their relationship always is a reciprocal one.

When an impasse occurs within the therapeutic relationship, a further occasion for experiencing shame emerges. Impasses in the relationship are inevitable and often triggered by mistakes made by therapists. Mistakes are natural, to be expected; they are even necessary. When therapists are able to recognize their mistakes, openly acknowledge them with their clients, and directly own them, then the relationship is restored: therapist and client become allies once again. But impasses will generate shame for therapists who cannot allow themselves to be human and imperfect. Their further refusal to acknowledge the natural shame initially caused by the impasse will prevent their restoring the relationship with the client. Relationships between adults thrive on sharing the power, on each person having equal power.

The inevitable limitations on therapist power round out the universal activators of shame. Therapists can effect change, but they are also limited in their power to do so. There was a time when I believed that I could "save" my clients. Gradually, I realized that I could not save anyone. Then I discovered that that illusion had only been replaced by another: now I was going to "rescue" clients. That, too, had to be relinquished. Then I faced my final illusion, that I had the power to "cure" clients.

A number of years ago I worked with a young man for some 18 months. Then he moved away to take another job. I was convinced I had not helped him. I had failed. Three years later he recontacted me when he was back in town. He said he came to tell me how much I had done for him. I was dumbfounded. He said it took him 3 years to assimilate the work we had accomplished during his therapy. I had offered him what I could, but he had to take it inside and grow with it.

Fully accepting our ultimate helplessness to cure is a difficult challenge confronting all practitioners of psychotherapy. The challenge facing therapists is to accept feeling limited without feeling *lesser* for the limitation. Herein lies a source of shame. The power to be healed or cured always is in the hands of the client. That is why I will often respond to clients with, "Feel free to stay neurotic, that's your right and choice." I can care about them and about their growth without feeling entirely *responsible* for either their progress or ultimate success. Therapists are always limited in their power to effect cure.

Activators of Shame Particular to Each Therapist

In considering activators of shame particular to each therapist, there are likely to be specific shame issues that become uniquely activated for different therapists. These are typically rooted in the therapist's own governing scenes. A useful starting point is attending to the actual feelings or needs expressed by clients that activate shame in the therapist. The process for the therapist is analogous to the one for the client.

Therapists have to be aware of their own Shame Profile. They must know how their shame manifests, what it actually feels like on the inside. Then they must be able to identify what events specifically activate their shame. Therapists must further examine their various reactions and responses to shame: secondary affects, constructed thoughts or images, retrieved memories, perceptions, and overt behavior. The effects of shame are multiple.

A young man I was working with came in one day and told me that he had just returned from visiting his parents. While there, he was finally able to express to his father how he truly felt about him, how important he was. His father had always been too busy with his work as a minister and had little time for his son. Along with telling me that, my client announced that he had completed what he needed to accomplish in therapy, and this was to be our last session. When it ended, I was aware that something had opened within me.

I sought out the individual who had been my mentor at the time, Dr. Bill Kell. As I sat with Bill, I struggled with mounting feelings of shame. I told him what had transpired with my client. Then I told him that I had never been able to do what my client had just now accomplished. And I told him that he, Bill, was important to me. He answered, "I've known that," as he turned to look out the window.

Still, I felt bound inside, struggling with shame. I said to Bill, "I do not feel resolved."

"You haven't said the words," he responded.

Then it came: overwhelming shame and paralysis. He moved his chair closer and touched my arm. For countless minutes I could not speak. I could not utter a word. It was agony. Then a knock at the door interrupted us, after which Bill returned to sit beside me. Finally, I struggled to speak the words, "I . . . love . . . you." Bill spoke only one word in response, "*Good*," as he smiled at me, his head gently nodding. His eyes gleamed with joy and his face radiated warmth and love. I felt *one* with him as I gazed deeply into his eyes and he into mine.

Therapists must differentiate the specific targets of shame in their own lives: their unique pattern of *shame binds*. They must also distinguish their particular identity scripts for reproducing shame. Finally, therapists must understand how they characteristically defend against shame. Defending strategies and scripts, as utilized by therapists, are critical signposts further illuminating the interpersonal process between therapist and client. Therapists who understand their own shame can guide clients to do likewise. They offer hope, so that clients may discover courage.

When Therapists Activate Shame Directly in Clients

We have been considering shame activation within the therapeutic relationship from the perspective of the therapist. Now we will examine it in reverse. Consider the client who is experiencing shame at the hands of his or her therapist. The first step is to actively approach the client's shame and openly validate it. Therapists need to say, in effect, "Yes, I see your shame, I see how badly you are feeling in response to my action." Therapists need to honestly *own* their part in activating their client's shame, and that is often difficult. In order to do so, therapists must be prepared, and willing, to admit their mistakes. Admitting mistakes is something that parents typically have been unwilling or unable to do in the first place. By admitting mistakes therapists acknowledge their part in the process; they share responsibility *with* their client.

Admitting mistakes further requires therapists to be able to tolerate their own shame. Responding to their own mistakes with shame is both natural and inevitable. The shame experienced, however, need not be overwhelming; it need not be magnified shame. However, shame in the form of simply feeling bad is the natural response to a mistake or failure. Insofar as magnified shame has been confronted and assimilated, therapists are more able to tolerate the recurrence of shame as an affect. If they can tolerate shame, then they can freely admit their mistakes.

Another feature of the healing process is accepting the client's anger. Rage, an inflation of anger affect, is a secondary reaction to shame. Therapists have to expect anger or rage in response to shaming and have to be prepared to absorb it, without becoming angry in response. I will say to clients, "Be as angry at me as you need to be, for as long as you need to be. Then, when you are finished being angry, let me know. Hopefully, you will come to forgive me."

Because I was late and felt hurried in my first interview with a young woman, I said something insensitive without realizing it. Suddenly she stood up and rushed from my office. I was perplexed. As I sat for a moment collecting my thoughts and reflecting on what to do, just as suddenly the door opened. She was back. "I just wanted to tell you exactly what I think of you before I leave," she shouted.

Then she proceeded to tell me exactly what she thought of me. I waited and listened. Then I answered, "I agree with you." She was speechless and her mouth gaped. "What?" she asked. "I agree with you," I said. Then she sat back down and we resumed the interview.

By letting themselves become known when a client is experiencing shame, therapists directly facilitate the healing process. Through appropriately sharing parallel experiences from their own lives, therapists become vulnerable along with their client. Therapists become human. Through permitting clients to actually know their therapists on the inside, clients are enabled to identify with them, to feel *one* with them. When shame activation is followed by directly restoring the interpersonal bridge, by renewed identification, shame becomes healed.

COMPETENCE IN CURRENT RELATIONSHIPS: DEVELOPING EQUAL POWER

Increasingly, the problems in living presented by individuals seeking professional assistance are the result of failures in parenting. Many of the clients we see now have not learned essential skills for building mutually satisfying relationships. These skills are eminently learnable. Offering clients guidance in living, guidance in building interpersonal competence, is a vital dimension of the therapeutic process. Guidance in living entails offering an identification model for how to function as a person, how to have sound relationships, how to live life effectively.

Psychotherapy is inherently a multidimensional process. Historical exploration, coupled with the recovering of governing scenes, is not entirely effective in the absence of an emotionally corrective experience within the therapeutic relationship itself. Yet both require the further translation of knowledge into action. This must occur in two domains: internally within the self and interpersonally with others. How the self actively relates to the self in the present must change, *and* how the self relates to others in the present also must change. Wisdom gleaned in the consulting room now must transfer into the actual living of one's life.

Psychotherapy must be action-oriented in order to complete the healing process. Clients need to be taught how to recognize situations of powerlessness. They need to learn how to take back the power directly in those situations whenever possible, or else regain power internally over their affective reactions to unavoidable powerlessness. The recent plight of the family farmer in middle America is a case in point. Individuals need to be educated in how to thrive.

Clients need to consciously identify their various needs and expectations in all kinds of relationships. The way to accomplish this is by observing their subliminal imagery, the actual flow of their internal *relationship scenes*. These scenes operate at the periphery of awareness, but directly observing them tunes them into fuller consciousness. I invite clients to consciously focus their attention inward whenever they are about to interact with others in order to *observe* the various images and scenes inside of them that involve that other person. Observing and distinguishing these varying relationship scenes is an important skill that develops only with practice. In order to further differentiate these often ambiguous scenes, I encourage clients to utilize as a psychological tuning fork the specific language of the self that distinguishes affects, needs, and drives.

The next step is learning to consciously observe the other person in order to know precisely what kind of person one is relating to. Much disappointment in relationships results from a mismatch between expectations and reality. My goal here is to teach clients how to realistically assess other people so that their specific needs and expectations strike a sounder match with the actual reality of the other. Too often the other person is either unwilling or unable to respond to particular needs or behave in an expected fashion. Learning how to match expectations with reality is a skill vital to living life with increasing effectiveness. Clients must be taught, first, how to clearly distinguish those needs and expectations and, second, how to match them with reality in particular relationships.

The process of consciously observing other people involves multiple aspects. I encourage clients to begin to observe the predominant affect communicated by particular people, by attending to their characteristic facial reactions. Then they are to observe how the other actually behaves. I also invite my clients to observe whether the words spoken by others match their actual forthcoming behavior. The next step is to observe whether the other is dependable and predictable, safe and trustworthy, capable of sharing the power in the relationship, capable of intimacy and vulnerability, and able to admit mistakes and apologize. I encourage clients not to avoid risks, but to risk consciously. Relationships require deliberate care and conscious effort over time in order to mature.

Consider the obverse situation. All too often individuals become infatuated with a virtual stranger and subsequently rush into a relationship prematurely. Just as depression is a negative affect spiral (shame conjoined with distress), infatuation is a positive affect spiral. The face of the other becomes an immediate and compelling preoccupation, eclipsing everything else and generating image after image involving intense positive affect, coupled with intense longing for the beloved and equally intense negative affect occasioned by the absence of the other. These intensifying scenes of enjoyment and excitement focused on the other spiral endlessly, triggering one another. Phenomenologically, the affect/scene spiral feels like *falling*. The common expression of "falling in love," therefore, is a direct consequence of conjoint affect and scene dynamics. One may indeed fall in love, just as one may fall in shame, or fall in hate.

Consider the phenomenon termed love more closely. Phenomenological analysis reveals it to be identification experiences of communion, or mutuality, amplified by enjoyment affect. The experience of union with another that we call love is produced by feeling *one* with the other, feeling identified; two separate beings now feel merged. This experience is amplified affectively by enjoyment affect. It is the shared enjoyment of mutual communion that we understand as love, and the face of the other is its primary activator as well as target. What we invariably long for, and often incessantly search for, is a particular *face*. What captivates us so completely is the actual face of another person, a face that indeed can launch "a thousand ships," one that resonates with another face embedded within a scene stored in memory.

Clients must be aided in distinguishing the faces that call to them, that compel them. They must also learn how to detach from infatuation spirals in order to distinguish between falling in love with an actual person and falling in love with one's own internal images of that person. Conscious observation of the other is a useful tool in that regard.

Critical to learning how to become vulnerable wisely is knowing when and how to remain *defended* interpersonally. Staying defended involves building a flexible conscious shield about one's innermost self, leaving one centered, fully conscious, and alert. Staying defended means temporarily not being vulnerable. It means not automatically taking inside and believing the messages communicated by others. Anything that hits one's shield bounces off rather than coming inside and disquieting the self. Staying defended further translates into not looking for anything, not expecting anything, and not needing anything from a particular individual, situation, or encounter.

REDEFINING RELATIONSHIPS IN THE FAMILY OF ORIGIN: ATTAINING EQUAL POWER

When clients remain trapped in shame-based relationships or situations, they have to be enabled to take back their rightful half of the power. As long as clients continue in shame-based relationships, psychotherapy cannot effect lasting change. Developing *equal power* is critical in current relationships and, especially, in the family of origin. Clients, as all individuals, need to develop equal power with their parents. This is not historical exploration so much as it is changing the actual relationship a client currently has with the parent. Through learning that one *now* can call the shots just as well as the parent, one is enabled truly to let go of the past and to live life in the present. It is this letting go that makes a different future possible. As long as clients remain stuck in the old relationship with parents, the original dynamics are being continually reenacted in the present. No amount of insight or internal change will be entirely effective until real change occurs in those actual, current relationships. Without action change, therapy is hobbled.

When clients feel powerless and trapped in a marriage or career, they need to discover tangible ways of similarly regaining personal power. And therapists must be their guides. The same principles apply to these situations, but we will consider here the particular context of the family of origin.

Relationships between parents and children must evolve into relationships between equal adults. This is the natural end toward which parenting itself must aim if parents are to raise autonomous individuals, capable of living their lives competently, with dignity and affirmation. Far too often, relationships with parents remain clouded, infantile, or burdened by guilty obligation.

Redefining relationships with parents translates into having power over one's half of the relationship. This must also include setting effective limits on the behavior of others in relation to oneself. If adulthood has any meaning, it must lie in attaining equal power in relation to both other adults and one's family of origin. Adulthood without equal power is a sham.

Relationship redefinition is a conscious process. The client consciously must consider what is actually "owed" to parents. The profound and difficult question each individual must examine is this: What do I feel I *owe* my parents considering what they gave me? Relationships between parents and children inevitably carry elements of obligation. It is imperative to distinguish between what the client feels is owed to parents and what the parents believe is owed them. Knowing precisely and specifically what actually is owed enables clients to know what they actually might freely want to share. They also must examine carefully the emotional costs to them of any continued interaction. Ultimately, each individual has the inalienable human right to terminate those relationships if continuing them means sacrificing their own emotional well-being.

There is no cultural model in Western or Eastern civilization for examining relationships with one's family of origin in a deliberately conscious and independent manner. Honor and obedience to parents have been an accepted ethical principle for centuries, handed down on tablets of stone. It is the foundation of family loyalty, of the family bond itself. Unfortunately, however, it has also rendered many adults emotional prisoners of their family. To challenge that ethical principle, to question its automatic assumption irrespective of particular circumstances, to independently examine the kind of relationship one now wishes to have or is willing to have with parents, is to commit heresy.

Too many individuals submit to that rule, Honor Thy Mother and Thy Father, without question. Even well after becoming adults, they continue being infantilized. They do not allow themselves honestly to consider the relationship with their parents as a relationship. Each client, each individual, needs to examine seriously what honoring their parents actually means. Only then will they be free to be true adults, their parents' equals.

In addition to the ties of obligation embedded in parental relationships, the lack of accepted and meaningful rites of passage in contemporary society further confuses the transition to adulthood. We are unclear and ambivalent as a society about the business of coming of age. The differing ages that exist for driving, voting, bearing arms, and drinking (both within and between various states) point to our cultural contradictions regarding the transition to adulthood. There can be no claim of adulthood until one actually begins behaving as an adult, with all its attendant rights, privileges, and responsibilities.

It is ultimately up to individuals to decide how exactly to honor their parents. One's conscience must be one's guide. This is a radical departure from custom and tradition, but it is required of clients if they are to become adults not just in name but in fact. Honoring parents, as an ethical principle and cultural rule, must be adjusted to match the honest reality of individual situations.

Attaining equal power with parents creates a different relationship. Client and parent become equals. Only then does making peace with the past become possible. Hopefully, clients will grow to accept their parents for who they are, and for what they were able to give. But that can only happen after attaining equal power. For some clients, acceptance may grow into actual forgiveness of their parents. However, that is more likely to happen when their parents also begin behaving differently in keeping with the changed relationship. When parents can begin to respect their adult children as equals, those children can begin to forgive them.

It must also be understood that some wounds are slow to heal, while others never do. Certain clients may indeed come to accept their parents' limitations, but will never forgive them. That is their right. Clients should not be pressured or admonished into forgiving their parents. That is tantamount to shaming them for still resenting and not forgiving the parent. Some acts may be unforgivable. Whether or not clients actually forgive either or both parents cannot be imposed. Forgiveness must happen of itself. To forgive one's parents is an act of reunion, just as to forgive oneself is an act of reunion with oneself.

The power to forgive always is in the hands of the client, and it must be up to the client to determine whether or when to forgive the parent. Inner healing does not require such forgiveness. It is more likely to occur when clients are enabled truly to let go of the past and to begin living their lives in the present. It is this letting go that makes a different future possible.

DEVELOPING EQUAL POWER: A CASE INVOLVING A DEPRESSIVE SYNDROME

In order to illustrate the foregoing principles regarding equal power and redefining relationships with parents, consider Emily, a middle-aged woman who sought therapy because of acute depression. Our first interview occurred immediately following a truly frightening incident in which she felt so utterly depressed that she could not get out of bed. It happened the evening previous to our first meeting when she had to prepare dinner for her young sons. Being unable to get out of bed and function as a parent caused her to seek immediate therapy.

Emily had always kept her own feelings buried inside and her concerns, however pressing, to herself. There was no one in her present life to whom she turned for emotional support. Emily was also a single parent living with her two sons, and she was devoted to them. Her depression had been building for quite some time.

When I first saw her, she was acutely depressed and on the verge of giving up hope. She felt there was nothing to live for. Initially, we examined her life to identify possible triggers for her depression and she related the following series of events. Eighteen months previously, she divorced her husband and subsequently required major surgery. Then a brother of hers was killed in a freak accident. Several months later her father suffered a heart attack. Emily began to wonder if she was just now beginning to experience consciously the emotional impact of that series of losses and disruptions in her life. This seemed quite likely to me.

Apart from the very real absence of emotional support in her life, Emily's recent divorce appeared to be the principal continuing source of major difficulties. She still felt guilty and ashamed about divorcing her husband and depriving her children of a home with two parents. Thus, she had not as yet fully resolved this matter for herself. Furthermore, relatives on both sides of the family continued to pressure her to become reconciled with her former husband, something he also had been pressuring her to do.

Emily's father was recovering well, and her own surgery was behind her. While the sudden death of her brother was unfortunate, none of these events accounted for the continuation of Emily's feelings of depression, hopelessness, and deepening despair. It was evident to me that she had been feeling powerless. When I suggested it to her, she readily agreed that this was her underlying feeling state. Naming it accurately was a vital first step.

Over the next several sessions, we worked to make the roots of Emily's powerlessness fully conscious. Once we understood the sources of her feeling hopeless and helpless, I explained, we could determine how to extricate her from this dangerously disabling position.

One of the facts that surfaced early on was that Emily's mother had walked out on the family when Emily herself was a child. From that point she had been raised by her father. Even prior to her mother's abandoning the family, Emily felt she could never please her mother, that no matter what she did or how she behaved, she was never good enough. Now we had uncovered one source of her shame. It was rooted in that series of governing scenes. Her mother's subsequent abandonment only confirmed Emily's abiding sense of inner deficiency. This was proof there was something wrong with *her*. Emily had internalized shame and it had then become even further magnified.

Emily later married a man who behaved in ways that were irresponsible and unpredictable. He repeatedly looked to Emily to make all the decisions, even to run interference for him at his job, to literally care for him the way a parent does for a child. He also engaged in a series of extramarital affairs, while always promising to stop. Without ever realizing it, Emily had reenacted her familial pattern by marrying a man who behaved in ways that were *analogous* to the ways her mother had behaved years before. Finally, Emily had enough and, after considerable inner struggle, decided to opt for divorce, though she continued to feel there was something wrong with *her* for not being able to make their marriage work. The failure was hers alone and she felt intense shame in response. The earlier failures in her relationship with her mother left Emily susceptible to experiencing the breakup of her marriage as another personal failure, another confirmation of shame. Finally, the recurring pressure from her ex-husband as well as many family members only confused her further and deepened her sense of shame about breaking up the family.

My efforts were initially directed toward helping Emily realize that she had indeed tried repeatedly to make her marriage work and, even further, that she herself truly felt she had *tried enough*. There was no sense in sacrificing her own well-being as well. Besides, she knew she would never reconcile with her former husband. There was nothing left inside her that wanted to try again.

The turning point in therapy came when Emily realized the impact of the failures in her relationship with her mother. She had to reexperience her shame. This enabled her to see how susceptible she was to repeating a similar pattern in her marriage. She could not see the behavior of the other person objectively, but always experienced herself as the failure, as inherently shameful. The shame surrounding her divorce had only magnetized the deeper shame from childhood. As long as she continued to feel shame in relation to her mother, she also carried the shame of her marital failure. If she could resolve and heal the early shame, then she would be able to let go of the other as well.

Once she came to fully realize the source of her long-standing sense of inner deficiency and recognize the truth about the particular man she had married, Emily was able to feel increasingly at peace about the divorce. Gradually her depression began to lift, particularly after she started paying conscious attention to what triggered her recurring depressive bouts. Once her eyes were opened, she began to consciously observe the actual sequence of events that resulted in her becoming depressed. This was critical because Emily had to be able to identify them. One day she came in and reported specific events in her present life that seemed to reactivate her depressive posture. Most notably, her depressions appeared to follow current interactions with either her mother or her former husband, the two individuals who had played a central role in her life.

Emily continued to feel powerless, in the present, in relation to her mother and her ex-husband. After a long absence, her mother was now pressuring Emily to resume their relationship; she was also pressuring Emily to bring her two grandsons to visit more often. Yet the predominant message from mother to Emily was exactly as it had been in childhood. If Emily called, her mother said she did not call enough. When Emily visited, her mother said she should visit more often. Basically, whatever Emily did was never enough or never good enough, thereby reopening the old wound and reawakening her sense of inner deficiency. In visiting her mother, her shame also was revisited.

What was to be done? Emily needed to consciously examine what she truly believed she *owed* her mother, considering what her mother gave her. This was not to be undertaken lightly because she had to be able to live with whatever conclusion she reached. After considerable and careful soul-searching, Emily realized that since no matter what she gave it was never enough anyway, she was going to give only what she truly wanted to, which was not very much. Besides, she had no real feeling at all for this person who was her biological mother. Emily decided she would simply behave toward her mother as though she were another adult. To strengthen her new determination, I offered Emily a *defense.* I suggested that whenever her mother gave the recurring message, "You're not good enough," Emily was to reply with, "Apparently, I'm a disappointment to you, but I do the best I can." It worked. Emily came away exhilarated; she no longer felt helpless with her mother.

The situation with her former husband was more complicated, since some interaction was necessary if only to arrange or accommodate visitation with the children. Whenever she saw him, her ex-husband would again pressure her for a reconciliation, in response to which Emily again tried to explain herself. This only left her once again confused, guilty, and resentful. He would also intrude on her privacy with questions or accusations about her personal life. Emily had been feeling powerless to stop these intrusions, thinking that if she were pleasant and rational he finally would understand. All that this accomplished was to reinforce the very pattern she abhorred.

When Emily's ex-husband came to pick up the children for visitation, often he would come quite late at night and then claim it was too late to take them. Then he asked if he could sleep there. If Emily said, "Get a motel room," he answered, "Well, I have no money." Finally she would back down and allow him to sleep in the living room. In return for her kindness, he played the television set all night, keeping her awake, and failed to leave in the morning with the children as planned. In fact, it was typically yet another day before he finally left, only after countless cross-examinations of Emily's comings and goings, and pleas for reconciliation—all, of course, for the good of the children. By this time Emily was enraged.

When he returned the children, often it was well past their bedtime; they were overtired and crabby, which further enraged Emily. "Why couldn't he be more responsible?" she would complain. "Why should this time be any different from all others?" I would answer. Emily had been expecting behavior from her former husband that he simply was incapable of.

On other occasions he actually would ignore the children, fail to call them for long stretches of time, even fail to show up as expected. All of this was an apparent attempt to hurt Emily through the children because he knew he could get to her that way. Emily cared that her sons had a father and a real relationship with him. Investing in that outcome was precarious for Emily because it was completely out of her control. Since it mattered to her, he was able to abuse the power she inadvertently gave him. Whenever she resisted his pleas for reconciliation, he ignored the children to get back at her.

Emily needed to take back the power directly in this situation. First, she needed to stop investing in *his* relationship with their sons because whether or not he saw them was out of her control. Whether their relationship with their father was ever meaningful or satisfying for the children was equally out of her control. Fully accepting this reality was a struggle for Emily, but she finally was able to.

Furthermore, Emily needed to name the particular behaviors of her ex-husband that gave her the greatest difficulty. In response to all inquiries concerning her personal life, Emily learned to answer, "That's none of your business." She learned to neither explain nor justify her actions or how she conducted her life.

Then came the matter of visitation. The next time he took the children, Emily told him to have them back before their bedtime or else take a motel room and return them in the morning, for she would not be home.

When he failed to return them by 8:30 p.m., Emily put a note on the door, locked it, and went to a friend's house for the evening. Her ex-husband was forced to spend the night in a motel with the children and returned them the next morning. From that point on, he brought them back on time, or even earlier, and he behaved in an increasingly responsible manner now that there were tangible consequences for his behavior.

He even began to see more of his children, since Emily was no longer invested in his doing so. She presented it clearly to him: "Whether you see them or not, or have anything with them, is entirely up to you from now on. I'm completely out of it." Now he could no longer hurt Emily by ignoring the children.

The next situation Emily learned to handle differently involved pressure from relatives wanting a reconciliation. Emily first needed to examine her varied choices for taking back the power. The basic message she needed to learn to give was that reconciliation was no longer a topic for conversation. She could respond with something like, "One of the things that happens when you get to be an adult is that you can make your own mistakes." This would sidestep the confrontation. Or she could respond with, "Even if remaining divorced is wrong, it's still my way and I guess I'm stuck with it." Following either response, she would then need to change the topic of conversation in order to behave the message as well. If unwelcome comments persisted, Emily could then say, "Hey, this is not a topic for conversation. If there's nothing else for us to talk about, I guess I'll go for a walk." Again she would have to actually behave the message whenever necessary. She could also choose to confront the matter more directly and say, "Look, I don't tell you how to live your life. Kindly don't tell *me;* it's none of your business." Finally, she could remove herself from the situation if that did not stop it: "Since you feel you have a perfect right to lecture me on what's good for me, I have a perfect right not to be around it." Emily was now armed with defenses. She knew her various choices for responding differently to unwelcome intrusions into her privacy. Instead of trying to justify herself, and feeling resentful, Emily felt a new sense of power in relation to all her relatives.

Emily's depression lifted completely. She felt freer, brighter, and had a renewed sense of hope. She had found tangible ways for taking back her rightful half of the power in all those situations that previously had left her feeling powerless and hopeless, depressed and inadequate. Emily had acquired vital tools for living her own life with increasing effectiveness.

She had discovered tools for resolving shame, coping with its sources, and developing equal power. At last Emily had learned how to preserve her dignity.

CONCLUSION: PSYCHOTHERAPY FOR SHAME-BASED SYNDROMES

Psychology requires a coherent image of the self as a process from which to evolve an accurate language of the self. To be useful, a language of the self must then translate into action. Implications for psychotherapy follow directly from that vision of how the self develops, functions, and changes. Psychotherapy must mirror development by actively engaging the identical processes that shape the self. It must attend to the full range of the primary affects by making each fully aware to the experiencing self. Psychotherapy also must provide a reparative, security-giving relationship that heals shame through identification. It also must directly engage imagery, not only language, in order to make conscious and reshape governing scenes. Mobilizing the developmental process facilitates the conscious integration of the self.

Affect, imagery, and language are as critical in the transformation of the self through psychotherapy as they are in its formation. By translating these concepts into action strategies for healing shame and building a competent self, an effective psychotherapy for shame-based syndromes emerges. Only through evolving an accurate language of the self will psychology have the necessary base from which to construct both a science of the self and a science of psychotherapy.

Ten

Time-Limited Group-Focused Treatment for Shame-Based Syndromes

Do not forget the most important fact that not hered-
ity and not environment are determining factors.
Both are giving only the frame and the influences
which are answered by the individual in regard to his
styled creative power.

ALFRED ADLER
The Individual-Psychology of Alfred Adler

In the previous chapters, we have considered four general process dimensions in the psychotherapy of specifically shame-based syndromes. Each process dimension is engaged at distinct points in the psychotherapeutic process. At the outset, creating the interpersonal bridge between client and therapist—who inevitably are strangers to one another—takes precedence over other therapeutic objectives. As trust becomes established, the focus shifts to examining the contextual life of the client in order to illuminate interpersonal and intrapsychic dynamics, historical as well as present. Conscious observation of the moment-to-moment interpersonal interaction provides important clues to the aforementioned dynamics. Careful observation of the interpersonal encounter, however, must be balanced by a studied attention to the therapist's inner experience. The therapist's attention should flow away from the client inward to the therapist's own imagery. This can be accomplished by momentarily breaking contact

237

with the client; gazing out the window or even closing one's eyes will deepen contact with imagery that generates directly in response to the client. The use of the therapist's own images is a potent therapeutic tool.

The focus of the therapeutic process continually shifts among the client's current life context, early significant relationships, the unfolding therapeutic encounter, and the client's patterns of inner relating. Returning internalized shame to its interpersonal origins itself is a multifaceted process that necessarily becomes interwoven with the other therapeutic processes. Attention to the inner life of the self illuminates the client's various negative identity scripts, while attention to the quality of significant relationships in the family of origin illuminates the client's Shame Profile. Inquiring specifically about the socialization of particular affects, drives, interpersonal needs, and purposes provides critical detail for that unfolding Shame Profile. Similarly, inviting clients to pay attention to how they both experience and express those affects, drives, and interpersonal needs engages them directly in continuing the therapeutic process between sessions. They become observers of their own experience.

The four fundamental process dimensions considered separately in previous chapters become gradually interwoven as psychotherapy unfolds. In this chapter, we examine their integration in two ways. First we explore particular aspects of psychotherapy that pertain to the various shame-based syndromes. Our purpose is to highlight the specific features that are salient in different syndromes. Next we examine a group-focused treatment approach for shame-based syndromes that synthesizes all of the facets of the psychotherapy process.

TREATMENT IMPLICATIONS FOR SPECIFIC SHAME SYNDROMES

Although the various therapeutic dimensions we have considered are general across all syndromes, critical aspects are more salient in certain instances. The actual patterning of psychotherapy is cocreated by therapist and client. The shifts in focus tend to be different, depending on the particular syndrome, and depending on the unique expression of that syndrome manifested by each client. Psychotherapy must be tailored to the syndrome, and to the individual client as well. Inevitably, the challenge for the therapist is finding an entrance to a closed system.

Physical Abuse Syndromes

In cases involving physical abuse, it is critical to make the shame-rage cycle conscious. This is true whether the client reenacts the abuse toward self, spouse, or children. The angry, punitive assault on another (or on self) is embedded in a sequence of events. Invariably, the abusive assault is preceded by shame. Awareness of that cycle is critical to releasing the self from automatically reenacting it.

It is equally imperative to recover the governing scenes mediating that reenactment. Orienting clients to the nature of scene reenactment is a necessary first step. Teaching clients to become observers of their own experience—in this case, the operation of governing scenes—is an essential component of psychotherapy. By learning to attend to the process, clients become able to follow their awareness back to inner events earlier in the sequence. Psychotherapy can be viewed as providing psychological reeducation.

In the case of clients who reenact those scenes by recreating analogous relationships in the present, which results in their continuing to be similarly abused by someone new, the recovery of governing scenes is absolutely crucial. Those scenes must be differentiated consciously from both current relationships and situations. Until that occurs, these clients will be compelled to return to those same abusive relationships again and again. Or, if they manage to escape, they will feel compelled to repeat those abusive scenes in yet another relationship. The *compulsion to repeat* is a direct consequence of the continued operation of unexamined governing scenes.

There are also necessary and sufficient activators of governing scenes, activators in the present, which then cause their importation into current interpersonal situations. These critical activators of governing scenes must be made fully conscious in order for clients to gain eventual mastery over their psychological black holes. One tool that can facilitate both the recovery of scenes and the identification of scene activators is the *journal.* By interrupting what has generally been an automatic process, clients focus attention on the stream of their awareness in order to identify the actual sequence of inner events. Writing in a journal about the abuse cycle begins to make it conscious and orients the self to the recovery of scenes operating at the periphery of awareness.

Eating Disorder Syndromes

Keeping a journal also can be an extremely useful adjunct to the therapy process for eating disorders because it provides clients with a vital tool to substitute for their automatic and driven behavior. Rather than ask bulimics, for example, to stop the behavior in question, bingeing or purging, I ask them to *delay* it. Even if they ultimately engage in it, I want them to learn to delay it long enough to focus attention on the intervening affective events. By writing in a journal about their experience just prior to bingeing, and then writing about their experience just prior to purging, the process of recovery of affects and scenes is initiated. Writing in a journal substitutes a conscious process for an otherwise driven and compulsive one.

Certain clients experience difficulties with this method. For some, writing is already associated with negative affect and they tend to resist the conscious use of the journal. Even when writing itself is not resisted, interrupting automatic, compulsive behavior is always a struggle.

Therapist availability is another feature of the process for bulimics. As discussed in previous chapters, the developmental process must be reversed by *substituting* reliance on the therapist for reliance on food as a sedative for intense or overwhelming negative affect.

As affects emerge, shame, dissmell, and disgust must be consciously differentiated. In bulimics, shame and disgust are critical; in anorexics, shame and dissmell are critical. Other negative affects will also surface and require precise differentiation.

Finally, positive affect body scenes must be created as body shame is made conscious and dissolved. The focus here is twofold: the internalized shame about the body has to be illuminated, brought into fuller conscious awareness; then positive affect has to be associated directly with the body. One way to facilitate this process is to invite clients to spend time during the week experiencing their bodies directly by looking in a mirror. Looking at themselves, preferably in a full-length mirror, will initially heighten shame and bring it into awareness. Once fully conscious, shame has to be validated and then assimilated. Positive affect about the body derives partially from the therapeutic relationship and partially from within.

Sexual Abuse Syndromes

In cases involving incest, governing scenes must be approached gently and gradually. It is imperative that clients who have been violated feel in control of the process: the client must not feel invaded once again. The therapist must avoid producing a repetition of a client's experiences of humiliation and powerlessness. Letting clients determine when they are ready to recover scenes communicates respect.

When a client is ready, both imagery and journal keeping are useful tools. Scenes can be recovered and relived, and their embedded affects assimilated, through either mode. Shame, anger, distress, and fear all will be reexperienced in this process. These negative affects will be encountered at heightened levels of intensity.

Addictive Syndromes

Dependence on the therapist gradually has to be substituted for dependence on the chemical (or other object) that characteristically has been relied upon to sedate overwhelming negative affect. This directly reverses the developmental sequence. In addictive scripts the self has become the agent of sedation and the capacity to rely on another person must be reawakened.

Internalizing the therapist as an inner ally is another crucial feature of the therapeutic process. Not only does the client begin to trust a relationship again, but that relationship increasingly is experienced as present within the self. Internalization is a direct outgrowth of identification.

The addictive client's tolerance for negative affect also must be increased. This can be facilitated by therapist and client together approaching negative affect scenes. Initially, it is the therapist who provides the necessary security for the client and conveys the confidence that negative affect *can* be neutralized by first enduring it. Reparenting imagery is an example of a specific tool that clients can be taught for assimilating negative affect.

The addictive client furthermore must develop as many alternative means as possible for managing negative affect. When numerous alternative means are available to the client for coping with negative affect scenes, the need for the addictive script is reduced. Various tools for effectively managing negative affect are presented later in this chapter when we consider the group-focused treatment program, but one tool—

refocusing attention—has already been discussed at length in chapter 7. This is an especially useful tool for coping more effectively with negative affect scenes in general and shame scenes in particular.

Phobic Syndromes

The first important task with phobic clients is to determine the specific affects embedded in the dreaded scene. Imagining the phobic scene during the therapy session is a vital tool for accomplishing that affective differentiation. Phobias are the result of phobic scripts, which inherently are avoidance scripts: the phobia guards against reexperiencing a negative affect scene. While active imagery allows the client to reexperience the avoided scene in the safety of the consulting room, the client ultimately will have to return to and face the actual scene to achieve complete recovery.

Consider, for example, a man who came into therapy because of a math phobia, which our exploration revealed had its sources in the fourth grade. That year his class was divided into groups based on ability, and he sat in the "dumb row," as his classmates called it, whenever arithmetic was taught. From that time forward, he avoided math and anything having to do with numbers. Whenever he was faced with having to perform mathematical procedures, he froze. While he certainly was fearful of math, his fear was anticipatory: he dreaded the reexperiencing of that early but deep, abiding sense of shame. Calling his impairment "math shame" would have been more accurate.

Therapy involved first recovering the governing scene and assimilating the shame embedded in that scene. He was next taught strategies for reentering the scene, for actually working with mathematics in ways that created positive affect that then would become associated with manipulating numbers.

Borderline Syndromes

So-called borderline clients have been deprived of appropriate and adequate parenting. Psychotherapy must create an analog of parenting in order for effective resolution of shame to occur. Therapy takes on essential elements of reparenting in this context.

Availability of the therapist between sessions creates an analog of the positive scene that clients subsequently can internalize, allowing them to experience the therapeutic relationship as actually present within.

Identification between client and therapist is an important dimension of the healing process. Having been deprived of positive identification, these clients actually require this form of relationship experience.

Finally, reowning disowned parts of the self is crucial to the eventual reintegration of the self. That alone will reverse the disastrous effects of splitting.

Sexual Dysfunction Syndromes

Refocusing attention is an effective tool for releasing shame directly in the sexual life. By refocusing attention onto one's sexual partner, and thereby experiencing mutual excitement and enjoyment, shame is interrupted and released.

It is imperative to enable the client to create sexual scenes of positive affect, because the sexual drive must become fused with excitement affect and enjoyment affect to function optimally. Enabling clients to share the power in their relationships generally, and in their sexual life specifically, is an important additional therapeutic objective.

Sociopathic Syndromes

There are three general dimensions of the therapeutic process necessary with sociopathic clients. First, identification with the therapist is vital in order to foster the eventual internalization of the therapist as a positive identification image.

There must also be an appropriate use of shame to foster the internalization of the shame response itself. A client who was highly sociopathic, for example, announced one day that he had just seduced his best friend's wife, and he was quite pleased with himself. People were merely objects for him to manipulate. My response was outrage at his behavior and I insisted that he feel shame.

"That's a despicable thing to have done," I said to him. "You don't treat your friends that way. You should be ashamed of yourself."

My response to his delight in his own behavior both surprised and confused him. Over the course of several years of therapy he gradually began to care both about me as a person and about what I actually thought of him. Creating the capacity for empathy, the third dimension, is indeed a challenge for psychotherapy.

Depressive Syndromes

To begin with, depression is a mixture of shame and distress. It is the conjoined magnification of shame and distress that produces the depressive mood. These affects must consciously be identified and clearly differentiated.

Typically, the anger frequently observed among depressives is more accurately viewed as *disgusted* anger, according to Tomkins. Distinguishing these affects is an important therapeutic objective.

Similarly, identifying the particular identity scripts that reproduce shame is vital in order to interrupt the depressive cycle. Self-blame, self-contempt and comparison making are the three most frequently observed negative identity scripts. By reproducing shame, any of these scripts will prolong shame into a continuing mood.

Schizoid Syndromes

For isolated and withdrawn individuals, therapy proceeds by renewing identification. Clients who have been emotionally isolated from an early age will need to experience a reciprocal relationship with their therapist. In the absence of true relatedness, therapy will not thrive. Such a relationship inevitably involves essential elements of reparenting.

Paranoid Syndromes

The paranoid script is rooted in shame, which must be made fully conscious to the client. Both the current experience of inferiority and its originating sources have to be brought into full awareness. Similarly, the blame-transfer defending script, which is the hallmark of the paranoid posture, must be recognized by therapist and by client. Providing the reconstructive therapeutic relationship and teaching more adaptive ways of coping with the alienating affect are central to the therapeutic process.

A STRUCTURED GROUP TREATMENT FOR SHAME-BASED SYNDROMES

The various syndromes that we have considered from the perspective of individual psychotherapy also can be treated effectively from the perspective of time-limited groups. These are not mutually exclusive modes of intervention, but instead complement one another. The in-depth individual psychotherapeutic relationship is a necessary form of treatment for entrenched shame-based syndromes. However, not all individuals can afford such a lengthy, time-consuming approach for various reasons, both personal and economic. Even in those instances where individual psychotherapy has occurred, there remains a need for group work to complete the resolution of shame. A combination of individual and group approaches is the treatment of choice with these manifold shame disorders.

In many centers of psychotherapeutic intervention, whether clinics, counseling centers, outpatient facilities, or even private practice, there has been in recent years a clarion call for short-term approaches to treatment. Practitioners increasingly are looking for new modes of treatment that are either group-focused or time-limited. This has been driven partially by financial considerations, including the increasing reluctance of treatment facilities to provide extended psychotherapy and the increasing reluctance of insurers to reimburse for unlimited psychotherapy. They also have been driven by the demands of the unserved, both the visible and invisible waiting lists that haunt every treatment facility. The waiting list, apparently, will always be with us. The mental health practitioner in any setting is thus faced with an ever-expanding clientele—individuals in distress, in need, clamoring for assistance, consumed by the pressures of living, hopeless and helpless, often desperate, often lacking the psychological sophistication that traditional forms of psychotherapy require. They pose new challenges as we approach the close of the 20th century.

The challenge we face is one of creating new forms for psychotherapy that will carry us into the next century. During the past 17 years I have developed a structured group-focused treatment approach for shame-based syndromes. The experiment began with a series of questions: Can we teach individuals psychological skills necessary for effective living? Can we translate psychological principles into practical tools that can be learned through practice? What evolved in response is a *psycho-educa-*

tional group program that can be implemented in either of two ways: directly as a curriculum within the educational system and directly as a mode of psychotherapeutic treatment. It has application for all of the disorders and syndromes that become organized around shame.

Both heterogeneous and homogenous groups can be accommodated by this particular program. It can be focused specifically for a group of bulimics or a group of adult children of alcoholics. Both survivors of incest and perpetrators of incest, as separate groups, can be taken through the program. It can be similarly adapted for physically abusive parents, depressive individuals, couples, families, or addicts. Individuals experiencing conflict about sexual orientation can be worked with as a group to facilitate the resolution of shame and the emergence of an integrated self-identity. There is particular value in working with a group displaying a common syndrome, source of shame, or focus of conflict; participating in such a group produces a rapid dissolution of the secondary shame about the syndrome itself.

The program's structure is a 15-week format that includes meeting twice a week for 90-minute sessions. Experience has demonstrated that for a time-limited program, a more intensive pace is more effective. Two-hour sessions could also be utilized. Fifteen to twenty participants can be accommodated in this particular program because of its psycho-educational focus. When offered in an educational mode, as an actual course, even larger groups have been reached effectively. When offered specifically in a treatment mode, smaller groups allow for more experiential processing.

The format of this program involves a combination of didactic and experiential work. Concepts are introduced each week, discussed, and then examined experientially; examples include powerlessness, shame, affect, and identity scripts. Fundamental principles of object relations theory, interpersonal theory, and affect theory are presented phenomenologically in order to provide a schema for participants to understand their own experience. The developmental theory of the self examined in these chapters is the theoretical foundation for this structured group treatment program.

The cognitive dimension of the program is balanced by translation of ideas into action. Change is a conscious process; it must be action-oriented. Each psychological principle is translated into a psychological "tool." Thus, we do not merely talk about self-esteem; we learn to *experience* self-esteem. These experiential tools are designed to engage affect and imagery as well as language. Because these three processes are central to the development and functioning of the self, each must be directly engaged in the treatment process. The purpose behind the tools is the eventual creation of new psychological skills that will both resolve shame issues and promote psychological health.

Principles and tools are presented each week and participants are expected to practice the various tools over the intervening days. They are also asked to record their observations in a journal. Writing serves several functions. It is a way of deepening conscious awareness of inner events. Writing also directly engages imagery because language is a powerful method for making images. And writing gives participants something active to do during the time between sessions. Change is a conscious, effortful process that writing directly mobilizes.

When the program is offered in an educational mode, as a course, two texts are used as companion readings [*Shame: The Power of Caring* (Kaufman, 1992) and *Dynamics of Power: Fighting Shame and Building Self-Esteem* (Kaufman and Raphael, 1991)]. When offered as either a workshop or treatment group, readings can be a valuable adjunct to the program's experiential component. Readings solidly ground the cognitive restructuring component of the program.

Embedded in this treatment program is a focus on the psychological reeducation of the self, a process that is necessarily affective every bit as much as it is cognitive. This focus evolved from the belief that if competence can be learned, it can also be taught; that psychotherapeutic intervention must be guided not only by an understanding of specific disorders, but also by a coherent vision of psychological health; that if knowledge is useful to the therapist, it can be equally useful to the client.

Psychological health encompasses five fundamental dimensions and each is structured as a three-week unit within the program. The first involves *powerlessness-affect-stress* cycles. The focus here is on the dynamics of power, powerlessness, affect, and stress. The second dimension is *shame and self-esteem.* The specific focus is on illuminating, for the participants, the role of shame. The next basic dimension is *identity development,* and identity is viewed from the perspective of the self's ongoing relationship with the self. The fourth dimension of the program is *affect management and release tools.* The final dimension involves the development of *interpersonal competence.* Taken together, these form a coherent theory of psychological health. By incorporating experiential tools, the program actively promotes health while simultaneously resolving shame issues.

Powerlessness-Affect-Stress Cycles

In the first phase of the treatment program, the concepts of power, powerlessness, affect, and stress are introduced. The need for power is inherently a need to predict and control. It is a need to experience inner control, in sufficient measure, over any sphere of life deemed significant. Life events that thwart one's ability to predict and control return one experientially to that primary scene of infant helplessness into which all humans are thrust at birth. As discussed in chapter 2, powerlessness is an activator of negative affect. The suppression of negative affect, in turn, results in backed-up affect, which then mediates stress.

Participants are encouraged to apply these ideas to their own lives by considering during the session various situations in which they feel powerless. Together we explore both the actual situation and their affective reactions during those situations. Then we strategize ways of actively regaining power, either directly in the situation or else internally.

The first set of tools involves compiling two lists during the course of each subsequent day. The first is a *Happiness List.* Participants are asked to make mental note of, then write down in their journals, five events in each day that leave them feeling happy, that put a smile on their face. The event is to be actually experienced when it occurs, mentally recorded as a positive affect scene, and then stored in memory. Writing down these particular events makes the entire process conscious and allows for recall of prior positive affect scenes at a later time.

While the Happiness List tool is designed to collect and store general feelings of enjoyment/excitement, the *Adequacy List* is designed to collect specific feelings of pride. The task here is to make mental note of five events in each day that leave one feeling proud of self. Participants first are to actually experience the feeling as the event is occurring, then to make mental note of it, and subsequently to record the event as a journal entry. While general happiness can be experienced in response to anything, specific feelings of pride are directly connected to one's actions or behavior. One must actually do something, handle a situation, or accomplish something in order to feel proud of self and thereby collect adequacy. Adequacy must also be collected from other sources than achievement. Learning to be proud of self independent of accomplishment is vital to broadening the sources of adequacy. Another objective is to develop an *inner* source of self-esteem, making self-worth no longer entirely contingent on either performance or the appraisals of others.

Consistent practice of these tools results in their eventual internalization. The self begins to collect and store positive affect—both general happiness and specific pride. These tools are not just a form of positive thinking. Cognition is certainly engaged, but these are affect tools; they operate primarily at the level of affect and imagery. Cognition actually plays a secondary role. These tools aim at a fundamental change in how the self collects, stores, and reproduces experience.

Working with these tools, however, accomplishes something else as well. The tools immediately illuminate each individual's characteristic pattern for undermining self-esteem. Some quickly become aware of subtly disparaging or criticizing their own successes. Others realize how stringent their criteria for adequacy are. By revealing these various means of sabotaging self-worth, these tools enable participants to discover how *they* have been participating in the process of their own psychological demise.

The Happiness/Adequacy tools are the first to be experienced. The next tool introduced in this phase of the program is the *Powerlessness Scene*. Participants are asked to identify a current situation of powerlessness and then describe it in writing. The purpose is to facilitate their ability to recognize and identify when they actually are experiencing powerlessness. Next they must identify their specific affective reactions during that particular scene. They are to use the language of affect theory in this context. Hence, they must consider the six negative affects (anger, fear, distress, shame, dissmell, and disgust) as equally potential responses to powerlessness. To learn to use the language of affect and to learn to differentiate among particular affects are important reasons for working with Tomkins's schema. Furthermore, participants learn through this tool to consciously observe the sequence of coassembled inner states: activator—affect—consequence. In this case, the activator is powerlessness. Finally, participants are instructed to identify two alternative options for coping with that situation that would enable them to take back the power. The purpose here is to learn how to overcome the sources of negative affect. This entire process is described in writing, which directly engages imagery while stimulating conscious reflection.

Generally, the Happiness/Adequacy tools are introduced the first week, the Powerlessness Scene during the second. Participants are given a week to work with each set of tools. These tools are offered as *psychological experiments;* the participants become observers of their own experience. Each session includes group discussion of their experiences working with that week's set of tools, including difficulties, successes, and discoveries. The group process can become as experiential as is deemed desirable. These general procedures are followed throughout the remainder of the program.

Shame and Self-Esteem

The second three-week unit of the program focuses on the dynamics of shame. Participants are introduced to the concept of shame, its facial signs, its phenomenology, and the various forms in which it manifests. The purpose is first to sensitize them to the operation of shame in their everyday lives. If they are to regain mastery over dysfunctional patterns such as addictions or abusive relationships, they must first understand the role of shame not only in their particular disorders but also as it relates to self-esteem generally. The dynamics of self-esteem are invariably the dynamics of shame. Issues around self-concept, self-image, body image, self-worth, self-doubt, even masculinity and femininity, dissolve into issues of shame.

The dynamics of addiction and stress are generally rooted in affect, with shame playing a more or less central role relative to other affects,. Self-sedation of negative affect via food, drugs, alcohol, or sex can only be mastered by first understanding how affect itself works. That understanding, that particular knowledge of self, must be affective as well as cognitive and must engage imagery, not language alone. The reeducation of individuals participating in this program is an emotional relearning experience. Simply enabling shame to become conscious is itself a significant accomplishment.

Following exposure to the nature of shame and detailed consideration of its sources throughout the life cycle, the following tool is introduced. Each participant is asked to identify and then describe in writing an old *Shame Scene* from childhood. The scene can represent any intensity or complex of shame (embarrassment, shyness, guilt, self-consciousness, discouragement, inferiority). The scene can also involve any interpersonal setting (family, school, peer groups). The task is to actually relive that scene, reflect on it in writing, and also describe specific affective reactions both during and following that scene. Participants must then describe how that old shame scene continues to influence them in the present, either positively or negatively. The purpose is to teach them how to recognize shame, retrieve shame scenes from memory, and then connect scenes in the past with their continuing influence in the present. These are translations of psychotherapeutic principles into learnable tools.

Some participants write about scenes involving sexual or physical abuse. Some pick scenes involving body shame or peer rejection, and others describe scenes in which they have injured someone else.

The next week is devoted to applying the *Shame Profile* to each participant's personality development. Following an in-depth consideration of the affect, drive, interpersonal need, and purpose systems (as already discussed in chapters 3 and 4), careful attention is given to the development of specific shame binds. Participants are taught the process by which shame becomes fused with particular affects, drives, interpersonal needs, and purposes. This sets the stage for self-examination of the impact of shame.

Participants are asked to apply the Shame Profile to their own personality. They must write about whatever affects, drives, interpersonal needs, and purposes have become bound by shame. Then they are asked to consider the higher-order scene dimensions in the Shame Profile: body shame, competence shame, relationship shame, and identity shame. The purpose of this tool is to illuminate the particular role shame has played in each person's life. By applying this tool, people become increasingly conscious of the pathways along which shame has developed. They begin to see *how* their adult forms of shame (body, competence, relationship, identity) actually evolved. In this way, together we are returning internalized shame to its interpersonal origins.

Identity: The Self's Relationship with the Self

The concept of identity gives personality a historical dimension. Each emerging self develops a separate and distinct identity as a self. Because identity connects the past with the present and future, identity reflects the history of each developing personality. The self evolves over time. Identity is not merely an individual's various and accumulating attitudes and thoughts, distinct impressions of self that are either mirrored back to the self or communicated to others. Identity is the conscious experience of the self together with the self's unfolding patterns for behaving inward toward the self. Identity is the set of coalescing scripts that give continuity to the self over time. These evolving identity scripts reproduce affect and simultaneously attempt to predict, control, interpret, or otherwise respond to any magnified set of scenes. Negative identity scripts invade the self.

The restoration of inner security depends on the conscious replacement of *self-blame, comparison making,* and *self-contempt.* These three identity scripts first generate in response to magnified scenes of shame but then function to reproduce shame. Observing inner voices is an important entrance to these scripts.

Following presentation of the concept of identity scripts and how they develop, participants are invited to imagine themselves in a series of universal situations that directly illuminate inner voices. The first of these is *looking into the mirror.* The purpose is to identify their characteristic ways of behaving toward themselves. The script involves language, affect, and imagery features. They are invited to imagine the scene of looking into the mirror and to consider how they typically react. Immediately, awareness of self-contempt or comparison making dawns.

A second situation involves *making mistakes, blunders, or even failing.* This is a typical activator of self-blame scripts, which are invariably accompanied by the words, "You should have known better."

The next situation imagined involves *success* or *accomplishment,* actually doing well. Here, the usual response is fault-finding. Individuals disparage their own accomplishments in various ways, calling it luck, believing it could have been done better, or feeling that however well they do is not good enough.

Another universal situation for the observation of inner voices involves *meeting strangers.* Upon leaving such an encounter, identity scripts become activated. Some individuals replay their real or imagined faux pas repeatedly in deepening mortification; others angrily find fault with themselves in a self-blame script. Some become mercilessly critical in a self-contempt script; others compare themselves to the stranger, feeling lesser for the comparison.

Receiving compliments is another critical situation because it universally activates shame. Most people feel undeserving of compliments and respond to them with embarrassment.

Actually being a *disappointment to others* or feeling *disappointed by others* are two additional situations that activate identity scripts. Generally, these scripts take the form of self-blame or self-contempt.

Following this introduction to the theory of identity scripts, participants are taught the process of changing negative scripts to self-affirming scripts. That process, as considered previously, involves a number of specific steps. The first is consciously observing the operation of identity scripts by attending to inner voices. In certain individuals, however, the process is not mediated by inner voices. Nevertheless, observing oneself in any of the aforementioned situations illuminates the process, whether or not it is mediated by an inner voice. The next step is *naming* the pattern accurately as either a form of self-blame, self-contempt, or comparison making.

In order to release these scripts, their *governing scenes must be recovered.* Participants are asked to attempt to visualize the voices they hear inside. Inner voices must be linked to their interpersonal origins. By observing inner voices whenever they occur, neither agreeing nor disagreeing with them, the imagery component of the scene is gradually recovered. Writing in a journal about whatever the inner voices say is an important tool that facilitates observing them. This is not a cognitive process, but a conscious one.

The final step is *creating new self-affirming identity scripts,* which is accomplished by engaging affect, imagery, and language directly. New scenes of positive affect for self must be created, accompanied by a new language of respect. Participants are given models: new words to say to themselves, new feelings to experience toward themselves, and a new voice to hear speaking inside. To complete the process they are invited to imagine someone else speaking to them inside, ideally someone older with whom they have had a mutually respecting relationship. In this way imagery is directly engaged in the change process.

Over the next week, participants are given an opportunity to work directly with the *Identity Scripts* tool. They are asked to experiment with observing and replacing their negative identity scripts. Their task is first to observe, then to accurately name, and finally to describe their prominent inner voices/identity scripts. They are further encouraged to attempt to recover the scenes in which these scripts are rooted and also to attempt to replace self-shaming with self-affirming scripts. Writing about their observations makes the entire process conscious. They are not expected to master the process, just to initiate it.

The process of recreating identity involves a number of dimensions, and replacing self-shaming identity scripts is the first. The next dimension involves developing an internal sense of how much is good enough. Rather than striving to be perfect, to feel compelled to excel at everything, individuals must adjust expectations to changing circumstances. The self must determine, *from within,* how much is good enough. Without that knowledge, the self remains forever caught between the inordinate demands of others and the pressure of deadlines. Only an *inner source* of that knowledge will free the self from the hopeless treadmill of perfectionism.

Distinguishing between two sources of shame/guilt is equally imperative to the creation of a self-affirming identity. Participants are asked whenever they experience guilt to further discover its source: disappointing self or disappointing another. That distinction, while less critical theoretically, is vital for the reeducation of the self. Typically, when individuals do experience a conflict of purposes with others, they invariably opt to disappoint themselves, reaping a harvest of discontent; disappointing another person is an anathema. Reversing this interpersonal polarity is central to maintaining the integrity of the self, to preserving the self in all relations with other persons.

In an analogous vein, the capacity to actively care for the self, to nurture the self, must be directly fostered. Participants are taught the *Self-Nurturing* tool and are asked to begin to actively nurture themselves on a daily basis. Cultivating tangible ways of doing so is critical for a self-affirming identity. They are further instructed that self-nurturing does not have to cost money or add calories. This tool engages participants directly in creating positive affect scenes.

Related to self-nurturing is self-forgiveness. Participants are taught that the resolution of shame depends on being able to forgive oneself for real or imagined wrongdoing, both "sins" of commission and "sins" of omission. Each individual must find a way to relieve the intolerable burden of guilt or shame by making peace within, by embracing the self once again, and thereby becoming whole. To borrow a metaphor from the judicial system, for every wrong there is a punishment and also a statute of limitations. There must come a time when the self says, "Now I have suffered enough; now I can forgive myself." When children do wrong and are given appropriate punishment, parents must further teach them to forgive themselves. In Western culture, atonement for wrongdoing is followed by forgiveness *from* an elder. Self-forgiveness is an analog of that process vital to the restoration of wholeness. The self must be taught how to forgive the self.

The next dimension involves the *Inner Child* concept and *Reparenting Imagery.* Participants are taught how to recontact earlier developmental phases of the self, either the child self or the adolescent self. The conception presented is one of selves within a self, and the inner child concept is introduced for several reasons. Life events that produce powerlessness activate the governing scene of primary infant helplessness, returning adults to that childlike state. Understanding how the child self can be reactivated and then intrude into adult consciousness is crucial to restoring security. Not only can the reparenting imagery tool restore security, but it can also facilitate the recovery of governing scenes in general. It can furthermore be used for the purpose of repairing or reshaping specific scenes of shame. By reparenting the child self through those scenes, shame becomes healed. Participants are taught the process of recovering and then healing scenes through reparenting imagery, which then creates a new scene.

During this phase of the program, for example, a young woman utilized reparenting imagery to rework an old shame scene. She accomplished the work on her own between sessions and reported on it in her weekly journal. The shame scene, which occurred when she was 10 years old, involved her best friend violating a confidence by revealing to the whole class that she liked a particular boy. She felt both humiliated and betrayed. Returning home, she sought out her mother, who, preoccupied with other matters, angrily told her to stop bothering her. The young girl withdrew into a closet, where she sat all alone in the dark, crying. During the reparenting imagery, she brought her adult self into the closet to find her child self and became the mother to that girl she had needed in the original scene.

The creation of a self-affirming identity is a synthesis of all these dimensions. The three specific tools for accomplishing the recreation of the self are identity scripts/inner voices, self-nurturing/self-forgiveness, and inner child/reparenting imagery. By creating new scripts and directly reparenting the inner child, individuals experience a rebirth of self. By writing new scripts and creating new scenes, individuals actually cocreate a new self-affirming identity.

Affect Management and Release

The next three-week unit focuses on the conscious differentiation of affects, drives, interpersonal needs, and purposes. The objectives are to teach participants a language of the self that will partition inner events precisely. In order to reverse the disowning process, it is necessary to first differentiate and then own specific affects, drives, and interpersonal needs. The first process learned, then, is *differentiated owning,* which includes three actions: experiencing, naming, and owning. It is a conscious process that enables the full expression of inner states by the self to the self.

A particular tool is also taught to facilitate the owning process. It involves directing the focus of attention inward in order to illuminate each motivational system. Participants are encouraged to spend 10 minutes every day focusing attention inwards in an activity called *Consulting Self.* Individuals are instructed to consciously attend to affects, bodily drives and states, interpersonal needs, and future scenes of purpose, as these were defined earlier. Their task is to distinguish both between and within these classes of inner events. During the following week, they are expected to practice this tool and write about their observations.

Following this instruction, participants are introduced to the process of *detachment.* Since affects, particularly negative ones, tend to spiral, it is necessary to learn how to detach from disturbing inner states. Being able to observe and let go of negative affect is crucial to its effective management and release. Addictive disorders and eating disorders develop in an effort to manage overwhelming negative affect. As Tomkins argues, "the more alternative means one possesses to deal with negative affect scenes the less the probability of addictive script formation" (1987b, p. 195).

A number of different types of *Detachment Tools* are presented, and participants are encouraged to experiment with them. First is *humor,* attempting to see the humor in upsetting situations. Humor enables one to observe the situation and thereby detach from it. Next is writing in a *journal* which directly engages imagery and simultaneously allows for the full release of affect. Writing a letter to somebody one is angry at or to somebody who has died are effective ways of releasing negative affect.

Another method is *refocusing attention,* as previously defined. *Imagery* can be directly engaged in various ways for the purpose of detaching. Imagining oneself on vacation at the seashore or mountains produces a calming effect by enabling the self to let go. Similarly, one can imagine worries placed in a shoebox in the closet, in a desk drawer, or in a back pot on a stovetop. Each image creates an imaginary container for doubts, worries, or preoccupations that frees one's conscious mind. One can also learn to time-limit worrying by setting aside a period of time, say, 15 minutes, specifically for "worry time," preferably not in the evening. Finally, *meditation* is taught as still another method of detaching, of letting go.

The process of *self-observation,* which rounds out this particular unit, involves consciously holding back a part of the self inside as a friendly observer. This creates a conscious *center* within the personality, around which all other parts of the self become integrated. Observing inner voices is one example of this process.

Participants practice the various detachment tools over the following week and then write about their experiences and observations in an effort to begin to master the tools. All of the tools considered facilitate the effective management of affect in multiple ways. By developing action-strategies for managing and releasing affect consciously, participants learn vital psychological skills for neutralizing negative affect scenes that are encountered during the course of living.

Interpersonal Competence

The final three-week unit of the program refocuses all of the preceding principles and tools directly into the interpersonal domain. Developing effective relations with peers, parents, and partners is the principal objective. The concepts of shame and power are revisited in the context of creating and maintaining sound relationships in all three contexts.

One of the central principles and tools is consciously *Observing Relationship Scenes.* In order to determine one's particular needs from or expectations of any given individual, one must attend to their *conscious* manifestation. Interpersonal needs and expectations become manifest in the form of specific or recurring scenes involving either a particular person or an imagined, even idealized stranger. By consciously attending to and observing over time these often subliminal relationship scenes, needs and expectations are made increasingly conscious.

The second fundamental principle is an extension of the first. Participants are instructed also to begin *Objectively Observing the Other Person* in the relationship. It is imperative that needs and expectations match reality. For a relationship to thrive, each person's needs must be in harmony with what the other person is actually capable of providing. By observing other people over time, distinct patterns of interaction emerge. One must maintain one's rightful half of the power while minimizing the potential for shame.

Participants are instructed to begin observing their own relationship scenes involving specific people they encounter. Before any interaction, they are encouraged to attend inward to what they imagine, anticipate, or hope for from that person. Observing scenes just prior to an encounter illuminates needs and expectations because these phenomena actually manifest as particular scenes.

Then, during the interaction, participants are encouraged to practice observing the other person in order to determine how that individual actually functions as a self. For example, they are asked to consider: Do I like, respect, or want to get to know this person? What is this individual's predominant affect? Is he or she capable of sharing the power, of admitting mistakes, of vulnerability? Is this person dependable, trustworthy? The process is one of making intuition conscious. When attention is focused directly on observing the other, power is kept in balance and shame is avoided. This is akin to the affect tool considered earlier, refocusing attention, but now applied directly to interpersonal relations.

Upon leaving the encounter with the other, participants are then encouraged to consider how well that person was able to provide whatever was needed or expected. They are taught to begin matching expectations with the reality of particular individuals. By observing first their scenes, then the other person, and finally the soundness of match between the two, a new approach to interpersonal relations emerges, one that is conscious in its attitude and operation, preserves dignity and self-respect, shares the power while never relinquishing half of the power, and minimizes the risk of shame.

All of the relationship principles considered in chapter 9 are introduced in this particular unit of the program. In addition, participants are asked to apply these ideas to three different current relationships—a friend, a family member, and a romantic partner. The specific relationship tools involve first determining particular *needs and expectations* in each of these relationships by observing the recurring relationship scenes. Next, participants must *objectively observe* each of the three individuals in order to determine how well their expectations (imagined scenes) match reality in each case. Finally, they are asked to examine each of the three relationships for *power/powerlessness* and for *shame.* Writing is again utilized to focus attention on these interpersonal dynamics and to make the entire process conscious. Participants are expected to work with these three sets of tools over a period of a week and then write about their observations. Group discussion of their experiences with the relationship principles during the subsequent meeting solidifies their grasp of the tools.

The program concludes with a review of all of the units, along with their accompanying concepts and tools. The purpose is to integrate specific ideas and their translations into action, and to demonstrate how different concepts interface and different tools interact, promoting competence.

Psychological Health and Self-Esteem

The program outlined above is a comprehensive group-focused treatment for shame-based syndromes. All of the principles and strategies discussed in the previous chapters on individual psychotherapy have been incorporated into this structured, time-limited treatment program. Essentially, participants are given all of the tools of psychotherapy but without the intensive psychotherapy relationship. The approach is psycho-educational because of its dual emphasis on experiential and cognitive learning. It aims at a fundamental reeducation of the self.

Psychotherapeutic treatment of shame-based syndromes is necessary for the eventual resolution of shame. Individual psychotherapy along the lines described earlier is an essential component of that treatment. Group psychotherapy, a support group, or the particular group-focused approach described above is equally important to complete the overall treatment of shame. The combination of individual and group approaches is the treatment of choice for shame-based syndromes. The unique advantage of the program presented above is that it is both structured and time-limited. It is also solidly grounded in affect theory and developmental self theory. Participants are taken through the process as though it were an analog of psychotherapy.

However, embedded in this program is an even larger vision. The program offers a comprehensive *curriculum for psychological health* that can be integrated not only in treatment centers but in educational settings as well. Psychology has unfortunately paid more attention to dysfunction than it has to health. The five units of the program comprise central dimensions of psychological health: stress, self-esteem, identity, affect management, and interpersonal relations. By translating theory into action tools, psychological principles are transformed into psychological skills that are eminently learnable.

It is to our schools that ultimately we must look if we have hopes of reaching the broadest population of individuals in need. At all ages, they are found struggling against powerlessness, drowning in overwhelming negative affect, struggling to overcome shame, searching for a coherent self, and striving for meaningful relatedness. Only knowledge will inoculate them against psychological disorder and dysfunction. Only knowledge will set them free, and that knowledge must be made universally available.

Eleven

A Language of the Self

Science then is not so much a model of nature as a living language for describing her. It has the structure of a language: a vocabulary, a formal grammar, and a dictionary for translation. . . . Thus science is a language whose structure mimics the behavior of the world; and when we use it, we acknowledge that we cannot separate ourselves from the behavior we describe, when we need a concept (like gravity) or discard one (like phlogiston). For every language is open, alive and changing; it has to invent new words and to experiment with new usages and thereby discover new meanings in what it can say.

JACOB BRONOWSKI
The Identity of Man

Both the process and ultimate effectiveness of psychotherapeutic intervention are directly dependent upon language, the bridge between different experiential worlds. The ability of the therapist to understand each client relies upon language to successfully translate one person's inner experience to another. How well that venture succeeds is determined by the accuracy of language first to partition and then to illuminate inner states. The therapist works with linguistic tools to hone the client's awareness of self and promote eventual mastery of life's problems. If the therapist's tools are faulty or imprecise, then the client's progress will be accordingly impeded. Language is the essential tool of psychotherapy and any form of psychotherapy succeeds or fails according to the effectiveness of its particular language. An accurate language of the self is as central to the science and practice of psychotherapy as it is to the science of the self. And only a unified language in psychology can be the basis of a general theory of the self.

The questions asked by any science must be answered through observations which can be repeated by other observers. The process of science involves a movement from accurate observation of particular phenomena through translation into words which, when taken together, become a living language for describing nature. The focus of psychology, as literature and all art, is knowledge of self. Other sciences seek the study of phenomena outside the self, whereas psychology becomes inevitably bound up with self-reference. Methods of scientific inquiry that extend the boundaries of knowledge in physics or in chemistry, therefore, may not be as readily transferable to the study of the observer. To become a science, psychology must first make accurate observations within its domain that then become translated into a useful language.

Psychology requires knowledge of three primary modes of experience: how the self actually functions, the nature of the process of development, and the determinants of the process of growth or change. In each of these endeavors, language must fit accurate names to observed experience, creating a tool. Language provides distinct tools of mastery when confronting the self's inner life. These tools, in turn, allow the scientific observer to perform inner operations, actual experiments, that then either confirm or refute previous observations.

Any scientific theory or language of the self must first be grounded phenomenologically. The inner experience of the self must remain the final test of these ideas. Psychology has unfortunately sought to imitate classical physics by applying the principles of quantification, specific predictability, and mechanical models to a domain of experience to which they do not readily apply, according to LeShan and Margenau (1982). Accurate observation of the self is the basis for constructing an accurate language of the self, which, in turn, is the foundation for knowledge. As the symbols for a language of the self continue to be verified and refined, understanding ultimately grows, and from understanding comes eventual mastery. This is knowledge, and this book is an experiment in knowledge.

PHENOMENOLOGY, LANGUAGE, AND EMPIRICISM

The vision of the self is both shaped and limited by language. Only by setting aside previously accepted vocabularies of the psyche and returning to accurate observation of inner experience can the self be perceived as an evolving process. When approaching the domain of inner experience, LeShan and Margenau (1982) believe that the psychologist must ask the identical questions the physicist asks: What are the observables here? What are the consistencies that can lawfully be related? Which are the experiences that belong together?

Each word or symbol in a language of the self—from identity and the unconscious to inferiority complexes, identification, affects, imagery, and consciousness itself—is a rearrangement of experience, an imaginative grouping, to echo Bronowski (1971). The concept signifies a particular phenomenological event and points to its relationship to other such events. Furthermore, if the symbol is to be useful, it must remain embedded within the experience it signifies. The word chosen to designate an inner state must allow other observers to experience that inner state directly through their own imagery. Because language itself creates imagery, these symbols become entrances to the self.

A science of psychology, studying the nature of the self, must begin by defining its domain. The particular domain of psychological inquiry encompasses how the self functions, the nature of the process of development, and the determinants of the process of change. A science of inner experience must then elaborate that domain through accurate observation of its particular phenomena.

Many models of the psyche currently exist, each with its own dictionary of essential terms and glossary of "discovered" relationships. In creating such a model, the psychological theorist is more accurately creating a functional language. That is what Freud did and Jung did, as did Adler, Sullivan, Fairbairn, and Tomkins after them. Each of our creative theorists began by making penetrating observations, but then filtered those perceptions through the existing language of their time. As Freud or Fairbairn each sought to fit particular words to their unique observations, the words chosen inevitably shaped perception itself. We in part detect, and in part create, perceived reality. Perceiving is not passive, not entirely receptive, but an active, *constructive* process in which we, the observers, participate.

When Freud conceived his *Id—Ego—Superego,* he created a unique image of the self, greatly enlarging prior conceptions. According to Bruno Bettelheim (1984), however, that particular choice of language was determined by Freud's translator; the original German is more accurately translated as the *It—I—Above-I.* Apparently, Freud wrote about the soul as well as the psyche. The changed words are not merely a question of semantics, but actually create different meanings, a different vision. This effect of language in shaping perception is central to Bronowski's (1971) view of science itself as a living language. Jung changed Freud's language and thereby created a different image of the self. Adler did the same. Each theorist partly perceived a different self, and partly created a different one through language.

Harry S. Sullivan's (1953a, 1953b) concept of *self-dynamism* created still one more qualitatively different vision of how human personality unfolds as well as how it becomes distorted. This particular model of the psyche is only another language, a different vocabulary of central concepts with different perceived relationships among its observables. For Sullivan, it is the network of recurring interpersonal relations that organizes inner experience. And one of his central concepts, *anxiety,* meant something different to him than it had to Freud. He saw new meanings in the word, used it differently, and so "discovered" new relationships between an old observable, anxiety, and new ones, such as the empathic relationship between infant and mother.

Language inevitably shapes perception in the struggle to organize inner experience. And the particular vision we reach through our concepts is as much created by us as it is detected. The vision reached in any age is further limited by the language of the times, by the existing vision of natural happenings in which we, the observers, are inextricably embedded. How we understand the universe, at any historical age, influences how we understand ourselves. Certainly Freud's language of the psyche was influenced by the language of classical physics prominent at his time.

A particular language may have evident blind spots, holes that hinder recognition of certain observables. A language of the self that has words for *guilt* or *anxiety,* thus according them the status of central concepts, but treats lightly the phenomena of *shame* or *powerlessness* is seriously lacking. Likewise, a psychology that considers only outward or "observable" behavior as relevant to inquiry, and so minimizes or ignores the role of *affect, imagery, consciousness,* and *purpose,* cannot be applicable to the study of the observer. These concepts are all relevant. Each refers to a particular observable within the domain of inner experience. None may be excluded or minimized. The pertinent questions remaining are: How do we understand these observables? How do they relate to one another?

If a language can have blind spots, accurately naming an inner state can also act to alter its very perception. Prior to Silvan S. Tomkins's *affect theory,* there was no language for differentiating primary affects from drives. The two were hopelessly confused. The perception of *affect* was hindered by the already existing concept of *drive* and by Freud's earlier concept of *libido,* which subsumed both.

Consider how the perception of *shame* has similarly been hindered by having a panoply of terms for designating different qualitative manifestations of that central human experience—words like embarrassment, shyness, guilt, inferiority, inadequacy, and self-consciousness. Such an array of words actually masks the underlying affect, which stretches through all these distinctly different experiences. Distinguishing shame, shyness, and guilt by giving them different names has greatly hindered accurate perception of these inner states. Language will either sharpen or cloud perception, but will, in any event, inevitably help to create it. Tomkins suspended traditional psychological categories, the accepted names for inner states, when he made the critical observation that shame, shyness, and guilt are, *at the level of affect,* one and the same affect. He created a changed vision of these inner happenings within the self, a rearrangement of experience.

Accurate naming of inner states provides the basis for a science of the self. Naming an inner state precisely focuses the spotlight of consciousness upon it, illuminating it in action. In order to be accurate, a name must create a metaphor of inner experience. The name functions as an *analog,* creating a harmonic image of one person's experience inside another. Language both creates and amplifies imagery.

Fairbairn's (1966) vision began by fitting new observations to a somewhat changed vocabulary, but still keeping well within the accepted psychoanalytic linguistic system. He observed that children needed to *feel convinced* they were loved as persons in their own right and needed to have their love accepted as good. He determined that having satisfying relationships mattered more than the satisfaction of drives. Security replaced gratification. He discovered the *anal phase* to be a developmental artifact, created by obsessive-compulsive mothering. And he gave us as a vision of the psyche an *internal saboteur,* an antilibidinal ego persecuting a libidinal ego within an interior landscape populated by bad objects.

Consider Fairbairn's image of the self in relation to Freud's, and also in relation to Erik Erikson's (1950) concept of *identity.* Erikson likewise made penetrating observations, crystalized in his concept of identity, yet he sought to describe those observations within the psychoanalytic linguistic system.

Why all the bother about a few words? Psychology is presently a babel of concepts. Investigators and theorists either use the same term to refer to different inner states or call the same phenomenon by different names. We have "depression" referring to everything from apathy to anger turned inward. Other investigators probe the distinctions between guilt and shame while calling these states guilt-anxiety and shame-anxiety, only confusing matters more. Certain theorists point to basic anxiety as the source of psychic disturbance; others point to insecurity. Some even use these two concepts interchangeably.

There is no organization to our language, no agreed upon set of observables, no accepted dictionary of central concepts referring to those observables, no set of precise definitions by which we can identify the concept described, let alone determine the accuracy of the observations referred to. So we have proceeded in a helter-skelter fashion, carving out grand models of the psyche, claiming for each a small corner of certainty. Or we have rushed pell-mell to empirically measure by robust experiment, to predict and control after the fashion of classical physics, whatever we could apply our paradigms to, before even agreeing on the set of observables within our domain and defining concepts with precision.

How can we engage in meaningful let alone empirical research before we have a coherent framework, an image of the self to guide us?

What psychology needs is an accurate language of the self in order to organize inner experience, to synthesize the set of existing observations, to bring into meaningful relation the net of observables already identified. We must first bring order to the linguistic chaos at hand if we are ever to create a general psychology, a true science of the self.

Organizing the domain of inner experience, creating a measure of order out of the present confusion, is one important reason for returning to accurate observation of the self followed by accurate naming. It is one reason for examining the existing psychological languages in order to begin the great task of synthesis: creating a coherent image of the self. Evolving such a language of the self is the only sound basis for a science. A second reason has already been alluded to: such a language will provide the needed framework to guide future study, investigation, and experimentation, but differently fashioned. The methods applicable to the study of inner experience are unlikely to be those of classical physics.

Finally, having an accurate language enables action. Language creates tools that allow one to act upon inner experience. Once a particular inner state can be observed consciously by having an accurate name that illuminates it, its intensity can be modulated, even its powerful hold released. The metaphor I use when teaching is that of learning to play an instrument, only the instrument in question is the self. There are many keys along the instrument (affects, drives, needs, scenes), which are either triggered accidentally or become activated automatically by external events. By giving each of these "keys" an accurate name, we discover its presence in consciousness and also how to activate or release it. We now have tied consciousness to language: through accurate naming we gain a vital measure of conscious control over what were perplexing inner states.

An accurate name makes a dimly felt inner state more fully aware to the experiencing self by creating a metaphor that resonates through imagery, suddenly illuminating what had previously been left in darkness. Metaphor reveals us to ourselves because naming sharpens clarity, hones perception. We learn to know ourselves through the images created by the names for our inner experience. Metaphor takes advantage of ambiguity to create knowledge of self.

Were Freud, Fairbairn, and Erikson observing parallel phenomena, but employing different symbols to signify them? Or were they actually perceiving distinctly different inner states? How can we verify which model, which language, is the more accurate and the more useful? Or might different languages simply be different views of the same inner reality? Where do the concepts, *ego—self—identity,* overlap? What are their commonalities? What are their differences?

Each of these linguistic symbols is a metaphor of the self. Each is a linguistic analogy of inner experience. In translating observations of inner experience into language, the scientist does what the poet does. The scientist paints an interior landscape with a particular language, which evokes a resonating image in all who listen. And those particular symbols which are accurate, which match individual experience, allow us to see deeper into ourselves by illuminating the self in action. They become entrances to the self.

We do not now have one unified psychology, but rather many subjective psychologies, each different in vital ways from the others, each collecting adherents into competing schools of thought. We have yet to begin the great work of synthesizing these conflicting models into a general science of the self. Synthesizing our many different psychological languages—from Freud's, Jung's, Adler's, Sullivan's and Horney's to Fairbairn's, Berne's, Kohut's and Kernberg's—is a critical task at this juncture. We lack precise definition of the central concepts in each of these theories. We need a dictionary of definition for each of these languages so that anyone could, in principle, observe the inner event referred to by the concept, thereby repeating the "experiment" and rechecking the observation. The tools of language enable us to perform inner operations, actual experiments, which then either confirm or refute previous observations. We also need a dictionary of translation so that we can move between different theories, different languages of the psyche: How does Freud's *id—ego—superego* correspond to Fairbairn's *libidinal ego—central ego—antilibidinal ego,* and how does each correspond to Berne's *parent—adult—child* ego states? Are these respected theorists employing a different language to describe identical or parallel phenomena? Or are they actually observing quite different facets of inner experience?

What psychology presently lacks, and decidedly needs, is a coherent image of the self as an evolving process. We must work diligently toward refining, sharpening, and finally integrating our many psychological languages. Once we have accurate names for inner experience that are generally agreed upon, we can develop methods of inquiry applicable to that profoundly unique and elusive domain, the self.

Part III

Contemporary Problems

All the negative affects trouble human beings deeply. Indeed, they have evolved just to amplify and deepen suffering and to add insult to the injuries of the human condition in several different ways. Terror speaks to the threat of death to life. Distress is the affect of suffering, making of the world a vale of tears. Shame is the affect of indignity, of defeat, of transgression, and of alienation, striking deep into the heart of the human being and felt as an inner torment, a sickness of the soul. But anger is problematic above all other negative affects for its social consequences. My terror, my distress, and my shame are first of all my problems. They need never become your problems, though they may. But my anger, and especially my rage, threatens violence for you, your family, your friends, and above all for our society. Of all the negative affects it is the least likely to remain under the skin of the one who feels it, and so it is just that affect all societies try hardest to contain within that envelope under the skin or to deflect toward deviants within the society and toward barbarians without.

SILVAN S. TOMKINS
Affect, Imagery, Consciousness

Twelve

Identity, Culture, and Ideology

The most important ideological transformations in civilization occurred when small game hunting became large game hunting and nomadic and when gathering became settled agriculture. In one . . . deities became masculine, sky-ward-transcendent, aggressive, possessive, intolerant, competing with men, taking sides in covenants with elected men against their enemies, punishing their favored men whenever they contested for divine power. In the other . . . deities became immanent earth or sea mothers, indulgent if sometimes capricious, a plenum which contracts and expands slowly (rather than quickly and destructively), more fixed than mobile, more conservative than radical and discontinuously creative, more cyclical than linear. In one, men dominate society. In the other, women dominate. One represents a magnification of excitement, the other a magnification of enjoyment.

SILVAN S. TOMKINS
Affect, Imagery, Consciousness

We have extensively examined the psychology of shame in three principal domains within our science: personality, psychopathology, and psychotherapy. Grounded in Silvan S. Tomkins's affect theory and script theory, the theoretical framework at the heart of this study rests on one fundamental principle: All experience becomes amplified by affect.

But the larger significance of affect theory and shame theory includes important implications that extend well beyond the development of individuals or even the functioning of the family. This new paradigm can be applied equally to culture and society as well as nations. We will examine the operation of three broad, interrelated phenomena that link individuals and families with the larger social milieu: identity, culture, and ideology.

THE DEVELOPMENT OF MINORITY IDENTITY

The development of any group-based identity is rooted in both positive and negative identifications with one's group. Shame is a principal source of identity for minorities because shame lies at the root of all negative self-images. These internalized negative cultural images have to be consciously confronted and assimilated in the search for a coherent, positive identity. The striving for identification is a need to feel a sense of pride in oneself precisely because of belonging to one's group. For particular groups in American society like Native Americans, African Americans, Asian Pacific Islanders, Hispanics, Jews, and lesbians and gay men, it is a need to create a positive, self-affirming identity, specifically as a member of that group. In every major culture around the globe, we can observe an analogous struggle experienced by that culture's particular subcultural groups.

Conflicting Identifications Complicate Identity Development

The positive and negative identifications from which identity evolves reflect experience that is both individually and group based. Just as a uniquely personal identity arises, so does an identity that is racial, ethnic, or religious. Individuals develop within overlapping social milieus, a family, peer group, an ethnic or religious community, as well as the culture at large. The need to identify presses for expression in each of these distinct interpersonal settings. We ultimately experience rootedness through feeling identified first with parents and peers, next with a particular ethnic, racial, or religious group, then with our own gender, and finally with the wider culture. But a sense of belonging grows only through positive identification with others. Any specific minority group—ethnic, racial, or religious—will inevitably be confronted by negative cultural images, and these images also become internalized.

The process is analogous whether the focus is ethnic, religious, racial, or sexual identity. A Native American man or woman struggling to reach a positive identification with other Native Americans as a racial group in a predominantly White racist culture will experience a process that is analogous to a Jewish man or woman grappling with identification with other Jews living within a predominantly Christian culture. Each has in varying ways felt like an outsider, each has to deal with historical patterns of oppression, hatred, and persecution, and each is journeying from being estranged to belonging.

The striving to experience positive identification with one's particular cultural minority group requires the creation of a self-affirming minority identity, experiencing a sense of pride in self precisely because of belonging to that group. Internalized negative cultural images about one's own cultural group will therefore have to be confronted directly, neutralized, and assimilated in the quest for a coherent self, a positive identification with that group, an equally positive self-image, and ultimately a secure identity.

Belonging to any minority group within a larger, dominant culture creates a conflict of identification. Members of minority groups inevitably experience conflicting identifications: pressures to embrace their particular group versus pressures to assimilate into the wider culture. When the barriers to assimilation into the wider culture are gradually removed, the pressure to assimilate and identify with the dominant culture often intensifies. For individuals living in contemporary American society, this conflict is further fueled by the three cultural scripts we explored in chapter 2 as additional sources of shame: to compete for success, to be independent and self-sufficient, and to be popular and conform. The awareness of being a member of a minority inevitably translates into being different, and therefore potentially inferior, in a culture prizing social conformity.

One cannot simultaneously belong to a minority group and the wider culture without some degree of conflict. It is that conflict which must be confronted directly if it is to be assimilated and eventually transformed.

Minority Identity Is Rooted in Scenes of Shame

For any minority group, negative identity is invariably rooted in scenes of shame. In American society, for example, the awareness of being an African American, Native American, or Jew calls inescapable attention to the self, exposing it directly to public view. Because of the fundamental equation of difference with shame, all minorities typically experience themselves as lesser in comparison to members of the majority culture. Inferiority is always rooted in shame. Members of minorities first compare themselves to members of the majority culture, and then feel deficient for the comparison.

Minorities are made poignantly aware of being different from others in various critical scenes around which shame accrues. In every instance there is a lasting impression of one's essential differentness from others, a difference that translates immediately into deficiency, into shame.

To illustrate the nature of the operation of such scenes, consider the experience of several groups living in contemporary America. In the case of Jewish children, for example, absence from school for Jewish holidays is one critical scene centered on the early awareness of being different. Going to synagogue is another critical scene involving a similar awareness of difference. Seeing a Hasidic Jew on the street, on television, or in a film is yet a third scene. Here, one is faced with perhaps the starkest contrast between being an American and being a Jew. Participation or nonparticipation in Christmas programs in school, along with that holiday's pervasive presence in American culture, confront the Jewish child with a celebratory pageant he or she is not part of. Finally, knowledge of the Holocaust may even bar identification entirely. These are a few of the critical scenes involving the early awareness of being different and through which feelings of shame about being Jewish begin to evolve. Jews living in other cultures, whether Anglo-Saxon, northern European or Latin, are just as likely to experience parallel scenes that set them apart as different from the dominant culture.

Knowledge of the Holocaust can produce for a Jewish child what knowledge of slavery does for an African American child, and what knowledge of Native American persecution and oppression accomplishes for a Native American child: warning against identification with a repudiated and victimized people. Other critical shame scenes for African Americans include ones less remote than slavery and lynchings: having to sit at the rear of buses, attending separate schools, living in separate neighborhoods, being beaten in civil rights demonstrations, having Black churches bombed, watching Black youths arrested for crimes on television. Scenes involving segregation were commonplace in the United States only 30 years ago. They remain poignant scenes of humiliation, lasting reminders for any African American.

Gay men and lesbians also experience shame scenes in the form of derision, ridicule, and often vicious contempt. These scenes occur during all developmental phases. Peers are generally merciless in persecuting anyone suspected of being gay or lesbian, and scenes of disparagement are universal for homosexuals. Youngsters learn at a very early age to avoid doing anything that will earn them the slur "faggot." Even when they do not understand the meaning of that particular insult, they learn quickly to avoid it. That word is wielded as a weapon to humiliate others. Being seen by one's peers as gay or lesbian, whether accurate or not, is equivalent to being a leper who is dreaded and shunned. And the phenomenon of gay bashing, which recently has become even further magnified in response to the AIDS crisis, is not unlike lynchings for African Americans and pogroms for Jews who lived in Eastern Europe. These are all magnified expressions of contempt for the outcast.

Scenes form around events in the past that become retold in the present, just as they crystallize around interpersonal events experienced more immediately. In either case, such graphic scenes become seared in memory.

Identity Scripts Reproduce Shame

Interpersonally based scenes of shame become internalized and subsequently reproduced. When specific shame experiences become magnified and fused, unrelated shame events become linked together, reinterpreted as signifying essential meanings about the self.

Attitudes of the wider culture become internalized through the various scenes of shame that are initially encountered in interpersonal settings. These scenes later generate scripts that give distinctive shape to minority identity as it emerges. First, avoidance and escape scripts develop in order to protect the individual from further encounters with shame at the hands of others. But those defending scripts, which initially are directed outward, now turn inward and invade the self, creating identity scripts. In turn, these scripts reactivate original scenes of shame and also reproduce them. By reproducing shame, these scripts become the source of the pervasive self-hatred attached to being a member of a given minority.

The predominant self-shaming scripts that reproduce shame for minorities are the same ones we considered earlier: *self-blame, self-contempt,* and *comparison making.* Now each script becomes activated by, and directly targeted to, being a member of a minority group; and each of these self-shaming scripts originates in governing scenes of shame. These scripts produce a shame-based minority identity.

These self-shaming scripts reactivate governing scenes of shame and thereby continuously reproduce shame. In so doing, these scripts become the source of all forms of internalized self-hatred connected to minority status—whether in the form of internalized racism, sexism, anti-Semitism, or homophobia.

Contempt as a Strategy Against Shame

Whenever people are relegated to an inferior status within a wider culture, they begin to doubt themselves and also question the worth of the group to which they belong. Whenever people are rejected because of belonging to a particular group, shame becomes radically magnified into inferiority. Whenever minorities like Native Americans in the United States, Gypsies in Romania, or Turks in Germany are targeted for persecution, humiliation is imposed with a reign of terror.

That is the reality of the minority experience around the globe, and in America it has ignited a search for cultural pride. It is no accident that the call for respecting multicultural diversity is being sounded widely throughout American society at exactly this moment in history. Valuing diversity and multiculturalism are this culture's responses to the ethnic and cultural shame connected to being different. Even more, multiculturalism is one route back to dignity, pride, and honor for society's outcasts. The resurrection of pride out of the ashes of shame is a consuming challenge for every ethnic and racial minority. But the struggle to secure pride is often beset by pitfalls. Foremost is a fundamental misunderstanding about the very nature of pride itself.

In their desperate search for pride, minorities all too often resort to contempt as a strategy against shame. But a persecuted or disenfranchised minority can insulate itself against humiliation by responding with contempt in very different ways. First, it can direct contempt toward the majority culture itself. In this case, contempt immediately elevates any minority group that employs it above all members of the majority living in the same society. By its very nature, contempt is an affect that partitions any social group into two distinct classes: the superior and the inferior. Whoever becomes the target of contempt is thereby rendered lesser, and the minority group employing contempt as a strategy feels superior.

By ending up feeling superior to the majority, an apparent sense of pride has been inculcated.

As an illustration, consider the question of race in American society. Even the change in language used in discussions of racial issues over the past 50 years in the United States—from colored people to Negroes to Black Power to Black Pride to African Americans to Afrocentrism—bears witness to the subtle influence of contempt. Afrocentrism, for example, seeks to turn the tables on White supremacy by asserting that the ancient Egyptians were Black and that Western culture really came from Africa because the ancient Greeks stole their culture from Egypt. Such a view directly targets the larger White racist culture, and contempt is the pivotal route out of shame: Contempt makes Blacks not just equal to Whites but superior by denigrating White culture at its very foundation. To "discover" that the true source of Western thought, science, and culture lies in Africa, not Greece, is the essence of Afrocentrism. But it is a racial solution to racial shame, one that can only remain viable as long as contempt is at the helm.

A similar use of the contempt strategy can also be seen operating in certain nations like Japan. Goodman and Miyazawa (1995) carefully document how various Japanese writers report having "discovered" evidence linking the Japanese people historically to ancient Israel. At work here is a solution to the Japanese sense of cultural shame, a solution based on contempt for all other nations and cultures. The antidote to cultural shame is cultural contempt: superiority over others. To see itself linked with "God's Chosen People" makes Japan the holiest of nations. The Japanese psyche is thus governed by both shame and contempt.

Contempt functions equally well in the formation of national identity, as in the case of the Japanese, as it does in the formation of racial identity. When shame requires an antidote, whether for nations or minorities, contempt is readily available and easily recruited.

There is a second way in which contempt operates to counteract shame. Contempt can be directed against other minority groups, not just the majority culture. A prime example of such a strategy is the use of contempt by the Nation of Islam, which it directs in particular against American Jews. Nation of Islam spokesmen have characterized Jews as conspiring against Blacks, as lying to and stealing from the Black race. They have labeled Judaism a "gutter religion." Nation of Islam "scholars" have portrayed Jews as descendants of cave-dwelling Neanderthals, slave traders who amassed their immense wealth by engineering the "Black African Holocaust," and by other demonic behavior like the massacre of American Indians by injecting smallpox into their blankets. The solution to their sense of racial inferiority is contempt for and a sense of superiority over American Jews. The Black race is found to be pure, better than, and superior—especially to Jews who are equated with vermin, parasites, and disease. Use of the image of filth goes right to the heart of the contempt strategy. That was true for the Nazis in 1930s Germany, and it is equally true for the Nation of Islam in 1990s America. The imagery of filth both expresses and further generates the affects of disgust and contempt in all who use it.

The contempt strategy has certainly appeared elsewhere. In the Nazi view, Germans were seen as the master race, inherently superior. But that constituted a reversal of roles. World War I had left Germany utterly defeated, stripped of both armaments and prestige, humiliated as a nation. The war guilt clause of the Versailles treaty further magnified Germany's national shame. What Adolf Hitler offered the German people was a heroic vision of pride and honor regained, not true pride, but arrogant contempt for all others. In order to confirm that they were indeed the master race, they had to actively repudiate other peoples, stamp out the impure in their midst, reject all who were contaminated—especially Jews, but also Communists, Jehovah's Witnesses, Gypsies, and homosexuals.

Contempt temporarily vanquished Germany's national shame, much as the Nation of Islam utilizes contempt to conquer racial shame, though in an entirely different context. What contempt accomplished for Germany's national identity during the Nazi era, contempt accomplishes for the Nation of Islam's minority identity today.

Contempt becomes the means of elevating an entire group of people above shame, of attempting the transmutation of shame into pride. It is the psychic equivalent of alchemy, one that is equally doomed to failure.

What is inherently lacking in all such attempts is the crucial distinction that must be drawn between pride and contempt. The two are not identical. Contempt will certainly yield a feeling of superiority, in this way momentarily displacing shame, but it can only hold shame at bay by continuing to disparage someone. The success of this contempt strategy depends on securing a particular group that is continually rendered inferior—equated with dirt, vermin, garbage. Contempt actually feeds on shame by distancing it, by locating its actual source elsewhere. For the

people employing contempt in this way, shame is not permanently dissolved, only temporarily dislodged by the reversal of roles that has been
accomplished: The inferior is now the superior.

Genuine pride has an entirely different nature. It is founded in positive
affect, not negative—in enjoyment and excitement about self. True pride
is not contempt-based at all. Because we have lacked the vital awareness
that springs from a knowledge of affect, in both our culture and science,
we have not understood the precise nature of pride and how different it is
from conceit, arrogance, and superiority—all of which are based in contempt. In an effort to quash all appearances of conceit and arrogance in
childhood, children have almost universally been shamed for *any* expression of pride. Yet in spite of all such efforts, conceit and arrogance remain
strong. What has unfortunately been lost is the awareness of what pride
really is and how to inculcate it, along with a recognition of the necessary
function of pride in both personality and culture. Expressing joy over
one's accomplishments, or because of who one is, is the essence of pride.
But feeling better than or superior over all others is the essence of contempt, and further, contempt demands that someone be rendered lesser.
Pride, in contrast, does not require anyone else to be diminished.

A Theory of Minority Identity Development: Shame and Contempt

The age-old questions "Who am I?" and "Where do I belong?" lie at the
very heart of minority identity. Answers to those questions are predominantly shaped first by encounters with shame that are directly connected
to minority status, and second by employing contempt as a strategy to
counteract shame. Various attempts have been under way to construct a
stage theory of minority identity, whether for African Americans or gay
men and lesbians. What these theories are actually attempting is to order
the range of experiences of members of a distinct minority group according to particular affect dynamics, but without any recognition of the primacy of affect in determining those experiences.

A general theory of identity development at the group level, either for
minorities or nations, must be solidly grounded in affect theory. This
means that affect must be our starting point for examining how group-
based identity is fashioned, and how it changes over time. In such an
endeavor we must attend both to shame and to contempt, the principal

affects governing identity formation. A general theory also ought to hold true across various minority groups, though such a theory must account equally for differences and for universals.

SHAME AND CULTURE

Cultures can be examined in order to identify their characteristic *sources* of shame, particular *targets* of shame, along with the various culturally patterned *remedies* for shame. Such an analysis can proceed by identifying for any given culture the predominant scripts that become organized around shame. Those *cultural scripts* dominating a particular culture, in turn, produce its *national character.* Modal personality characteristics will vary widely in response to those cultural scripts. These scripts also determine any culture's patterning of interpersonal relations specific to its targets of shame. Just as misunderstandings arise between individuals and even families in response to shame, certain misunderstandings between nations will likely occur partly because of failures in sensitivity to each culture's unique sources of shame and to its equally unique, culturally patterned scripts governing shame.

Sources of Shame

To illustrate how such an affect analysis might proceed, consider the culture of modern Iraq and, by extension, Arab culture in general. Accomplishing such an objective requires intimate knowledge of the culture in question. Sana al-Khayyat (1990) conducted a fascinating study of shame and honor in modern Iraq through in-depth interviews designed to probe experiences of shame. The most important meaning of honor in the Arab world occurs in connection with the sexual behavior of women, according to al-Khayyat (1990). If a woman brings shame on her family by her sexual conduct, she brings shame and dishonor on all of her kin. Therefore, the honor of a man in Arabic society depends almost entirely on the honor of the women in his family. Either actual sexual misconduct by women or merely the suspicion of misbehavior is a source of profound shame for the entire family in the Arab world. Parents, brothers, and other adults therefore seek to control young girls for a single purpose: to protect male honor.

Targets of Shame

A definite gender socialization pattern is evident, according to al-Khayyat (1990), which is rooted in the widely held cultural belief in the superiority of men and the equally natural subservience of women. From an early age, a girl is taught to be obedient and is punished if she refuses to obey. It is, in fact, deemed shameful for a girl to disobey, but not necessarily so for a boy living in the same family. A specific code of behavior is taught to girls from an early age: be careful how you walk or talk, avoid letting your skirt ride up when you sit, avoid crossing your legs, don't wear tight or revealing clothing, and never meet the eyes of strangers. Girls are brought up to avoid any behavior defined as sexual, according to al-Khayyat, because an honorable girl "ought not to do anything which might lead men to desire her" (1990, p. 81).

In contrast to boys, girls are also systematically shamed for expressing anger verbally or physically, and also just for raising their voices. Good girls always stay home; they are shy and polite, and never mix with other children. From an affect theory perspective, then, both anger and excitement affects are targeted for shaming when expressed by girls. The demands for obedience, coupled with restrictions on virtually everything, also reveal that the need for power is severely shamed whenever young girls attempt to assert power. Strict control over girls is paramount. The need for identification is similarly shamed, as are the needs for relationship and touching/holding. In everyday life, al-Khayyat points out, very little embracing takes place after childhood; special celebrations are, however, an exception to that rule. The mother-daughter relationship is not a particularly close one either; the mother's duty is to inculcate in her daughter certain rules and a code of behavior in order to protect the family honor. Thus an individualized relationship has only the remotest chance of developing.

Women are taught to view sex as sinful, as both filthy and shameful; still, sex is their duty to their husbands. But if a woman experiences any sexual desire herself, she must never admit it even to her husband. For women, sex is completely bound by shame.

Remedies for Shame

In a culture in which male honor must be upheld above all else, and in which women carry the family's honor, a principal remedy for having dishonored the family is the "honor crime": a relative kills the woman who has sexually misbehaved. Such an action is the culturally prescribed remedy for this profound family shame. According to al-Khayyat (1990), such honor crimes typically occur more frequently in rural areas and among the less educated.

Cultural Scripts

The scripting of women's role in society in Iraq illustrates the operation of cultural scripts in one particular culture. Such scripts operate in every society, and they embody specific rules that govern affectively charged scenes of cultural significance. A particular subset of those scripts deals with the operation of shame at the wider cultural level.

Three prominent cultural scripts in contemporary American culture, previously discussed in chapter 2, are to compete for success, to be independent and self-sufficient, and to be popular and conform. These three scripts function to prescribe certain behaviors deemed culturally acceptable and to proscribe others that are negatively sanctioned.

These three cultural scripts influence the development of personality by utilizing the affect of shame to negatively sanction undesirable behavior. These scripts are cultural rules for action, decision, and interpretation within particular life contexts. They shape the contours of identity within American culture by placing a distinctive cultural stamp upon personality, one that is also differential by gender.

But other scripts will likely arise and dominate in various cultures and thereby place a different cultural stamp upon their people. Even within a particular culture, there are markedly distinct subcultural groups. Within American culture, there are Asian Pacific Islanders, Native Americans, and Chicanos, for instance, and each group organizes shame somewhat differently.

How the Eskimos socialize their children offers another illustration of the use of cultural scripts to reinforce social control. Young children are taught to discriminate thin ice from solid ice by means of public shaming at the hands of the entire family; this group shaming occurs the very first time the young child's foot slips through thin ice into water (English, 1975). The family quickly gathers around the child, no matter how young, laughing and teasing. They all point at the child who is now humiliated for a seemingly innocent mishap. But the child learns an important lesson: never again to mistake thin ice for solid ice. Slipping through ice into water has become bad, shameful, the worst thing imaginable. It must be avoided at all cost. Perception about how solid the ice on a lake is has become radically magnified, and that heightened awareness will become second nature. An obvious survival skill in this way becomes indelibly learned. At work here is the internalization of social control through the operation of cultural scripts.

Patterning Affect Expression

The particular affects that are deemed appropriate for expression—such as anger, distress, and joy—reflect culture-specific patterns, as do the scripts governing the expression and public display of affect. What is judged to be acceptable varies widely across cultures. In some Mediterranean cultures, for example, distress affect is publicly displayed in response to the death of a loved one; even the specific cry of distress affect largely remains uncensored. Contrast this for a moment with American culture where the "stiff upper lip," the antidistress response, is the governing rule for mourning, certainly in public and often in private as well, because distress affect has been systematically and uniformly shamed. Remember President Kennedy's assassination in 1963; news commentators repeatedly remarked with approval how "strong" Jacqueline Kennedy was because she did not cry.

Among the British, the expression of enjoyment affect in the form of noisy laughter is strictly controlled in certain situations, notably, social entertainments like plays. On a recent visit to England, I observed how restrained the audience was during the theatrical performance of a comedy; when I laughed out loud I was greeted with embarrassment and looks of disdain. I had unknowingly violated a cultural taboo. At least in this particular circumstance, expressing enjoyment affect facially and vocally—smiling widely, laughing loudly—is deemed shameful. All such expressions are controlled by shame. Certainly, class status will play an important role in determining the rules that govern affect expression, mediating what is acceptable where and when. The expression of affect in England will vary according to one's social class as well as the particular situational context, both of which are patterned distinctively by the culture.

Different affects have even dominated in Eastern and Western cultures generally. For example, in China the affect of enjoyment has predominated, bringing an investment in sameness and tradition. According to Tomkins, the Chinese particularly enjoyed "the land which they inherited from their ancestors, who had loved it before them" (1991, p. 250). In contrast, the affect of excitement has predominated in the West, and especially in the United States, bringing an investment in transformation and change.

Patterning Drive Expression

Differential shaming across cultures also targets the expression of affect about the hunger drive, and in particular, the behavior of individuals when eating in public. As a culture, for example, the French seemingly have no shame about eating food, and no shame about eating in public. They can eat and be seen eating without shame; perhaps this accounts for the many sidewalk cafés. Strangers passing by typically look directly at people who are eating, and they also look directly at the plates of food before those dining. The passersby display no shame at looking, and the people who are eating display no shame at being looked at, seen. What's more, even strangers are apt to express enjoyment at the food served to someone else. Contrast this with the cultural rules governing public eating in American culture, where eating is considered private, not to be intruded on by strangers. Countless people experience acute shame in this culture when eating in public, or when being seen eating. To verify this observation, simply violate the cultural rule and look directly at the food on someone's plate as you pass by their table. This will undoubtedly activate shame (possibly other affects as well) for the person who is eating, just as it may for the person who violates the rule.

Patterning Interpersonal Need Expression

The primary interpersonal needs will vary widely in expression from one culture to another. Touching will be considered quite acceptable in certain cultures—even between members of the same sex in public as is the case in Thailand—while in others it will be negatively sanctioned, even abhorred.

The needs for identification and differentiation also become differentially magnified across cultures. In the West, for example, it is the need to differentiate, both to separate from others and also acquire mastery, that has marked Western culture so distinctively. In the East, in contrast, it is the need to identify—to merge with others, with the group, and in so doing, to belong—that instead has dominated that culture for centuries. Differentiation is fueled by the affects of excitement and disgust whereas identification is amplified by enjoyment affect. The differential magnification of affects and interpersonal needs is a principal determinant of cultural development.

The degree to which identification with the group becomes magnified in a given culture is itself an enormously important dynamic. The Japanese culture is probably the most extreme example of this particular phenomenon. The Japanese are systematically socialized to identify totally with their families, and then with various other groups including employers as well as the wider culture. In this way, the individual becomes completely merged with the group. Identification with the group will influence everything about the culture, even how shame itself is experienced. The individual's experience of shame is thus tightly linked with the family's or groups's shame. It therefore becomes virtually impossible for any person to experience shame in isolation. Because the experience of shame is always two-faced—both the self and other are simultaneously exposed—shame must be avoided at all cost.

Consider the need for identification more closely, and in particular, its expression through mutual facial gazing. At work here first is curiosity about the face of the stranger, which is an expression of the affect of interest. Enjoyment follows interest. The mutual enjoyment of communion expressed through the facial embrace culminates in the two individuals becoming fused as one through their eyes. Yet this universal experience of facial gazing is socialized somewhat differently across cultures. Native American children, for example, are typically socialized to keep their heads down and not look too directly into the face of strangers. In their culture, doing so is a sign of respect. Contrast these attitudes toward facial gazing for a moment with those embedded in French culture, where looking into the eyes of strangers is culturally permitted to a greater extent even than is true of American culture in general. As a further contrast, in Israel looking directly into a stranger's eyes and holding that gaze occurs freely between men and also between women, including strangers, and to an even more extraordinary degree than in France. Israelis simply have not been shamed for mutual facial gazing, whereas Native Americans have been shamed for looking too directly into the eyes of another, particularly a stranger's, because doing so is deemed "disrespectful" in Native American culture. But setting aside judgments of what is respectful or disrespectful, mutual facial gazing always becomes interrupted for the members of any culture only by directly shaming its expression.

Invariably, the head-down posture is a shame posture. When Native Americans hold their heads down as a culturally scripted sign of respect, they are nevertheless expressing shame, albeit in a particular social context. Even the head bowed before royalty or deity is a shame posture. We always pay homage by publicly displaying the head bowed in shame. It is the very essence of both humility and awe.

How Different Cultures Pattern Shame

Previous attempts to classify cultures as either guilt or shame cultures are, from an affect theory perspective, obsolete and misguided—as Peristiany and Pitt-Rivers (1992) also conclude. We can readily observe the dynamics of shame in every culture, though differently patterned. Both Mediterranean and Eastern cultures are shame-honor cultures, though what becomes shameful in one culture need not be deemed necessarily shameful in another. In these particular cultures, shame is quite visible; it is neither hidden nor disguised. American culture, in contrast, is simply organized much less openly around shame.

To bring shame upon oneself in traditional Japanese culture, for example, inevitably means bringing shame, and therefore dishonor, upon one's family and ancestors. As in many other shame-honor cultures, in Japanese culture there are prescribed rules for either purging shame, avenging dishonor, or restoring honor. Traditionally, ritual suicide, or hara-kiri, was the only culturally prescribed remedy for loss of face in Japan, the principal route for returning to honor from the feudal to the modern era. One of the most dreaded sources of loss of face among the Japanese is the look of disgust on the face of anyone of equal or greater status than oneself. In Tomkins's view "this heightened the necessity to smile and reassure the other as it also magnified the vigilant scanning for the possibility of either contempt, disgust, or dissmell on the face of the other" (1991, p. 25). Such dangers are carefully warded off by the culturally scripted behaviors of apologizing, bowing, and smiling—all of which are highly ritualized, social requirements. The Japanese must act so as never to give offense to the stranger or guest, to one's equal or superior. To provoke their contempt is to immediately lose face. All social relations are orchestrated precisely to avoid contempt from others.

Even in the southern states in the United States, there still exists a distinctive shame-honor culture. Here the Civil War continues to live on and play out. The humiliation handed the South by the North during and after that great conflagration, now well over 100 years in the past, has been neither entirely redeemed nor forgiven. The Confederate battle flag still flies proudly across the South. People living in the southern states today replay the great battles of that divisive era, and relive its deepest passions as though it were only yesterday. The return to dignity, honor, and pride is a long and lonely journey, for individuals and for nations. Yet for many, repairing shame is never fully completed. For them, shame lives on if only in memory.

Culture and Personality

The socialization of affect scenes, drive scenes, interpersonal need scenes, and purpose scenes will determine their differential magnification for individuals living within a given culture, just as their socialization within a particular family is a prime determinant for any individual family member. The socialization of various individuals within any culture, then, will vary from the modal pattern observed for that culture. Socialization variants will be further influenced by minority group status within a particular culture. The socialization pattern and consequent shaming patterns observed for Asian Pacific Islanders or Hispanics living in contemporary American culture are therefore likely to vary somewhat from the modal pattern observed for the culture at large.

Culture influences personality development through the operation of cultural scripts, which are the equivalent of cultural rules for the governance of various types of affect-laden scenes. Cultural scripts are the socialization tools of culture. One particular set of cultural scripts develops in response to shame scenes, and these scripts function to control the experience of shame at the wider cultural level. While different cultures will certainly organize shame differently—with different cultural sources and targets as well as vastly different rules governing the return to honor—shame is nevertheless a dynamic observed in all cultures.

Just as culture significantly impacts the expression of personality and the development of identity, culture also becomes impacted in vital ways at the same time. Both the human being and culture are continuously and reciprocally evolving. The broader sociocultural milieu that exists in a given society, along with the more limited family and peer group milieus, all interact in the evolution of both the self and civilization. Culture and identity are thus forever joined.

Even forms of psychopathology have changed over the last 100 years. The acceleration of eating disorders over the past 20 years demonstrates the impact of cultural values regarding appearance and thinness on both personality and psychopathology. The disorders prominent today are unlikely to be exactly the same ones observed 20 years from now. Human beings adapt to their environment, which is both physical and interpersonal. They live in a social group. Because people strive to identify with others in their group, to belong, culture is able to wield considerable power over any individual person.

The emergence of a highly technological society has created the necessity for that lengthy cultural apprenticeship known as higher education. Such a cultural development has itself prolonged and transformed the developmental epoch of adolescence. The presumably innate progression of developmental phases has thus been directly altered by sociocultural changes.

This lengthening of adolescence, in turn, accords the peer group even greater influence over personality formation. Certainly Harry S. Sullivan was one of the first personality theorists in the early decades of this century to recognize the enormous importance of peer relations. That Sullivan's own early development was marked by an absence of peer relations should come as no surprise. He constructed a theory of personality that first of all accounted for his own experience, for the lacks in his development.

Yet the role and impact of the peer group in a highly technological society is vastly different from that in an agrarian society, or even in an industrial society like the one Sullivan knew. How much more different will the peer group's influence be in the Information Age that has since dawned?

The peer group that has evolved in contemporary American culture now rivals the family in its power to socialize adolescents. Youths and teenagers are increasingly turning to their peer group to meet primary interpersonal needs that their families no longer provide. The family in contemporary society is in disarray. Parents are overburdened by the demands of their own lives, or ill prepared to parent effectively. Too often they abdicate their role entirely, and that vacuum is quickly filled by older peers who then become the equivalent of parent figures. The emergence of powerful urban gangs, and their gradual spread beyond the inner city, is a direct result of these various interacting forces.

No single factor is responsible for the rise of gangs. Returning women to the home will not solve our social problems, nor will turning single-parent families back into two-parent households; believing that either is a viable solution simply overlooks the enormous complexities involved.

Multiple forces have been at work, each one influencing the others and simultaneously being influenced by them: the developmental epoch of adolescence itself has been prolonged; higher education is now a prerequisite for thriving in the Information Age; women have not only entered the work force but also pursue their own careers coequally with family life; the stigma surrounding divorce has been lifted; people are encouraged to leave marital relationships that are unsuitable or destructive; the demands of parenting now outweigh the preparation, skills, and resources that parents actually receive; last century's safety net of an extended family kinship clan surrounding each biological family unit has disappeared largely in response to greater societal mobility; the very concept of family itself is undergoing transformation as the nuclear family gives way to a panoply of single parent families, stepfamilies, blended families to which each parent adds children from previous marriages along with their own additions, and lesbian and gay families; women are having children through sperm donors, often without any active participation of men.

Only by positing a theory of the reciprocal evolution of personality and culture are we able to arrange all of these disparate forces into a meaningful and coherent whole. We can no longer continue to view culture and personality as entirely separate domains, devoid of complementary influence. The recognition of how culture determines personality, coupled with how personality impacts culture, also places the development of identity itself on an entirely new footing. Identity is an expression of personality in action, just as it is a comparable articulation of culture. Although both individuals and cultures develop distinct identities, exactly how the two domains interact has not yet been systematically examined with regard to the unfolding of identity in either context. What has so far been lacking in all such endeavors is the missing link bridging those domains: scripts. These are the vital rules for dealing with scenes, both in the psyche and in culture. These rules govern affect-laden scenes embedded in the collective life of each culture every bit as much as they govern magnified scenes embedded in the memory of individual persons.

AFFECT AND IDEOLOGY

The cultural scripting of shame as well as every other facet of life points to the primacy of scripts as fundamental ordering principles. Scripts order affectively charged scenes. Above all other types of scripts, one class is foremost: *ideological scripts.* We inherit ideological scripts by belonging to a particular nation, religion, gender, or class, and also because we live during a particular historical time.

Three main characteristics distinguish ideological scripts. They define one's general orientation in the universe, in a particular society, and in relationship to other members of that society. They embody values and injunctions by evaluating what is good and what is bad. And they also embody sanctions, positive ones for the fulfillment of central values and negative ones for their violation.

Ideological scripts are the most important class of scripts "because they endow fact with value and affect," according to Tomkins (1991, p. 229). These scripts imbue impartial facts, like the termination of pregnancy, for instance, with intense affect and therefore with enormous value. Ideological scripts become fundamental matters of faith, and, according to Tomkins, faith is something "without which human beings appear unable to live" (1991, p. 229). These unique scripts are the particular faiths by which human beings live and die—whether in the clash of nationalities in the recent Balkan War or in the increasingly violent abortion controversy in America—and thus are the principal agents of bonding and division among all peoples. Ideological scripts are both self-validating and self-fulfilling because, for all individuals, they divide what is true and good from what is false and bad, and they are lived out *as if* true, while all other competing scripts are refuted *as if* false.

The Bifurcation of the Affects

To understand where and how ideology originates, we have to examine the origin of social stratification that predates it. The stratification inherent in society in the form of social classes and the stratification that has existed between the sexes both have their origin, according to Tomkins, in "the affect stratification inherent in adversarial contests" (1991, p. 236). During the early evolution of civilization, Tomkins argues, the perception of scarcity, together with the reliance on violence to reduce such scarcity, ultimately generated contests in which there were victors and losers. The spoils always went to the victors. As Tomkins views it, when "the relatively undifferentiated hunter-gatherers split into predatory big-game hunters and sedentary agriculturalists, differentiation ultimately became increasingly specialized and finally stratified into warrior nomads who subjugated peasant agriculturalists in the formation of states, empires, and civilizations" (1991, p. 234).

The intensification of violence first against big game animals, followed by warfare against human beings, eventuated in the now universal bifurcation, polarity, and stratification of the full spectrum of the innate affects into two distinct sets, according to Tomkins: excitement, surprise, anger, dissmell, and disgust versus enjoyment, distress, fear, and shame. The man/warrior is excited, ready for surprise, angry, contemptuous, fearless. In contrast, losers in adversarial contests are timid, loving, distressed, shy and humble, fearful, ashamed. It is for that reason that an effeminate man can be viewed only as a loser. But even warriors necessarily remain deeply ambivalent about mothers who are loving rather than risk taking, empathically distressed rather than hostile, modest, and shy rather than judgmental and distancing, timid and fearful rather than competitive and dangerous. Because of the magnification of the warrior affects, the feminine affects become alien in Tomkins's view. That is why an overly masculine female is as repellent as an overly effeminate male to the warrior, and by extension to men in general.

This polarity in "families of affect" appeared next in cosmology and the nature of the gods: masculine, skyward, transcendent, and possessive, on the one hand, versus immanent earth or sea mothers, indulgent, and cyclical, on the other. The polarity in families of affect also appeared in the relationship between the sexes: in the dominance of one sex and the submission of the other. This polarity finally appeared in secular ideology, particularly regarding the stratification between the classes in a given society.

Once the full spectrum of the innate affects became partitioned into two distinct sets—the masculine/warrior affects and the feminine/loser affects—the affects of surprise, excitement, anger, dissmell, and disgust were assigned to warriors and to men. The remaining affects of enjoyment, fear, distress, and shame were assigned to the losers in adversarial contests, next to women because they were easily defeated by men in physical combat, and by extension to children and ultimately the lower classes.

The major dynamic of ideological differentiation and stratification, according to Tomkins, arises "from perceived scarcity and the reliance upon violence to reduce such scarcity" (1991, p. 235). Violence becomes the principal means to allocate scarce resources disproportionately to the victors in adversarial contests. Social stratification therefore derives from the affect stratification inherent in adversarial contests.

We can see the dynamic of perceived scarcity, coupled with the ensuing reliance on violence to reduce scarcity, operate in more contemporary contexts, for example, in the ethnic cleansing that has taken place in Bosnia, in the opposition to affirmative action because it threatens "White" jobs, and in the opposition to gay rights because it extends "special" rights. We are still locked in adversarial contests for scarce resources, and the victors continue to oppress the losers. Not much has changed since the early evolution of civilization.

The Humanistic and Normative Orientations

Tomkins argues that the ideological polarity between the "left" and the "right" did not exist before social stratification and is, in fact, a derivative of social stratification and exploitation. The left has always represented the oppressed; the right, the oppressors. Whenever groups or classes protest their inferior status, the debate between the left and the right is engaged anew. That was true during the 1960s civil rights protest in the United States, and it is equally true of the 1990s gay rights movement.

Tomkins has presented a theory of the structure of ideology and a theory of the relationship between ideology and personality (1991; 1965; 1963b). He traced a recurrent polarity between the humanistic and normative orientations, between "left" and "right," in diverse fields including theology, metaphysics, foundations of mathematics, political theory, epistemology, theory of perception, theory of aesthetics, theory of value, theory of child rearing, theory of psychotherapy, and theory of personality.

In the normative ideology—on the right—punishment is used to socialize affect during childhood, whereas on the left, in the humanistic ideology, affects are socialized in a much more rewarding fashion. Normatively orientated parenting is marked by an intolerance for negative affect displays by the child—particularly distress, fear, and shame—along with an overriding concern for punishment of norm violation. Humanistically oriented parenting, in contrast, is marked by empathic distress for the distress of the child, or empathic shame for the child's shame, coupled with relatively lesser importance given to punishment for violating norms. The child's feelings simply take precedence. These different patterns of affect socialization produce distinctively different sets of ideas about which feelings are appropriate and when. Affect socialization is the birthplace of ideology.

Parental child rearing practices determine a particular pattern of affect socialization. This differential socialization pattern generates the child-rearing practices that will, in turn, be utilized with the next generation by those very same children when they themselves become parents. Child rearing and affect socialization are thus locked in continuous and reciprocal interaction across the generations.

But the resulting socialization of affect also determines such widely diverse phenomena as political and parenting philosophies, attitudes toward law and order, social welfare, abortion, and religion. Even attitudes toward dividing areas of responsibility are determined by affect socialization—whether those attitudes arise in a committed relationship between two autonomous people or in the political relations between the various sovereign states and the federal government. All of these issues are sources of debate and contention in the political life of nations, just as they can be sources of conflict in intimate relationships. Ideas, values, and attitudes in all of these different arenas, and numerous others as well, are generated in response to "ideo-affective resonance" (1991, p. 230)—feeling more in tune with certain ideas than others—which itself is grounded in affect socialization.

Tomkins further demonstrated a "deep coherence between the differential magnification of specific affects and quite remote ideological derivatives" (1991, p. 232). For example, if you believe that when life is disappointing, it leaves a bad taste in your mouth rather than a bad smell, then you are also likely to believe all of the following: that it is distressing rather than disgusting to see an adult cry, that human beings are basically good rather than evil, that numbers were created rather than discovered, that the mind is like a lamp rather than a mirror, that the promotion of social welfare by government is more important than the maintenance of law and order, and that play is important for all human beings rather than childish. Each of these examples juxtaposes two alternatives: Preferences for the first set of ideas correspond to the humanistic orientation while preferences for the second set correspond to the normative. Ideas about feelings, play, and law and order become loosely organized into a coherent script that can wield enormous influence in the life of every individual as well as in society at large.

There is, of course, a mixed ideological type that represents a blend of the two principal orientations. That type is produced, for example, when one parent displays a strong normative ideology while the other displays an equally strong humanistic ideology. The child is then exposed simultaneously to both orientations and is, therefore, more likely to develop a mixture of the two.

From Ideological Scripts to an Ideology

The ideological humanist, according to Tomkins (1991), is positively disposed toward others in expressed affect, perceptions, and cognitions whereas the ideological normative is negatively disposed. Either type resonates to a particular ideology because of a distinctive script, a somewhat loosely organized set of feelings and ideas about feelings or an "underlying ideo-affective posture" toward the world (Tomkins, 1991, p. 230). This "ideological" script itself is the direct result of the differential socialization of affect.

An ideology, in contrast, is a much more systematic and tightly organized set of beliefs that capture and dominate an individual's life, one which is also self-validating. Ideological scripts evolve into ideologies, and ideologies are principally fueled by affect, though they certainly become further shaped by language and cognition.

Ideology, in turn, plays an enormously important role in all social relations. Every person will struggle with certain ideas about affect: which feelings and interpersonal needs are acceptable, according to one's sex, and which are unacceptable. Even attitudes about various sexual practices like masturbation reveal the operation of a deeply entrenched ideology that can forbid any such expression. Conflicts frequently break out between relatives and between friends concerning politics, religion, or social welfare. Controversies centering on environmental interests versus business interests, at either the individual or societal level, also reveal the underlying role of ideology. If two individuals in a relationship are engaged in raising children, then the possibilities for an ideological clash over child-rearing practices become endless. One parent might be much more concerned about empathizing with the child's feelings in response to misbehavior, whereas the other parent might be more concerned that the child had violated a rule or norm, and so must be punished.

Two individuals whose ideological orientations conflict sharply can become embroiled in endless conflict throughout the course of their relationship. The degree to which their ideologies are in harmony or instead collide will be a decisive factor in determining the future course of their relationship.

All of these various ideological clashes originate in an ideological polarization, which itself is rooted in prior child rearing practices.

Ideology as a Dynamic in Science

To illustrate the operation of ideology within scientific disciplines, consider what happens when new scientific evidence is published that suggests a possible genetic predisposition for at least some male homosexuals. Verification and replication of the findings along with further research are obviously necessary before firm conclusions may be drawn, and comparable studies of lesbians also must be completed. Despite the lack of such definitive conclusions, homophobic ideologues begin fixing on these very preliminary findings as comparable to evidence for a genetic contribution to alcoholism. Their swift response reveals the power of ideology to seize upon and reinterpret any emerging new data as proof of what is already believed to be true. Ideology inevitably places blinders on the very perception of reality. Once again, homosexuality is being likened to a disease, as though that were the only possible comparison. The implication always drawn in these arguments is that the "homosexual lifestyle" is sick and deviant, a contaminant. There is no room in such an ideology for any alternative perspective, no possibility for viewing homosexuality as anything but aberrant.

Scientists studying the nature of sexual orientation are not the only ones who have been caught in the vise of ideology. In the early 17th century, for example, Galileo Galilei was the first person to use the telescope to study the skies and thereby prove, contrary to accepted belief, that the earth indeed revolves around the sun and is not the center of the universe. A noted Italian mathematician, astronomer, and physicist, he had confirmed by astronomical observation the Copernican theory that the planets revolve about the sun, a radical departure from accepted thought. Galileo's research and conclusions so challenged the accepted ideology of his day that he was tried for heresy by the Inquisition in Rome, ordered to recant, and forced to spend the final years of his life under house arrest.

That was less than 400 years ago, but we are no further along with regard to examining the accumulating evidence from the social and natural sciences concerning sexual orientation. Ideology was as much in charge of the 1993 United States Senate hearings on the military ban on gays as it was in Galileo's day. Believing that gays ought to serve openly in the military is a conclusion drawn from reasoned and dispassionate examination of the evidence in the same way that Galileo's conclusions were made. When the Pentagon's favorite think tank—The Rand Corporation—issued a study against the ban, it was rejected by the Pentagon.

Ideology: Polarization and Dispute

The controversy surrounding gays serving openly in the military brings us to the larger issue of ideological dispute. The current dispute raging about abortion in the United States is an example of an extremely polarized, ideological dispute, and the individual's right to die promises to become another. Still other ideological disputes are looming on the horizon, most notably, centering on introducing self-esteem curricula in the elementary school classroom, gay rights, and affirmative action.

Medical science has given us birth control, which has effectively disconnected procreation from sexual pleasure. It has also given us safer methods of abortion, and that has ignited a deep ideological dispute concerning reproductive rights for women. The scenes of protest and violence at abortion clinics recall other scenes of violent protest decades earlier at the height of the civil rights movement. The claims made to nature and particularly to Christian morality—for the preservation of natural order—by those opposed to abortion are fundamentally no different than the claims made over a century ago in defense of slavery, and when that institution fell, in defense of segregation. Slavery was always justified by Christian doctrine and by reference to biblical texts (Wood, 1990).

These are the same claims also being made today against gay rights, but now the claim is made in defense of "family values," as though only last century's family form actually constitutes a true family value. These claims are even appearing in the context of the individual's right to die, whether involving doctor-assisted suicide or not. By advancing knowledge and lengthening the life span, medical science has paradoxically rendered living more problematic for many. The choice to terminate one's own life by means of suicide challenges received religious wisdom concerning the natural order.

All of these oppositions are rooted in an ideology that both underlies and unites those varied claims. If all individuals were allowed freedom of choice, with regard to abortion, suicide, procreation, sexuality in all its forms including homosexuality, as well as marital and family forms, then what would happen to the social order we have inherited?

Another ideological dispute is quietly at work in American society. This one concerns the wisdom of including self-esteem curricula in our public schools. Some people are ideologically opposed to children feeling too good about themselves and being allowed too much inner control. These individuals oppose mandated self-esteem curricula in the public schools largely on religious grounds. Not only should self-esteem education be left to the family, so their argument goes, but if it is done at all it should conform to a particular religious posture—an ideology.

What lies at the heart of all such ideologies is the claim of moral infallibility (Wood, 1990, p. 250). There can be no reasoned debate, therefore, nor any alternative view that is judged morally equivalent. One God, one morality—one interpretation that holds true for all people and that can never be questioned. Not surprisingly, those who are opposed on ideological grounds to self-esteem being taught in the public schools tend to be the same people who are ideologically opposed to anyone having the right to abortion, to the individual's right to die under any circumstances, and to gay rights of any kind.

The latest addition to this catalogue of ideological disputes is affirmative action. The validity of affirmative action programs itself is coming under increasing fire as the dispute heats up. What had previously been a more-or-less accepted principle for redressing the effects of racial discrimination in American society has paradoxically now become viewed by a growing number of people as a form of reverse discrimination, and therefore has become suspect. What is inflaming this newest dispute, and thereby further polarizing people on opposite sides of the controversy, is affect.

Ideology and Hatred

While hatred and violence have recently plagued abortion clinics in the United States, as well as doctors who perform abortions, this is not the only ideological arena in which intense affect boils over, igniting destructive action. The hatred and violence that have historically played out between various groups is inextricably rooted in the dynamics, not only of identity and culture, but of ideology as well. Ideology is equally central to the problem of intergroup hatred.

Ideologies transcend both the person and society, linking them tightly together within a cosmology that both communicates and defines each person's place in the universe, delineates how to evaluate what is good and what is bad, and determines positive sanctions for conforming to the prescribed ideology and negative sanctions for deviating too sharply from it. Ideology unites identity with culture.

The ideology of intergroup hatred and violence is directly fueled by three critical affects: shame, anger, and contempt. Hatred is only partly an intensification of anger. Shame almost always underlies that rage, and contempt further compounds it. Racism, sexism, anti-Semitism, heterosexism, and homophobia are particular examples of the ideology of group hatred that manifests first as prejudice and then translates into violence. These forms of group-based hatred are not just made up of anger in the extreme but, more important, are governed by contempt.

Belonging to a particular ethnic, racial, or religious group is equivalent to being seen as different, and therefore lesser, in any culture that devalues differences. That equation is made doubly true in a culture that also derives all self-esteem from the necessary disparagement of certain groups. Then, enhancing one's own good feeling can only occur at the expense of someone else's. The sense of inferiority, alienation, and feeling outcast that is almost invariably experienced by members of distinct minority groups is the direct product of the affect of shame, further compounded by contempt from the majority culture for all perceived differences. Because contempt always partitions the inferior from the superior in any culture or nation, contempt is the principal affect dynamic fueling prejudice and discrimination. The seeds of later hatred are inevitably sown in that process.

How are the affect dynamics of hatred scripted? Only the affect of contempt causes the punitive distancing of the repudiated other, who is now deemed unfit for the human community. The contaminant must be permanently distanced via dissmell, and just as severely punished via anger (the two affects that combine in producing contempt). The key to understanding all forms of hatred directed at certain groups is the magnification of contempt into a distinct ideology of superiority—whether White supremacist, Afrocentric, Nazi, or Serbian. Distinctive ideologies of superiority, founded in contempt as a strategy to counteract an underlying sense of shame, now fuse directly with rage, fomenting hatred. The violence that, in turn, spills from hate is always directed at certain groups who are perceived to be the cause of one's shame—the betrayers, conspirators, and oppressors, whatever their guise. The actions and reactions that subsequently play out between particular groups in a given society are always scripted actions. Each participant, each group, enacts its uniquely scripted part.

People who belong to different cultural and racial groups, and who feel outcast or inferior because of it, live lives of unrelenting exposure to shame. Humiliation is always a fertile breeding ground for hatred and vengeance. But it is aided, and doubly magnified, by powerlessness. Whenever a group of individuals feels persecuted, disenfranchised, or looked down upon, their resulting shame and powerlessness inevitably become fused. Eventually, shame turns to rage, followed by contempt for their perceived humiliators—their particular oppressors. Powerlessness and humiliation are thus the principal sources of violence.

Only when rage becomes further magnified by contempt for one's perceived humiliators do they cease being fellow human beings deserving of respect, but instead become inconsequential objects to be destroyed. Only when such unrelenting contempt is directed toward others can they be treated with brutality, whether in the inner city or in Bosnia. The recurring cycle of hatred and violence that plays out repeatedly between different ethnic groups in so many countries will not stop until we understand the cycle of shame, rage, and contempt that invariably fuels it.

To effect the resolution of continuing intergroup hatred and violence, whether in the United States, Northern Ireland, the Balkans, or in the former Soviet Union, the psychology of personality must evolve into a psychology of peoples.

Thirteen

Governing Scenes in Personality and Culture

A nuclear family of scripts . . . must continue to grow in intensity of affect, of duration of affect, and in the interconnectedness of scenes via the conjoint promise of endless, infinite, unconditional ends, of more positive affect and less negative affect, with endless conditional necessity to struggle perpetually to achieve (against lack), to maintain (against loss or threat), and to increase (against deflation and adaptation) the means to such a magnified end. They matter more than anything else, and they never stop seizing the individual. They are the good scenes we can never totally or permanently achieve or possess. . . . If they reward us with deep positive affect, we are forever greedy for more. . . . If they punish us with deep negative affect, we can never entirely avoid, escape, nor renounce the attempt to master or revenge ourselves upon them despite much punishment. If they both seduce and punish us, we can neither possess nor renounce them. . . . These are the conditions par excellence for unlimited magnification.

SILVAN S. TOMKINS
Affect, Imagery, Consciousness

Three distinct processes interact in the initial construction and subsequent reactivation of scenes: *affect, imagery,* and *language.* Just as any of the affects present during any event that occurs become imprinted directly into the scene, both images and language also become embedded in the scene. That includes any people who were present, their facial expressions or the actions they performed, even spoken words, sounds, or smells. In this way, all experience becomes stored in memory in the form of very specific and quite separate scenes, scenes which also comprise important visual, auditory, and kinesthetic features. In most cases, the scene itself eventually recedes from full conscious awareness, increasingly operating only at the periphery of consciousness.

Scenes are later reactivated by the occurrence of new situations that are sufficiently similar to those original scenes, but also different from them in one or more important ways. If instead of containing critical differences, the new situations were always exactly identical to the original scenes, then their reactivation and further magnification would simply not occur. "Scenes are magnified not by repetition but by repetition with a *difference.* . . . Sheer repetition of experience characteristically evokes adaptation which attenuates, rather than magnifies, the connected scenes" (Tomkins, 1991, pp. 87-88). Magnification thus feeds on repetition with a difference, and that is the decisive factor in Tomkins's view.

Another way in which new repetitions of old scenes can be synthesized is mediated by language; this occurs, for example, when we say the identical phrases to ourselves now that were previously said to us by others. Language is one way in which we actually reactivate scenes and thereby reproduce the feelings originally experienced in those scenes. When a scene is reactivated through either mode, it will intrude directly into present-day consciousness—usually with little or no awareness that this is happening—and we then relive that scene in the present with all the force of its original affect fully reawakened.

For a large group of individuals, only the language component of the scene remains completely available to conscious awareness. These individuals typically experience an inner voice, which is the scene's conscious residue. This voice is the language or auditory component of the scene. The inner voice that some people experience in this way can be the actual voice of a particular person embedded in the original scene. Or it can be a particular word or phrase permanently attached to the scene that is repetitively spoken internally. Imagine the following situation. A boy grows up in a family in which his father calls him "Stupid" whenever he assists his father in any way. No matter what this boy does, his father responds with, "You're hopeless, you're clumsy, you're stupid," or other words communicating the same message, clearly evoking shame. And each time this happens, the young boy hangs his head in shame in response. This particular boy will likely grow up hearing a voice inside saying, "You're stupid." That inner voice he now must live with once belonged to a particular face—his father's face—that also looked angry, disgusted, and contemptuous while it was speaking. The voice he hears inside that calls him disparaging names, thereby reproducing shame, is merely the conscious remains of the scene that operates beneath the surface of consciousness.

For this first group of individuals, therefore, only the language channel remains both open and connected. Through this channel, which is mediated by the inner voice, the entire scene itself can be reactivated, even out of full conscious awareness, though the affect embedded in the scene typically is always fully reexperienced. Their experience of scene reactivation is essentially auditory.

A second group actually hears no inner voices, but has full visual recall of the scene. Their images of earlier events can be crisp and vivid, rich in detail, but they lack any affect when picturing those events. For these individuals the imagery channel remains open and connected, while the affect and language channels are largely blocked. These individuals are able to vividly recall and describe, often in precise detail, even the most traumatic or shaming events without any affective experience connected to those events. They are able to picture disturbing events they had previously experienced but without feeling disturbed by them in the present. And when new repetitions of old scenes occur, generated by new situations sufficiently similar to them, their experience is equally bleached of affect.

There is a third group of individuals who hear no inner voices and experience no visual images, yet they become overwhelmed by intense affect, often for no apparent reason. For these people the process of scene reactivation is essentially silent because the language and imagery channels have both been disconnected. Any new situation sufficiently similar to an old scene can prompt its immediate reactivation and return. When that occurs, no inner voice is heard and no visual recall of the old scene occurs, but the affect embedded in that scene forcefully intrudes. It is as if these particular individuals become unexpectedly taken over or swept away by affect storms.

In order to illustrate this phenomenon, let's consider sexual abuse. A woman who was sexually abused by her father during childhood may eventually lose all conscious recollection of violation. As an adult, she no longer has any memories of abuse. But whenever her boyfriend touches a particular part of her body, whether or not it occurs during lovemaking, the original scene of violation, powerlessness, and shame is immediately reactivated because of the inherent similarity between her early scene and the present circumstance. That scene now intrudes directly into her adult consciousness, however subliminally. Even when that governing scene itself remains completely blocked from awareness, the affect embedded in that scene can nevertheless forcefully intrude. That is why her response to even an invited caress can be so inexplicable.

Psychological health depends on the conscious recovery of scenes and the complete reconnection of all three channels—affect, imagery, and language—by which scenes become reactivated. In accomplishing this objective, it is necessary to utilize whichever channel is initially connected or open for any given person, thereby gradually working toward accessing those blocked.

INTRUSION OF GOVERNING SCENES IN POSTTRAUMATIC STRESS DISORDERS

The experience of unrelenting terror conjoined with humiliation, in Tomkins's view (1963a), can potentially induce psychosis in human beings. Scenes of terror and shame, terror and rage, or terror and endless crying in distress can become seared in memory. These scenes of unending and unrelenting affect replay in nightmares, in night terrors, and in waking fantasy, as if they were actually happening all over again.

Posttraumatic stress disorder is organized around recurring scenes of overwhelming negative affect that have not been completely assimilated, but instead continue to seize the individual. These scenes can be historical in nature, as in the case of childhood sexual abuse, or they can be immediate and contemporary, as in the case of surviving a natural disaster like an earthquake. Scenes can be old or current; they can be banished from consciousness as a result of repression or disowning or they can be intrusive in the form of night terrors; they can operate only at the periphery of awareness or intrude directly into full waking consciousness like a living nightmare. Whether it is past or current scenes that intrude, they invade forcefully. They are being continually reactivated, imported directly into present-day consciousness with all of the raw affect reexperienced fully and completely, utterly unnerving the person they hold captive. We are immediately swept up in the scene, and we become lost in it.

The following clinical case illustrates this process of *scene intrusion* that is so characteristic of posttraumatic stress disorder. As a child, Theresa was sexually molested repeatedly by her father, beginning as early as age five. Her father would enter her bedroom each night and slip into bed with her, forcing Theresa to submit to various sexual acts. In response she felt deeply humiliated and utterly to blame. Increasingly she came to loathe herself.

Physically violating the body invariably generates profound shame; in response to shame one naturally feels to blame.

If Theresa tried to get away, her father would pull her back harshly by her hair. If Theresa tried to cry out, he quickly covered her mouth tightly with his hand or a pillow. Theresa became instantly terrified because she could not breathe; she felt like she was choking. Each night the scene of conjoined shame and terror played itself out—for well over five years. After he was finished with her each night, he silently left her room. Theresa remained there alone, crying. Then she crept to the bathroom and hid under the sink. For this woman, terror and shame became magnified conjointly.

Theresa had blocked these memories from consciousness for many years and had also resorted to alcohol in order to deaden the pain and shame. Alcohol became her sedative; eventually she became addicted to it. Several years into therapy, and only after she became sober, Theresa began to recover her memories of having been sexually abused. At the time I began working with her, Theresa had already undergone several years of psychotherapy, had successfully been able to maintain sobriety, and already knew consciously that she had been abused.

When I looked into Theresa's face, I saw terror as well as shame. Both affects were still present. During one of our earliest therapy sessions, I suggested to Theresa that we would eventually need to reenter those abuse scenes in order to heal her shame. Theresa quickly blurted out, "But I'm already there—I'm in them right at this moment. I'm in that room while I'm speaking to you—and he's coming in, he's climbing into my bed. Now he's grabbing me, hurting me. *I can't get him out!*"

Theresa was vividly reexperiencing those terror/shame scenes in full waking consciousness. She also indicated that these scenes could recur unexpectedly at any time, even daily, often several times each day. On every occasion, she would feel overwhelmed, terrorized, and deeply humiliated.

I knew that I needed to intervene. As I continued to gaze into her face and into her eyes, I said, "Imagine me right there beside you as your ally, right there in that room with you. I want you to picture me standing there. Can you see me?"

After a pause, Theresa slowly nodded her agreement, her eyes closed. "Yes . . . I can see you . . . with me."

"Now, I'm pushing him out of your bedroom," I continued. "He doesn't belong there, and I'm stronger than he is. I'm pushing him back through the doorway, back into the hallway, and now I'm closing the door and locking it. He will not come back in. He won't be able to hurt you while I'm here. And I'm going to stay right here in this room with you for as long as you need me. I will guard the door and I will protect you. It's safe now."

Theresa visibly relaxed. I further suggested to her that she imagine me right there guarding the door whenever the disturbing abuse scene returned and intruded itself. Theresa said she would try to do so. She immediately began utilizing this particular imagery on her own. It took a number of months for Theresa to gain confidence in using it.

In most cases I will have my client imagine his or her adult self actually present in the original shame scene, and then imagine becoming the protecting, nurturing parent to the child self in that scene, thereby transforming the traumatic scene. I did not utilize this form of *reparenting imagery* in the above case because there are times when clients will not be able to imagine a nurturing, protective self of any kind. In these instances I have learned that I must first involve myself directly in the traumatic scene, before my client is ever able to do so. In effect, what I am doing is "modeling" self-protection as a way to transform scenes.

Several sessions later, I suggested to Theresa that we actually construct in her imagination a new house for that abused girl still locked away inside of her, because the only home she had known was filled with terror and shame. The necessity for doing this became evident during an imagery experience we shared on one occasion. Theresa was imagining herself as a young girl sitting on a fence watching the sunset with me beside her. She was feeling a quiet calm inside, contentment, only to become instantly terrified and ashamed upon realizing that sundown had always lowered a blanket of gloom. Sundown, Theresa told me, had always inexplicably terrified her as a child. Now she understood the reason for it: Sundown signaled her imminent return to the family home—and then to her bedroom.

Following my suggestion, Theresa became excited and joyful at the prospect of actually creating a new house. I suggested that she could use crayons or paints to draw it, or she could use cardboard or wood to actually build it. And it was to be a safe place, one where only she could live. In *this* house Theresa had the power to let inside only safe individuals that she truly wanted to allow inside.

After several months, Theresa was able to feel increasing inner peace and freedom. Our work together was certainly far from finished, but she was now able to imagine me as a protector in the troublesome scene, her ally. Scenes of her father no longer intruded quite so unexpectedly. When they did, Theresa quickly imagined me present in the scene, stopping the abuse, or instead she fled the scene for her new safe house. We had been able to successfully create a *container* for those acutely disturbing childhood scenes of abuse.

This clinical case suggests a potential treatment approach that can be adapted for working with many other forms of scene intrusion. The reactivation and intrusion of affect-laden scenes is the principal dynamic that occurs in various kinds of posttraumatic stress disorders, from survivors of a disaster to survivors of battle. Two fundamental principles must be engaged in any psychotherapeutic treatment approach: conscious containment of the scene and transformation of the traumatic scene. Imagery is a valuable tool for creating a container for the disruptive scene that has been able to unexpectedly intrude like an emotional tornado. Doing so, however, must be adapted individually for each unique situation.

This case not only illustrates the application of the above principles to a specific person with a particular traumatic scene, but it also reveals more general features of the therapeutic process of scene containment. Transforming the traumatic scene is equally unique for every given circumstance. Crucial to this process is learning to increasingly tolerate the original scene in full consciousness, while the affect embedded in that scene is also fully reexperienced and thereby progressively neutralized. Then a container must be created for the troublesome scene so that the individual concerned gains increasing conscious control over the prior automatic nature of scene intrusion. We have to be able to contain the scene in order to interrupt scene intrusion. Next, the scene itself must be transformed by creating a new scene that continues the old scene but transmutes it. This new scene must be fused with intense positive affect, enjoyment and excitement—in the form of safety, protection, nurturing, love, support, or power. Powerlessness scenes must be transformed into scenes of power. Abuse scenes must be stopped and replaced as in the example above. How to adapt these principles for any given case is the fundamental therapeutic challenge facing every clinician.

In every case of survival of group trauma, a trauma which some survive while others do not, there will also be *survivor shame.* Whether it is an earthquake, airplane crash, or the Oklahoma City bombing, those who survive the disaster will experience shame—not guilt—because they are still alive. They will be plagued with unanswerable questions: "Why me? Why did I live? Why didn't I die too?" The joy of rescue is thus tarnished by the shame of surviving. If all survive, then all can rejoice together. But if some survive when others do not, then any rejoicing can only be bittersweet. When the fact of having survived itself becomes a new source of shame, living inevitably is made deeply ambivalent. This shame, produced because one has survived when others did not, itself will have to be assimilated and resolved. Neutralizing survivor shame is an important therapeutic objective that must be aimed for in addition to actively containing the intrusion of scenes in which the disaster is continuously relived. No longer so tormented by having survived a horrific event, the survivor must be aided in eventually securing a measure of inner peace.

HOW MEMORIES CAN BE REAL AND FALSE

During the process of therapy in the above case, one day Theresa reported the intrusion of an entirely new scene, not previously conscious. She remembered how one night after her father had left her bedroom, she crept through the dark to the bathroom as usual. There she collapsed on the cold floor, sinking between the sink and the toilet. With her knees pulled up to her chest and her arms locked about them, she sat in that cold, dark bathroom and cried. Suddenly the door opened, and the silhouette of her father appeared in the doorway. She froze in terror. Then he came closer, silently. He stood over her for a moment. All she felt was the cold of the floor and of the sink behind her. Without a word, her father began to urinate all over her. Theresa felt the urine splashing in her face, filling her eyes, even her mouth, dripping through her hair. She was drenched, and she stank. When he was finished, he simply left the bathroom without a word. That was her scene.

Was her scene real, or was it false? Was the entire pattern of childhood sexual abuse at the hands of her father real or false?

Because of recent litigations involving recovered memories, these have become disturbing questions for psychotherapists, memory researchers, the legal establishment, and society at large. But true versus false in a legal sense is not exactly the same question psychologically speaking. We have to step back from these particular questions and from the controversy surrounding recovered or repressed memories itself, to examine the nature of memory storage and retrieval. Affect theory has a unique perspective to offer on this vitally important and timely issue.

Memory is essentially a duplicating mechanism according to Tomkins (1963a; 1992). The ability to learn from experience depends on the ability to duplicate the past; what we duplicate in consciousness therefore has to be preserved. It is for this reason that, as Tomkins puts it, "a memory mechanism that grossly distorted the information it stored or made available in retrieval would have proved biologically bizarre and useless" (1992, p. 116). Recovered memories are not simply fabrications or gross distortions, conscious or otherwise. They are also not just the product of heightened suggestibility, even though suggestibility is itself a real phenomenon. Nor are recovered memories merely fantasy creations, even though certain individuals have considerable difficulty in accurately distinguishing between fantasy and reality. All of these factors, important as they are in their own right, are still extraneous to the whole question of how memories are stored and retrieved.

Tomkins contrasts the automatic storage of information with the learned retrieval of information. Not all of the information that continually bombards the individual is permanently stored in memory. Only information that has been transmuted into a conscious report "is automatically sent first to reverberating transient storage, then to longer-term storage, and then to permanent storage" (Tomkins, 1992, p. 124). Simply put, what is conscious is stored, and what is automatically stored in Tomkins's view is a constantly changing set of scenes.

The retrieval of earlier memories that have been stored in the form of scenes has to be learned based on their relevance for ensuing information and future purposes.

> How any unique experience will be remembered is a joint function of how it was originally experienced and to what extent succeeding inputs are experienced as similar. This is inevitably so, because of the necessity to match succeeding experience by past stored experience. In the process of such retrieval, there is the conjoint transformation of past memories and present percepts. . . . what we learn to remember for purposes of recognition depends upon the continuing relevance of the initial experience to related, later experience. (Tomkins, 1963a, pp. 385–386)

What we learn to retrieve, then, is not the original experience per se, but instead what that experience *becomes* as we attempt over and over to retrieve information that is relevant to our present needs. The only way we can "isolate past experience so that it is uniquely retrievable is through the complex compression-expansion transformations used in rote memorizing" (Tomkins, 1963a, p. 386).

To use an example that Tomkins also employs, if we have had an initial encounter with a person who appears delightful on first impression, we cannot readily recover the original memory and affect if we later learn that we had actually misread that person completely. Conversely, if we feel intense negative affect toward someone on the first encounter but later learn that this person is only superficially abrasive and really delightful through and through, we cannot readily perceive this person the way we did originally, divorced from our current feelings and knowledge.

> What is live among my memories, and readily retrievable, are the present cumulative totals. . . . what are retrievable are incomplete and somewhat indeterminate fragments which can become complete and determinate in a variety of ways, depending upon the nature of succeeding demands on retrieval by succeeding sensory inputs. It is not simply that the first experience is changed, but rather that it has to be radically supplemented before it can learn to be retrieved. . . . Not all that is first stored may be retrieved unless succeeding inputs demand the learning of such retrieval skill. (Tomkins, 1963a, p. 388)

In the case discussed above, Theresa clearly learned to retrieve scenes from early childhood that had, as their central unifying component, sexual abuse involving her father. As she began to relinquish alcohol as a sedative for her shame and terror, those affects increasingly became conscious. Her growing awareness of affect allowed her to link those now conscious feelings with their sources—both in the present and in the past. She began to "learn" how to retrieve early scenes partly through the example set by her first therapist, partly by initial success in recovering certain scene fragments, and partly by necessity. Life was simply too unbearable the way it was. It is conceivable that the very first scene she retrieved (which occurred prior to our working together) became immediately coassembled with additional memory fragments, even ones unrelated to the actual abuse, and also with additional affect. Then, when that newly recovered scene was subsequently stored in memory, it was stored as a somewhat changed scene because it had already been supplemented by new information. She was now "primed" to retrieve similar scenes. Their relevance for Theresa's present life misery had also been made unmistakably clear to her. Theresa's alcoholism, depression, and self-loathing were all rooted in events that had happened years before, and the way out of that quagmire lay in recovering more scenes. It was her realization of this vital emotional connection during her first therapy that subsequently demanded her further learning of memory retrieval skill. She had become truly motivated to retrieve scenes because her early experience had been made relevant to her later experience.

What Theresa thus stored in memory after retrieving her first memory fragment was a somewhat changed scene. It had been radically supplemented. But the storage of this recovered scene, in turn, influences the retrieval of additional scenes.

> The relationship between storage and retrieval is collusive in that what is retrieved becomes more and more what is stored, and so becomes more and more what is retrieved, to be then stored again in an ever-expanding family of somewhat similar and somewhat different engrams in storage. In this way the individual becomes slowly both the beneficiary and the victim of the world he has most often experienced and remembered. He is its beneficiary when the stored scenes have been positive-affect scenes. He is its victim when the stored scenes have been negative-affect scenes. He feels "free" when he retrieves (and somewhat transforms) the good scenes. He feels victimized when he retrieves (and

somewhat transforms) the bad scenes. . . . One's freedom is sharply limited by the automatic storage of all of one's experience. This limitation is never nakedly apparent because of the increased degrees of freedom in learning to retrieve from storage and in transforming what has been retrieved. (Tomkins, 1992, pp. 125-126)

As Theresa began to recover more and more memories of abuse, those memories next became directly fused together, creating a family of abuse scenes. This new, magnified scene constellation now invaded her consciousness on a continual basis. The magnification of her scenes was an internal process, not a property of the event (sexual abuse) as it occurred. That her "recovered memories" took the particular form of scene intrusion, with these now intrusive scenes literally possessing a life of their own—disturbing her tranquility seemingly at will—was a function of how Theresa's scenes became additionally magnified after their initial reactivation.

Theresa had indeed become a victim of her abuse scenes. Further, she experienced considerable loss of freedom because those abuse scenes could intrude anywhere and anytime. Scene intrusion could occur while she was driving her car, and she'd have to pull to the side of the road, shaking in terror. Or it could occur while she was shopping; on one occasion she left her grocery cart fully loaded in the middle of an aisle as she fled the store in a panic.

Because the complex, shifting set of scenes is only loosely matched with actual events, the accuracy of stored information is limited. That accuracy, however, can be continually improved or instead made much worse. But the connected history of our scenes with all of the people who have mattered deeply to us—as we experienced them—are indeed real to us, irrespective of what those encounters actually were. Hence, the real structure of our experienced scenes is difficult to discover. The "retrieval and recruitment of past information, together with its further analysis and synthesis, radically changes what is then *stored* about any scene" (Tomkins, 1992, p. 127). Thus, we are quite capable of retrieving from memory either a "false" love or a "false" hate. But the criteria by which we judge the objective reality of such "memories" must not ignore their entirely separate subjective meaning for us or their subjective reality among our various percepts and memories. Objective truth, as used in the legal sense or applied in a court of law, is not exactly the same thing as subjective truth, nor does the objective criterion necessarily or always supersede the subjective. That it does so in the legal domain is obvious, but the objective is not necessarily the superior or preferred criterion in the psychological domain.

Our accumulating scenes define our experience, the fundamental truth about who we are and how we experience both ourselves and our world— our scenes are our inner reality, our subjective truth. That is the case even when our scenes do not exactly match the objective reality of particular people or the objective truth of events as they had indeed happened, were an impartial observer present to record them.

Were Theresa's scenes of abuse real? Did they happen exactly the way she remembered them? These are not the same questions. Her scenes were indeed real for her, emotionally and subjectively. They comprised her narrative truth, the way she had come to understand and explain who she was. But her abuse scenes also possessed the ring of truth—they felt real to me as a participant observer.

Every psychotherapist confronts the question of veracity: Is this person's report true? In answering that question we coassemble various observations including facial expressions, verbal descriptions, behavioral mannerisms, coupled with our own internal empathic responses. It is the assemblage of those percepts that generates congruence, creating the felt authenticity of experience.

I had no reason to doubt or question the veracity of Theresa's experience, not even when she revealed the scene in which her father had urinated on her. Having now heard similar accounts from more than one client who had been sexually abused as a child by their fathers helps confirm at least the possibility of such an occurrence—or else implies parallel fabrication independently by people who are complete strangers to each other.

Therapeutically speaking, the challenge is to confront Theresa's magnified scenes in the precise form they had evolved into, and then work actively toward transforming them. That is not the same objective when the question of real versus false is transposed to a court of law. In the legal domain the question of truth takes on a somewhat different meaning. Yet there is a real point of convergence. Clients feel an inordinate need to make sense out of their lived experience, and to arrive at a coherent explanation for what has occurred in their lives—to both legitimize their pain and connect it meaningfully to real events that have happened. Not just any narrative explanation will do. Though we all strive for truth in the search for understanding who we are (truth in the objective sense), what we in fact discover is a rearrangement of events, an explanation or theory that suddenly makes everything fit into a coherent whole—but it is always partly an interpretation of those events, a script in Tomkins's sense, ideally one that is alive, open, and changing.

Were Theresa's recovered memories real? That question is not easily dismissed. She believed they were, and I also believe they were. Recovering and then transforming her governing scenes had definite therapeutic import for her present life. Her psychic pain diminished, and her interpersonal relationships improved. Further, she eventually found out from her two younger sisters that their father had sexually abused them as well. Is that confirmation of Theresa's scenes of abuse? Proof? That depends on what question you are asking, and in which domain. Do Theresa's scenes, either with or without her sisters's confirmatory experiences, constitute "evidence" that would stand up in a court of law? That is doubtful.

What is equally important to address is the prior question about whether recovered memories should ever be brought as "evidence" into a court of law in the first place. Different domains have different observables, to echo LeShan and Margenau (1982), and different rules of correspondence apply in each of those domains.

Had Theresa's intrusive scenes derived not from sexual abuse that was kept secret from everyone else at the time, but instead from a trauma that was publicly witnessed and shared by an entire group—like the Oklahoma City bombing in April 1995—then all questions about real versus false would immediately become self-evident. Of course the event was real—everyone saw it take place. Even a shared trauma like a flood, earthquake, or airplane crash can generate scenes of such intense affect that they become either blocked from memory entirely or else repetitively and disturbingly intrusive. Whether that public trauma, in contrast to a private or hidden one like sexual abuse, occurred in childhood or adulthood, its effects could still be long-lasting in the form of either complete repression or more-or-less conscious scene intrusion. Soldiers returning from combat confront an analogous psychological reality; they struggle, often for years, with disturbing intrusions of battle scenes, which are unexpectedly reactivated. And for many Vietnam veterans, the 1991 Gulf War reactivated their particular old scenes, ones long since dormant. In all of these instances, determining whether the trauma was objectively real or false is largely irrelevant. The publicness of the event, the existence of many others who also suffered from it, and the presence of witnesses all make the horrific event consensually valid, obviating all questions about whether it did in fact occur.

What we can say with certainty is that trauma does occur, and that traumatic events are stored in memory in the form of specific scenes. How those scenes are later retrieved from storage, in what form, with what further degree of magnification, whether with or without the repression of key elements, only as scene fragments, in a repetitively intrusive manner, or not at all—these are the principal questions for further study on a case-by-case basis.

But the memories that are stored for any given person, in fact, may or may not be actually retrievable; in part that depends on the presence and location of their *name* in memory storage. Even if a particular memory is retrievable, it may only rarely be retrieved. *Memorability,* by which Tomkins refers to the probability and frequency of actual retrieval, is not fixed; a scene may, in fact, continually increase or decrease in memorability. The memorability of any event depends on both its distinctiveness and its magnification.

The distinctiveness of any event about to be stored, which is the first critical factor influencing memorability according to Tomkins, refers to its *difference* from other events already stored in memory. The distinctiveness of an event is actually enhanced by increasing the relatedness and connectedness of that event to all other events because we cannot continue to remember any particular scene in exactly the same way throughout our lives. Typically, any given memory is retrieved less and less often from its memory address. Only when a memory becomes a necessary part of many different wholes—that is, scene constellations—will the memory endure almost intact.

The second critical factor influencing memorability is the degree of its magnification. Not simple repetition, but repetition with a difference is the determinant of magnification. The magnification of memorability for any particular scene is therefore based upon the creation of an ever expanding family of somewhat similar and somewhat different scenes. The detection of similarity in otherwise very different scenes involves the creation of *analogues* of those scenes, while the detection of difference in otherwise very similar scenes involves the creation of *variants* of those scenes. These are the two principles by which magnification grows.

Negative affect scenes become magnified mainly by the creation of analogues, while positive affect scenes grow principally through the production of variants.

Now contrast magnification with attenuation, which occurs in addiction. When scenes are endlessly repeated, as they are in any addictive process, their memorability actually is reduced. The cigarette addict is unaware of smoking for the majority of the time—until he or she stops smoking. Addiction is a habitual skill, like walking, that is only occasionally interrupted by "memorable" intrusions.

> Memorability grows through magnification. . . . Every time an individual scans a scene for its *possible* similarity or difference to any particular scene, *that* scene has been made more memorable no matter what the outcome of the comparison. This is not to say that this is usually a conscious memory that is retrieved. What *is* conscious is the present scene *transformed* as guided by the variant or analogue. (Tomkins, 1992, p. 171)

One implication of Tomkins's theory of memory is that the fruits of psychological investigation, valuable as they are for personality theory and psychotherapy, are not readily transferable to the legal domain, certainly not for the principal purpose that occupies attorneys, juries, and judges—the determination of someone's guilt or innocence. Reality and truth take on very different meanings in the two domains, and the criteria by which we judge truth are necessarily different as well.

TRAUMA AND SCENE MAGNIFICATION

An important consequence of affect theory's perspective on memory is that events are not necessarily traumatic at the precise moment they occur, but instead become traumatic later—after magnification is under way. Tomkins argues that "there is no such thing as a traumatic experience. An experience has to *become* traumatic by being further transformed both in content and in retrievability by succeeding experience" [emphasis mine] (1963a, p. 386). Thus, being in an automobile crash is not inherently traumatic when the event occurs; it is not even necessarily traumatic at all. Events become traumatic only after the future happens—after they are transformed in meaning or interpretation and further linked to new scenes (what Tomkins means by the term succeeding experience), all of which markedly increase their retrievability.

Such "succeeding experience" can occur as a result of environmental support in the form of new experience that is sufficiently similar to the original event, as in the case of humiliation that is later repeated in some form. Or such succeeding experience can occur without further environmental support; in this case succeeding experience can be in the form of prior experiences, already stored as scenes, that are sufficiently similar to the event in question. No repetition of an event in reality is absolutely necessary because that repetition can occur wholly internally. But in either case—with or without additional environmental support—this transformative work has to take place in order for any given experience to become traumatic.

An event of intense negative affect is stored in memory as a scene. That scene is then reenacted when the event is actually repeated in analogous form; it must not be repeated identically but with sufficient similarity, because only repetition with a difference is decisive for magnification. The scene can also be reenacted when the original event is later relived in memory, not actually repeated; each time the scene is replayed and reviewed internally the initial affect is reexperienced, deepened, drawn out over a considerably longer period of time. Internal repetition of a scene both prolongs and intensifies the affect of the original event, thereby magnifying it. Its reenactment in imagination also links the event directly with other events that were previously unrelated, causing a set of isolated scenes to now become more permanently interconnected. This resulting family of scenes defines the process of psychological magnification—the fusion of unrelated scenes. There is yet a third distinct feature of this process: the addition of fresh affect, not present in the event when it actually occurred, to this emerging new family of scenes.

In the case of an automobile crash, for example, the actual event as stored in memory in the form of a scene next has to be supplemented by new information: by reliving that scene over and over, intensifying its affect; by linking that scene to other similar scenes that happened previously; by assembling the scene with new interpretations about who might have caused the accident, any loss of life that may have occurred, or attributions of self-blame; and by adding entirely new affect to this growing scene constellation, affect not embedded in the original scene, upon each review in memory.

Trauma is actually the result of any one of these factors or a product of some combination of them. The traumatic impact of any given experience is therefore unpredictable at the time it occurs. Its ultimate impact can only be known after reenactment and magnification have taken place.

RECOVERING MEMORIES: IMPLICATIONS FOR PSYCHOTHERAPY

In his theory of memory, Tomkins (1992) delineates specific conditions under which the retrieval of early memories can be directly activated. Let's proceed by way of example. If you were instructed to write your name very slowly, at the rate of about 3 seconds per letter, you would observe several phenomena. Your handwriting would closely resemble your childhood handwriting, not your adult handwriting. Only after completing the task would you recognize it as early handwriting. You might also hold the pencil the way you did as a child, and you might even retrieve early memories of your first-grade teacher or classroom. The instruction was not to recall early memories of learning to write, but simply to write your name very slowly.

Why are early memories retrieved? Because the early, childhood performance is slow in the case of handwriting, while the later, adult performance is more rapid. Speed, thus, is a *distinctive name* that retrieves the early performance. But speed alone is not sufficient to retrieve early handwriting. What is necessary is a *conjoint distinctive name,* as in the above instruction to "write . . . your name . . .very slowly"; any single component alone will not recall early handwriting, though other memory traces might return. Only the combination of all three components is effective in activating the particular early memory of interest. A conjoint distinctive name is a group of names for early memory traces that, taken together, are capable of activating one and only one particular memory.

Consider a second example. If you were instructed to perform before a group and shout as loudly as possible the phrase "No, I won't," again you would make certain observations. You might feel shy and too inhibited to comply at all, or the very idea itself might produce fear or shame. Your facial expression upon shouting the above phrase might even give the appearance of a defiant, pouting child, because your lower lip would protrude immediately after speaking. You might also reexperience the childhood affects of distress and anger along with specific incidents, long since forgotten, in which those affects were triggered. On the other hand, your face might express the smile of triumph instead of a pout, along with joy and anger instead of distress and anger.

Why are such early memories retrieved? Because the early performance is considerably louder than the later, adult performance. In the case of speech, the most critical discontinuity is the loudness or intensity of speech. The instruction to shout at the top of the voice is effective because of this discontinuity, but it is not always effective; for example, it is not effective for people who continue to shout as adults. "In general, the more the voice was soft-spoken in adulthood, the more this method unlocked a flood of early memories if there was compliance" (Tomkins, 1992, p. 204).

If we focus on the learning skill required in retrieving early memories under conditions of supplying the correct instruction, as evidenced by the necessity of learning the conjoint distinctive name for the memory trace in question, "then it is clear that the debate about primacy versus recency, early versus late experience," according to Tomkins, "is a mistaken polarity and that the nervous system is quite capable of supporting two independent sets of traces under certain conditions" (1992, p. 206). Thus, in the case of early and late handwriting two independent organizations exist side by side with little interaction in either direction. "Early memory here does not influence later memory, nor does later memory alter early memory" (Tomkins, 1992, p. 206).

Extending these principles to the recovery of affectively laden scenes from childhood requires that we first carefully consider the parameters that are likely to be unique in childhood. Relative size is the first such parameter. Since the child is so much smaller than the adult, and objects in the child's environment are considerably larger, bringing an adult into a room that would duplicate the spatial relations of early childhood—a room about two and a half times normal size in all dimensions including furniture—would directly activate early memories. Why? Because relative size is one discontinuity between infancy and adulthood that holds true in the experience of all individuals, independent of culture or family. But spatial relations are not the only distinctive feature of childhood.

> In addition to living in a space that is relatively larger, there are many types of experience peculiar to infancy and childhood, such as being alone in the dark in a crib; nakedness; being fondled; being tweaked on

the face; being wet; being hungry and wet; being sated and cuddled; being in a crib; being looked at intently by adults; smelling urine and feces, talcum powder, mother's body odor; falling while walking; being moved passively; being rocked; being read to sleep at night; being bathed; being undressed; hearing lullabies; being read fairy stories; hearing the variety of talk directed toward infants and children; being tickled and teased; being spanked, being made to stand in a corner as punishment, being made to write 1,000 times "I will not pick my nose," being sent to bed without supper, being subject to castration threats, and so on. (Tomkins, 1992, p. 213)

These are all distinctive experiences of childhood and, therefore, can be utilized for the purpose of retrieving early memories, of recovering scenes. The child also actively emits a number of responses that are just as characteristic of childhood, like sucking fingers, mouthing objects, biting, rolling over in a crib, talking baby talk, crying, screaming, breaking things, falling down, splashing water in a tub, being dirty, urinating and defecating in the presence of an adult, playing with food, rolling in mud, jumping rope, and so on. These are equally distinctive of childhood, and thus potential activators of early scenes. "If, then, we place the adult in the milieu of the infant or child, bombard him with the messages peculiar to the milieu, and permit, require, and urge him to emit the behaviors characteristic of infancy and childhood, we should be able to activate traces that have been dormant for most of the individual's lifetime" (Tomkins, 1992, p. 214).

Similarly, an adult could be subjected to a variety of "lectures" that reproduce the identical experience with parents, teachers, and peers during childhood. Examples would include punishment, cleanliness, conscience, achievement, respect, and tenderness lectures.

By replicating various conditions that are unique to early childhood, the conjoint distinctive name can be utilized in order to reactivate a particular memory. The discontinuity between childhood and adulthood is what makes possible the recovery of scenes.

Still other discontinuities are present. One particular discontinuity that is universal for every adult is reactivated on the occasion of becoming a parent. What is reactivated in this case is the unexpected reliving of infancy and childhood precisely in the role of being a parent. The discontinuity between early and late experience itself is what prompts the sudden intrusion of affects, attitudes, and reactions long forgotten. What occurs is surprising to the individual, often startling. "Many a parent is hurled back into his past and held as in a vise. . . . The parents may relive not only the role of themselves as children but also the roles of their own parents" (Tomkins, 1992, p. 218). When we are parents we relive our own childhoods in two distinct ways: from the perspective of ourselves as children and from the perspective of our own parents. Thus, we may reenact an old scene from our own childhood, but when we play that scene out in relation to our children we, in fact, can take the part of one of our parents in the original scene. It is the very nature of parenting that guarantees such an intrusion of early scenes.

Another distinctive discontinuity between childhood and adulthood concerns the condition of powerlessness, which is a regressive experience. Whenever adults are rendered powerless in any situation or context, their early scenes of infant helplessness are immediately reactivated. That scene intrudes directly into adult consciousness. Thus, rejection, failure, loss of love, illness, surgery, hospitalization, financial loss, defeat by a rival in love or by a competitor in business, loss of status, destruction of one's home by natural disaster or fire, the anticipation of death, and aging can all activate powerlessness in characteristically active and competent adults. And we are apt to experience powerlessness in adulthood with any combination of negative affects, depending on the particular current situation confronting us and the particular early scene that is reactivated and subsequently invades our experience.

Finally, we can reactivate the early childhood experience of interpersonal intimacy by requiring two strangers to stare continuously into each other's eyes. When they are able to comply with this instruction, the individuals usually report an unexpectedly intense feeling of intimacy. Why? Because there is a distinctive discontinuity that is created between early and late experience through the universal taboo on mutual facial gazing. It was the mother and child, and in some cases father and child as well, who first gazed continuously and lovingly into each other's eyes. But older children are systematically shamed into not looking too directly into the eyes of others. In spite of some variability across cultures in how much mutual looking is actually permitted, all cultures inhibit the eye-to-eye scene at least some degree. The taboo on mutual looking arises because of shaming, and it operates in order to inhibit facial gazing in later childhood and throughout adulthood. While the child may continue for some years to stare into the faces and eyes of strangers as well as others, the facial gaze is not likely to be returned because of the successful operation of the taboo among adults.

Adults have internalized sufficient shame about looking too directly into each other's eyes, so they learn to look into each other's faces only tangentially. They do not look continuously into both eyes at the same time. Instead, adults look at the space between the eyes of the other person, either above or below the eye, at the eye of the other person when it is not focused on one's own eyes, at the top of the nose or tip of the nose, at the forehead, or by fixating on the face as a whole. In all of these ways, adults cooperate in maintaining the taboo on mutual facial gazing by attenuating interocular intimacy. When, however, the eyes of two adults do, in fact, meet in a continuous mutual gaze, they become suddenly lost in each other's eyes; and they will feel like they are falling in love because they are immediately returned to the earlier, more intimate communion that they previously enjoyed as children. "Eyes meeting eyes is the name of these early feelings," according to Tomkins (1963, p. 340), the conjoint distinctive name that will reactivate only this memory.

The therapeutic process outlined previously in chapter 8 for recovering scenes, along with the reparenting imagery process designed to transform those scenes, is based directly on the foregoing principles of memory storage and retrieval. The reason why the client is asked to imagine lying down on the floor in the reparenting imagery script, thereby enabling recall of how gigantic everything seemed as a child, is in order to reproduce the spatial relations of childhood. Similarly, other features of the reparenting imagery process are designed to stimulate other distinctive discontinuities that would reactivate various governing scenes or memory traces.

What is of utmost importance is that the therapist not impose a particular meaning or preconceived interpretation on a series of reactions or scene fragments. There are always multiple pathways into any particular syndrome. Every individual who was sexually abused as a child is by definition shame-based, but not everyone who is shame-based has to have been sexually abused in childhood. The dynamics of shame can be produced by any number of constellations of factors. Overinterpreting the presence of any single predisposing factor, like parental physical or sexual abuse, is therefore a serious therapeutic error. Therapists must understand the dynamics of affect in order to understand particular syndromes because psychopathology is principally a disorder of the affective life.

The recovery of scenes ought to be encouraged, not forced. The therapeutic key is discovering the distinctive discontinuity for this unique individual, and for this person's particular set of experiences—the one critical feature that, once identified, will unlock the doors of memory.

In another therapeutic case, a woman I was working with remembered a scene fragment of a particular experience that she was attempting to recall more completely. It was important to Joyce to ascertain whether her father had been home at the time of the event in question. She knew her mother was not home, and later she had been blamed by her mother for something that had happened to her younger brother. Knowing whether her father had also been home at the time of the event in question meant the difference between feeling herself totally responsible for the mishap that had occurred and being able to let herself off the hook. Her memory fragment did not include her father or any information pointing to his presence.

I first asked her to visualize the family home and to retrace her steps just prior to the event in question. She closed her eyes and began picturing her home in vivid detail, verbalizing what she saw. She next descended the staircase to the main floor, saw herself coming around the corner, and then came to a small but open room—and there she saw her father busying himself. He had been there all along! She opened her eyes, feeling immense relief, now able to finally assimilate the previously troubling scene that had occurred after her mother returned home.

Another client, Peter, recalled hearing the words "You're an idiot" whenever his father spoke to him as a child. Each time the words recurred in adulthood, he froze and went blank. I encouraged Peter simply to observe those words whenever they returned, and to observe them very consciously each time they did so. At first he could hardly tolerate hearing the voice inside utter those words, but with increasing exposure to his inner voice, his tolerance grew. Gradually, Peter was able to hear the words, experience the shame induced by them, then actually picture the face of his father and hear his father's voice as he was speaking inside. Peter was becoming increasingly conscious of his internal process for reproducing shame. Over time, additional fragments of his original scene returned; he recalled more about what had happened both before and after the words "You're an idiot" were actually spoken by his father during the childhood event in question.

SCENE REENACTMENT IN THE SUPERVISORY PROCESS

Just as a client's scenes can reactivate scenes in a therapist, the scenes playing out between therapist and client are also reenacted in the supervisory relationship. Such *parallel process* phenomena, well known to more experienced clinical supervisors, are actually a special case of the more general process of scene reenactment that occurs in virtually all relationships, from parenting to intimate ones. Scenes are reenacted everywhere and all the time. We are simply oblivious to its occurrence usually.

On occasion, the scenes that are reenacted between the supervisee and supervisor are analogous to the scenes being enacted between the supervisee and client. The supervisory relationship in this instance becomes a mirror of the therapeutic relationship, and a vehicle for demonstrating how to resolve the scenes now playing out between therapist and client. Jonathan is a novice therapist. In supervision he described a troublesome encounter with a particular client, Anne. His client was overly demanding in their most recent session, pressing him for advice and direction about exactly how to handle her relationship with her boyfriend. She became quite insistent, leaving Jonathan feeling confused and unsure of how to respond. Then she stormed out of his office. Jonathan felt badly about how he had actually handled the situation at the time. He felt like a failure as a therapist.

Later in supervision, Jonathan reenacted that scene directly with his supervisor. He wanted his supervisor to tell him what to do and kept insisting on receiving specific answers to his dilemma with his client. His supervisor listened empathically, and Jonathan felt his experience validated, understood. By not allowing Jonathan's demandingness to control him, his supervisor "showed" Jonathan how to respond to his demanding client. And by not shaming Jonathan for insisting on receiving answers, his supervisor showed him how to avoid shaming his client.

There are other times when the supervisee may stimulate scenes directly from the supervisor's own life. In this case the scenes that are imported into their relationship, and subsequently reenacted, are historical, not current. And the reverse can obviously also happen. When the supervisor stimulates the reactivation of scenes from the supervisee's own early life, those scenes are apt to invade their present relationship, initially prompting confusion. In either case, distinguishing the supervisor's or supervisee's governing scenes from their current real relationship is a critical part of the supervisory process.

GOVERNING CULTURAL SCENES

The scenes that are stored in memory are dynamic in every sense. Not the equivalent of static photographs at all, they fuse directly together, becoming increasingly interconnected and growing in their power to capture and dominate us. Scenes operate in the lives of individuals, families, even nations. Governing scenes compel reenactment. They govern identity and intimacy both for individuals and relationships, directing action as well as imagination, defining the good life and how it should be lived from now until the end of days. Governing scenes, to put it simply, govern us completely.

We may know an individual by his or her principal scenes, those which direct, unite, dictate, or even fragment a life. Scenes are like the unifying thread that stretches through time, the distinctive marker for each unique individual.

What is a people if it is not a group bound by a collective scene of riveting impact? Shared group scenes that have reached a level of intense magnification have enormous power over entire peoples, equal to the power of governing scenes in the lives of individuals. Governing group scenes are the motive power that fills the sails of culture, propelling civilization. They are the collective scenes that are reenacted in the daily lives of a group of people who have become bonded together by virtue of sharing a common language, distinct traditions, particular rituals, and a uniform set of beliefs.

Culture bonds a people together, embracing special symbols, holidays, and heroes. That bonding is secured through retelling a people's history and reliving its heritage in stories read at bedtime; in literature listened to, studied, and learned in school; in epic films depicting memorable events, both victories and defeats, in the life of a people; and through participating in its hopes and dreams as well as its humiliations. Binding the tapestry of a culture is a set of shared scenes that is laden with intense and enduring affect.

Archeology is the science of ancient cultures. An archeological dig is a place where artifacts, the products of human activity, are sought and eventually uncovered; like portals in time, they provide vital glimpses of past civilizations. Just as archeology is the scientific study of the remains of a people's culture, psychology is the scientific study of the self. Here we are engaged in a kind of "psychological archeology" in that we are studying an analogous set of artifacts: the residue of experience in the psyche. Governing scenes are thus the psychological equivalent of artifacts unearthed at a dig. And this is precisely the point at which the study of personality and the study of culture converge: governing cultural scenes are the psychological artifacts of culture, just as individual governing scenes are the psychological remains of experience for specific persons.

A culture's governing scenes always live on in collective memory. They are kept alive by remembering them, by making them not merely remote events in a distant past but immediate and compelling experiences for everyone living today, and especially for the children of tomorrow. Cultural scenes are here—they are now. Collective scenes depend on the group remembering them in order to survive into the future, to be equally alive for future generations.

Each nation, each ethnic group, has its own distinctive scene or set of scenes that marks it as unique among all other peoples. Elias Canetti (1962) offers a perspective on the psychology of nations that maps particularly well onto Tomkins's theory of scenes. The distinctive character of a nation, in effect, becomes its faith, what it believes in unshakably or holds especially dear. Usually, this almost religious aspect of a nation's "soul" is seen most sharply only when it goes to war. What every citizen of a nation, and by extension every member of a cultural group, feels personally related to is its *crowd symbol.* That is the foundation of Canetti's schema. Individuals picture themselves in a fixed relationship to the specific symbol that has assumed central significance in the life of the nation or group. Each nation's crowd symbol reappears from time to time when necessity requires it, and its recurrence is the source of the continuity of national feeling. "A nation's consciousness of itself changes when, and only when, its symbol changes" (Canetti, 1962, p. 171). For Canetti, crowd symbols possess the characteristics of crowds: "density, growth and infinite openness; surprising, or very striking, cohesion; a common rhythm or a sudden discharge" (1962, p. 170). These qualities are also analogs of affect. In the distinguishing affect attributes of crowds also lie the seeds of cultural memory.

What Canetti described in terms of crowd symbols can be equally well described in terms of affectively charged scenes that have become widely shared by an entire people. To think of these phenomena as "crowd scenes" instead of crowd symbols—or to be more precise, as governing cultural scenes—bridges Canetti and Tomkins. Cultural scenes, whether of a particular ethnic group or an entire nation, become deeply and permanently embedded in the group's collective memory. It is those shared scenes of enormous affect that become a people's crowd symbols. Symbols stand for scenes and also reproduce them. Crowd symbols, in Canetti's sense, ignite group memory, and thereby reactivate the group's cultural scene.

What are some examples of governing cultural scenes? Canetti describes specific crowd symbols/cultural scenes for various nations. For example, England is an island nation, and its crowd symbol is the *captain on his ship sailing the sea.* To command a ship and rule the seas is an image that goes to the very heart of the English psyche. Hence the historic power of the English navy as a symbol of English might, of the English soul. The Dutch, in contrast, had to win their land from the sea. The dikes are thus an eternal symbol of Dutch national life: the barrier erected to protect them against the sea. Thus, *dikes erected against the sea* is the crowd symbol of the Dutch. "Nowhere else has the feeling of a human wall opposing the sea been so strongly developed" (Canetti, 1962, p. 172). While the English subjugated the sea through ships which they commanded at will, the Dutch always had the sea at their backs. If their dikes failed, their land was imperiled. Danger was thus always at their backs as well, whereas the English were safe on their island and in their ships. When their island was threatened with attack, they counted on the sea with its storms to protect them. For the Dutch, the sea always meant jeopardy.

The French have a very different crowd symbol, their *revolution.* The storming of the Bastille is synonymous with the French Revolution itself: "The crowd, for centuries the victim of royal justice, takes justice into its own hands" (Canetti, 1962, p. 174). That historic event is branded in memory for all time. The people storming the Bastille captures the essence of the crowd feeling embodied in the Revolution, just as it expresses the continuing national feeling of the French as a distinct people. It marks the birth of their identity.

While the English have their captains on their ships ruling the sea, and the Dutch have their dikes erected as barriers against the sea, the French have their Revolution, symbolized in the storming of the Bastille. Each embodies specific places, times, and events filled with intense, enduring affect. Each is both symbol and scene—something capable of evoking fervent national feeling at a single stroke and, at the same time, a shared cultural memory.

For the Jewish people, the *Exodus from Egypt* is their crowd symbol. "The image of this multitude moving year after year through the desert has become the crowd symbol of the Jews. It has remained to this day as distinct and comprehensible as it was then. The people see themselves together before they settled and then dispersed; they see themselves on their migration. In this state of density they received their law. If ever a crowd had a goal, they had. . . . This long wandering inflicted as a punishment contains all the torments of later migrations" (Canetti, 1962, p. 179). Freedom from bondage, coupled with the multitude wandering in the wilderness, is a widely shared group scene of enormous power in the lives of Jews everywhere. Moreover, it is the defining event for the Jewish people—the critical moment when their identity as a people was born. But another governing cultural scene emerged in the late 1960s, one drawn from more contemporary times that has since become equally compelling for Jews—the *Holocaust.* That is a scene of humiliation and terror par excellence, and it is not easily reconciled with the primary crowd symbol of wandering in the wilderness; they are not equivalent. Nor can the Holocaust be subsumed into the Exodus from Egypt symbol as though it were simply another "migration" scene. Whether the crowd symbol of the Jews is changing still remains to be seen, but the Jewish people's consciousness of itself as a people will never again be the same as it was before the Holocaust.

To extend Canetti's formulation to other ethnic minorities, consider the experience of African Americans as a racial group living in a predominantly White society. For all Black Americans, *slavery* is a collective scene of immense resonance. That scene lives on in the memories of Black Americans. More recent scenes of segregation, commonplace in the southern states only 30 years ago, have been largely absorbed into the prior and more compelling scene of slavery. All of those scenes, intensely charged as they are with the affect of humiliation, have become fused into one interconnected family of scenes—and slavery is both its symbol and its name. Both the Nation of Islam and Afrocentrism are equally scripted yet entirely different cultural responses to this compelling, governing collective scene.

A further example of the power of cultural scenes that are widely shared by a given people can be seen in the recent Balkan war. The Serbian people continue to be gripped by an enormously powerful scene deeply embedded in their collective memory. That scene occurred six centuries ago when the Serbs were utterly defeated by the Turks in the Battle of Kossovo. Applying Canetti's theory of crowd symbols to the Serbian people, Robert Kaplan identifies the crowd symbol of the Serbs: "*Kossovo Polje,* the 'Field of Black Birds,' where the Turks delivered the final defeat to the Serbs on June 28, 1389, leaving their bodies for carrion birds to devour" (1993, p. 35). At that moment, Kossovo Polje entered myth, and permeated the Serbian consciousness. That humiliation is as vivid for Serbs living today as it was for the Serbs who actually witnessed the calamity directly. There are two particular pictures which hang in home after home among the Serbs: "The Maiden of Kossovo" and "The Moving of the Serbs." The first depicts a young woman giving a wounded Serbian warrior a drink from a jug on the battlefield of Kossovo in 1389 with slain Turks all around, and the second portrays the Serbian Orthodox Patriarch, surrounded by mounted soldiers, women holding babies, and flocks of sheep, leading the Serbian people on a long trek after later Serbian revolts failed.

These images are more than just Serbian equivalents of Washington crossing the Delaware or Texans remembering the Alamo. They are icons of the 500-year struggle of the Serbs against the Ottoman Turks, and they ignite nationalist feeling comparable to religious zeal. Prince Lazar's defeat by the Turks is still venerated today by the Serbs. When the 600-year commemoration of Prince Lazar's martyrdom at Kossovo Polje approached, his coffin began a tour of every town and village in Serbia on June 28, 1988, drawing huge crowds of wailing mourners dressed entirely in black (Kaplan, 1993). For the mourners, Kossovo Polje was only yesterday. For the Serbian people humiliation always lives on in memory, and that governing scene continues to compel reenactment—to avenge defeat and reclaim Greater Serbia. The essence of Serbian national feeling, it is one motive fueling the war that has wreaked havoc in the Balkans recently.

America has its own crowd symbol, and its seeds lie in civil protest, in its war culture, and in revolution. What James Gibson refers to as

America's "creation myth" is another way of describing its special crowd scene: "the story of independent gunmen defeating evil enemies and founding a new society" (Gibson, 1994, p. 18). The "shot heard 'round the world" at Lexington and Concord is the very essence of both scene and symbol—of myth. The *American Revolution,* as crowd scene/symbol, was the product of the lone gunman; the revolutionary army was less an army than a militia of mobilized citizens, according to Gibson. Dreams of being a warrior thus became deeply embedded in the American crowd scene. This governing cultural scene was relived again and again through the image of the frontiersman who fought in the Indian wars, and later, in virtually every war this nation fought. Like the revolutionary militias before them, American military forces have always been portrayed as virtuous defenders of a just cause. Thus, Americans have always believed that they deserved to win all their wars because their cause was always just.

In closing our examination of crowd symbols/scenes, let's probe Canetti's perspective further by studying the character of the German people, and how their crowd symbols have shaped the course of human events. While their crowd symbol eventually became the *army,* it began as the *marching forest.* "In no other modern country has the forest-feeling remained as alive as it has in Germany" (Canetti, 1962, p. 173). For the Germans, the forest holds a deep, mysterious delight. In contrast to the English, who love to imagine themselves at sea, the Germans prefer to imagine themselves deep in a forest. But an entirely new crowd symbol formed after Germany became unified as a nation: the army. Pride in their army was universal among Germans after the end of the Franco-Prussian War of 1870–71. Being surrounded by soldiers, protected by the mass of uniforms of an army, was to Germans just like being surrounded by dense trees, feeling *one* with the trees. These two distinctive images or crowd symbols, the army and the marching forest, soon became completely fused together for the German people: either could stand equally well as the crowd symbol of the nation. Forest and army were identical, creating a single forest-army symbol of the German nation.

At the outbreak of World War I, according to Canetti, Adolf Hitler "fell on his knees and thanked God. It was his decisive experience, the one moment at which he himself honestly became part of a crowd. He never forgot it and his whole subsequent career was devoted to the re-creation of this moment, but *from outside.* Germany was to be again as it was then, conscious of its military striking power and exulting and united in it" (1962, p. 181).

But something else happened that made Hitler's dream possible: the Treaty of Versailles disbanded the German army. That prohibition robbed the German people of their vital crowd symbol, without which they could have no national feeling whatsoever. To the German people, Versailles became synonymous with the prohibition of sacred practices without which they could not imagine life. Versailles meant less of a national defeat than the prohibition of something akin to a religion. "The faith of his fathers had been proscribed, and it was every man's sacred duty to re-establish it" (Canetti, 1962, p. 181). This was the birthplace of the Nazi regime.

Hitler's use of *Versailles* as his chief slogan and rallying cry was propitious: Each time it was used it reopened the nation's wound, making healing impossible. Even further, *Versailles* reminded Germans not only of their latest humiliation as a nation, but it also summoned up other portentous scenes in German history. It was at Versailles that Bismarck proclaimed the German Empire, and Versailles was also the seat of Louis XIV, the one French ruler besides Napoleon who had most deeply humiliated the Germans. The name *Versailles* was thus synonymous with the greatest triumph of modern German history and also with its single greatest humiliation. Every time Hitler spoke the word *Versailles,* the memory of Bismarck's triumph was reawakened, and it electrified his audience as a promise that defeat would again be turned into victory, and humiliation into triumph—with the prohibited army recreated for this very purpose. The German crowd symbol/scene had to be set free from its shackles in order for the German people to regain their national feeling, their essential identity as a people, but its consequences were disastrous.

Because there is no delete key for consciousness, there is no way to permanently erase scenes from memory, not for individuals and certainly not for nations. Depriving a nation of its crowd symbol by prohibiting it is dangerous; Germany illustrates that much. Governing group scenes will always survive in the collective memory of a people, but those scenes can be transformed.

Exactly how to transform such compelling scenes as slavery, the Holocaust, and Kossovo Polje, scenes of such intensity and import that they are capable of capturing and swaying whole crowds of people instantaneously, is a challenge that must be faced directly by all concerned if cultural conflict is ever to be finally resolved. But the solution will continue to evade our grasp until we learn how to take the principles for the transformation of scenes at the individual level and successfully adapt them for entire peoples and even nations.

The resolution of cultural and national shame, at the group level, is one of the principal challenges of the 21st century. Resolving that shame means transforming those governing cultural scenes that lie at its heart, the collective scenes that function like a cauldron inflaming action as well as imagination. Transforming cultural scenes will begin the process of interrupting the recurring cycle of shame and rage, and the ensuing violence and war to which those affects inevitably give rise.

The affect of anger, particularly when externalized in the form of overtly expressed violent aggression, has been acutely disruptive throughout all of human history. We have not learned how to tame anger, nor to contain angry aggressive eruptions. Explosive anger continues to evade all attempts at the peaceful solution of grievances. That is true in the lives of individuals and families, and it is equally true in the lives of nations.

When anger and contempt further combine in the form of virulent hatred, and when these volatile affects are deeply embedded in governing cultural scenes, scenes so widely shared that they possess the power to seize an entire people in their grip, and further, when the scripted response to those scenes is unrelenting opposition to whoever terrorizes or humiliates, the enemy, however perceived—when all of these conditions hold true, then the situation is ripe for the outbreak of hostilities: violence between individuals, war between nations, and war between distinct peoples living within the same geographic region.

It is precisely here that identity, culture, and ideology collide—in the boiling cauldron of hatred and the destructive violence that spills over.

Will we be able to transform scenes that defy the erosion of time, that govern experience and imagination for an entire people? Will we be able to eventually stop the recurring cycle of shame and rage that war is heir to? Will we be able, finally, to contain anger effectively as a society—without having to deflect it either toward deviants in our midst or toward barbarians outside our borders?

And will we, in some still unseen future, be able to one day live more or less in harmony with each other—with our differences intact—without the necessity of having one group or another to hate and feel superior to?

Bibliography

Adler, A. (1930). Individual psychology. In C. Muchison (Ed.), *Psychologies of 1930*, 395–405. Worcester, MA: Clark University Press.

Adler, A. (1933). Advantages and disadvantages of the inferiority feeling. In H. L. Ansbacher and R. Ansbacher (Eds.), *Superiority and social interest.* Evanston, IL: Northwestern University Press, 1970.

Adler, A. (1959). *The practice and theory of individual psychology.* Patterson, NJ: Littlefield, Adams and Co.

Adler, A. (1966). The psychology of power. *Journal of Individual Psychology, 22,* 166–172.

Alexander, F. (1938). Remarks about the relation of inferiority feelings to guilt feelings. *International Journal of Psycho-Analysis, 19,* 41–49.

Al-Khayyat, S. (1990). *Honour and shame: Women in modern Iraq.* London: Saqi Books.

Amsterdam, B. K., & Levitt, M. (1980). Consciousness of self and painful self-consciousness. *The Psychoanalytic Study of the Child, 35,* 67–83.

Ansbacher, H. L., & Rowena, R. (Eds.) (1956). *The individual-psychology of Alfred Adler.* New York: Basic Books.

Angyal, A. (1965). *Neurosis and treatment: A holistic theory.* New York: Da Capo Press.

Anthony, E. J. (1981). Shame, guilt, and the feminine self in psychoanalysis. In S. Tuttman, C. Kaye, & M. Zimmerman (Eds.), *Object and self: A developmental approach.* New York: International Universities Press.

Anthony, E. J. (1981). The paranoid adolescent as viewed through psychoanalysis. *Journal of the American Psychoanalytic Association, 29,* 745–787.

Ausubel, D. (1955). Relationships between guilt and shame in the socializing process. *Psychological Review, 62,* 378–390.

Barry, M. J. (1962). Depression, shame, loneliness and the psychiatrist's position. *American Journal of Psychotherapy, 16,* 580–590.

Bassos, C. A., & Kaufman, G. (1973). *The dynamics of shame: A therapeutic key to problems of intimacy and sexuality.* Paper presented at the meeting of the American Psychological Association, Montreal, Canada.

Bettelheim, B. (1984). *Freud and man's soul.* New York: Vintage Books.

Bronowski, J. (1971). *The identity of man.* Garden City, NY: Natural History Press.

Bronowski, J. (1973). *The ascent of man.* Boston: Little, Brown.

Broucek, F. J. (1982). Shame and its relationship to early narcissistic developments. *International Journal of Psycho-Analysis, 63,* 369–378.

Broucek, F. J. (1991). *Shame and the self.* New York: The Guilford Press.

Buss, A. H., & Plomin, R. (1975). *A temperament theory of personality development.* New York: John Wiley.

Buss, A. H. (1980). *Self-consciousness and social anxiety.* San Francisco: Freeman.

Canetti, E. (1962). *Crowds and power.* Trans. by Carol Stewart. New York: Viking Press.

Colby, K. M. (1977). Appraisal of four psychological theories of paranoid phenomena. *Journal of Abnormal Psychology, 86,* 54–59.

Demos, E. V. (1995). *Explolring affect: The selected writings of Silvan S. Tomkins.* Cambridge: Cambridge University Press.

Ekman, P. (1971). Universals and cultural differences in facial expressions of emotion. In J. K. Cole (Ed.), *Nebraska symposium on motivation,* Vol. 19, 207–283. Lincoln: University of Nebraska Press.

Ekman, P. (1982). *Emotion in the human face.* Cambridge, MA: Cambridge University Press.

Ekman, P., Levenson, R. W., & Friesen, W. V. (1983). Autonomic nervous system activity distinguishes among emotions. *Science, 221,* 1208–1210.

English, F. (1975). Shame and social control. *Transactional Analysis Journal, 5,* 24–28.

Erickson, M. H. (1954a). Special techniques of brief hypnotherapy. *Journal of Clinical and Experimental Hypnosis, 2,* 109–129.

Erickson, M. H. (1954b). Pseudo-orientation in time as a hypnotherapeutic procedure. *Journal of Clinical and Experimental Hypnosis, 2,* 261–283.

Erickson, M. H. (1964). The confusion technique in hypnosis. *American Journal of Clinical Hypnosis, 6,* 183–207.

Erickson, M. H., Haley, J., & Weakland, J. (1967). A transcript of a trance induction with commentary. In J. Haley (Ed.), *Advanced techniques of hypnosis and therapy.* New York: Grune & Stratton.

Erickson, M. H., & Rossi, E. (1979). *Hypnotherapy: An exploratory casebook.* New York: Irvington.

Erickson, M. H., & Rossi, E. (1983). *Healing in hypnosis.* New York: Irvington.

Erickson, M. H., Rossi, E., & Rossi, S. (1976). *Hypnotic realities.* New York: Irvington.

Erikson, E. H. (1950). *Childhood and society.* New York: Norton.

Erikson, E. H. (1968). *Identity: Youth and crisis.* New York: Norton.

Erikson, E. H. (1977). *Toys and reasons: Stages in the ritualization of experience.* New York: Norton.

Erickson, E. H. (1980). *Identity and the life cycle.* New York: Norton.

Fairbairn, W. R. D. (1966). *Psychoanalytic studies of the personality.* London: Routledge and Kegan Paul.

Fisher, S. F. (1985). Identity of two: The phenomenology of shame in borderline development and treatment. *Psychotherapy, 22,* 101–109.

Fossum, M., & Mason, M. (1986). *Facing shame.* New York: Norton.

Frankl, V. E. (1962). *Man's search for meaning—An introduction to logotherapy.* Boston: Beacon Press.

Frankl, V. E. (1968). *Psychotherapy and existentialism.* New York: Simon and Schuster.

Frankl, V. E. (1969). *The will to meaning: Foundations and applications of logotherapy.* New York: World.

Frankl, V. E. (1975). Paradoxical intention and dereflection. *Psychotherapy: Theory, Research and Practice, 12,* 226–237.

Freud, S. (1914). *On narcissism: An introduction.* Standard edition, 14, 73–102. London: Hogarth Press, 1957.

Freud, S. (1923). *The ego and the id.* Standard Edition, 19, 1–66. London: Hogarth Press, 1961.

Freud, S. (1930). *Civilization and its discontents.* Standard edition, 21, 59–145. London: Hogarth Press, 1961.

Freud, S. (1933). *New introductory lectures on psycho-analysis.* Standard edition, 22, 58–182. London: Hogarth Press, 1964.

Gibson, J. W. (1994). *Warrior dreams: Violence and manhood in post-Vietnam America.* New York: Hill & Wang.

Gilligan, C. (1982). *In a different voice.* Cambridge, MA: Harvard University Press.

Goodman, D. G., & Miyazawa, M. (1995). *Jews in the Japanese mind: The history and uses of a cultural stereotype.* New York: The Free Press.

Greenberg, J. R., & Mitchell, S. A. (1983). *Object relations in psychoanalytic theory.* Cambridge, MA: Harvard University Press.

Guntrip, H. (1961). *Personality structure and human interaction.* New York: International Universities Press.

Guntrip, H. (1969). *Schizoid phenomena, object-relations and the self.* New York: International Universities Press.

Guntrip, H. (1971). *Psychoanalytic theory, therapy and the self:* New York: Basic Books.

Horney, K. (1937). *The neurotic personality of our time.* New York: Norton.

Horney, K. (1945). *Our inner conflicts: A constructive theory of neurosis.* New York: Norton.

Horney, K. (1950). *Neurosis and human growth. The struggle toward self-realization.* New York: Norton.

Izard, C. E. (1977). *Human emotions.* New York: Plenum Press.

Jacoby, M. (1994). *Shame and the origins of self-esteem: A Jungian approach.* London: Routledge.

Johnson, G., Kaufman, G., & Raphael, L. (1991). *A teacher's guide to stick up for yourself.* Minneapolis, MN: Free Spirit Publishing.

Jung, C. G. (1923). *Psychological types.* Trans. H. G. Baynes. London: Routledge & Kegan Paul.

Jung, C. G. (1965). *Memories, dreams, reflection.* Trans. Richard & Clara Winston. New York: Vintage Books.

Jung, C. G. (1968). *Analytical psychology: Its theory and practice.* New York: Pantheon.

Kaplan, R. D. (1993). *Balkan ghosts: A journey through history.* New York: St. Martin's Press.

Kaufman, G. (1974a). The meaning of shame: Towards a self-affirming identity. *Journal of Counseling psychology 21,* 568–574.

Kaufman, G. (1974b). *On shame, identity and the dynamics of change.* Paper presented in Symposium, D. L. Grummon (Ch.), Papers in Memory of Bill Kell: *Issues on Therapy and the Training of Therapists.* Symposium presented at the meeting of the American Psychological Association, New Orleans.

Kaufman, G. (1986). Dynamics and treatment of shame-based syndromes. In *Proceedings of the Eighth and Ninth Annual Adult Psychiatric Day Treatment Forum.* Minneapolis: University of Minnesota.

Kaufman G. (1987). Disorders of self-esteem: Psychotherapy for shame-based syndromes. In P. A. Keller and S. R. Heyman (Eds.), *Innovations in clinical practice: A source book,* Vol. 6, 53–62. Sarasota, Florida: Professional Resource Exchange, Inc.

Kaufman, G. (1990a). *The role of shame in the differential patterning of gender socialization: A new psychological perspective.* Paper presented at the National Conference on Re-Visioning Knowledge and the Curriculum: Feminist Perspectives. Michigan State University, East Lansing, MI.

Kaufman, G. (speaker). (1990b). *From shame to self-empowerment: Origins, healing, and treatment issues.* Newton, MA: Lifecycle Learning Cassettes.

Kaufman, G. (speaker). (1991). *Shame-based syndromes: Theory and treatment.* Robesonia, PA: Logan Audio Publishing.

Kaufman, G. (1992). *Shame: The power of caring.* (3rd Ed.) Rochester, VT: Schenkman Books.

Kaufman, G. (1993). *Journey to the magic castle.* Sepulveda, CA: Double M Press.

Kaufman, G. (1995). Men's shame. In R. U. Schenk & J. Everingham (Eds.), *Men healing shame.* New York: Springer.

Kaufman, G., & Bly, R. (1995). Healing internalized shame. In R. U. Schenk & J. Everingham (Eds.), *Men healing shame.* New York: Springer.

Kaufman, G., & Raphael, L. (speakers). (1983). *Listening to your inner voices* (Cassette Recording No. 20275). Washington, DC: Psychology Today Tapes.

Kaufman, G., & Raphael, L. (1984a). Relating to the self: Changing inner dialogue. *Psychological Reports, 54,* 239–250.

Kaufman, G., & Raphael, L. (1984b). Shame as taboo in American culture. In R. Browne (Ed.), *Forbidden fruits: Taboos and tabooism in culture.* Bowling Green, OH: Popular Press.

Kaufman, G., & Raphael, L. (1987). Shame: A perspective on Jewish identity. *Journal of Psychology and Judaism, 11,* 30–40.

Kaufman, G., & Raphael, L. (1990). *Stick up for yourself! Every kid's guide to personal power and positive self-esteem.* Minneapolis, MN: Free Spirit Publishing.

Kaufman, G., & Raphael, L. (1991). *Dynamics of power: Fighting shame and building self-esteem,* (2nd Ed.) Rochester, VT: Schenkman Books.

Kaufman, G. & Raphael, L. (1996). *Coming out of shame: Transforming gay and lesbian lives.* New York: Doubleday.

Kell, B. L., & Burow, J. M. (1970). *Developmental counseling and therapy.* Boston: Houghton Mifflin.

Kernberg, O. F. (1975). *Borderline conditions and pathological narcissism.* New York: Aronson.

Kernberg, O. F. (1976). *Object relations theory and clinical psychoanalysis.* New York: Aronson.

Kinston, W. (1983). A theoretical context for shame. *International Journal of Psycho-Analysis, 64,* 213–226.

Kohut, H. (1971). *The analysis of the self.* New York: International Universities Press.

Kohut, H. (1972). Thoughts on narcissism and narcissistic rage. *The Psychoanalytic Study of the Child, 27,* 360–400.

Kohut, H. (1977). *The restoration of the self.* New York: International Universities Press.

Laing, R. D. (1960). *The divided self.* New York: Pantheon.

Leites, E. (1986). *The puritan conscience and modern sexuality.* New Haven: Yale University Press.

Lewis, M. (1992). *Shame: The exposed self.* New York: The Free Press.

LeShan, L., & Margenau, H. (1982). *Einstein's space and VanGogh's sky: Physical reality and beyond.* New York: Macmillan.

Levin, S. (1967). Some metapsychological considerations on the differentiation between shame and guilt. *International Journal of Psycho-Analysis, 48,* 267–276.

Levin, S. (1971). The psychoanalysis of shame. *International Journal of Psycho-Analysis, 52,* 355–362.

Lewinsky, H. (1941). The nature of shyness. *The British Journal of Psychology, 32,* 105–112.

Lewis, H. B. (1971). *Shame and guilt in neurosis.* New York: International Universities Press.

Lewis, H. B. (1981). Shame and guilt in human nature. In S. Tuttman, C. Kaye, and M. Zimmerman (Eds.), *Object and self: A developmental approach.* New York: International Universities Press.

Lewis, H. B. (Ed.) (1987a). *The role of shame in symptom formation.* Hillsdale, NJ: Erlbaum.

Lewis, H. B. (1987b). Shame and the narcissistic personality. In D. L. Nathanson (Ed.), *The many faces of shame.* New York: Guilford Press.

Lynd, H. M. (1958). *On shame and the search for identity.* New York: Harcourt, Brace.

MacCurdy, J. T. (1965). The biological significance of blushing and shame. *British Journal of Psychology, 71,* 19–59.

Mahler, M. S., Pine, F., & Bergman, A. (1975). *The psychological birth of the human infant.* New York: Basic Books.

Marsella, A. J., Murray, M. D., & Golden, C. (1974). Ethnic variations in the phenomenology of emotions: Shame. *Journal of Cross-Cultural Psychology, 5,* 312–328.

Modigliani, A. (1968). Embarrassability and embarrassment. *Sociometry 31,* 313–326.

Modigliani, A. (1971). Embarrassment, facework, and eye contact: Testing a theory of embarrassment. *Journal of Personality and Social Psychology, 17,* 15–24.

Money, J. (1987). Homosexual gender identity and psychoneuroendocrinology. *American Psychologist, 42,* 384–399.

Money, J., & Ehrhardt, A. (1972). *Man and woman, boy and girl: The differentiation and dimorphism of gender identity from conception to maturity.* Baltimore: Johns Hopkins University Press.

Montagu, A. (1972). *Touching: The human significance of the skin.* New York: Harper and Row.

Morrison, A. P. (1983). Shame, ideal self, and narcissism. *Contemporary Psychoanalysis, 19,* 295–318.

Morrison, A. P. (1989). *Shame: The underside of narcissism.* Hillsdale, NJ: Analytic Press.

Mueller, W. J., & Kell, B. L. (1972). *Coping with conflict: Supervising counselors and psychotherapists.* New York: Appleton-Century-Crofts.

Nathanson, D. L. (1987a). A timetable for shame. In D. L. Nathanson (Ed.), *The many faces of shame.* New York: Guilford Press.

Nathanson, D. L. (1987b). The shame/pride axis. In H. B. Lewis (Ed.), *The role of shame in symptom formation.* Hillsdale, NJ: Erlbaum.

Nathanson, D. L. (1992). *Shame and pride: Affect, sex, and the birth of the self.* New York: Norton.

Nuttin, J. (1950). Intimacy and shame in the dynamic structure of personality. In M. L. Reymert (Ed.), *Feelings and emotions.* New York: McGraw-Hill.

Pelletier, K. (1977). *Mind as healer, mind as slayer: A holistic approach to preventing stress disorders.* New York: Dell.

Peristiany, J. G. (1974). *Honour and shame.* Chicago: University of Chicago Press.

Peristiany, J. G., & Pitt-Rivers, J. (1992). *Honor and grace in anthropology.* Cambridge: Cambridge University Press.

Perlman, M. (1958). An investigation of anxiety as related to guilt and shame. *Archives of Neurological Psychiatry, 80,* 752–759.

Piers, G., & Singer, M. B. (1953). *Shame and guilt: A psychoanalytic and a cultural study.* Springfield, IL: Charles C Thomas; reprint ed. (1971). New York: Norton.

Rank, O. (1964). *Will therapy.* New York: Norton.

Raphael, L. (1991). *Edith Wharton's prisoners of shame: A new perspective on her neglected fiction.* New York: St. Martin's Press.

Riezler, K. (1943). Comment on the social psychology of shame. *American Journal of Sociology, 48,* 457–465.

Riezler, K. (1951). Shame and awe. In *Man: Mutable and immutable.* New York: Henry Regnery.

Rotenstreich, N. (1965). On shame. *Review of Metaphysics, 19,* 55–86.

Rothstein, A. (1984). Fear of humiliation. *Journal of the American Psychoanalytic Association, 32,* 99–116.

Sattler, J. (1965). A theoretical, developmental, and clinical investigation of embarrassment. *Genetic Psychology Monographs, 71,* 19–59.

Scheff, T. J., & Retzinger, S. M. (1991). *Emotions and violence: Shame and rage in destructive conflicts.* Lexington, MA: Lexington Books.

Schneider, C. D. (1977). *Shame, exposure and privacy.* Boston: Beacon Press; reprint ed. (1992). New York: Norton.

Shapiro, K. J., & Alexander, I. E. (1975). *The experience of introversion: An integration of phenomenological, empirical, and Jungian approaches.* Durham: Duke University Press.

Singer, J. L. (1974). *Imagery and daydream methods in psychotherapy and behavior modification.* New York: Academic Press.

Singer, J. L. (1980). The scientific basis of psychotherapeutic practice: A question of values and ethics. *Psychotherapy: Theory, Research and Practice, 17,* 372–383.

Singer, J. L., & Pope, K. S. (1978). *The power of human imagination.* New York: Plenum.

Spero, M. H. (1984). Shame: An object-relational formulation. *The Psychoanalytic Study of the Child, 39,* 259–282.

Spiegel, L. A. (1966). Affects in relation to self and object: A model for the derivation of desire, longing, pain, anxiety, humiliation, and shame. *The Psychoanalytic Study of the Child, 21,* 69–92.

Stamm, J. (1978). The meaning of humiliation and its relationship to fluctuations in self-esteem. *International Review of Psycho-Analysis, 5,* 425–433.

Stern, D. N. (1985). *The interpersonal world of the infant.* New York: Basic Books.

Stierlin, H. (1974). Shame and guilt in family relations. *Archives of General Psychiatry, 30,* 381–389.

Straus, E. (1966). Shame as a historiological problem. In *Phenomenological psychology: Selected papers.* Trans. Erling English. New York: Basic Books.

Sullivan, H. S. (1953a). *Conceptions of modern psychiatry.* New York: Norton.

Sullivan, H. S. (1953b). *The interpersonal theory of psychiatry.* New York: Norton.

Sullivan, H. S. (1956). *Clinical studies in psychiatry.* New York: Norton.

Sullivan, H. S. (1972). *Personal psychopathology.* New York: Norton.

Thomas, A., & Chess, S. (1977). *Temperament and development.* New York: Brunner/Mazel.

Thrane, G. (1979). Shame and the construction of the self. *Annual of Psychoanalysis, 7,* 321–341.

Tomkins, S. S. (1955). Consciousness and the unconscious in a model of the human being. In *Proceedings of the 14th International Congress of Psychology.* Amsterdam: North-Holland Publishing Co.

Tomkins, S. S. (1962). *Affect, imagery, consciousness: The positive affects,* Vol. 1. New York: Springer.

Tomkins, S. S. (1963a). *Affect, imagery, consciousness: The negative affects,* Vol. 2. New York: Springer.

Tomkins, S. S. (1963b). The right and the left: A basic dimension of ideology and personality. In R. W. White (Ed.), *The study of lives.* New York: Atherton.

Tomkins, S. S. (1965). Affect and the psychology of knowledge. In S. S. Tomkins & C. Izard (Eds.), *Affect, cognition and personality.* New York: Springer.

Tomkins, S. S. (1971). A theory of memory. In J. Antrobus (Ed.), *Cognition and affect*, 59–130. Boston: Little, Brown.

Tomkins, S. S. (1975). The phantasy behind the face. *Journal of Personality Assessment, 39,* 551–562.

Tomkins, S. S. (1979). Script theory: Differential magnification of affects. In H. E. Howe and R. A. Dienstbier (Eds.), *Nebraska Symposium on Motivation,* Vol. 26, 201–236. Lincoln: University of Nebraska Press.

Tomkins, S. S. (1981). The quest for primary motives: Biography and autobiography of an idea. *Journal of Personality and Social Psychology, 41,* 306–329.

Tomkins, S. S. (1982). Affect theory. In P. Ekman (Ed.), *Emotion in the human face.* Cambridge, MA: Cambridge University Press.

Tomkins, S. S. (1984). Affect theory. In K. R. Scherer and P. Ekman (Eds.), *Approaches to emotion.* Hillsdale, NJ: Erlbaum.

Tomkins, S. S. (1987a). Shame. In D. L. Nathanson (Ed.), *The many faces of shame.* New York: Guilford Press.

Tomkins, S. S. (1987b). Script theory. In J. Aronoff, A. I. Rabin, & R. A. Zucker (Eds.), *The emergence of personality.* New York: Springer.

Tomkins, S. S. (1991). *Affect, imagery, consciousness: The negative affects—anger and fear,* Vol. 3. New York: Springer.

Tomkins, S. S. (1992). *Affect, imagery, consciousness: Cognition—duplication and transformation of information,* Vol. 4. New York: Springer.

Tomkins, S. S. & McCarter, R. (1964). What and where are the primary affects? Some evidence for a theory. *Perceptual and Motor Skills, 18,* I 19–158.

Wallace, L. (1963). The mechanism of shame. *Archives of General Psychiatry, 8,* 80–85.

Ward, H. P. (1972). Aspects of shame in analysis. *American Journal of Psychoanalysis, 32,* 62–73.

White, R. W. (1959). Motivation reconsidered: The concept of competence. *Psychological Review, 66,* 297–333.

Winnicott, D. W. (1975). *Through paediatrics to psychoanalysis.* New York: Basic Books.

Wood, F. G. (1990). *The arrogance of faith: Christianity and race in America from the colonial era to the twentieth century.* New York: Alfred A. Knopf.

Wurmser, L. (1981). *The mask of shame.* Baltimore: Johns Hopkins University Press.

Index

Springer Publishing Company

MEN HEALING SHAME
An Anthology

Roy U. Schenk & **John Everingham,** Editors
Featuring **Robert Bly** and **Gershen Kaufman**

In this pioneering work, the editors and contributors identify the underlying (previously hidden) social and cultural causes of shame in men's lives, as well as its effects, and then discuss theoretical models and methods of treatment to help men process their shame. This volume also considers the possible impact of the women's movement on men's feelings of shame and is inspired by the current men's movement in psychology. This volume will be of interest to psychologists and professionals who counsel men.

Partial Contents:

Preface, *R. Schenk and J. Everingham* • Some Basics about Shame, *J. Everingham* • Shame in Men's Lives, *R. Schenk* • Men's Shame, *G. Kaufman* • Seven Sources of Men's Shame, *R. Bly* • Healing Internalized Shame, *G. Kaufman and R. Bly* • Men Facing Shame: A Healing Process, *J. Everingham* • Involving Men in Healing their Wounds of Socialization, *compiled by R. Schenk* • On Men, Guilt, and Shame, *F. Baumli* • Basic Male Shame, *J. Gagnon* • Male Initiation: Filling the Gap in Therapy, *C. Miller* • A Shame-Based Model for Recovery from Addiction, *G. Lindall* • Grandiosity: The Shadow of Shame, *D. Lindgren* • The Rescue Triangle: Shame Update, *J. Everingham* • Forgiving the Unforgivable: Overcoming Abusive Parents, *J. Giles* • Inadvertent Shaming: Family Rules and Shaming Habits, *J. Everingham* • Men and Goodness, *A. Heuer* • Men and Intimacy, *P. Dougherty* • Shame, Initiation, and the Culture of Initiated Masculinity, *M. Greenwald*

Springer Series: Focus on Men
1995   352pp   0-8261-8800-1   hardcover

536 Broadway, New York, NY 10012-3955 • (212) 431-4370 • Fax (212) 941-7842